God, Knowledge, and the Good

God, Knowledge, and the Good

Collected Papers in the Philosophy of Religion

LINDA TRINKAUS ZAGZEBSKI

Oxford University Press is a department of the University of Oxford. It furthers
the University's objective of excellence in research, scholarship, and education
by publishing worldwide. Oxford is a registered trade mark of Oxford University
Press in the UK and certain other countries.

Published in the United States of America by Oxford University Press
198 Madison Avenue, New York, NY 10016, United States of America.

© Oxford University Press 2022

All rights reserved. No part of this publication may be reproduced, stored in
a retrieval system, or transmitted, in any form or by any means, without the
prior permission in writing of Oxford University Press, or as expressly permitted
by law, by license, or under terms agreed with the appropriate reproduction
rights organization. Inquiries concerning reproduction outside the scope of the
above should be sent to the Rights Department, Oxford University Press, at the
address above.

You must not circulate this work in any other form
and you must impose this same condition on any acquirer.

Library of Congress Control Number: 2022902482
ISBN 978-0-19-761238-5

DOI: 10.1093/oso/9780197612385.001.0001

1 3 5 7 9 8 6 4 2

Printed by Integrated Books International, United States of America

Dedicated to the memory of Marilyn McCord Adams

Contents

Introduction   1

I. FOREKNOWLEDGE AND FATALISM

1. Divine Foreknowledge and Human Free Will (1985)   15
2. Eternity and Fatalism (2011)   36
3. Divine Foreknowledge and the Metaphysics of Time (2014)   54

II. THE PROBLEM OF EVIL

4. An Agent-Based Approach to the Problem of Evil (1996)   75
5. Good Persons, Good Aims, and the Problem of Evil (2017)   88
6. Weighing Evils: The C. S. Lewis Approach (2007)   103
   Coauthor Joshua Seachris

III. DEATH, HELL, AND RESURRECTION

7. Sleeping Beauty and the Afterlife (2005)   115
8. Religious Luck (1994)   132

IV. GOD AND MORALITY

9. The Virtues of God and the Foundations of Ethics (1998)   151
10. The Incarnation and Virtue Ethics (2002)   168

V. OMNISUBJECTIVITY

11. The Attribute of Omnisubjectivity (2013, 2016)   187

VI. THE RATIONALITY OF RELIGIOUS BELIEF

12. The Epistemology of Religion: The Need for Engagement (2004)   213

13. First-Person and Third-Person Reasons and Religious Epistemology (2011)   229

14. Religious Diversity and Social Responsibility (2001)   245

VII. RATIONAL RELIGIOUS BELIEF, SELF-TRUST, AND AUTHORITY

15. A Modern Defense of Religious Authority (2016)   263

16. Epistemic Self-Trust and the *Consensus Gentium* Argument (2011)   273

VIII. GOD, TRINITY, AND THE METAPHYSICS OF MODALITY

17. What if the Impossible Had Been Actual? (1990)   291

18. Christian Monotheism (1989)   306

Bibliography   323
Sources   333
Index   337

Introduction

My life in philosophy of religion did not begin until after graduate school, when I joined the Society of Christian Philosophers and started writing papers and commentaries for meetings. My first major conference was an important philosophy of religion conference funded by the National Endowment for the Humanities (NEH) and organized by Robert Audi at the University of Nebraska in 1984. Most of the philosophers in the United States doing philosophy of religion at that time were in attendance, as well as a few like me who were just entering the field. Another highlight for me, as well as for many people in the field, was the Institute in Philosophy of Religion organized by William Alston and Alvin Plantinga in Bellingham, Washington, in 1987, also funded by the NEH. The 1980s and 1990s were vibrant decades. That period produced the first generation of publications and conferences that applied the distinctive knowledge and techniques of analytic philosophy to issues in philosophy of religion, some of which connected philosophy with Christian theology. I was blessed to have distinguished mentors and many friends in philosophy whose intellectual paths invigorated my own. I know that my thought and my life would have been much poorer without them.

The papers in this collection span thirty-five years. I have divided them into eight topical categories: (I) Foreknowledge and Fatalism; (II) The Problem of Evil; (III) Death, Hell, and Resurrection; (IV) God and Morality; (V) Omnisubjectivity; (VI) The Rationality of Religious Belief; (VII) Rational Religious Belief, Self-Trust, and Authority; and (VIII) God, Trinity, and the Metaphysics of Modality. There are eighteen papers in total, numbered as Chapters 1–18 in this volume. All are at least lightly revised. One paper is coauthored. I have not included papers published in reference books, and I have left out a few papers mentioned in the following summaries of each section. Some of my papers in religious epistemology are published in the collection of my epistemology papers, *Epistemic Values* (2020).

I. Foreknowledge and Fatalism

Chapter 1: "Divine Foreknowledge and Human Free Will," originally published in *Religious Studies*, 21 (Fall 1985), 279–298.

I have found this topic gripping since later childhood and I have never heard of a solution that is fully satisfying. This chapter was my first full-length journal article and the topic of my first book, *The Dilemma of Freedom and Foreknowledge* (Oxford University Press, 1991). The paper was written in the early 1980s when the problem of foreknowledge and free will was becoming one of the most hotly discussed topics in American philosophy of religion. In this paper I canvas the literature on the topic since Nelson Pike argued for the inconsistency of infallible divine foreknowledge and human free will in his landmark 1965 paper, "Divine Omniscience and Voluntary Action." I defend the logical compatibility of infallible foreknowledge and free will, but I conclude that showing logical consistency is not sufficient for resolving the tension between them. For that, we need a broader theory in theological metaphysics that shows that divine foreknowledge and human freedom are mutually plausible. I still accept most of the arguments of that first paper and first book, but the range of options that I think are both viable and useful has been considerably narrowed, and I discuss that in the next two papers.

Chapter 2: "Eternity and Fatalism," originally published in *God, Eternity, and Time*, edited by Christian Tapp and Edmund Runggaldier (Ashgate, 2011), 65–80.

Both the past truth of propositions about the future and God's past infallible knowledge of the future seem to lead to fatalism, and in both cases it is tempting to think that fatalism can be escaped by escaping time. If propositions are timelessly true, rather than true in the past, the logical fatalist argument apparently collapses. If God's knowledge of our future is timeless rather than in the past, the theological fatalist argument apparently collapses. I argue that escaping fatalism by escaping time succeeds only if the timelessness move can overcome two hurdles: (1) There must be no temporal counterpart that permits a reformulation of the fatalist argument. The timeless truth of propositions cannot overcome this hurdle. The timeless knowledge of God can overcome this hurdle, but only if there are restrictions on the knowledge of Jesus Christ, who is incarnated in time. (2) There must be no reason to think that the timeless realm shares with the past the feature of being outside our control. I argue that the timelessness move does not overcome this hurdle for either argument. I extend an argument I first presented in *The Dilemma of Freedom and Foreknowledge* (chapter 2, sec. 3.5) that there is a principle of the Necessity of Eternity that permits the formulation of a parallel timeless truth dilemma and a parallel timeless knowledge dilemma. I conclude that the escape from fatalism does not turn on the issue of temporality versus timelessness. There are many reasons why a Christian philosopher would be attracted to the traditional conception of divine timelessness, but the need to escape fatalism should not be one of them.

Chapter 3: "Divine Foreknowledge and the Metaphysics of Time," originally published in *God: Reason, and Reality*, edited by Anselm Ramelow, in the *Philosophia* series: Basic Philosophical Concepts, Philosophia Verlag (Munich, 2014), 275–302.

In this paper I argue that when we examine the traditional dilemma of infallible divine foreknowledge and human free will, we uncover a deeper dilemma that has nothing to do with God, infallibility, or free will. Many historically important ways out of theological fatalism are irrelevant to this problem, which arises within the metaphysics of time. The assumption that the past has a kind of necessity that the future lacks is inconsistent with the principle that temporal necessity is transferred over entailment and the possibility that a proposition about the past entails a proposition about the future. I argue that the most reasonable response to this dilemma is to reject the view that the necessity of the past is a purely temporal modality; in fact, it is not a form of necessity in the formal sense of necessity. Rather, I propose that it reduces to the metaphysical thesis that the past is causally closed. With this interpretation of the necessity of the past, the argument for theological fatalism must be revised in a way that reveals confusions in our notions of causality and the arrow of time. I conclude that well-known fatalist problems are interwoven with problems about time that are easier to see in the context of theism, but which would be there anyway. This problem shows us one of the ways in which philosophical theology has important implications for secular metaphysics.

This paper incorporates parts of the argument of an earlier paper, "Omniscience and the Arrow of Time" (2002a). That paper is not included. It is reprinted in Fischer and Todd (2015).

II. The Problem of Evil

Chapter 4: "An Agent-Based Approach to the Problem of Evil," originally published in *International Journal for the Philosophy of Religion*, 39 (June 1996), 127–139.

This paper was written while I was writing *Virtues of the Mind* (1996a), at a time when I was exploring different forms of virtue theory. It argues against one of the supplementary premises in the logical problem of evil—the premise that a good being is motivated to produce good and to prevent or eliminate evil. That premise assumes that the good or evil of the state of affairs is primary, and the goodness of agents is at least partly derivative from the good or bad of the state of affairs they aim to bring about or to prevent. This was the first paper in which I began exploring what I later called Divine Motivation theory, a theory that bases good and bad on the motivational states of God. God is good in the primary sense, and the good and bad of everything else is derivative from God's motives, which include permitting his creatures to be free persons. What makes free will necessary is not that God sees its goodness, but that God is motivated to have a relationship with creatures who have free will. Freedom is necessary because it is a condition for a personal relationship, not because of its goodness. God's motives express the divine nature, and we find out what good motives are by looking at the motives of God as expressed in what God does, not by conceptual analysis.

Chapter 5: "Good Persons, Good Aims, and the Problem of Evil," originally published in *Ethics and the Problem of Evil*, edited by James Sterba (Indiana University Press, 2017), 43–56.

This paper was written twenty years after essay 4, revisiting an assumption that most formulations of the problem of evil take for granted: a good person aims at producing good and preventing evil. That is generally interpreted as (a) a condition for being a good person is that she aims at producing good states of affairs and preventing evil states of affairs. An alternative interpretation I defend is (b) a condition for something being a good state of affairs and something else an evil state of affairs is that a good person aims at producing the former and preventing the latter. This paper explores the relationships between the goodness of persons, the goodness of aims, and the goodness of states of affairs, and argues that the problem of evil looks very different when the metaphysics of good and evil is interpreted in the way I have defended here, which is intended to be a clearer and improved version of an argument contained in my book *Divine Motivation Theory* (2004a).

Chapter 6: "Weighing Evils: The C.S. Lewis Approach," coauthor Joshua Seachris, originally published in *International Journal for Philosophy of Religion* 62.2 (October 2007), 81–88.

It is often argued that the great quantity of evil in our world makes God's existence less likely than a lesser quantity would, and this is presumably because the probability that there are some gratuitous evils increases as the overall quantity of evil increases. Often an additive approach to quantifying evil is employed in such arguments. In this paper, Joshua Seachris and I examine C. S. Lewis's objection to the additive approach, arguing that although he is correct to reject this approach, there is a sense in which he underestimates the quantity of pain. However, the quantity of pain that exists does not significantly increase the probability that some pain is gratuitous. Therefore, the quantitative argument likely fails.

III. Death, Hell, and Resurrection

Chapter 7: "Sleeping Beauty and the Afterlife," originally published in *God and the Ethics of Belief: New Essays in the Philosophy of Religion*, edited by Andrew Chignell and Andrew Dole (Cambridge University Press, 2005), 59–76.

This paper tells a fairy tale aimed at making sense of the idea of a resurrected body identical to the one that died. We have inherited two strands of thought about human persons that are in tension with each other and force us to make some hard choices. One is the motive to think of human beings as organisms, part of the natural world. The other is the motive to think that an individual person is the sort of thing that is necessarily distinct from everything else in the world, including every other person. A person has determinate persistence conditions and is not replicable. In my story I propose that it is possible that nature cooperates with the strong distinctness of persons. There might be a substantial form that is a non-duplicable particular, but which cannot exist without informing matter. A certain person exists when and only when that person's substantial form informs some matter. This interpretation makes the resurrection of that person possible.

Chapter 8: "Religious Luck," originally published in *Faith and Philosophy*, 11.3 (July 1994), 397–413.

In this paper I argue that the problem of moral luck, made famous by Joel Feinberg, Thomas Nagel, and Bernard Williams, exists for Christian moral theory and practice, and I argue that the problem is magnified by certain aspects of Christian theology, including the doctrine of grace and the doctrine of an eternal heaven and hell. I then consider five solutions to the problem, all of which involve modifying in one way or another either traditional Christian doctrines or common views on the grounds of moral evaluation.

IV. God and Morality

Chapter 9: "The Virtues of God and the Foundations of Ethics," originally published in *Faith and Philosophy* 15.4 (October 1998), 538–552. (Special issue on "Virtues and Virtue Theories from a Christian Perspective").

This paper outlines an early form of my Divine Motivation (DM) theory (see Chapters 4, 6, and my 2004 book). In this theory, all moral concepts are derivative from the concept of a good motive, the most basic component of a virtue, where what I mean by a motive is an emotion that initiates and directs action toward an end. I argue that the motivations of one person in particular are the foundation of all moral value: God. The theory I outline is structurally parallel to Divine Command (DC) theory, but it has several advantages over DC theory without the well-known problems. DM theory does not face a dilemma parallel to the famous Euthyphro problem, nor does it have any difficulty in answering the question whether God could make cruelty morally right. Unlike DC theory, it explains the importance of Christology in Christian ethics, and it provides a unitary account of all evaluative properties, divine and human.

Another paper on Divine Motivation theory, written at about the same time, is "Perfect Goodness and Divine Motivation Theory" (1997). In that paper I propose that DM theory offers a natural way to solve four traditional puzzles involving the attribute of perfect goodness: (1) the apparent incompatibility between perfect goodness and omnipotence, (2) the apparent incompatibility between perfect goodness and God's freedom, (3) the apparent self-inconsistency of the concept of perfect moral goodness, and (4) the problem of evil (related to Chapter 4). A discussion of these four puzzles about perfect goodness also appears in *Divine Motivation Theory* (2004), Chapters 7 and 8.

Chapter 10: "The Incarnation and Virtue Ethics," originally published in *The Incarnation*, edited by Stephen T. Davis, Daniel J. Kendall, SJ, and Gerald O'Collins, SJ (Oxford University Press, 2002), 313–331.

An advantage of DM theory is its capacity to insert imitation into a narrative ethical structure. This paper shows how DM theory can make the Incarnation central and the imitation of Christ the basic normative idea. At the time I was writing that paper, narrative ethics was getting a lot of attention, but its defect was the lack of a structure that would make it a viable competitor to leading moral theories. Divine Motivation theory is a theological form of the general type of ethical theory I later called "exemplarism" or "exemplarist moral theory." The theological form became *Divine Motivation Theory* (2004), while the general form became *Exemplarist Moral Theory* (2017). This paper argues for the advantage of this kind of theory for the distinctive goals of Christian ethics. It is a theoretical structure in which the motive to be moral is a component of the theory. The motivating feature was emphasized in the later book through its focus on admiration, a state that attracts us to the exemplar, and in which admirability is the theoretical focus of the theory. For a brief summary of these theories, see "Divine Motivation Theory and Exemplarism" (2016d).

V. Omnisubjectivity

Chapter 11: "The Attribute of Omnisubjectivity," an expanded version of *Omnisubjectivity: A Defense of a Divine Attribute*, Aquinas Lecture 2013 (Marquette University Press, 2013).

I first proposed and defended the attribute of omnisubjectivity in "Omnisubjectivity" (2008). In that paper I argue that the property of having a complete and perfect grasp of the subjective states of all beings with subjectivity from the first-person perspective of those beings is entailed by omniscience. I expanded the argument and argued that omnisubjectivity is also entailed by omnipresence and is implied by common practices of prayer in my 2013 Aquinas Lecture. I included some reflections on the implications of omnisubjectivity for the doctrine of the Trinity in "Omnisubjectivity: Why It Is a Divine Attribute" (2016b). The chapter in this book is primarily an edited version of the Aquinas Lecture, with the addition of a section from the 2016 paper. I have also modified the argument to account for problems in using the model of human empathy for God's grasp of our subjective states. As several people have pointed out to me, the indirectness of human empathy, in which we rely upon our own previous experience to understand another person's mental state, leads to confusion about the way in which God grasps anything, whether it is objective facts or subjective states. God's grasp is direct. In this paper I have included a longer account of how God grasps the subjective states of other beings. My aim is to explain how omnisubjectivity is possible without merging the mind of God with the minds of creatures.

In my most recent book, *The Two Greatest Ideas: How Our Grasp of the Universe and Our Minds Changed Everything* (2021), I have begun exploring intersubjectivity as an antidote to the conceptual and practical problems that have arisen in Western history because of the particular way we have put together two great ideas: the idea that the human mind can grasp the universe, and the idea that the human mind can grasp itself. For long periods of history, the first idea was primary, but the second idea became dominant starting in the Renaissance in art and literature, and in the early modern age in philosophy and science. Our inability to put the two great ideas together has led to failure in understanding how subjective and objective reality can be combined in a conception of the world as a whole, and it has led to our current moral and political conflicts. At the end of the book, I propose that the possibility of intersubjectivity deserves to be the third greatest idea. Omnisubjectivity, or the God's-eye view of all subjective reality, would be the ultimate goal of subjective inquiry. Curiously, what is usually called "the God's-eye view" is a total grasp of objective facts, the ultimate goal of objective inquiry. But objective reality is not all of reality. I believe that we will not make substantial progress in grasping all of reality without an extended development of the study of intersubjectivity. Omnisubjectivity is the perfection of intersubjectivity.

VI. The Rationality of Religious Belief

Chapter 12: "The Epistemology of Religion: The Need for Engagement," originally published in *Proceedings of the Twenty-Sixth Annual Wittgenstein*

Symposium: Knowledge and Belief, edited by Winfried Loffler and Paul Weingartner (Holder-Pichler-Tempsky, 2004), 386–398.

This paper was written for an American Philosophical Association Author-Meets-Critics session on Alvin Plantinga's book, *Warranted Christian Belief*, and was given in an expanded form at the twenty-sixth annual Wittgenstein symposium in 2004. Plantinga's three warrant books offer a sustained and influential theory of knowledge and rational belief that has the consequence that theism is rational and, given some factual assumptions about God's design of the universe, constitutes knowledge. The third book in the sequence, *Warranted Christian Belief*, extends the earlier line of argument to a defense of distinctively Christian beliefs, arguing that for Christians in certain circumstances, belief in Christian doctrines is rational in multiple senses of rationality and constitutes knowledge. In this paper, I argue that Plantinga's strategy lacks the social usefulness we would expect if rationality is a common human property that requires us to engage in open discussion and evaluation in competition with alternative theses. The Plantinga approach is purely defensive and leads to a kind of epistemic isolationism. His approach to external rationality has the consequence that Christian beliefs are rational if *and only if* they are true. His approach to internal rationality makes the conditions for that kind of rationality so easy to satisfy that many beliefs of extremists are internally rational. That makes it very difficult for us to use social responses as a way to judge the possession of a property that ought to be recognizable by normal human beings. The social dimension of rationality is something I find important because we live in a world of increasing global interaction by even ordinary people. I welcome the confidence that Plantinga gave Christian believers in convincingly arguing that Christians have a solid line of defense against attack. What I find missing is the importance of the commonality of all human beings in their rational nature. When that is missing, we become more and more separated and even polarized in moral, religious, and political beliefs.

Chapter 13: "First Person and Third Person Reasons and Religious Epistemology," originally published in *European Journal for Philosophy of Religion*, 3.2 (Fall 2011), 285–304.

In this paper I argue that there are two kinds of epistemic reasons. One kind is irreducibly first personal—what I call deliberative reasons. The other is third personal—what I call theoretical reasons. I argue that attending to this distinction illuminates a host of problems in epistemology in general and in religious epistemology in particular. These problems include (a) the way religious experience operates as a reason for religious belief, (b) how we ought to understand religious testimony, (c) how religious authority can be justified, (d) the problem of religious disagreement, and (e) the reasonableness of religious conversion. As a reasonable person I must figure out how to answer for myself my own religious questions without ignoring the fact that the contents of my beliefs are also the property of all reasonable persons in their common attempt to find the truth.

In addition to this paper, I use the distinction between first person and third person reasons in a paper that is not included in this collection: "Trust, Anti-Trust, and Reasons for Religious Belief," in *Religious Faith and Intellectual Virtue* (2014b). I also use the distinction to solve the problem of the infinite regress of reasons in (2014c), reprinted in *Epistemic Values* (2020). In *The Two Greatest Ideas* (2021, chap 6), I argue that there are also second-person reasons, reasons that I propose to you or you propose to me, that are reducible neither to first-person nor to third-person reasons. I believe that these reasons are important for the intersubjective aspect of rationality.

Chapter 14: "Religious Diversity and Social Responsibility," originally published in *Logos: A Journal of Catholic Thought and Culture*, 4.1 (2001), 136–156.

This paper explores what I call the second-person approach to rationality as it applies to the diversity of religious beliefs. I propose that rationality gives us social responsibilities, and that leads to some principles governing discourse across religious cultures. One is the *Culture-Sensitivity Principle*: Persons should treat the members of other cultures and religions as though they are *prima facie* as rational as themselves. A second is the *Rational-Recognition Principle*: If a belief is rational, its rationality can be recognized, in principle, by rational persons in other cultures engaged in sympathetic contact with each other. I also refer to these principles in Chapter 10 of *Epistemic Authority* (2012).

I have another paper on religious diversity that I have not included: "Self-Trust and the Diversity of Religions" (2006); reprinted in Weithman (2008). This paper includes a portion of an argument in *Epistemic Authority* (2012) that self-trust logically commits us to basic trust in others when I see that they have the same properties I trust in myself. I argue also that epistemic admiration for others commits us to a greater degree of trust than that to which we are committed by consistent self-trust. This paper overlaps some of the arguments of the papers in section VII.

VII. Rational Religious Belief, Self-Trust, and Authority

Chapter 15: "A Modern Defense of Religious Authority," originally published in *Logos: A Journal of Catholic Thought and Culture*, 19.3 (2016), 15–28.

This paper summarizes a central argument defending epistemic authority in *Epistemic Authority*, chapter 5, and then applies it to authority in the domain of religious belief. The argument uses well-known principles of authority proposed by Joseph Raz in his defense of political authority on a liberal basis, and then argues that those principles show that religious authority can be defended under the modern liberal assumption that the ultimate authority over the self is the self. According to Raz's Normal Justification Principle, the normal way to show that one person has authority over another is to show that the subject is more likely to act for her own ends if she accepts the directives of the alleged authority and tries to follow them, rather than to try to act for those ends directly. When this principle is formulated in the first person, we see how the subject's own self-direction can justify her acceptance of authority in the moral and religious domains as well as in the political domain.

Chapter 16: "Epistemic Self-Trust and the *Consensus Gentium* Argument," originally published in *Evidence and Religious Belief*, edited by Kelly Clark and Raymond van Aragon (Clarendon Press, 2011), 22–36.

In this paper I argue that (1) epistemic self-trust is more basic than what we take to be reasons for belief, and (2) consistent self-trust commits us to trust in others. This argument was subsequently developed in chapters 2 and 3 of *Epistemic Authority* (2012). Epistemic self-trust is inescapable, given that the search for reasons leads to epistemic circularity, and given the more basic fact that we have no way to tell that there is any connection at all between reasons and truth without trust in ourselves when we are epistemically conscientious. I then argue that when we are conscientious we will inevitably come to believe that other persons have the same quality of conscientiousness in virtue of which we trust ourselves, and so we owe them epistemic trust in advance of reasons for thinking that they are reliable. The fact that someone else has a belief gives me a *prima facie* reason to believe it, and the reason is stronger when large numbers of people share the belief. The conclusion is that consistent epistemic self-trust supports common agreement arguments, in particular, a new form of the *consensus gentium* argument for theism, based on self-trust.

VIII. God, Trinity, and the Metaphysics of Modality

Chapter 17. "What if the Impossible Had Been Actual?," originally published in *Christian Theism and the Problems of Philosophy*, edited by Michael D. Beaty (University of Notre Dame Press, 1990), 165–183.

This early paper was written while I was doing research for *The Dilemma of Freedom and Foreknowledge* (1991), and was thinking about propositions of the form "If God were not omniscient, then . . ." Under the assumption that God exists necessarily and is essentially omniscient, the antecedent of any such proposition is necessarily false. I called counterfactual conditionals with necessarily false antecedents "counterpossibles." These conditionals are pertinent to many areas of the metaphysics of theism, not only discussions of omniscience. The problem is that on the standard semantics deriving from David Lewis and others, all counterpossibles are trivially true. But there ought to be a way to interpret a proposition such as (1) *If God were not good, then there would be more evil in the world than there is* as non-trivially true, and (2) *If God were not good, then there would be less evil in the world than there is* as non-trivially false. I argue that it is a mistake to treat all necessary falsehoods as logically equivalent, and I propose a way to extend the semantics of counterfactual conditionals to account for the intuition that (1) is true and (2) is false in a metaphysically significant sense.

Chapter 18: "Christian Monotheism," originally published in *Faith and Philosophy*, 6.1 (January 1989), 3–18.

In this paper I argue that there can be no more than one God in a way that allows me to give the doctrine of the Trinity logical priority over the attributes traditionally used in arguments for God's unicity. My argument that there is at most one God makes no assumptions about the attributes included in divinity. It uses only the principle of the Identity of Indiscernibles and a Principle of Plenitude. I then offer a theory on the relationship between individuals and kinds that allows me to offer an interpretation of the Trinity.

I use a similar form of argument in another paper, "Individual Essence and the Creation" (1988), which was written close to the same time. In that paper I argue for the existence of individual qualitative essences in the strong sense that each object in each possible world has a set of qualitative properties that is essential to it and which is possessed by no other object in any world. I then argue that if these individual essences are identified with ideas in God's mind in a traditional account of creation, an important objection to this account can be answered.

It has been almost a half century since philosophy of religion became a distinct field of philosophy in the English-speaking world. My career started in philosophy of religion, both because of my religious commitments, and because of the influence on me of the many fine philosophers whose work created exciting research programs that lasted more than a generation. Because of their work I was led to epistemology, which led me to propose a new form of epistemology in my version of virtue epistemology, and since virtue epistemology is an instance of virtue theory in general, I was led to virtue ethics, and my desire to design a new form of virtue ethics led me to what I call exemplarist moral theory. I examined epistemic authority because I wanted to defend religious epistemic authority, and I examined the metaphysics of modality because I wanted to defend traditional doctrines of foreknowledge and divine goodness. I examined omnisubjectivity because I thought that the modern discovery of subjectivity required a re-evaluation of omniscience, and I am thinking about intersubjectivity because my work on omnisubjectivity made me think that our own intellectual goals have been severely constrained by the mistaken view that the world is the same as the objective world. I know that readers perusing these papers will find many strands of thought that I did not pursue or did not pursue far enough, and I know that this collection reveals how unfinished a body of work must be. But I hope that readers will find something of interest in these papers that they might not have noticed before the papers were collected, and I hope to see the paths that readers are taking on these topics, as well as topics I have not thought of.

Santa Fe, New Mexico
May 26, 2021

I
FOREKNOWLEDGE AND FATALISM

1
Divine Foreknowledge and Human Free Will (1985)

1.1. The problem of reconciling foreknowledge and freedom

If God knows everything, he must know the future, and if he knows the future, he must know the future acts of his creatures. But then his creatures must act as he knows they will act. How then can they be free? This dilemma has a long history in Christian philosophy and is now as hotly disputed as ever. The medieval scholastics were virtually unanimous in claiming both that God is omniscient and that humans have free will, although they disagreed in their accounts of how the two are compatible. With the Reformation, the debate became even more lively since there were Protestant philosophers who denied both claims, and many philosophers ever since have either thought it impossible to reconcile them or have thought it possible only because they weaken one or the other.

In this paper I wish to argue for the consistency of the two claims:

(1) God is essentially omniscient

and

(2) Human beings have free will.

I am taking each of these claims in the strongest sense. That is, I take it to follow from (1) that God knows all true propositions and believes no false ones. I assume that propositions are omnitemporally true or false, an advantage to logic and the theory of truth, and I assume that propositions can be expressed by tensed sentences, some of which are in the future tense. So one and the same proposition can be variously expressed by future-tensed, present-tensed, or past-tensed sentences, depending upon the temporal relation between the knower and the event which the proposition is about. It follows from (1) that God knows all true propositions expressed by sentences in the future tense and since he is *essentially* omniscient, he knows them at all times in all possible worlds.[1] In addition, I am taking (2) in the strong sense sometimes referred to as incompatibilist free will, or the sense of free will which is incompatible with determinism. That is, there are times when person A does x at time $t2$, and it would be correct to say that given the entire causal history of x and the world's causal laws, A could nevertheless have refrained from doing x at $t2$.

If we give (1) and (2) these strong interpretations, it follows that even if God knows at $t1$ that A will do x at $t2$, A nevertheless can refrain from doing x at $t2$. I will attempt an explanation of foreknowledge that removes conceptual difficulties in this assertion. An argument for the truth of (1) and (2) in addition to their consistency would have to be much more elaborate and is beyond the scope of this paper.

1.2. Some unacceptable solutions

There are several attempted solutions to the problem of reconciling divine foreknowledge with human free will that are unacceptable given the interpretation of (1) and (2) just offered. These are ones that weaken one or the other of the two claims. One set of solutions weakens the notion of human free will. St. Augustine's solution in *On Free Will* and *The City of God* is of this type. In *On Free Will* he says that even though God's foreknowledge means that a person's will to sin must come to pass, he nevertheless does so voluntarily, and hence freely, since "who but a raving fool would say that it is not voluntarily that we will?" (1953, 175). His argument seems to involve an account of what it is to will. To will just *is* to act voluntarily, and this in turn means to have it within our power. He thinks this is so because our wills can be contrasted with things that are obviously not in our power, such as growing old. So for Augustine, any act of will by definition is a voluntary act and a free act. But this does not preclude the necessity claimed by the determinist, as he argues in *The City of God*:

> For if that is to be called *our necessity* which is not in our power, but even though we be unwilling effects what it can effect—as, for instance, the necessity of death—it is manifest that our wills by which we live uprightly or wickedly are not under such a necessity; for we do many things which, if we were not willing, we should certainly not do. This is primarily true of the act of willing itself—for if we will, it *is*; if we will not, it *is* not—for we should not will if we were unwilling. But if we define necessity to be that according to which we say that it is necessary that anything be of such a nature, or be done in such and such a manner, I know not why we should have any dread of that necessity taking away the freedom of our will. (1948, 68)

The same approach can be found in contemporary philosophy. Anthony Kenny (1979) argues in his book *The God of the Philosophers* that divine foreknowledge is incompatible with indeterministic free will, and he favors a deterministic notion of freedom.[2] He makes this move largely because of his objections to Plantinga, which I will discuss in section 1.8. Many other philosophers, of course, have taken this approach for other reasons. However, I wish to consider a version of (2) that denies any form of determinism.

A second set of solutions that would be unacceptable on the strong interpretations of (1) and (2) are those that weaken the scope of divine omniscience. They do this either by (a) denying that future contingent propositions have a truth value, or by (b) claiming that while future contingent propositions may be true, they are nonetheless unknowable. The former either deny the law of excluded middle, which has led to multi-valued logics, or they deny the omnitemporality of truth, which has led to tense logics. An example of someone in the recent literature who denies that future contingent propositions have a truth value is Joseph Runzo (1981). I will discuss some of the points in his paper in sections 1.5 and 1.8. The claim that while future contingent propositions may be true, they are nevertheless unknowable, was argued by Richard Swinburne (1977). His reasons will be discussed in section 1.7.

It should be apparent that this set of solutions not only greatly restricts the range of divine omniscience, but it also complicates logic. The fact that a view complicates logic is, of course, not a refutation of it, but it does suggest that the resort to such moves is something that should be done only when one is forced into it by some philosophical problem. Certainly, those who have appealed to such exotic logics have done so because they do feel forced into it by problems such as the one addressed in this paper, but if it could be shown that the problem of divine foreknowledge can be resolved without giving up the law of excluded middle or the omnitemporality of truth, that would be an advantage. The matter of weakening divine omniscience may be more serious. The notion of omniscience that Runzo uses, for example, is not unreasonable, and it would not be fair to call it a weakening of omniscience if the future is truly unknowable, but he makes it clear that he believes we are forced into it by considerations on the logic of knowledge. If we can make sense of knowledge and contingency without weakening the notion of omniscience, as I hope to show, so much the better.[3]

1.3. Aquinas's solution

There is one classic solution to the problem of reconciling divine foreknowledge with human free will that does not weaken either (1) or (2), but which is not the one I wish to pursue in this paper. That is the solution of Thomas Aquinas.

Following Boethius, Aquinas argues that God's knowledge is timeless, not in the sense of being omnitemporal, but in the sense of being outside time.

> Things reduced to actuality in time are known by us successively in time, but by God they are known in eternity, which is above time. Whence to us they cannot be certain, since we know future contingent things only as contingent futures; but they are certain to God alone, Whose understanding is in eternity above time. Just as he who goes along the road does not see those who come after him; whereas he who sees the whole road from a height sees at once all those travelling on it. (Aquinas, *Summa Theologica*, reprinted in Brody (1974), 392)

To put Aquinas in the modern idiom, not only is the assertion that God knows p, where p is future-tensed, ill-formed, it is never correct to speak of God's knowing p *at* a time t. That is, not only is the proposition God knows not expressible by a tensed sentence, but his act of knowing cannot be related to a moment of time either. So since God's knowledge is not only outside the chain of causes leading up to an act, but is outside the temporal chain altogether, there is no worry that God's knowledge prevents the contingency of the act.

This solution deserves a thorough inspection, but I suspect that it ultimately will not work. One reason is that even if God's act of knowing is timeless and the object of his knowledge is not properly expressible by a future-tensed sentence, we can nevertheless ask if the proposition expressed by "God timelessly knows p" is omnitemporally true. If it is, as we would expect, then it was, of course, true prior to the event described by p, and the problem of divine foreknowledge is generated again. If that proposition is not omnitemporally true, it could not be for the reasons Aquinas has given.[4] Second, even if this solution did solve the logical problem of divine foreknowledge, it still may not be the most desirable. Many people, including Anthony Kenny and A. N. Prior, doubt the coherence of the concept of timeless knowledge. Kenny repeats Prior's oft-quoted objection that it seems an extraordinary way of affirming God's omniscience if a person, when asked what God knows *now*, must say "nothing," and when asked what he knew *yesterday*, must again say "nothing," and must yet again say "nothing" when asked what God will know *tomorrow* (Kenny 1974, 409). For those who share their misgivings about this approach, a solution that understands God's foreknowledge in a way that is closer to the ordinary conception would be preferable. Nelson Pike (1970) and Anthony Kenny (1974) claim that the doctrine of the timelessness of God's knowledge is inessential to Christian theology anyway.[5] In fact, a strong case can be made for the opposite view, since Christians want to say that God interacts with human history, and so must have known certain things at those times. In any case, the timelessness solution is commonly offered when the other solutions are perceived to fail.[6] However, my purpose in this paper is not to attack such a solution, but to argue that it is not necessary since there is no incoherence in claiming God knows at each moment of time all events that will follow it in time, even when some of those events are free human acts.

1.4. Some pseudo-problems

Some philosophers have thought that the simple omnitemporal truth of a proposition or the truth of a future-tensed proposition is sufficient to preclude free will. This seems to have been a widely held belief in antiquity. There are indications of it in Aristotle's sea-battle argument in *De Interpetatione* Bk 9, where on one common interpretation of that argument, he is asserting *p* or not *p* (the law of excluded middle) for contingent future-tensed propositions, while denying the truth of either of the disjuncts taken individually (the principle of bivalence). The Stoics associated their determinism with the truth value of future-tensed assertions, while Epicurus thought that in order to maintain the doctrine of free will, he had to deny the truth value of such propositions. In this century, J. Lukasiewicz conceived the idea of a three-valued system of logic to handle future contingents since he thought the truth of future-tensed propositions would entail determinism.[7]

This position seems to me to be a mistake. The truth or falsity of a proposition *p* is a semantical property of *p* distinct from the necessity or contingency of *p*. It is not an event or state of affairs, and it has no causal effect on the world, except incidentally. Furthermore, if we accept a correspondence theory of truth, the truth of a proposition is explained by the fact that the state of affairs it describes takes place, not the other way around. Some true propositions are also necessarily true, meaning they are true in all possible worlds. Some false propositions are also necessarily false, meaning they are false in all possible worlds. Contingency and non-contingency are properties that can be ascribed either to propositions or to events/states of affairs. A proposition is non-contingent if and only if it is either necessarily true or necessarily false. A proposition is contingent if and only if it is neither necessarily true nor necessarily false.

The contingency or non-contingency of events is more complicated. One approach would be simply to say that an event or state of affairs that corresponds to a contingent proposition is contingent, while one that corresponds to a non-contingent proposition is non-contingent. Let us call this the notion of logical contingency. However, we need another, much more rigorous notion of contingency for the free will advocate. Suppose we wish to say that the event of Jane's marriage to Harry at *tn* is a contingent event in the sense that they could have refrained from marrying under the circumstances. We clearly do not wish to assert merely that Jane and Harry's marriage is neither logically necessary nor logically impossible. Although true, such a claim is trivial and irrelevant to the question of free will. For the advocate of free will, to say that the marriage is a contingent event is to say that the marriage is neither logically nor causally necessitated by the events making up the causal history of the marriage at *tn*. It is common to conclude from this that none of the events in the temporal history of the world at *tn* is sufficient to necessitate the marriage at *tn*. In other words, there is some possible world with a temporal history identical to that of the actual world at *tn* in which Jane does not marry Harry at *tn*. Let us call this the notion of causal contingency. We will need to amend this notion later, but this account should be adequate to show the distinction between truth and contingency as needed in the foreknowledge dilemma. The omnitemporal truth of the proposition that Jane marries Harry at *tn* is no problem if, as stated earlier, truth is not an event, does not enter causally into the world, and does not thereby prevent the contingency of events.

Necessity, therefore, should not be confused with truth. Furthermore, it should not be confused with certainty. Certainty is a psychological state of the knower, whereas necessity is a property of a proposition. Necessary truths are often more certain than contingent truths, but this need not be the case. Descartes has convinced readers for over 300 years that "I think" and "I exist" are among the most certain of all the propositions I know, though they are by no means necessary since I do not exist in all possible worlds. On the other hand, there are undoubtedly theorems of mathematics which have not yet been proven and about which no one is yet certain, but which are necessarily true.

If necessity should not be confused with truth or certainty, it also should not be confused with inalterability or the related notion of accidental necessity that comes from William of Ockham.[8] There is a sense in which the entire past is inalterable. Given that certain events have already occurred, I cannot now make it happen that those events did not occur.[9] I cannot go back in time and make something that did happen not happen. Some writers, such as Kenny and Prior, would also say that the future is inalterable in the same sense. I cannot go into the future and make something that will happen not happen. That is because, arguably, the future is what *will* come to be after we've made all our choices, just as the past is what came to be after we made all our choices.[10] With this interpretation, inalterability becomes a vacuous notion since all events, past, present, and future, would be equally inalterable. But whether or not inalterability is broadened in this way, it is distinct from the notion of causal necessity as contrasted with causal contingency. The causal contingency of an act is a property of that act. It does not lose that property after it is performed. Causal contingency is defined in terms of the relations between an event and other events or states of affairs occurring previous to it. This relation always remains the same and is not affected by whether the event is past, present, or future. There are causally contingent events in the past and causally necessary events in the future. Hence, if the past is inalterable, that cannot be because it is causally necessary. Causal contingency and necessity must be distinguished from Ockham's notion of the inalterability (accidental necessity) of the past.

1.5. The real problem

Truth is not an event and does not enter causally into the world. Knowing, however, is an event, and I have been assuming that God's knowing is an event that occurs at moments of time in the actual world.[11] By the criteria for causal contingency given previously, to say that Jane can refrain from marrying Harry at tn is to say that there is a world with a past exactly like the actual world up to $tn-1$, in which Jane does not marry Harry at tn. But one of the events in the actual world up to $tn-1$ is the event of God's infallible knowing that Jane will marry Harry at tn, and this is incompatible with Jane's refraining from marrying Harry at tn since on all accounts of the meaning of "infallibly knows," the proposition that S infallibly knows p entails p.[12] So there is no world *exactly like* the actual world up to $tn-1$ in which Jane does not marry Harry at tn. Hence, it looks as if the marriage is not causally contingent and Jane and Harry are not really free not to marry after all. This is basically the argument presented by Nelson Pike (1977, 216) in his argument against Alvin Plantinga and endorsed by Joseph Runzo (1981, 143) as an effective rebuttal to the compatibility of (1) and (2).

Not only do I find this argument inconclusive against the compatibility of (1) and (2), but I believe it shows a misunderstanding of the meaning of the subjunctive statement:

(3) Jane could have refrained from marrying Harry at tn,
upon which the claim of incompatibilist free will rests.

Consider the proposition expressed by the sentence:
(4) Jane marries Harry at tn.

Let us call the actual world α. If God's knowing (4) is a fact about α before tn, then the marriage occurs at tn. But this is no problem because what we mean to imply by (3) is that *if* Jane were to decide not to marry Harry at tn, then it *would have been the case that* God did not know (4) before tn. He would have known the negation of (4) instead. But that is only to say that the actual world would have been a different possible world than this one. When we assert a subjunctive statement of the form of (3), we are in effect asserting what would be the case if a different possible world had been actual instead of this one. In describing such a world we are entitled—in fact, required—to make the minimal changes in the description of that world compatible with the change from (4) to (not-4). If we assume the existence of an essentially omniscient God, then necessarily, if (4) God knows (4), and if (not-4) God knows (not-4). To look for a world exactly like this one with the sole exception that the truth of the proposition (4) is changed from true to false is to look for a logically impossible world. It is unreasonable to include God's foreknowledge of which of all possible worlds will be the actual one as part of the description of the past of this world and then to ask if an alternative possible world is compatible with *that*. It is to ask if there is a possible world β in which God knows the actual world is α, and of course the answer is no. So the mere fact that God infallibly knows (4) before the event described by (4) occurs should not in itself prevent that event from being contingent.

Yet God's knowledge of (4) before tn does preclude the causal contingency of (4) on the criterion of causal contingency given in the previous section. It is not true that there is a possible world exactly like the actual world up to $tn-1$ where Jane and Harry do not marry at tn. In the next section I will suggest a change in the definition of causal contingency that I think is reasonable given the intuitions I have just discussed on the meaning of the subjunctive assertion (3).

1.6. The logical and causal contingency of propositions about future human choices

The free will advocate needs to establish that any proposition describing a future free human act such as (4) is both logically and causally contingent. Let us first consider the argument that it is logically contingent.

Let Ox: x is an omniscient being
g: God
Kxp: x knows p

It is a necessary truth that:

$(x)(Ox \to (Kxp \leftrightarrow p))$.

That is, there is no possible world in which an omniscient being x exists and either Kxp and not-p or not-Kxp and p. If we assume that God exists in all possible worlds and is omniscient in all possible worlds, then we get

$\Box (Kgp \leftrightarrow p)$.

So the propositions *Kgp* and *p* are logically equivalent. But this does not show that the fact that God knows *p* makes the event described in *p* logically necessitated. There is a difference between the proposition

(5) $\Box (Kgp \to p)$

and the proposition

(6) $Kgp \to \Box p$.

(5) is true and is required by the logic of knowledge. It shows a logically necessary connection between anybody's knowledge of *p* and the truth of *p*. Proposition (5) is perfectly harmless and is simply a special case of the logical truth

$\Box [(\exists x) Kxp \to p]$.

(6) is needed for the denial of logical contingency, but it is false. If God knows *p*, it does not follow that *p* is a necessary truth. Applying this analysis to the proposition (4), it turns out that there is an ambiguity in the sentence:

(7) Jane could have refrained from marrying Harry at *tn* even though God knew that she would.

The ambiguity stems from an ambiguity in the scope of the modal operator "could have." We do *not* mean:

(7') It could have been the case that: Jane does not marry Harry at *tn* and God knows she marries Harry at *tn*.

This is logically contradictory. We do mean:

(7") It could have been the case that Jane does not marry Harry at *tn*; and God does in fact know that she will marry Harry.

(7") could be true. Interpreted in terms of possible worlds, (7') says that there is a possible world in which Jane does not marry Harry at *tn* and yet God knows that she does in that world. There is obviously no such world. (7") says that there is a possible world in which Jane does not marry Harry at *tn*, and yet God knows that she does in the actual world. This seems quite plausible and is innocuous.

The distinction in the scope of the modal operator expressed in (5) and (6) was understood by Aquinas (Brody 1974, 392) and was used by him as a suggested solution to the problem of divine foreknowledge. However, he was prevented from using it as his ultimate solution because he decided that Kgp is a necessary truth (Brody 1974, 391). Unfortunately, this produces the problem all over again, since from (5) and $\Box\ Kgp$ it follows that $\Box\ p$. That led Aquinas to the solution mentioned in section 1.3, which is simply to deny the truth of Kgp when Kgp is tensed on the grounds that in such a case Kgp is ill formed.

It follows from this analysis that in order to maintain the position that any true proposition describing the occurrence of a future free act is logically contingent, we must also maintain that the proposition Kgp is itself a logically contingent truth. This is what we would expect, given the analysis we have already discussed. The proposition Kgp is not true in all possible worlds, nor is p true in all possible worlds. Hence, both p and Kgp are logically contingent.

Next let us look at the argument that p is causally contingent; that is, the event described by p is not causally necessitated by any event or set of events, including God's knowledge that p. One way to make this seem plausible is to argue, as Alvin Plantinga does, that the contingency of Kgp is dependent upon the contingency of p, not the other way around. So if Jones performs a free act at $t2$, it was within his power at that time to do something else such that if he had done it God would have had a different belief at $t1$. To say this is to deny what John Martin Fischer (1983) calls the Fixed Past Constraint:

(FPC) A person never has it in her power at t so to act that the past (relative to t) would have been different from what it actually was.

In the rest of this section I will defend the reasonableness of denying FPC.

First, it is important to see that the denial of FPC neither entails that there is temporally backwards causation nor that one can alter the past. To say that a person has it in her power to do something such that had she done it the past would have been different from what it was is not to make the stronger claim that she has the power to do something that would have *brought it about that* the past was different from what it was.[13] The stronger claim might also be true and its coherence will be discussed in the next section. However, a denial of FPC does not entail it and my analysis does not rest on an acceptance of the stronger claim. The denial of FPC involves a claim of temporally backwards contingency, but such contingency need not be causal.

Still less does the denial of FPC entail that the past can be altered. I assume that once an event occurs, it is fixed. There is only one past and it cannot be changed. But that does not mean that a full explanation of the occurrence of the event might not refer to something in its future.

The denial of FPC, however, is not sufficient to show causal contingency in the sense needed for free will. It is not enough that there be *some* possible world in which Jones does something at $t2$ which is such that God's belief that not-p at $t1$ in that world is contingent on it. If we use the definition of causal contingency given earlier, at least one of the worlds of that description must be exactly like the actual world up to just before $t2$. The reason for this is that we want the two worlds to have the same causal history.[14] If all such worlds have been eliminated by the events up to $t2$, then Jones really does not make a free choice at $t2$. But all such worlds have been eliminated if we use our earlier definition since one of the events up to $t2$ is God's knowing that p, and that is incompatible with not-p. The definition of causal contingency will have to be modified, and we can see that it is reasonable to do so since the motivation for maintaining that the temporal history of the two worlds must be exactly the same up to just before $t2$ is simply that we want their causal history to be identical. But identity of temporal history is not necessary for identity of the causal history relevant to some event. Also, since in the next section we will want to leave open the question of whether there is temporally backwards causation, we must allow for the possibility that temporal identity up to $t2$ is not sufficient for causal identity either.

The definition of causal contingency should therefore be modified in the following way: At least one possible world in which Jones does something at $t2$ upon which God's belief not-p at $t1$ is contingent has exactly the same causal history as the actual world has at $t2$. The only differences between the two worlds are that (1) p is true in the actual world and false in that world, and (2) that world must be a logically consistent world. Of course, possible worlds are by definition logically consistent, so clause (2) merely calls attention to the fact that the change in the truth value of a proposition p from true in the actual world to false in some other world will entail a change in the truth value of an infinite number of other propositions as well. As long as the changes necessary to maintain logical consistency do not affect the exact identity of the causal history of the two worlds or their causal laws, we can still say that the proposition p in question is causally contingent. These intuitions can be used to define the notion of maximal similarity:

> Two possible worlds, w and w', are maximally similar relative to p if and only if they share the same causal history relative to p.

We can now define causal contingency as was promised in section 1.5:

> A proposition p true in a world w is causally contingent in w if and only if there is a possible world w' maximally similar to w relative to p in which p is false.

Now take the following three propositions which we will assume to be true in the actual world: (1) God is essentially omniscient; (8) God believes (4); (4) Jane marries Harry at tn. To say that (4) is causally contingent on the new definition is to say that there is a possible world maximally similar to the actual world relative to (4) in which (4) is false. But if (4) is false, then either (1) or (8) must also be false by the requirement of logical consistency. Since (1) is true in all possible worlds, (8) is false and we have a coherent interpretation of causal contingency that denies FPC.

1.7. A red herring: Backwards causal contingency

In the previous section I argued that there is nothing inconsistent in the assertion that God infallibly foreknows a causally contingent act, at least not by the definition of causal contingency I proposed. I argued that this does not entail the stronger assertion that such an act can "make it happen" that God foreknows it; at least there is no reason to think such an entailment holds unless and until we have a complete account of the nature of knowledge that shows the relation between the object of knowledge and the act of knowing to be fundamentally causal. I do want to say that an earlier event (God's knowledge) can be contingent on a later one (my act) in the following sense: In every possible world in which the later event occurs, the earlier event occurs. The later event is sufficient for the earlier. (Of course, the earlier is likewise sufficient for the later.) I do not know if the contingency I have just described is causal contingency, but I do want to say that my act is responsible for God's previous knowledge of it, that God would not have foreknown it if I had not done it. I do not think this entails backwards causation, but let us look at the stronger causal assertion anyway to see what the objections might be.

Plantinga's (1974a) assertion about the relation between my act and God's knowledge is the following:

(9) It was within Jones's power at $t2$ to do something that would have *brought it about that* God did not hold the belief that he did hold at $t1$.[15]

In this section I would like to examine the grounds for thinking that (9) is incoherent.

Richard Swinburne (1977) argues that it is logically impossible to cause or in any broader sense "bring about" the past. He says, "We must understand here by a state of affairs x being a logically possible state of affairs after T that x be not merely logically possible and after T but also that x be a state of affairs logically compatible with all that has happened at and before T" (Swinburne 1977, 151). Swinburne concludes from this that affecting the past is a logical impossibility. In particular, a person cannot bring about that God held a certain belief in the past. By her choice a person has it in her power at $t2$ to make the beliefs held by a being at $t1$ true or false, but she does not have it in her power at $t2$ to make it the case that a being has a certain belief at $t1$. This would be affecting the past and would be a logical impossibility (Swinburne 1977, 160). He concludes that God does not know everything true, but everything true that it is logically possible to know by the preceding definition. Since he thinks it is not logically possible to know a future contingent by that definition, God does not know future contingents.

Swinburne's point is ambiguous, however. He is right that it is logically impossible to do x after T if God knows before T that x will occur. It has already been pointed out that given that some particular set of events is in the past, it is logically impossible now to alter that past and make it happen that God did not know what he knew after all. But (9) is not a claim about altering the past. Since we do not always know what makes a particular event occur, why couldn't it be something in the future? Could it still be the case that the past wouldn't be the past that it is if some event did not happen in the future? If such a thing is impossible, it could not be simply on the grounds of logical impossibility since an account of what it is to say the past is contingent on the future was given earlier. The further claim that the past is *causally* contingent on the future should not be rejected out of hand either until we get an analysis of causality which demonstrates that it is logically necessary that a cause be temporally prior to its effect. But Swinburne does not give such an analysis.

On the contrary, recent literature on the causal relation includes a number of philosophers interested in giving an account of causality that permits an effect to be temporally prior to its cause.[16] For example, Douglas Ehring (1982) has presented a new account of causality that does not depend on an assumption of temporal priority of causes to effects. It is important to note that in the case of Ehring and others interested in the general topic of causation, the considerations that lead them to allow backwards causation are much broader than a concern with defending divine foreknowledge. At the least, this shows that temporal order is not a closed issue and that foreknowledge is not the sole kind of case in which we might be led to say that an effect can be prior to its cause.

Whenever we put together an argument that can go in more than one direction, there is always a problem in weighing the likelihood of alternative premises. To take a well-known example, we can argue that an all-good and all-powerful God would not permit evil; therefore, there is no such God. Alternatively, we can argue that since there is such a God, an all-good and all-powerful God must have a reason to permit evil. The choice of which way to argue depends upon the level of prior certainty of the different premises. Analogously, we could argue either that because there is precognition of a free act, there must be backwards causation, or we could say that since there is no backwards causation, there must be no precognition of contingent events. Since a full account of the nature of causation is still wanting, it is not fair to opt for the second approach without independent reasons for thinking that a premise that there is no backwards causation is more plausible than a premise that says precognition of free acts is possible.

In any case, as I have already said, it is not clear that my account is committed to saying that my act "causes" God's prior knowledge of it anyway. It is only necessary to say that God's knowledge is contingent upon my act. Section 1.9 will begin a discussion of how this is to be interpreted.

1.8. Another red herring: The problem of counterfactuals

Assertion (9) brings up yet another problem. This is the analysis of subjunctive counterfactual conditionals. I hope to show next that (9) also survives the objection that it is committed to incoherent counterfactual claims.

The truth of (9) seems to entail the truth of the following counterfactual:

(10) If Jones had done x at $t2$ (making p false), God would not have believed p at $t2$.

Because (10) is backwards-looking and we may want a version of the subjunctive conditional that is not time-relational, perhaps the following would be more perspicuous:

(10') If it were the case that Jones does x at $t2$, it would be the case that God would not believe p at $t1$.

I do not see any problem in maintaining the truth of (10') (and (10) also, given the necessary temporal qualifications). But (10) and (10'), unlike many other counterfactuals, are easy to analyze. They seem to be true because in all possible worlds in which the antecedent is true, the consequent is true. That is, in any world in which Jones does x at $t2$, God does not believe p at $t1$. This follows immediately from the fact that God is essentially omniscient.

I would also expect that it follows from God's essential omniscience that God is able to comprehend a complete description of all possible worlds, not only the actual world. This means that for every possible event, God knows whether that event does or does not take place in any given possible world. That would mean that there are counterfactuals of another type which God would know, such as:

(11) If world β had been actual, Saul would have besieged the city.
(12) If world γ had been actual, Saul would not have besieged the city.

My analysis is committed to the truth of counterfactual propositions of the form of (11) and (12), but this is because (11) and (12) are simply alternative ways of describing different possible worlds. (11) and (12) are equivalent to:

(11′) In world β Saul besieges the city.
(12′) In world γ Saul does not besiege the city.

These are innocuous.

Some counterfactuals, however, are not innocuous. As Robert Adams (1977) has pointed out, a problem arises in the analysis of the following:

(13) If David stayed in Keilah, Saul would besiege the city.

Adams argues, and I think rightly, that if such a counterfactual is true, at least on the Stalnaker account of counterfactuals, human beings do not have free will. This is because, according to Stalnaker, a counterfactual conditional is true in world w just in case in the world that is most like w up to the time of the counterfactual event and in which the antecedent is true, the consequent is true. But this means that if (13) is true, Saul's siege would not be a causally contingent event and Saul would not be acting freely. The reason for this is that on the notion of contingency I have given, if Saul exercises free will when he does x at $t1$ in world w, we want to say there are two worlds maximally similar to w except in one world Saul does x at $t1$ and in the other Saul does y at $t1$. Let us consider those worlds in which David stays in Keilah. If Saul exercises free will when he decides whether to besiege the city in those worlds, that is to say that in one world he does besiege the city and in another maximally similar world he does not. But this precludes (13) from having a truth value if subjunctive conditionals are analyzed in Stalnaker's way. Therefore, the believer in free will who also accepts Stalnaker's account of the truth conditions of counterfactuals would want to deny that propositions such as (13) are true. This is in fact what Plantinga (1974b, chap 9) does.

None of this in any sense hinders God's foreknowledge. It is surprising, then, that Anthony Kenny (1974, 67) bases his argument against Plantinga, whose account he calls the most sophisticated attempt to reconcile foreknowledge and indeterminism, on the impossibility of God's knowing counterfactuals such as (13). The source of the confusion could be that Plantinga's views on God's knowledge about all possible worlds bear a striking resemblance to the doctrine of middle knowledge advanced by the later scholastic philosophers Suarez and Molina, a similarity noted earlier by Robert Adams. According to the doctrine of middle knowledge, God knows what every possible free creature would freely do in every situation in which that creature could possibly find herself. Molina thought that foreknowledge proceeded by way of counterfactuals, but Plantinga does not think this way, nor do I.

In short, to say that God is omniscient and knows all true propositions, including those about the contingent future, is not to commit us to saying that God knows propositions like (13). If some propositions in counterfactual form are true, God would, of course, know them. I have already said (10′) is one such proposition. If God's omniscience includes knowing a complete description of every possible world, God would also know propositions like (11) and (12). Again, I have no objections. If other kinds of counterfactual propositions are true, God would know those also, but a list of them awaits a satisfactory account of counterfactuals, and this is independent of the topic of this paper. So just as the objection to backwards causation is a red herring, so is the objection to Plantinga's account of counterfactuals. In neither case is (9) committed to objectionable claims.

I have said that God knows a complete description of all possible worlds and knows which of these is the actual world. But this is not to say that God chose a particular possible world to create. Such a view, I believe, is incompatible with the contingency of events. The reason is as follows: At any given moment of time there is an infinite number of possible worlds compatible with everything that has occurred up to that moment. It is human free choices that determine that the actual world is, say, α rather than β or γ. This means that God does not choose to create an entire world α, but chooses only to create a portion of a world—certain physical and non-physical substances and laws setting things in motion, as well as perhaps some plans of a very general nature such as a plan of Redemption, but all of this is still compatible with an infinite number of possible worlds, and it is up to the inhabitants of the created world-fragment to bring about one world rather than another.

1.9. God's foreknowledge and the theory of explanation

So far, I have argued that God's foreknowledge of an event does not prevent either its logical or its causal contingency. I also have argued that there is nothing incoherent about backwards contingency or the idea that an event is contingent upon an event occurring after it in time, which may or may not be the same as backwards causation, and I have argued that even if God knows what a person freely does in every possible world, this is not the same as knowing a problematic counterfactual such as (13). Problems in the assignment of a truth value to (13), then, pose no problems for my account. My arguments have been primarily negative since I have intended only to show that the attempt to reconcile (1) and (2) will not get us into trouble, as some philosophers have thought. In this section I would like to begin a sketch of my positive account, arguing that a person's free choice can explain God's previous foreknowledge of that choice, and God's foreknowledge does not explain a person's free choice. So even though God's foreknowledge of p is contingent on p just as much as p is contingent on God's foreknowledge of p, the order of explanation is asymmetrical.

On the account I have given, my act ∅ is both necessary and sufficient for God's previous foreknowledge that I would do ∅. This is because if I had not done ∅ now, God would not have known that I would do ∅ before, and if God had not known that I would do ∅ before, I would not have done ∅ now. Another way to put this is to say that my act and God's foreknowledge of it are logically equivalent events. They occur in exactly the same possible worlds. A plausible possible worlds account of causation goes as follows: To say A causes B in $w1$ is to say that in every world with the same physical laws as $w1$ and where A occurs, B occurs. This is the same as saying A is a causally sufficient condition for B. Now, whenever A is a causally sufficient condition for B, B is a causally necessary condition for A. But this does not express the fact that the causal relationship (and the relationship of contingency between events in general) is not symmetrical.

The concept of causally necessary and sufficient conditions does not express the asymmetry of causality. To see that, consider the following case: Suppose that A is the cause of B. On the account of causality just given, this is to say that A is causally sufficient for B and B is causally necessary for A. Suppose further that A is the only thing that *could* cause B. A would not only be sufficient for B, it would also be necessary. But by the same token, if A is necessary for B, B is sufficient for A. Thus, A is both necessary and sufficient for B and B *is* both necessary and sufficient for A and the relationship looks symmetrical. There is no way to tell which is cause and which is effect. Of course, there *is* a sense in which the relationship is symmetrical as the possible worlds analysis demonstrates. But there is more to the relationship between cause and effect, or more generally, between an event and another event upon which it is contingent, than is expressed in the possible worlds relationship, and this is not symmetrical. Suppose A is God's willing to create material beings and B is the coming into existence of material beings. A and B are logically equivalent events; A is necessary and sufficient for B and B is necessary and sufficient for A. But this does not capture the fact that God's will to create explains the existence of the material world in a way in which the existence of the material world does *not* explain God's will to create.

This asymmetry can hold between other states of affairs than events. Consider, for example, the property of being water, call it A, and the property of being H_2O, call it B. Even though A and B may go together in all possible worlds—A is a necessary and sufficient condition for B and B is a necessary and sufficient condition for A, being H_2O explains what it is to be water in a way in which being water does not explain what it is to be H_2O.

Analogously, I want to say that a contingent event ∅ involving a human free choice explains God's foreknowledge of ∅ in a way in which God's foreknowledge does not explain the event ∅. Explanation involves an asymmetrical relationship that is not captured by the concepts of necessary and sufficient conditions, nor by an account in terms of possible worlds as standardly understood.

To take a simple metaphor, suppose that a seer gazing into a crystal ball perceives propositions, and that every proposition such a seer sees is true. Suppose further that every true proposition can be perceived in this way. The fact that the seer sees the proposition is both necessary and sufficient for the truth of the proposition and the truth of the proposition is both necessary and sufficient for the seer's seeing it, but the relationship of explanation is not symmetrical. It would not be an explanation of the truth of some proposition to simply point out that the seer sees it in the ball. On the other hand, it would be an explanation of the fact that the seer sees the proposition, or at least a partial explanation, to say that the proposition is true. The seer's seeing ability does not make the proposition true, but the fact that the proposition is true in part makes the seer see it.

To get a really clear grasp of how it is that my act explains God's foreknowledge, whereas God's foreknowledge does not explain my act, it would be necessary to appeal to a general theory of explanation, something I am not able to do. However, I hope it would be useful to at least outline the considerations that such an account may involve. The main thing that an explanation does, I take it, is to make coherent some set of beliefs. This means that the *explicans* is logically or ontologically prior to the thing it explains. An *explicans* makes the *explicandum* understandable.

Even though we are talking about metaphysical rather than scientific explanation, it might be helpful to look at the classical account of the nature of explanation set out by C. G. Hempel. Let C = a group of events or states of affairs, one of which may be selected as "the" cause. Let L = a set of natural laws or principles, normally in the form of universal generalizations. Let E = some event or state of affairs that needs explaining. We then say that C and L explain E if E follows deductively from C and L.

The application of the Hempelian model to a metaphysical explanation of divine foreknowledge might be as follows:

Let C = the event of a person A performing a free act x.
L: the metaphysical or theological principle that God is omniscient
E: the event or state of affairs of God's knowing that A does x.

Since E can be deduced from L and C, we are entitled to say that L and C explain E on the Hempelian model. However, the order of deduction can just as well go the other way since C can be deduced from L and E. What right do we have to say that *L* and *E* do not really explain *C* the way *L* and *C* explain *E*? Although I do not have an answer to this question, I think it is important to see that this is not a problem peculiar to the matter of divine foreknowledge, but it is a general problem in the theory of explanation. The Hempelian model has sometimes been criticized because it allows us to explain effect by cause as well as cause by effect. Perhaps this is an example of the more general criticism that Hempel's model does not illustrate the asymmetry between *explicans* and *explicandum*. If so, the fact that in my account there is no clear way to tell that my act explains God's foreknowledge of it, but not conversely, may be a symptom of a general problem in the theory of explanation and is not a special weakness of this account of foreknowledge. In order to develop a theory of explanation that would be useful for the account I have given, I think it would be worthwhile to notice that a particular temporal order is not in general necessary for explanation. The only kind of explanation that might require a certain temporal order is causal explanation, and even that may not do so either, as I indicated in section 1.7.

I have argued that God's foreknowledge of my free act depends upon or is contingent upon my act. I do not know whether it is correct to say that my act causes the foreknowledge, but I suspect that this question is ultimately not very important since it is the general form of an asymmetrical explanation that is needed, whether or not it is called causal. This point is important when we remember that the only reason of logic that has ever been given for rejecting the claim that my act explains (brings about, causes) God's foreknowledge of it is the temporal order.

Second, a useful theory of explanation should pursue the insight that the *explicans* and *explicandum* function very differently in a theory. The expressions "water" and "H_2O" function very differently in a theory, even though I believe it is the case that in any possible world, something is water if and only if it is H_2O. Similarly, the proposition that *p* and the proposition that God knows *p* will function very differently in a metaphysical theory even though they are true in the same possible worlds. The problem for divine foreknowledge and human free will, then, is not that they are incompatible, but that we need to explain one in terms of the other; we want an explanation in which a human act "comes first" in the order of explanation, and this requires a general account of the theory of explanation.[17]

To show that divine foreknowledge and human free will are not logically incompatible, then, is not yet to resolve the tension between them. Philosophical understanding seeks harmony, and the fact that two beliefs do not turn out to exhibit the worst kind of disharmony is not to say that they are harmonious. A full explanation of (1) and (2) would imbed them both in a wider theory within which they both seem not only possible but plausible. Such a theory would involve a general account of God's attributes in which an eternal and immutable

God can be related to contingent events. Knowing is only one way God is related to the contingent. Willing is another.[18]

Notes

1. It is not actually crucial to my analysis to accept the omnitemporality of truth. There does not have to be a tenseless proposition true at all times corresponding to every fact. All that is necessary is to accept that if (1) is true, then God knows the truth of future contingents, whether these are properly expressed in a tensed or a tenseless form.
2. Kenny seemed to express more hope for reconciling the two in an earlier article, Kenny (1974).
3. After the publication of this paper, William Hasker (1989) published an influential book arguing that the future is unknowable infallibly because of the incompatibility of infallible foreknowledge and free will. I summarize the enormous literature on both sides of the problem in my Stanford Encyclopedia of Philosophy entry, "Foreknowledge and Free Will." <https://plato.stanford.edu/archives/spr2021/entries/free-will-foreknowledge/>.
4. Alvin Plantinga has pointed out to me this difficulty with the timelessness solution. In a later paper of mine, "Eternity and Fatalism" (Chapter 2 of this book), I argue that the Plantinga response shows at best that the timelessness move will not avoid logical fatalism, which is fatalism allegedly entailed by the past truth of propositions. The foreknowledge problem, however, is not about the past truth of propositions, but about God's past infallible belief states.
5. In addition to Pike and Kenny, see Stephen T. Davis (1983) chapter 1, and Nicholas Wolterstorff (1975).
6. An example of this view is Richard Purtill (1974), 319.
7. See William and Mary Kneale (1962), 48, for a brief discussion of these points. Lukasiewicz is discussed on pp. 569–570.
8. Ockham's notion of accidental necessity is a type of necessity that attaches to the past simply in virtue of its being past. For a good early discussion of this notion, see Freddoso (1983).
9. Jonathan Edwards confuses necessity and inalterability in *Freedom of the Will* (1754), sec. 12, reprinted in Brody (1974), 393.
10. Anthony Kenny in Brody (1974), 411.
11. By saying that God's knowing is an event that occurs at moments of time, in fact all moments of time, I do not mean to preclude the possibility that in addition, God's knowing may occur in a sense that goes beyond time. I am sympathetic with St. Anselm's account in *Monologium*, chap. XXII, of the sense in which God can exist both within time at every moment as well as outside time.
12. It has sometimes been observed that "knows *p*" entails "*p*," and therefore, ordinary human knowledge of the future ought to be fatalistic according to the argument we

are considering. It is true that knowledge entails truth, but the fact that someone's belief state in the past about a future event is a state of knowledge is not inalterable, and hence, does not produce a fatalist problem. For instance, we say that I know the date that classes end at my university provided that the belief is true and I have the other conditions for knowledge—the belief is justified, I believe, in a virtuous way, etc. But since I am not infallible, the fact that my belief state about the future is a state of knowledge is not inalterable since it is still possible that classes do not end on that date. The infallibility condition in the theological fatalist argument is therefore crucial.

13. See Alvin Plantinga (1974a), 71.
14. Nelson Pike (1977) seems to be calling for just such an analysis. He thinks, however, that it is not possible.
15. The year after I published this paper, and twelve years after *God, Freedom, and Evil* (1974a), Plantinga published "On Ockham's Way Out" (1986), which defended a weaker interpretation of backwards contingency than the version in his 1974 book discussed in this section.
16. George Mavrodes (1984) does this in a theological context. Others who take seriously the possibility of backwards causation include Mackie (1966) and von Wright (1971), as well as Ehring (1982), discussed later.
17. Alvin Plantinga makes a similar point in his Aquinas Lecture (1980).
18. I am grateful to a number of people for their meticulous comments on an earlier version of this paper, particularly Alvin Plantinga, George Mavrodes, Joseph Runzo, James Hanink, and Mark Henninger. I also benefited greatly from the discussions of the paper when an earlier version was read at the Philosophy of Religion Society meeting in Claremont, California, October 1983, and at the Society of Christian Philosophers meeting at the University of Notre Dame, March 1984.

2
Eternity and Fatalism (2011)

2.1. The fatalist argument

Fatalism is the thesis that we have no control over future events. Since the past used to be future, fatalism is actually the thesis that we do not have control over any events and never did. But the influential fatalist arguments conclude that we do not control *future* events. The futurity of the fated events is essential to the claim that they are fated. We allegedly have no control over the future because we have no control over the past and we do not control the connection between past and future identified by the fatalist. In the first part of this paper I want to investigate this link between fatalism and temporality, and I will then explore the issue of what happens to fatalist arguments when we move outside the temporal domain.

At the most general level, the three historically most important fatalist arguments all have the same form: We cannot control the past; the past entails the future; therefore, we cannot control the future. This is the basic form of standard arguments for logical fatalism, for theological fatalism, and for causal fatalism. In each case, the proponent of the argument is usually *not* a defender of the fatalist thesis. Rather, the proponent typically takes for granted that the fatalist conclusion is false and proposes the argument as a way to force us to reject one or more premises of the argument. Other philosophers reject the validity of the arguments. I am not going to focus on the specifics of either of these responses since I am interested in investigating the general form of the fatalist threat and its connection with time.

Although the standard fatalist arguments say, in effect, that we cannot control the future because we cannot control the past, none of the arguments says that we cannot control the future only because we cannot control the past. Each of the arguments identifies something else that we cannot control in addition to the past. The argument then has the form: (1) We cannot control the past, and we can't control x. (2) The past + x entails the future. Therefore, (3) we cannot control the future. Let us look briefly at how each kind of fatalist argument has this structure.

Logical fatalism

The logical fatalist argues that we cannot control the past truth of propositions about the future, nor do we have any control over the fact that the truth value of a proposition is immutable. Together these assumptions entail that the future will be what it will be. Therefore, we cannot control the future.[1]

Theological fatalism

The theological fatalist argues that we cannot control the fact that God had the beliefs he had in the past, nor can we control the fact that God is infallible. God's past beliefs together with his infallibility entail the future. Therefore, we cannot control the future.[2]

Causal fatalism

The causal fatalist argues that we cannot control the state of the world billions of years ago, nor can we control the laws of nature or the principle of determinism (which we presuppose for the purposes of the argument). The state of the world in the distant past plus the laws of nature entail the future, given determinism. Therefore, we cannot control the future.[3]

Given the assumption that the conclusion is false, a common strategy is to use the argument as a way to force the denial of one of the premises—e.g., the truth of propositions about the contingent future, divine foreknowledge, or the thesis of determinism. Each of these arguments has a large literature, particularly the second and third. Curiously, many philosophers take the first argument to be fallacious on its face, yet rarely does anybody make the same claim about the second or third argument.

I have presented the general structure of these arguments to highlight the fact that each argument crucially depends upon the assumption that we cannot control something in the past. Presumably we cannot control it *because* it is past. In addition, each argument depends upon the assumption that there is something else we cannot control—a principle about the fixity of the truth value of propositions, God's nature, or causal determinism and the laws of nature. In each case the argument gets its conclusion by using a transfer of necessity principle. The principle is modeled on axiom K, an axiom of every system of modal logic:

$$\Box (p \supset q) \supset [\Box p \supset \Box q]$$

It is tempting to accept principles of this form for types of necessity other than logical necessity, including principles that substitute the informal operator "we cannot control the fact that p" for "$\Box p$" in the consequent of axiom K. If we make that substitution, we get the following Transfer of Lack of Control principle (TLC):

TLC: □ (p ⊃ q) ⊃ [We cannot control the fact that p ⊃ We cannot control the fact that q].

Fatalist arguments use this principle or some variation of it. There are objections to TLC, but it has many variants,[4] and my focus in this paper is not a critique of TLC.

Is there any way we could get a plausible and important argument for fatalism without the assumption that we cannot do anything about the past? I do not know of any historically important argument that does not include lack of control over the past as a premise, and lack of control over the future as a conclusion, but notice that there is nothing in TLC that refers to temporality. The past is allegedly one of the things we cannot do anything about, but there are others. I think that we should keep in mind that the fatalist argument relies on TLC or a variation of it since later we will discuss the possibility of an argument for fatalism that makes no reference to time.

I have drawn attention to the similarities among the arguments for logical, theological, and causal fatalism, but I do not want to exaggerate the similarities. It could turn out that one argument is invalid or has a false premise, but another does not. Perhaps the argument for theological fatalism fails to show that infallible foreknowledge leads to fatalism, but the causal fatalist argument succeeds in showing that causal determinism leads to fatalism. Or perhaps the logical fatalist argument fails to show that past truth about the future leads to fatalism, but infallible foreknowledge does lead to fatalism. My point in calling attention to the similarities in the structure of the arguments and their assumptions about the past is not to claim that they stand or fall together, but to reveal the reference to past and future in fatalist arguments, and to raise the question whether reference to temporality is crucial in generating a fatalist argument.

2.2. Escaping fatalism by escaping time

The logical fatalist and theological fatalist arguments have something in common that distinguishes them from the causal fatalist argument. The former arguments have a premise that we cannot control something in the past that arguably is not in the past because it is not in time. Propositions can be plausibly understood as non-temporal entities, if they are entities of any kind, and if so, they do not have properties in the past. If so, a proposition *p* was not true yesterday, nor is it true today, nor will it be true tomorrow. Similarly, according to an important tradition in Christian philosophy notably defended by Boethius and Aquinas, God is not in time and so he does not have beliefs in time.[5] There is nothing God believed yesterday, nor does he believe anything today, nor will he believe anything tomorrow. So one traditionally important way out of both logical and theological fatalism attempts to escape fatalism, not by denying TLC, nor by denying the assumption that we cannot do anything about the past, but by denying the pastness of that which we allegedly do not control as presented in the first premise of the respective arguments.

Notice that the denial that God is in time need not involve any positive claim about the nature of divine eternity in order to avoid commitment to the fatalist conclusion in the argument for theological fatalism. For example, God need not be eternal in the full Boethian sense of having the complete, simultaneous, and perfect possession of illimitable life.[6] It is sufficient that God has no temporal properties and, in particular, God did not have beliefs in the past. Similarly, the denial that propositions have truth values in time need not involve any commitment about the nature of propositions beyond the claim that they have no properties in time.

There are some differences between the use of the timelessness move to avoid logical fatalism and the use of the move to avoid theological fatalism. Here is one difference. Even if propositions are outside time, they seem to have temporal correlates—sentence tokens, or perhaps more obviously, utterances. An utterance occurs at a particular moment of time and utterances seem to be the sorts of things that are true or false. You can speak truly or you can speak falsely, and if what you say is true, being true seems to be a property of the utterance at the time of the utterance, which may be in the past. So even if propositions are timeless entities, what you said yesterday was true yesterday. If so, the logical fatalist gets his argument. He only needs to formulate it in terms of utterances, or what people say, rather than propositions. In contrast, if God's beliefs are timeless, there is nothing that is a temporal correlate of God's timeless beliefs. That is to say, there is no x that occurs in time and is related to divine timeless beliefs as utterances are related to timeless propositions, and which permits a reformulation of the fatalist argument. In this respect the timelessness move looks better as a way out of theological fatalism than as a way out of logical fatalism.

But isn't there something in the past correlated to God's timeless beliefs in the relevant way? Suppose I make the utterance, "God timelessly believes p." Isn't my utterance true or false for the same reason that my utterance "p" is true or false? If my utterance yesterday that God timelessly believes p was true, doesn't that mean that there is something in the past that we do not control due to its pastness, and which permits a reformulation of the fatalist argument? If so, the eternity move does not help.[7]

But that response is too fast. The theological fatalist argument is a different argument than the logical fatalist argument. The former begins with the pastness of God's past beliefs; the latter begins with the pastness of the past truth of propositions—or utterances, in the revised version. If God (with his beliefs) is outside of time, then there is a straightforward escape from the theological fatalist argument. The reply that it falls prey to an argument about the past truth of utterances about God's timeless beliefs is just the reply that this way of escaping theological fatalism is not also an escape from logical fatalism. But the defender of divine timelessness as a way out of theological fatalism can quite rightly point out that he was not offering a way out of logical fatalism. He was responding to a standard form of theological fatalism, and that is given by the doctrine of divine timelessness. What remains is not an argument about God or his infallible beliefs, but an argument about the past truth of utterances, and that is a different problem which has, presumably, a different solution. The problem with the past truth of the utterance "God timelessly believes p" is the same as the problem with the past truth of the utterance "p." It is the same problem and it has the same solution, if there is one. I think, then, that if God's beliefs are timeless, we do not yet have a reason to think that they are tied to something in time in a way that permits a reformulation of the theological fatalist argument. Divine timelessness does not escape the argument for logical fatalism, but we knew that anyway.

There is, however, a way God's timeless beliefs could be tied to something in time in a problematic way. Under the assumption that God infallibly knows outside of time that an event occurs at time t, couldn't he reveal his knowledge to a temporal being prior to t? Suppose God infallibly and timelessly believes that the Treaty of Versailles is signed on June 28, 1919. Surely, God could reveal this knowledge to a human being a hundred years before the signing of the treaty. Or suppose, as Peter van Inwagen imagines, that God causes a monument to come into existence *ex nihilo* in 1900 on which is inscribed the following words: "On 21 September, 1942, a human being named Peter van Inwagen will be born. On 23 December, 2006, at 11:46 a.m. Eastern time, he will have to choose between lying and telling the truth. He will choose to lie" (Van Inwagen 2008, 219). Van Inwagen argues that this possibility poses a fatalist threat for a timeless being. He says, "Is it true in any of the possible continuations of the then-present state of affairs that the words inscribed on the monument did not express a true proposition? No, for in that case God would either have been mistaken or have been a deceiver, and both are impossible. My act (telling the lie) was therefore not a free act." Van Inwagen goes on to say that "a divinely inspired human prophet who has foretold certain actions of human beings would also be a Freedom-denying Prophetic Object" (2008, 219). He concludes that the foreknowledge problem can be reconstructed for a timeless deity and retains "much of the force" of the original argument.

Let us look more closely at whether the possibility of a revelation of the future in the form of van Inwagen's monument permits a reconstruction of the theological fatalist problem. Since it is belief in what the monument says that leads to a foreknowledge dilemma, let us begin by considering the reason why fallible human knowledge of the future does not pose the same fatalist threat as infallible foreknowledge. Whether a fallible human belief about the future is one of knowledge depends upon how things turn out. For instance, suppose I believe in September 2008 that final exams in the fall semester at my university end on December 19, 2008, and suppose that the belief is true and that it is warranted or justified or has whatever other property knowledge requires in addition to truth. In that case, I know that final exams end on December 19. But since I am fallible, no matter how justified I am in my belief in September, there is no guarantee that my belief is true. There might be a big ice storm that results in the cancellation of the last day of finals, or the university president might, on a whim, move the exams up a week. Of course, that probably will not happen, and so it will probably turn out that my state of belief in September is one of knowledge. But if finals do not end on December 19, it will turn out that I did not know in September that finals would end on that day even if I was as justified as I can be in such matters. Possessing the best of justification or whatever other property knowledge requires in addition to truth is compatible with having a false belief. Of course, since knowing entails truth, it is necessary that *if* I know, I have a true belief, but it is not necessary that my state of believing in September is one of knowing since I am not infallible, and so it is not necessary that I am in a state of believing what is true.

That is the reason the problem of divine foreknowledge rests on the combination of the pastness of God's beliefs and their infallibility. Although we cannot do anything about the fact that somebody in the past believed what he believed, we sometimes *can* do something about the fact that the belief he had was true and was a case of knowing—if the belief is about something that has not yet happened. Somebody can, in principle, make a belief that final exams end on December 19 false by canceling the exams, in which case they also make it the case that anybody who believed that exams end on December 19 did not know that they do. But unfortunately, we do not have this power when the belief is infallible. There is nothing anybody can do to make an infallible belief false.

Now let us go back to van Inwagen's monument. Is there anything anybody can do to make a belief in what the monument says false? Given that the words on the monument are written by God in plain English, and assuming some human Sam is a normal English speaker and the monument is easy for him to read, and assuming also that Sam believes the inscription is veridical, then if Sam reads it and comes to believe what he thinks is written there, there is not much chance he will make a mistake in believing what God timelessly believes and which was divinely inscribed on the monument in 1900. But even though there is not much chance, there is nonetheless *some* chance. Given the fallibility of Sam's powers and the lack of a perfect match between him and his environment and his understanding of the intentions of the inscriber, it is still possible that what he comes to believe when he reads the monument is false. If so, the state he is in does not entail the truth of what he believes, and so his believing in 1900 that van Inwagen will tell a lie in 2006 does not entail that van Inwagen will tell a lie.

Van Inwagen asks, "Is it true in any of the possible continuations of the then-present state of affairs that the words inscribed on the monument did not express a true proposition? No, for in that case God would either have been mistaken or have been a deceiver, and both are impossible" (Van Inwagen 2008, 219). But there is a confusion in this claim. There *is* a possible continuation of the then-present state of affairs in which the words that Sam *believes* are inscribed on the monument do not express a true proposition. God cannot be mistaken, but Sam can. Since God is not a deceiver, we can assume that God makes sure that Sam believes the truth. Even so, God does not make Sam believe infallibly. So long as we interpret the monument example as one in which a timeless infallible God reveals the future to fallible temporal beings, there is no fatalist dilemma arising from believing the inscription on the monument. And the same point applies no matter how a fallible being obtains knowledge from God. If the recipient is fallible, we do not get a problem like the problem of theological fatalism.

But there is another interpretation of van Inwagen's claim that has nothing to do with God being a deceiver because it has nothing to do with the belief of a human knower. When van Inwagen says that there is no possible continuation of the then-present state of affairs in which the monument did not express a true proposition, he might think that the mere existence of the monument poses a fatalist problem even if nobody reads it and comes to believe the inscription. Perhaps he thinks of the monument as a piece of a vast History of the World, containing all true propositions about the past, present, and future, and no false ones. In that case, fatalism seems to be implied by the *truth* of the inscription which records a particular proposition God infallibly believes and which he inscribes with perfect accuracy. On this interpretation of the monument example, infallibility is not relevant since infallibility is a property of a conscious believer, not a property of inscriptions or of the propositions expressed on inscriptions. On this interpretation, if there is a fatalist problem, it arises from the fact that a truth about the future is "written" and cannot be unwritten or changed; truth necessarily stays the same forever. On this interpretation, the problem of the monument is the problem of logical, not theological fatalism, and as I have said, the two problems are distinct and should be treated separately. The problem of the monument is therefore either a version of logical fatalism, which has nothing to do with anybody receiving a revelation from God, or it is not a fatalist problem because the recipient is not infallible. Either way, it is not the problem of infallible foreknowledge.

So far we have not found a reason to fear that if God is timeless, his timeless knowledge can have a temporal counterpart, thereby generating another version of theological fatalism. Surely, God can reveal his knowledge to a temporal creature, but so long as the creature is fallible, that creature's epistemic state will not entail the truth of what he believes. But this leads to a harder problem. Can't we imagine that God reveals his knowledge to an infallible temporal being? To make the strongest case for a temporal correlate of timeless knowledge, all we need to do is postulate the possibility that God himself enters time with his infallible knowledge intact. And that is exactly what some versions of the doctrine of the Incarnation maintain. If Jesus Christ had a divine mind in time that knew the future infallibly, there is a threat of theological fatalism even if we accept the doctrine of divine timelessness.[8] Of course, there might be reasons why this version of the doctrine does not make sense, but the worry is that if it does make sense, it would mean that the doctrine of divine timelessness loses any advantage it would otherwise have in solving the problem of theological fatalism.

Furthermore, I suspect that the problem exists as long as it is even *possible* that God enter time with infallible foreknowledge, and this point can be generalized. Van Inwagen makes it clear that he is not worried that God's inscription on the monument would prevent human freedom only if God actually created such a monument. Presumably, he thinks that there is no such monument, but he thinks the mere possibility of the monument threatens fatalism. And this is the usual position of incompatibilists about infallible foreknowledge and free will. If I am right about that, we cannot save the timelessness solution as a way out of fatalism unless it turns out that it is not even possible that a timeless God enter time with infallible foreknowledge, nor can he reveal his foreknowledge to an infallible temporal being.

In this section I have argued that the timelessness solution to the foreknowledge dilemma succeeds in evading the theological fatalist argument only if there is no temporal counterpart of divine timeless knowledge, and I think that the defender of the Boethian way out can succeed in avoiding such a temporal counterpart under the assumption that the incarnate Son of God does not have infallible knowledge at moments of time, and could not have such knowledge, nor can any other temporal being have infallible foreknowledge. But in the next section we will look at a different reason for thinking that escaping time does not escape fatalism.

2.3. Fatalism and a timeless knower

If fatalism is a problem about the relation between past and future, escaping time ought to escape the fatalist threat. But we do not yet have a secure solution to theological fatalism unless the timeless realm does not also have a problematic relationship to human contingent acts. In past work I have argued that the Boethian moves avoid one fatalist argument only to fall prey to another (Zagzebski 1991, 60–63). To identify the problem, let us go back to the essential idea of fatalist arguments in TLC: If p entails q, then if we cannot control p, we cannot control q. Standard fatalist arguments begin with the fact that we cannot control the past and we cannot control something else, and argue from there to the conclusion that we cannot control the future. But TLC does not include any reference to time, and I think that the lack of reference to time in TLC is important. There are many things we cannot control, in addition to the past. The fatalist arguments themselves rely upon premises referring to our lack of control over things other than the past—the laws of physical nature, the laws of God's nature, and the logical principles used in the arguments. Presumably, there are many other things we do not control as well. One would think that a paradigm case of something we cannot control is anything in the timeless realm. How could finite temporal beings hope to have power over a transcendent domain, a domain wholly outside of time (and, presumably, also outside of space)? The prime candidates for timeless objects—properties, propositions, numbers, possible worlds—are as necessary as anything can be. I am not suggesting that God's timeless beliefs are abstract objects like numbers and propositions. Nonetheless, there is a *prima facie* connection between the timeless realm and the realm of what we cannot do anything about, a connection that requires a closer look.

One way to examine our intuitions about what we can and cannot control is to think about why we believe we cannot control the past and why we think that it is at least arguable that we can control the future. We can then apply these intuitions to the timeless realm.

I think there are two different reasons why we believe we cannot do anything about the past. The first is the metaphysical principle that there cannot be backwards causation. This principle is often thought to be intuitively obvious, but there are at least two distinct ways the principle can be understood:

(i) A cause cannot be later in time than its effect.
(ii) A cause must be prior in time to its effect.

Most philosophers who discuss causation distinguish (i) and (ii) only because they notice that (ii) rules out the possibility that a cause is simultaneous with its effect, whereas (i) does not. I doubt that in the context of most discussions another difference is noticed: (ii) rules out a causal relation between a temporal event and something outside of time, whereas (i) does not. The principle that there cannot be backwards causation rules out a temporal cause and a timeless effect only if the principle is interpreted as (ii). Furthermore, it is not clear that either version of the principle is relevant to the issue of whether we can have some control over the timeless realm since *doing something about x* or *having some control over x* is broader than *causing x*. Causing *x* is one way to have some control over *x*, but it is not the only way. Even if we do not and cannot cause God's timeless beliefs, it might still be the case that God believes what he believes *because of* something we do; perhaps he believes timelessly *in virtue of* something we do in time. I am not able to offer an account of the because-of relation, but I think that it is worth noticing that whatever the relation is, it is very doubtful that it reduces to the causal relation. So if the principle ruling out backwards causation is interpreted as (i), it does not rule out causing something in a timeless domain, and even if the principle is interpreted in the strong sense of (ii), that does not rule out the possibility that something in the timeless domain occurs because of something in the temporal domain, under the assumption that the because-of relation is not causal.

I conclude that if our lack of power over the past is due to the principle that there cannot be backwards causation, there is no reason to think that we lack power over the timeless realm. At least, it would take quite a bit of work to demonstrate the application to the timeless realm. However, this point may be irrelevant because there is a second reason why we believe we cannot do anything about the past that comes much closer to applying to the timeless realm.

Writers on time and fatalism sometimes refer to the idea that the past is ontologically determinate, fixed, complete, whereas the future is ontologically indeterminate, unfixed, in need of completion by an injection of free choice (and maybe also pure chance) into the ontological mix.[9] This point is often associated with the claim that the past is more real than the future. These claims are obviously vague, but they are probably clear enough to permit the following conjecture. The reason why we can't do anything about the past is that there is nothing left to be done; the past is complete. We can in principle do something about the future because the future is in process of construction. It is in need of something to complete it.

This reason for thinking we cannot do anything about the past certainly appears to apply to the timeless realm. The timeless domain is at least as real as the past. In fact, the origin of the idea of the timeless realm in Parmenides and Plato suggests that it is *more* real than anything temporal. Furthermore, the timeless domain is determinate, fixed; it has no need for something outside of it to make it complete. It surely does not need the temporal domain. It would exist just as it is even if no temporal domain existed at all. At least, it is tempting to think that. And that suggests that on grounds of ontological reality and fixedness, the timeless realm is like the past and unlike the future. In fact, it has more of what makes the past beyond our power than the past does. So if we think we cannot control the past, we have at least as much reason to think that we cannot control the timeless domain. Therefore, if God's beliefs are outside of time, it appears that we would have no more control over them than we would if God's beliefs were in the past. Both are in the category of what we cannot do anything about.

I think that this means that we have reason to adopt a principle of the Necessity of Eternity that is parallel to the principle of the Necessity of the Past. Admittedly, the two principles differ in their hold on our intuitions. The latter is enshrined in such commonsense aphorisms as "There is no use crying over spilled milk," whereas there is no parallel aphorism that says there is no use crying over some timeless state. But that should not make us feel any more secure about our ability to influence the timeless realm. People do not have sayings about our relation to the timeless realm only because most of us have very few ideas at all about the timeless realm. Philosophers do not have much to say about it either, but I have suggested that what philosophers say pushes us in the direction of thinking that we have no control over it. I am not arguing that the principle of the Necessity of Eternity is true. In fact, I hope that it is false. My point is that it is supported by some of the same intuitions that support the Necessity of the Past, and for that reason should be taken seriously.

The principle of the Necessity of Eternity permits the formulation of a fatalist argument for timeless knowledge parallel to the argument from infallible foreknowledge. To formulate both arguments, we need three principles:

(1) Either the necessity of the past or the necessity of eternity
(2) TLC
(3) A principle that Quine called "semantic shift" (1970, 12).

By "semantic shift," I mean a principle permitting semantic ascent or semantic descent. An illustration of semantic ascent is standardly given by the following:

If snow is white, the proposition that snow is white is true.

Semantic descent is the converse:

If the proposition that snow is white is true, then snow is white.

We can now formulate two fatalist arguments, one for a temporal deity, and one for a timeless deity. Take an example of a future human act that is intuitively freely chosen, if anything is. Suppose it is my act of flying to Los Angeles on

December 23, and let F be the proposition I express by the sentence, "I will fly to L.A. on December 23."

The argument in which God has beliefs in time runs as follows:

Theological fatalist argument for temporal deity

(1) God infallibly believed F in the past. (Assumption)
(2) I cannot do anything about the fact that God infallibly believed F in the past (Necessity of the Past and lack of power over God's infallible nature).
(3) Necessarily, if God infallibly believed F in the past, then F is true (definition of "infallibility.")
(4) If (2) and (3), then I cannot do anything about the fact that F is true (TLC).
(5) Therefore, I cannot do anything about the fact that F is true. (2, 3, 4 *modus ponens*)
(6) Therefore, I cannot do anything about the fact that I fly to Los Angeles on December 23 (semantic shift).

An exactly parallel argument with the assumption that God is timeless runs as follows:

Theological fatalist argument for timeless deity

(1') God infallibly believes F timelessly (assumption).
(2') I cannot do anything about the fact that God infallibly believes F timelessly (Necessity of Eternity and lack of power over God's infallible nature).
(3') Necessarily, if God infallibly believes F timelessly, then F is true (definition of "infallibility").
(4') If (2') and (3'), then I cannot do anything about the fact that F is true (TLC).
(5') Therefore, I cannot do anything about the fact that F is true (2', 3', 4' *modus ponens*).
(6') Therefore, I cannot do anything about the fact that I fly to Los Angeles on December 23 (semantic shift).

In offering these arguments, I am not proposing that there are no ways to escape their conclusion. My view is that there are ways out of the temporal version of theological fatalism, and I also think there are ways out of the timeless version. My point here is that timelessness itself does not solve the dilemma and it may not even have any advantage in escaping theological fatalism. Possibly a stronger case can be made for the rejection of (2′) than for the rejection of (2), given the fact that the Necessity of Eternity has a weaker hold on our intuitions than the Necessity of the Past. Even so, the intuitions supporting (2′) are strong enough that it cannot be rejected out of hand. The Boethian solution to the problem of infallible foreknowledge cannot be declared victorious without further argument.

2.4. Logical fatalism and timelessness

Does the timelessness move do any better as a solution to logical fatalism? I argued in section 2.2 that even if propositions are timeless, there are temporal counterparts to propositions that permit a reconstruction of the argument for logical fatalism, so we already have one reason to think that timelessness is not useful in avoiding the problem. The argument of section 2.3 gives us another reason to think that timelessness does not escape logical fatalism. If the timeless realm is as fixed as the past, the timeless truth of propositions about the future are as fixed as the past truth of propositions. So if the timelessness move generates a parallel dilemma of theological fatalism, it would also permit a parallel dilemma of logical fatalism. As we will see, however, there is an interesting difference in the timeless truth dilemma. The fatalist argument it generates is much shorter than the arguments for temporal utterances.

Let F be my utterance, "I will fly to Los Angeles on December 23, 2008," or alternatively, the proposition I express by that utterance.

Logical fatalist argument for temporal propositions (or utterances)

(1L) F was true in the past (e.g., the time of utterance) (assumption).

(2L) I cannot do anything about the fact that F was true in the past (Necessity of the Past).

(3L) Necessarily, if F was true in the past, F is true forever (immutability of truth value).[10]

(4L) If (2L) and (3L), then I cannot do anything about the fact that F is true forever (TLC).

(5L) Therefore, I cannot do anything about the fact that F is true forever (2L, 3L, 4L, *modus ponens*).

(6L) Therefore, I cannot do anything about the fact that I fly to Los Angeles on December 23 (semantic shift).

The principle of the Necessity of Eternity permits a much shorter fatalist argument for timeless propositions, without requiring the Transfer of Lack of Control Principle (TLC):

Logical fatalist argument for timeless propositions

(1L′) F is timelessly true (assumption).
(2L′)   I cannot do anything about the fact that F is timelessly true (Necessity of Eternity).
(3L′)   I cannot do anything about the fact that I fly to Los Angeles on December 23 (semantic shift).

If propositions are timeless, and assuming that the semantic shift at line (3L′) is innocuous, it follows that premise (2L′) had better be false. We can see, then, that the move from (1L) to (1L′) is hardly an advantage! The timelessness move either has no advantage in escaping either kind of fatalism, or only a weak advantage due to the somewhat weaker intuitive support for the Necessity of Eternity over the Necessity of the Past.

2.5. The urgency to find a compatibilist solution to the timeless knowledge dilemma

Let us return to theological fatalism. So far, we have seen that the doctrine of divine timelessness escapes theological fatalism only if it can overcome two hurdles. The first is that there must be no temporal counterpart to timeless knowing that permits a reconstruction of the temporal fatalist argument. I have argued that it can overcome this hurdle. The second is that there must be no apparent fatalist consequence of timeless knowing. In the previous section I argued that the doctrine does not overcome this hurdle since there is a timeless knowing dilemma parallel to the foreknowledge dilemma. That does not prove that timeless knowing leads to fatalism, but it does mean that there is a fatalist argument for a timeless deity that requires a response, just as there is a fatalist argument for a temporal deity that requires a response. Perhaps it is easier to get out of the timeless knowledge dilemma than the temporal knowledge dilemma. Nonetheless, a way out is required, and timelessness does not escape fatalism in one move. If the doctrine of divine timelessness comes out ahead of the doctrine of divine temporality with respect to fatalism, it is only by the extent to which the Necessity of the Past is more compelling than the Necessity of Eternity. I will leave it to my readers to decide how much that is, but in this section I want to argue that there is one respect in which the timelessness doctrine has a disadvantage when compared with the doctrine of a temporal deity.

The problem is this: There is no incompatibilist fallback position if God is timeless. Christian philosophers who believe that infallible foreknowledge is incompatible with human free will typically conclude that free will exists, but there is no divine foreknowledge. That is, the incompatibility they perceive between foreknowledge and free will is resolved in favor of free will. The denial of divine foreknowledge, then, is a backup position for those philosophers who want to retain as much of the traditional conception of God as they think they can, while retaining the belief in human freedom. This is the position taken by Peter van Inwagen in the paper mentioned earlier, and it has been defended by philosophers, such as William Hasker, who advocate "Open Theism" (Hasker 1989); see also Pinnock et al 1994). Hasker's idea is that an omniscient deity forgoes possessing infallible foreknowledge of human choices in order to save human freedom. God has complete, detailed, and infallible knowledge of the past and present and the tendencies of each creature, which allows him to know the objective probability of each possible future event and the gradually changing likelihood of each possibility's being realized. But God does not know the contingent future infallibly. Christian philosophers who take this position typically also say that nothing of religious importance is lost by this qualification of God's omniscience. God's ultimate control over the world does not require meticulous knowledge and control over every detail of the creation. We can still trust in God and rely upon his providential care even without infallible foreknowledge (Hasker 1989, Chap. 10).

Now notice that there is no analogous incompatibilist position on timeless knowledge that preserves free will. If a timeless knower "gave up" timelessly knowing the contingent future, he would have to give up all infallible knowledge of human contingent affairs. For a timeless God, there is no possibility of temporarily forgoing an infallible grasp of the future. Either a timeless God infallibly knows that I fly to Los Angeles on December 23 or he does not. Either he infallibly knows van Inwagen tells a lie on a certain date in 2006 or he does not. And the same point applies to every other act in human history. On the view of incompatibilists like the Open theists, God eventually finds out what happens in the world when it occurs, and ever afterward he knows it infallibly. But if God is timeless and does not know human free acts infallibly, he never knows infallibly. The unavoidable conclusion is that human free will had better be compatible with infallible timeless knowing because if it is not, there is no incompatibilist qualification of omniscience that will save anything close to the traditional conception of a God for the adherent of divine timelessness.

I have presented this feature of the timeless knowledge dilemma as a disadvantage of the doctrine of timelessness, but that judgment may not be fair. If you are confident that there is a good compatibilist solution to the problem, you will not be dismayed by the fact that there is no appealing fallback position. Or maybe you think the fallback position is not very appealing anyway, so the foreknowledge dilemma is no less threatening than the timeless version. But for people who are attracted to divine timelessness and would like a fallback position, the lack of a fallback position makes the need to resolve the timeless knowledge dilemma urgent.

How urgent is the need to solve the dilemma of logical fatalism? It seems to me that the fallback position that propositions or assertions about the contingent future have no truth value is not very appealing. There are good logical reasons for accepting that propositions are either omnitemporally or timelessly true, so there is a pressing need to solve the logical fatalist problem. Given a choice between the position that propositions are timeless and the position that they are temporal, I have argued that there is no reason to prefer the view that propositions are timeless because of its alleged advantages in escaping logical fatalism. We should acknowledge that if any human being can do anything about anything, there is a proposition the truth of which somebody has some control over. If propositions are temporal entities with truth values that remain fixed throughout time, then somebody can do something about something in the past. Alternatively, if propositions are timeless entities with timeless truth values, then somebody can do something about something in the timeless realm. Is the latter implication any easier to accept than the former? Or to pose the question the other way around, is the former implication any harder to accept than the latter? I think not, and I think the situation is much the same with the problem of divine foreknowledge. How much harder is it to say that God knew p in the past because of something that happens in the future than to say that God knows p timelessly because of something that happens in time?

2.6. Conclusion

Every historically important argument for fatalism argues that we have no control over the future because we have no control over the past. In this paper I have concentrated on the arguments for logical and theological fatalism. The past truth of propositions about the future and God's past infallible knowledge of the future both seem to lead to fatalism, and in both cases, it is tempting to think that fatalism can be escaped by escaping time. If propositions are timelessly true rather than true in the past, the logical fatalist argument appears to collapse. If God's knowledge of our future is timeless rather than in the past, the theological fatalist argument appears to collapse. But I have argued that escaping fatalism by escaping time solves the fatalist problem only if the timelessness move can overcome two hurdles: (1) There must be no temporal counterpart that permits a reformulation of the fatalist argument. I argued that the timeless knowledge of God can overcome this hurdle, provided that we accept a view of the Incarnation that denies infallible foreknowledge to Jesus Christ, but the timeless truth of propositions cannot overcome this problem. (2) There must not be a reason to think that the timeless realm shares with the past the feature of being outside our control. I argued that the timelessness move does not overcome this hurdle for either argument. There is a principle of the Necessity of Eternity that permits the formulation of a parallel timeless truth dilemma and a parallel timeless knowledge dilemma. The necessity of eternity may have a weaker hold on our intuitions than the necessity of the past, and to that extent the timeless knowledge argument for fatalism may be easier to escape than the temporal version, but the timeless knowledge problem is worse in one respect: there is no fallback position that saves human free will by qualifying divine omniscience. If God is timeless, there had better be a mistake in the timeless knowledge argument.

I conclude that the escape from fatalism does not turn on the issue of temporality versus timelessness. There are many reasons why a Christian philosopher should be attracted to the traditional conception of divine timelessness, but I do not think the need to escape fatalism is one of them.

Notes

1. The Master Argument of Diodorus Cronus was widely discussed by post-Aristotelian logicians and its general form has remained unchanged for millennia. The argument is roughly of the form given here.
2. The foreknowledge dilemma is mentioned by Cicero in *De Fato* and by Augustine in *On the Free Choice of the Will*. The contemporary version, of course, has an enormous literature.
3. A well-known variation of this argument is given by Peter van Inwagen (1983). It has been called the consequence argument for the incompatibility of causal determinism and free will.
4. Variations include the stipulation that p is true, or the stipulation that q is false. Another variation requires that q is about something later in time than p. For the latter proposal, see Timothy O'Connor (2002), chap 1.
5. Boethius, *The Consolation of Philosophy*, Book V, Prose vi. One passage in Aquinas that adopts the Boethian position on divine timelessness is *ST* Ia, q. 14, a. 13, reply obj. 3.
6. Ibid.

7. Plantinga gives a version of this objection to the timelessness move in Plantinga (1986). I endorsed it in "Divine Foreknowledge and Human Free Will" (Chapter 1 of this volume), but subsequently decided that the objection does not succeed.
8. I am thinking of a position like the two minds view of Thomas V. Morris (1986), 102–107, or the divided mind view of Richard Swinburne (1994), 194–209.
9. The traditional contrast between past and future given here does not mention the present. Recently, presentism, the view that only the present is real, has gained popularity. I will not discuss presentism in this paper.
10. A variation of the view that propositions are immutably true is that there are truth value links between tensed versions of the same proposition that hold necessarily. Michael Dummett (2003) argues for these links.

3

Divine Foreknowledge and the Metaphysics of Time (2014)

3.1. Introduction

Most philosophers assume that philosophical inquiry into the nature of God is important only for theists or those who at least find theism tempting. In this paper I will argue that when we examine the traditional dilemma of infallible divine foreknowledge and human free will, we uncover a deeper dilemma that has nothing to do with God, infallibility, or free will. Many historically important ways out of theological fatalism are irrelevant to this problem, which arises within the metaphysics of time. I will then argue that the most reasonable response to the dilemma is to reject the idea that the necessity of the past is a purely temporal modality; in fact, it is not a form of necessity in the formal sense of necessity. Rather, I propose that it reduces to the metaphysical thesis that the past is causally closed. With this interpretation of the necessity of the past, the argument for theological fatalism must be revised in a way that has a peculiar and problematic feature. My conclusion is that well-known fatalist problems are interwoven with problems about time that are easier to see in the context of theism, but which would be there anyway. Unraveling the dilemma of foreknowledge and free will shows us one of the ways in which philosophical theology has important implications for metaphysics.

3.2. What is the dilemma of foreknowledge and free will about?

In this section I will argue in three stages that the apparent incompatibility of infallible divine foreknowledge and human free will is an instance of a much more general problem that is far wider in scope than a problem about God or free will. In the first stage I will argue that the problem is not uniquely about God; it is about infallibility and free will. In the second stage I will argue that it is not limited to a problem about free will because it leads to a general dilemma about infallibility and temporal necessity. In the third stage I will argue that the problem is even broader than that because infallibility is not an essential component of the problem. A form of the dilemma arises directly from the idea of temporal necessity.

3.2.1. Is the problem uniquely about God?

Let us begin with a standard argument for theological fatalism. Assume that God exists and is infallible. That is to say, necessarily, if God believes that *p*, then *p*. Assume also that God existed in the past and had beliefs in the past about future human acts.

In addition, assume the necessity of the past. As we will see, there are a number of confusions about this type of necessity, and one important ambiguity. On the one hand, the necessity of the past can be interpreted as the thesis that there is no backwards causation. We can neither cause nor prevent the past. However, in many contemporary debates, the necessity of the past has been treated as a special kind of necessity that the past has simply in virtue of being past. This type of necessity is not about causes. Unfortunately, the old adage, "There is no use crying over spilled milk," can be interpreted either way. It might mean that we have no power to cause or prevent the past spilling of milk, or it might mean instead that the pastness of the spilled milk confers a special type of necessity on it just because it is past.

We can see the second interpretation of the idea of the necessity of the past in the influential treatment of it by William of Ockham, who called the necessity of the past "necessity *per accidens*," or "accidental necessity." According to Ockham, what makes the necessity of the past accidental is that a proposition acquires it only at a certain moment of time. Ockham accepted the view (also common among contemporary philosophers) that a proposition never changes truth value. It is either true at all times or false at all times. However, Ockham thought that a proposition changes its modal status at the time of the event the proposition is about. For example, the proposition *The Battle of Hastings occurs in 1066* is always true, but it is accidentally contingent until the time of the battle; thereafter, it is accidentally necessary.[1] What makes *The Battle of Hastings occurs in 1066* accidentally contingent up to the moment of the battle is that prior to the battle, there is a potency in things for both the truth and the falsehood of the proposition *The Battle of Hastings occurs in 1066*. Once the battle occurs, the potency for the falsehood of the proposition is lost, and the proposition then becomes accidentally necessary. The necessity of the past, then, is one side of a modal arrow of time. Time moves in a direction that goes from the temporally contingent to the temporally necessary.

It is important to see that the kind of necessity that the past has simply in virtue of being past is not the same as the causally necessary. Causal necessity exists because of the relation between an event and its prior causes. An event is causally necessary when conditions sufficient for its occurrence precede the event. An event is causally contingent if there are no conditions sufficient for its occurrence prior to the event. Causal contingency and necessity, therefore, are determined by the relation between an event and events prior to it. That relation never changes. In contrast, the accidental necessity or contingency of an event (or the proposition that says the event occurs) changes over time. When the event is in the future, it is accidentally contingent. When it is in the past, it is accidentally necessary. Accidental necessity is therefore distinct from causal necessity.

Ockham also maintained that accidental necessity has the formal features of the logically necessary, and this also is widely accepted in the contemporary literature. If *p* is accidentally necessary, *not p* is accidentally impossible. If both *p* and *not p* are accidentally possible, *p* is accidentally contingent. In short, what makes accidental necessity accidental is that a proposition acquires it at a certain moment of time. It does not have that property at all times. What makes accidental necessity a form of necessity is that it has the formal features of necessity.

In this section I will proceed under the assumption that the necessity of the past is a purely temporal modality, and that it has the formal features of necessity, inter-definable with possibility, impossibility, and contingency. I will return to the interpretation of the necessity of the past as the denial of backwards causation in Section 3.3.

Assume next the following Transfer of Accidental Necessity principle:

$$[Nec_{ac} p \;\&\; \Box (p \rightarrow q)] \rightarrow Nec_{ac} q,$$

where "Nec_{ac}" is accidental necessity or the necessity of the past. This principle is the exact analogue of axiom *K*, an axiom of standard versions of modal logic.[2] That axiom says that if it is necessary that *p* and *p* entails *q*, then it is necessary that *q*. The use of this principle in fatalist arguments makes it clear that the necessity of the past as used in those arguments is intended to be a kind of necessity, possessing the same formal features as logical necessity.

Finally, assume the Principle of Alternate Possibilities (PAP): If some person *S* does *A* freely, *S* can refrain from doing *A*. There is a large literature on PAP, leading to numerous variations of the principle, but the precise formulation of PAP will not play a role in the arguments of this paper.

With the preceding assumptions, we can formulate a standard argument that infallible divine foreknowledge is incompatible with human free will as follows:

(1) Suppose God believed yesterday that *S* will do *A* tomorrow.

From the principle of the necessity of the past we get

(2) It is now-necessary (accidentally necessary) that God believed yesterday that S will do A tomorrow.

From the definition of divine infallibility we get

(3) Necessarily, if God believed yesterday that S will do A tomorrow, then S will do A tomorrow.

From 2, 3, and the Transfer of Accidental Necessity principle we get

(4) It is now-necessary that S will do A tomorrow.

It follows from definition of accidental necessity that

(5) If it is now-necessary that S will do A tomorrow, then S cannot refrain from doing A tomorrow.

The Principle of Alternate Possibilities states that

(6) If S cannot refrain from doing A tomorrow, then S does not do A tomorrow freely.

By 4, 5, 6, and hypothetical syllogism we can conclude

(7) S does not do A tomorrow freely.

Now suppose that God is not only infallible about some given belief, but is essentially omniscient. That is to say, necessarily, God believes p if and only if p. Then, for every human act, God had a prior belief that the act would occur, and no human act is free by this argument. Global fatalism seems to follow.

This argument is usually treated as a dilemma because few people are willing to accept the conclusion. That is, very few people actually use it as an argument in defense of fatalism. But many people begin with a previous inclination to accept both divine infallible foreknowledge and human free will. An argument like the preceding seems to force them to give up one or the other. Historically important "solutions" to the dilemma aim at defending the compatibility of divine foreknowledge and free will, and so they attempt to find some place at which the argument goes wrong.

The traditional and contemporary ways out of the dilemma almost always fall into one of the following categories:

(A) Future contingent propositions have no truth value, and so God does not infallibly believe such propositions. This move makes premise (1) false (the Aristotelian solution).
(B) God is outside of time and his beliefs are outside of time, so God did not believe anything in the past. This solution also makes premise (1) false (the Boethian-Thomistic solution).
(C) Although God is in time and had beliefs in the past, the fact that God had these beliefs does not have the necessity of the past, so premise (2) is false (the Ockhamist solution).
(D) The Principle of Alternate Possibilities (PAP) on line (6) is false.[3]

The foreknowledge literature also prominently includes Molinism, the view that God knows the actual contingent future through his Middle Knowledge. I will not discuss that solution here since it does not attack any particular premise of the theological fatalist argument.[4]

If we look at the preceding argument as a whole, it might appear that it is an argument specifically about God, but actually it is not. Notice that there is nothing in the argument that appeals to the personhood of God or to the attributes of God other than infallible foreknowledge. The argument is clearly intended to demonstrate an incompatibility between infallible foreknowledge by any being whatsoever, and human free will. Of course, God is the primary candidate for a being with infallible foreknowledge, and so the version of the argument that focuses on God has obvious theological importance for traditional theists. But the focus on theological fatalism can easily hide the fact that there is a metaphysical problem revealed here that would exist whether or not there is an infallible God.[5] The argument purports to show that it is metaphysically impossible for free will and infallible foreknowledge to coexist. If free will exists in the world, it is metaphysically impossible that anybody is infallible or becomes infallible in their knowledge about free acts. But the alleged connection between the ability to act freely and the epistemic ability of a completely independent being is exceedingly strange. Surely there is a *prima facie* principle that knowing p does not affect the truth of p. Usually it is thought to be the reverse. Of course, the adherent of the incompatibility of infallibility and free will does not deny this principle in general. It is only in the special case in which knowing is infallible that the principle does not hold. But that makes the peculiarity of the argument even more striking since a knowing ability that in every other case has no power over the object known allegedly does acquire such a power in the unique case in which the knowing power attains the highest degree, namely, infallibility. It seems to me that this is a problem with deep significance for our understanding of the connection between the way the world is and the powers of knowing minds. It is a problem for anybody, not just theists, and it is a problem whether or not one ultimately judges that infallible foreknowledge is compatible with free will. The fatalist argument threatens our conception of the relation between mind—any mind—and the world.

The preceding theological fatalist argument therefore reveals an underlying metaphysical problem in addition to the theological problem, a problem that can easily go unnoticed by non-theists and metaphysicians who are not interested in the traditional doctrine of divine omniscience. Unfortunately, theists who discuss theological fatalism often do not notice the metaphysical problem either, and they offer solutions that are effective only against the theological form of the problem. The view that God is timeless is in this category. Timelessness is a traditional attribute of God that is not connected to the attribute of infallibility. God's timeless knowledge allegedly escapes fatalist consequences, but notice that that is irrelevant to the issue of whether infallible *fore*knowledge is incompatible with free will.[6] The adherent of the timelessness solution needs a response to the metaphysical argument. If she thinks that the argument succeeds in showing that infallible foreknowledge by a temporal being is incompatible with human free will, that places restrictions on what she can say about the knowing power of temporal beings. In particular, she seems to be prevented from maintaining the possibility of an incarnate infallible foreknower.[7] On the other hand, if she thinks the argument fails to show the incompatibility of infallible foreknowledge and free will, there has to be a solution to the dilemma other than divine timelessness. Either way, the adherent of the timelessness solution must face the metaphysical dilemma because not only is the metaphysical problem a different problem, but her response to it can affect the viability of her response to the theological dilemma or her other theological claims.

Consider also the Ockhamist solution according to which God's foreknowledge in the past does not have the necessity of the past. If that is due to infallibility per se, then the Ockhamist solution works as a solution to the metaphysical dilemma if it works for the theological dilemma. But if God's foreknowledge lacks the necessity of the past because of something unique to the nature of God, then the solution is inadequate for the metaphysical problem. This objection applies to the solution I called "Thomistic Ockhamism" in Zagzebski (1991, chap 3). There I argued that if we accept the way in which God has knowledge according to Aquinas, God's knowing does not have the necessity of the past even if God is in time. The same point applies to the position of William Alston (1986) that God knows by immediate awareness and does not have beliefs. In each of these cases, the solution proposed applies only to God, and it does not address the deeper metaphysical issue.

The moral of the first stage of my argument, then, is that the dilemma of divine foreknowledge and human freedom is easily generalizable to a problem that is not uniquely theological, but metaphysical. If the fatalist argument with which we began succeeds, it succeeds in showing that infallible foreknowledge is incompatible with human free will, apart from anything specific to the nature of God. This is a problem of wide-ranging interest because it purports to show a logical incompatibility between the existence of human freedom, the conditions for which are presumably metaphysical, and an epistemic power of some independent being. No matter what one's theological commitments, this argument seems to force us into a very strange view of the world, one that conflicts with the intuitively plausible principle that the truth of p comes first in logical order; knowing p comes second. I also mentioned a corollary of the principle: knowing has no effect on what is known, no matter how perfect one's knowing power. Of course, I am not defending the principle or its corollary, only pointing out that the theological fatalist argument requires a confrontation with the principle, and that is not a problem unique to theists.

3.2.2. Is the problem uniquely about infallibility and fatalism?

Is the problem, then, essentially a conflict between infallibility and free will? The answer is no. The problem can be generalized in a way that has nothing to do with free will. To see how, go back to the assumption of the necessity of the past, or accidental necessity.

Allegedly the past and future are modally contrastive in that there is a kind of necessity that the past has simply in virtue of being past, whereas the future is contingent with respect to that kind of necessity in virtue of being future. This is not to deny that the future can have some other kind of necessity, such as causal necessity, nor is it to deny that the past can have some other kind of contingency, such as causal contingency. Nonetheless, the suggestion is that the past carries with it a distinctive type of temporal necessity that the future lacks. Indeed, if we follow Ockham, one of the main ways in which the past is distinguished from the future is by the presence or absence of accidental necessity. The past is accidentally necessary, whereas the future is accidentally contingent.

It can be shown that the existence of an infallible foreknower is incompatible with the existence of the modality of accidental necessity/contingency, apart from any considerations about free will:

(1) Suppose that there is (and was before now) a believer B who has an infallible belief whether F, where F is about something in the future. So:
(2) Either B believed F before now, or B believed not F before now.

From (2), the Principle of the Necessity of the Past, and constructive dilemma, we get

(3) Either it is now-necessary that B believed F before now, or it is now-necessary that B believed not F before now.

From (1) and the definition of infallibility it follows that

(4) Necessarily (B believed before now that $F \rightarrow F$), and necessarily (B believed before now that not $F \rightarrow$ not F).

By the Transfer of Accidental Necessity principle, we get

(5) Either it is now-necessary that F or it now-necessary that not F.
(4) is logically equivalent to
(6) Either it is not now-possible that F or it is not now-possible that not F.

From the Principle of the Accidental Contingency of the Future it follows that

(7) It is now-possible that F and it is now-possible that not F. But (7) contradicts (6).[8]

This dilemma rules out another important response to the standard dilemma of theological fatalism: the denial of the Principle of Alternate Possibilities (PAP). I defended this solution in Zagzebski (1991, chap 6), and it has been defended by David Hunt (1999).[9] Notice, however, that this solution is irrelevant to the preceding dilemma since that dilemma is not about free will, and PAP makes no appearance in the argument. Indeed, there are not many ways out of this particular dilemma. The problem arises from the combination of infallibility with respect to some proposition about the future, and the purely temporal modality of accidental necessity and contingency that Ockham describes, with the assumption that there is a Transfer of Necessity principle for accidental necessity parallel to a standard axiom of modal logic. So the thesis that there is a kind of necessity that is purely temporal and that has the formal features of necessity conflicts with the possibility of infallible foreknowledge.

3.2.3. Is the problem uniquely about infallibility and time?

From what we have seen in the second stage of my argument, the problem of infallible foreknowledge can be generalized to a dilemma of infallible foreknowledge and a temporal modality, where the past has temporal necessity and the future does not. But the dilemma can be generalized further. A form of the problem arises whenever a proposition about the past entails a proposition about the future, when combined with this temporal modality. The deeper metaphysical problem is not about free will. It is not even about infallible foreknowledge.

The problem is that it is impossible for there to be a type of modality that has the following features:

(i) The past and future are asymmetrical in that the past is necessary with respect to this type of modality, whereas the future is contingent with respect to this type of modality.
(ii) The Transfer of Necessity principle applies to this modality.
(iii) There are true propositions about the past that entail propositions about the future.

Propositions (i)–(iii) form an inconsistent triad. Specifically, let P = some true proposition about the past. Assume that the past is now-necessary (accidentally necessary) and the future is now-contingent (accidentally contingent). This is not to deny that past events may be contingent in some other sense such as causal contingency, and future events may be necessary in some other sense such as causal necessity, but we are considering temporally relative necessity and contingency.

Now let F = a proposition about the future that is entailed by P. The argument is as follows:

(1) P
(2) It is now-necessary that P (necessity of the past).
(3) Necessarily $(P \rightarrow F)$ (assumption).
(4) It is now-necessary that F (Transfer of Necessity principle).

But by the Principle of the Contingency of the Future, we get

(5) It is now-contingent that F. But (5) conflicts with (4).

The conclusion is that there cannot be a temporally asymmetrical modality like Ockham's accidental necessity/contingency with a transfer principle as long as any proposition about the past entails a proposition about the future. Infallible foreknowledge is just one instance in which a proposition about the past entails a proposition about the future, but there can be many others. For instance, consider the principle of the ancient Atomists that matter is indestructible, or Spinoza or Leibniz's principle that substance is indestructible. Any such principle requires that many propositions about the past—e.g., *Matter (substance) existed before now*—entail propositions about the future—*Matter (substance) will exist in the future*. There are, of course, propositions about God that are also in this category, e.g., *God is everlasting*. However, it is not necessary to look at rarified metaphysical theses for examples of propositions about the past that entail propositions about the future. Arguably, much more mundane examples are at hand. In a different context, John Martin Fischer (1983) has argued that the proposition *Jones sits at t1* entails *Jones does not sit for the first time at t2*.[10] Given the pattern of argument Fischer uses, every proposition about the past entails some proposition about the future. If so, the denial of (iii) is not an option. But even leaving Fischer's argument aside, examples of propositions about the past that entail propositions about the future are plentiful. I assume, then, that denying that any proposition about the past entails a proposition about the future is not very promising.

It follows that there is no more reason to deny that God knows the future infallibly on the grounds of the theological dilemma as interpreted in the preceding paragraphs than to deny that God is everlasting or that substance is indestructible or that Jones sits at *t*1. Infallibility is a fascinating property for both metaphysical and theological reasons, but it is not unique in leading to a dilemma when combined with the notion of the necessity of the past as a purely temporal modality. In fact, if I am right that the fatalist dilemma is actually just a particularly vivid example of the dilemma of this section, then the dilemma of this section is the deeper problem, a problem that does not require us to retract a thesis about the possibility of infallibility without retracting a host of other theses.

Assuming, then, that we do not want to deny (iii), it follows that there is no type of modality that is temporally asymmetrical (the past has it, the future does not), and for which the Transfer of Necessity principle holds. Either there is no such modality, or if it exists, the transfer principle fails for it. If the transfer principle is part of the logic of necessity and possibility, it is hard to deny the transfer principle without turning the necessity of the past into something other than necessity. That, of course, is an option, and we will look at that option in the next section, but we can conclude at this point that there is no temporal necessity as described by the conjunction of (i) and (ii). The necessity of the past is incoherent if it is intended to distinguish past from future, and if it is a real type of necessity, inter-definable with the concepts of possibility and contingency, and to which an analogue of the modal axiom *K* applies.

3.2.4. Conclusion to section 3.2

In this section I have argued that the traditional dilemma of divine foreknowledge and human free will can be generalized in three ways. First, I argued that the problem is not unique to divine infallible foreknowledge, but applies to infallible foreknowledge by any being whatever. That means that solutions to the problem that refer to something distinctive about the divine nature will not escape the more general problem. That includes the traditional timelessness solution, some forms of the Ockhamist solution, and the view that God does not have beliefs. Second, the problem is not limited to future human free acts, but can be extended to a problem about the contingency of the future. Solutions that involve disputing the Principle of Alternate Possibilities or any other principle about the nature of free will do not escape the argument of section 3.2.2. Third, I argued that the problem is not even limited to infallible foreknowledge, since it can be generalized to a dilemma for any thesis according to which a proposition about the past entails a proposition about the future. I conclude that there is no purely temporal form of necessity/contingency for which the standard Transfer of Necessity principle applies.

3.3. Back to the necessity of the past

3.3.1. The necessity of the past without the arrow of time

I have given an interpretation of the necessity of the past as a purely temporal modality, and then argued that it is incoherent. It is doubtful that there is any purely temporal form of necessity. But before we can draw that conclusion, I want to mention an interpretation of the necessity of the past that makes it purely temporal, and which is not inconsistent with the thesis that there are propositions about the past that entail propositions about the future.

The Ockhamist view of the necessity of the past I have been using expresses the intuition that there is a modal arrow of time. There is a modal *difference* between the past and future. As Ockham describes it, accidental necessity is a property that a proposition acquires only after a certain time. While the proposition is about something still in the future, it is accidentally contingent. Once the event the proposition is about occurs, the proposition becomes accidentally necessary. The fact that accidental necessity and contingency are temporally contrastive in this way is an intrinsic feature of this modality. The necessity of the past and the contingency of the future are two sides of the same coin.

But we need to consider the possibility that the necessity of the past is one side of a coin with an indeterminate other side. Fatalist arguments of all kinds, whether logical, theological, or causal, begin with an intuition that the past has a kind of necessity in virtue of being past, and nothing is said about the future. Perhaps the modal status of the future is up in the air. When the fatalist argues to the conclusion that the future has the same kind of necessity as the past, he can say that he has discovered that the other side of the coin looks the same as the first: the future is modally just like the past. Of course, this way of thinking requires a rejection of the idea that the necessity of the past is "accidental." It means that a true proposition is accidentally necessary at all times. It does not acquire accidental necessity at the time of the event the proposition is about. There is no contingency of the future. There is only the necessity of both past and future, a necessity that is endowed on the future by the combination of the necessity of the past and the Transfer of Necessity principle, given in the argument for theological fatalism at the beginning of section 3.2.1.

As I have mentioned, we are probably confused about the necessity of the past, and no doubt there are many different interpretations of it. My view is that we would not talk about the necessity of the past at all were it not for the fact that we think that the past and future are distinguished by a difference in modal properties. The necessity of the past, accompanied by the contingency of the future, is one of the ways in which time allegedly has directionality. Time moves in a certain direction, from what is first contingent to what is then necessary, and that is why fatalist arguments have usually been treated with suspicion. These arguments begin with the intuition of the necessity of the past—one side of the modal arrow of time—and use a formal Transfer of Necessity principle to get a conclusion that denies the modal arrow of time. Clearly, something sounds right about the way those arguments look at the necessity of the past; otherwise, fatalist arguments would not exist. However, there is an equally long history of philosophers who have thought that something must be amiss in these arguments. It is not just that the conclusion is unappealing. The arguments themselves seem to reveal a confusion that is hard to identify.

I think, then, that this matter cannot be settled without a closer look at the way ordinary people think about the past. When we do so, I think we find an easier way to see that the necessity of the past is not a purely temporal modality.

3.3.2. The denial of backwards causation

Let us go back to the adage "There is no use crying over spilled milk." I suggested at the beginning of section 3.2 that this adage can be interpreted either as the claim that the past has a form of necessity simply in virtue of being past, or as the intuition that the past is causally closed. By that I mean that nothing can either cause or prevent what has already happened. On the second interpretation, the necessity of the past is neither a purely temporal modality, nor is it a type of necessity.

It is hard to know how we can determine what ordinary people think, but it seems to me unlikely that people who say there is no use crying over spilled milk mean to say that the past is "necessary" in the sense in which the necessary can be inter-defined in standard ways with the possible, the impossible, and the contingent. For instance, if a proposition *p* is necessary, *p* is possible, but if milk was spilled, do ordinary people say that the proposition *Milk was spilled* is possible? The negation of a necessary truth is impossible, but would they say that *Milk was spilled* is necessary, and *Milk was not spilled* is impossible? They might, but it would be very unusual to say such things. What is more likely is that both *Milk was spilled* and *Milk was not spilled* are put in the category of what we cannot do anything about. We can neither cause the past spilling of milk now, nor can we prevent it now. Both the actual past and alternative pasts are beyond our causal power. In fact, the actual and counterfactual pasts are beyond the causal power of anything, not just human agents. This interpretation of ordinary intuition casts doubt on the idea that the necessity of the past is actually about *necessity*, and it casts doubt on the idea that the necessity of the past is a purely temporal modality. Instead, it suggests that the necessity of the past is just the intuition that the past is causally closed.

A test of whether I am right in this conjecture is the intuitive response to a world in which there *is* backwards causation. Suppose we can make such a world coherent. What would we say about the necessity of the past in that world? Would we say that the past has a kind of necessity in virtue of being past even though it is possible to cause what has already happened or to prevent what has already happened? It seems to me that the answer is no.

Without a causal arrow, there would be no adage about spilled milk. Of course, maybe we cannot make sense of such a world at all. I am not denying that. My point is only that I do not see anything in addition to the denial that this is such a world in the idea of the necessity of the past.

My interpretation of the "necessity" of the past preserves the intuition that the necessity of the past is connected with an arrow of time. It is very likely that there is a causal arrow. Past and future are contrasted in that if some event E is in the past, E is not now causable, and not E is not now causable. If some event E is in the future, E is now causable by something, and it is at least arguable that not E is causable by something. Whether an alternative future is causable is an important issue, but we need not settle that to see that there is a causal asymmetry between past and future as long as the future is causable and the past is not.

3.3.3. Back to God

Using this interpretation of the necessity of the past, we will need to make a significant modification to the theological fatalist argument with which we began. First, let us define causal closure:

Definition of causal closure
E is causally closed = There is nothing now that can cause E, and there is nothing now that can cause not E.

Replace the principle of the necessity of the past with the following principle:

Principle of the Causal Closure of the Past
If E is an event in the past, E is causally closed.

Next, the Transfer of Necessity principle must be replaced by a Transfer of Causal Closure principle.

[E occurred and is causally closed and $\Box$ (E occurs $\rightarrow$ F occurs)]. $\rightarrow$ F is causally closed.

The argument for theological fatalism would then need to be recast as follows:

(1) Suppose God believed yesterday that S will do A tomorrow.

From the causal closure of the past, we get

(2) There is nothing now that can cause God to have believed yesterday that S will do A tomorrow, and there is nothing now that can cause God not to have believed that S will do A tomorrow.

From the definition of divine infallibility we get

(3) Necessarily, if God believed yesterday that S will do A tomorrow, then S will do A tomorrow.

From 2, 3, and the Transfer of Causal Closure principle we get

(4) There is nothing now that can cause S to do A tomorrow and there is nothing now that can cause S not to do A tomorrow.

But nobody would accept (4) since (4) denies that there are causes of the future. Certainly it is uncontroversial that something now, whether agents or events, can cause future events.

The problem here is that the principle of the causal closure of the past has two conjuncts. One is the following:

Principle of the Non-causability of the Past

If E is an event in the past, nothing now can cause E.

The relevant half of the Transfer of Causal Closure principle for this conjunct is the following Transfer of Non-causability Principle:

[E occurred and is now non-causable, and $\Box$ (E occurs → F occurs)] → F is now non-causable.

But nobody would argue as follows:

(1) Suppose God believed yesterday that S will do A tomorrow.

From the principle of the non-causability of the past, we get

(2) There is nothing now that can cause God to have believed yesterday that S will do A tomorrow.
(3) Necessarily, if God believed yesterday that S will do A tomorrow, then S will do A tomorrow.

Therefore,

(4) There is nothing now that can cause S to do A tomorrow.

However, if we take just the second half of the principle of the causal closure of the past, we get an argument for fatalism that many philosophers treat seriously:

Principle of the Unpreventability of the Past

If E is an event in the past, nothing now can cause not E.

The relevant half of the Transfer of Causal Closure principle gives us the following Transfer of Unpreventability principle:

[(E occurred and it is not now causable that E does not occur), and $\Box$ (E occurs –> F occurs)]
–> it is not now causable that F does not occur.

This principle is virtually identical to the Transfer of Unpreventability principle proposed by Hugh Rice (2005) in his response to a paper of mine. Rice's principle is the following:

[U p and $\Box$ ($p \rightarrow q$) and p is true] -> U q[11]

It is also equivalent to a strengthened version of Peter van Inwagen's well-known rule beta.[12]

Using this principle, we get the following argument for theological fatalism:

(1′) Suppose God believed yesterday that S will do A tomorrow.

From the principle of the unpreventability of the past we get

(2′) There is nothing now that can cause God not to have believed that S will do A tomorrow.

From the definition of divine infallibility we get

(3′) Necessarily, if God believed yesterday that S will do A tomorrow, then S will do A tomorrow.

From 2′, 3′, and the Transfer of Unpreventability principle we get

(4′) There is nothing now that can cause S not to do A tomorrow.

From a variation of the Principle of Alternate Possibilities, we get

(5′) If nothing can cause S not to do A tomorrow, then S does not do A tomorrow freely.

From (4′) and (5′), we get

(6′) S does not do A tomorrow freely.

This is the strongest argument for theological fatalism I know of. Given the arguments of this paper, we can see one way in which this fatalist argument is better than the standard theological fatalist argument with which we began. If I am right that a purely temporal necessity is incoherent, this argument is better than our original argument in that it does not refer to a purely temporal necessity in the second premise. But if I am also right that the relevant necessity of the past is not a form of necessity in the formal sense, but is instead the thesis that the past is causally closed, then the transfer principle licensing the crucial inference to (4′) is not a transfer of necessity. Unlike the Transfer of Accidental Necessity principle in our original argument, it is not a variation of axiom K, and therefore it is far from indisputable. Nonetheless, as I have indicated, it has strong defenders.

However, it seems to me that there is a remarkable weakness in the preceding argument. It argues for fatalism by using one half of the principle of the causal closure of the past. That principle is the thesis that the past can be neither caused nor prevented. No one would license a transfer principle for the uncausability of the past because it leads to the uncausability of the future, and nobody denies that the future is causable.[13] But then why should we license a transfer principle for the unpreventability of the past when it leads to the unpreventability of the future? If those who think the actual future is causable have reason to deny the Transfer of Non-causability principle, then it seems to me that those who think that alternative futures are now causable have reason to deny the Transfer of Unpreventability principle.

Here is a reply I would expect: "Well, we all agree that something can cause the future, and so the Transfer of Non-causability principle is clearly invalid, but we do not agree that things can cause alternative futures, and so the Transfer of Unpreventability principle cannot be rejected on the grounds that all agree it endorses inference from a truth to a falsehood." But notice that this answer cuts both ways. It makes it clear that the fatalist conclusion of the preceding argument is not something to which we are forced by principles we all endorse. Rather, the transfer principle that endorses the fatalist conclusion is as disputable as fatalism. The uncausability of the past and the unpreventability of the past are both part of the same intuition that the past is causally closed. Neither transfer principle is a principle of logic like the Transfer of Necessity principle, and both principles license an inference to a metaphysical conclusion that is unacceptable to most or many people. It seems to me that what this shows is that philosophers ought to do a lot more work to uncover what is going on in the intuition of the causal closure of the past. It is surely not enough to note that the argument supports fatalism when half of the intuition generating the argument has consequences that are unacceptable to virtually everyone.

I think we can see that the idea of the necessity of the past is confused. I have suggested that the confusion surrounding it weakens fatalist arguments, although nothing I have said tells us what the ultimate verdict on these arguments will be. But I believe it is not sufficient to give an argument using a principle that seems plausible in isolation, but which arises from a problematic view on the modal status of the past. It is even worse if the argument refers to an incoherent form of the necessity of the past, as we saw in section 3.2.

3.4. Conclusion

I have argued that the traditional dilemma of divine foreknowledge and human free will arises from deep problems in the nature of time. It is a mistake to treat the theological dilemma as simply an "in house" problem in Christian theology. Of course, I do not deny that there is a particular version of this dilemma that strikes at the heart of deep beliefs within the Christian worldview, but I think that some of the arguments in this paper reveal problems and confusions in our notions of causality and the arrow of time, problems of a strictly metaphysical nature. I hope that more metaphysicians will work on these issues, whether or not they are theists, and I hope that the relevance of work on the theological dilemma to these broader issues will be noticed. Throughout the history of Western philosophy, Christian theists have made major contributions to metaphysics in the course of working on theological problems. Some of their work then became part of the legacy of Western philosophy. For instance, the topic of free will in its modern form became important largely due to theological debates over theological determinism and the Pelagian heresy. A long era of dissection of the notion of free will ensued, apart from theological considerations. I think that the debate over foreknowledge and fatalism can serve a similar role in stimulating and serving debate on causality and the arrow of time.

Notes

1. Of course, Ockham did not think that all propositions are about events at specific moments of time, so his idea of accidental necessity does not apply to all propositions.
2. To my knowledge, I am one of the few people who have suggested that the Transfer of Accidental Necessity principle might be false. I argue that briefly in Zagzebski (1991), chap 6.
3. David Hunt calls this the Augustinian solution in Hunt (1999). I defended this solution in Zagzebski (1991), chap 6, but I did not attribute it to Augustine.
4. Middle Knowledge is defined as God's knowledge of what every possible free creature would freely choose in every possible circumstance. Contemporary discussions derive from Luis de Molina (1988). For a good defense of Molinism, see Flint (2006).
5. David Hunt has aptly argued that the metaphysical problem and the theological problem of fatalism are distinct problems in Hunt (1998).
6. My purpose here is not to discuss the issue of whether the timelessness of God escapes theological fatalism. I argued in Zagzebski (1991), chap. 2, and more recently in Zagzebski (2011), Chapter 2 of this collection, that there is a timeless knowledge dilemma parallel to the traditional foreknowledge dilemma, so the timelessness move is not sufficient to escape theological fatalism. My point here is that even if the timelessness move succeeds in escaping theological fatalism, the adherent of timelessness needs a response to the more general metaphysical argument.

7. I argued in Zagzebski (2011), Chapter 2 of this collection, that a proponent of the timelessness solution to the foreknowledge dilemma is committed to a view of the Incarnation according to which the incarnated Son of God did not have infallible foreknowledge at moments of time.
8. I presented a dilemma very similar to this in the appendix of Zagzebski (1991), as well as in other places subsequently. See also Zagzebski (2002).
9. The denial of PAP was made famous by Harry Frankfurt (1969), and, like Frankfurt, those who deny PAP are generally determinists. I have argued for the position that PAP is false even though determinism is false also in Zagzebski (1991) and in Zagzebski (2000). David Hunt (2000) has also defended the position, as does Eleonore Stump (1990).
10. Presumably, it is true that Jones does not sit for the first time at $t2$ whether or not Jones sits at $t2$ and whether or not $t2$ occurs.
11. At the end of his paper, Rice defines "U p" as "it is not causable that not p," and then proposes the preceding Transfer of Unpreventability principle. He gives his principle in terms of propositions, whereas mine is in terms of events. I do not see any difference in the two ways of formulating the principle, although it is probably closer to ordinary usage to speak of causing and preventing events rather than causing or preventing the truth of propositions.
12. Peter Van Inwagen proposes his rule beta as a rule of inference rather than as a principle modeled on a modal axiom. Van Inwagen's rule beta is the following: Np & $N(p \rightarrow q)$ /: Nq, where $Np = p$, and no one has or ever had any choice about whether p. The replacement of the second premise by "$\Box (p \rightarrow q)$" was proposed by Finch and Warfield (1999) to avoid objections. Timothy O'Connor (1993) suggested adding that p is made true earlier than q to avoid other counterexamples. Adding that clause does not affect the arguments of this paper since all arguments in this paper are of cases in which p is made true earlier than q.
13. Ben Polansky has suggested to me that a defender of the form of argument I am criticizing might agree that there are no causes of the future if nothing now can cause the past. The consequence would be that there is only one cause at the beginning of time. Perhaps the causal determinist would accept that.

II
THE PROBLEM OF EVIL

4
An Agent-Based Approach to the Problem of Evil (1996)

4.1. Introduction: The logical problem of evil

The problem of evil is a serious challenge to the belief that there is an omnipotent, omniscient, and perfectly good God. In its potentially most devastating form, the problem is that there seems to be an inconsistency between these attributes and the existence of evil. The inconsistency is not straightforward, but requires supplementation by additional premises, usually involving what an omnipotent being would be able to do and what a perfectly good being would be motivated to do. In addition to the logical form of the problem, there are other forms that challenge the religious believer in her ability to confront and handle evil in an effective and satisfying way. Solutions to the problem range from the purely formal demonstration that the propositions generating the dilemma are not logically inconsistent[1] to the generous use of substantive religious beliefs in an attempt to show that within a background of Christian theology, we can shed light on the existence of evil and our ability to face it.[2] In this paper I will make a direct attack on one of the supplementary premises used to generate the logical problem of evil; namely, the premise that a good being is motivated to produce good and to prevent or eliminate evil.[3] This premise, or a variation of it, is virtually always used in the argument for the inconsistency of the existence of an omnipotent, omniscient, and perfectly good God and the existence of evil, and it is almost always taken for granted by all parties to the dispute.

The logical problem of evil can be stated as follows:

(1) A perfectly good being would be motivated to eliminate all the evil he can.
(2) An omniscient being would know of the existence of any evil and how to eliminate it.
(3) An omnipotent being would be able to eliminate all the evil he knows about and knows how to eliminate.
(4) So if there were a being who is perfectly good, omnipotent, and omniscient, this being would be motivated to eliminate evil, would know of its existence and how to eliminate it, and would be able to eliminate it.

(5) But if there were a being who was motivated to eliminate evil, knew of its existence, knew how to eliminate it, and was able to do so, evil would not exist.
(6) But evil does exist.

Therefore,

(7) There is no being who is perfectly good, omnipotent, and omniscient. The traditional Christian God does not exist.

The most common response to this argument on the part of theists is to claim that evil is worth accepting for the sake of some good. Theistic philosophers then go on to look for a reason why a God who has the attributes just described would permit evil for the sake of some good for which the evil is a logically necessary prerequisite. The way in which these responses are developed can be quite elaborate, but premise (1), which gives us the motivational requirement that a good God would want to produce good and to eliminate evil, is rarely if ever questioned.

The intuition behind premise (1) is an ethical one, but it is not self-evident. Premise (1) assumes that what is good or evil is not made to be such by the motivations of good beings. Something would count as good or evil independent of anybody's motives. In fact, part of what makes a being good, it is usually maintained, is that such a being is motivated to produce good and to prevent evil. That this intuition is not self-evident can be seen from the fact that Divine Command theories of morality deny no self-evident truths, even if they are implausible. According to such theories, what is right or good is determined by the will of God, so such theories deny premise (1) as it is intended in the generation of the dilemma. That is, they deny the claim that a perfectly good God is motivated to produce something good, where good is understood to be independent of God's will. Divine Command theories accept (1) only in the trivial sense that since good just is what God wills, and since it is trivially true that God is motivated to will what he wills, then God is motivated to will good. But of course, in this sense of (1) there is no dilemma.

Many people believe that Divine Command theories are false, but these theories cannot be accused of failing to comprehend some alleged universal understanding of the independent existence of good and evil. The problem of evil is built upon many assumptions, not only about what the attributes of perfect goodness, omnipotence, and omniscience mean, and the psychology of what a being with these attributes would do, but it is also built upon significant ethical assumptions. To say that good and evil exist in a way that is independent of anybody's will or motivations is a substantive claim that needs defense. The commonality of its acceptance is admittedly a defense of sorts, but it has recently been challenged by a form of virtue ethics that is new in the West, but perhaps not new in Chinese ethics. This theory ought to be of particular interest to Christian philosophers for at least two reasons: (1) it is the most natural way to interpret the metaphysical status of good and evil within traditional Christian theology, and (2) it permits a new and interesting approach to answering the problem of evil. In addition, this type of ethical theory can be defended purely within ethics as a rival to the leading ethical theories in contemporary Western philosophy, a claim traditional Divine Command theories cannot make.

4.2. Agent-based ethics

The type of theory I want to describe is a strong form of virtue ethics lately called "agent-based virtue ethics."[4] Like all virtue theories, this theory focuses its analysis on a person's inner traits—their virtues and vices, and on the components of virtues and vices, particularly motivations. Virtue theories do not derive the concept of a virtue from the concept of a right act, either as a disposition to perform right acts, or by any other relation to right acts. Stronger and weaker forms of virtue theories can be identified by the way each theory relates the fundamental moral concepts of a virtue, the good, and a right act. Consider first the way a virtue theory relates the concept of virtue to the concept of a right act. A weak form of virtue ethics maintains that the rightness of an act is independent of the existence and operation of virtues, but it is appropriate for theoretical ethics to focus attention on the virtue since the behavior of a virtuous person gives us the best criterion for the rightness of acts. A stronger form of virtue ethics maintains that the concept of a right act is strictly derivative from the concept of a virtue. The motivations or behavior of virtuous persons is what makes an act right. An act would not be right if it were not for its relation to virtue or virtuous motivation. Agent-based ethics makes the stronger claim on the relation between virtue and rightness.

Virtue theories can also be compared with respect to their stand on the relation between the concept of a virtue and the concept of the good or of a good life. Common teleological forms make the concept of a good life the fundamental ethical concept, and a virtue is explicated in terms of its contribution to a good life, either as a means to it or as a constituent of it. Aristotle's ethics is of this kind. A more radical, non-teleological form of virtue ethics makes the virtues or other internal properties of the agent ethically fundamental, and the good is treated as a derivative concept. This is what I am calling "agent-based ethics." It is a theory that takes the stronger position on the relation between virtue and the good, as well as on the stronger position on the relation between virtue and the right. Virtues or other internal properties of the agent, such as the agent's motivations, are treated as the fundamental, bottom-level moral concepts, and all other moral concepts are treated derivatively. So, for example, in an agent-based theory, the virtue of benevolence or the motive of benevolence would be treated as good in the primary sense, not because of the connection between benevolence and the happiness or well-being of human beings or because of its connection with the good in some other sense, and not because of the connection between benevolence and the performance of right acts. Benevolence would be good intrinsically.

Instances of agent-based ethics in the history of Western philosophy are hard to find, but there is possibly a form of it in Duns Scotus, and a clear form of it in the ethics of the nineteenth-century philosopher James Martineau, and in this century, in Josiah Royce's philosophy of loyalty. The earliest occurrence of agent-based virtue ethics may be in Chinese philosophy in the work of Confucius and Mencius. Lately I have begun working on a version of this theory for the purposes of epistemology as well as ethics.[5]

What are the reasons for preferring an agent-based ethical theory? Perhaps the most compelling reason is experiential. Many of us have had the experience of meeting persons whose goodness simply shines forth from the depths of their souls. If this can happen, it suggests that it is possible to know a person is good before we investigate her behavior or observe the outcome of her acts. She may simply exude inner peace or have a "glow" of nobility or fineness of character. If we then attempt to figure out what it is about her that makes her so good, we may be able to identify that goodness as involving certain inner qualities, for example, feelings of compassion, an attitude of self-respect and respect for others, motives of benevolence, sympathy, or love. In each case we need not determine that her love, compassion, or benevolence is good because of its relation to things independently identified as good. We simply see that these motivations, feelings, or attitudes are the traits whose goodness we see in her. Alternatively, we may focus our attention first on the motivation itself and see that it is good, and again, we may see this independently of any evaluative judgment about the acts or consequences to which this motivation gives rise. That is, we see that there is something intrinsically morally good about the motivation of love itself.

An agent-based approach also is attractive from the point of view of theoretical ethics. One appealing aspect of this kind of theory is its ability to systematically unify ethical phenomena. Moral judgments about motives, virtues, acts, and the good life are derived from the primary concept of a virtue or its motivational constituent. This is an important consideration in a moral theory. Even classical act utilitarianism, a theory which goes far in the direction of unifying moral phenomena, has trouble handling the evaluation of moral motives.[6] Contemporary utilitarians judge the moral value of such motives as benevolence, love, and caring solely in terms of the consequences of the motives, a view that conflicts with the common-sense idea that what is praiseworthy or blameworthy about motives is at least largely a matter of the condition of the heart. Deontological theories also have difficulty in explaining the importance of these motives in the moral life and either reject them entirely or make them subservient to the motive of duty. This has led to well-known objections to this class of theories.[7] Virtue theories in general are preferable to consequentialist and deontological theories in their ability to deal with the moral importance of motives.

In addition to the support for agent-based theories from our moral experience of persons and from theoretical ethics, this class of theories should be of particular interest to Christian philosophers since it is the most natural way to understand ethical concepts on the traditional Christian view of God's goodness. During the high era of Christian theology, God was understood to be identical with perfect goodness and the source of all goodness outside himself, and even now this position is the dominant one in Christian philosophical theology. But notice what this view on the metaphysics of goodness indicates for ethics. It implies that when the agent of whom we are speaking is God, goodness is not something external to his nature that becomes the object of his motivation. The medieval philosophers explained the link between the divine nature and the created world more in terms of the divine will than divine motivation, and the claim in that period was that God's will is expressive of internal features of his nature within which perfect goodness resides. But since the challenge of the problem of evil is put in terms of motivation, it is useful to focus on the connection between God's motives and his goodness. God has motives that are purely expressive of his nature. These motives are good for reasons purely internal to God's nature, and the objects of these motives are good in a derivative sense. That means that at least as far as the ethics of God's behavior is concerned, the most natural way to understand it is agent-based. It is much harder to explain the connection between God's internal perfect goodness and the ethics of divine action in a consequentialist or a deontological fashion.

Furthermore, if all normative judgments ultimately derive from the goodness of God, this suggests that ultimately all normative judgments are not only agent-based, but are based in one agent: God. Not only are judgments of goodness analyzed in a way that is based in the internal properties of God, but so are the moral laws and judgments about the rightness of acts. This leaves open the possibility of attaching a Divine Command theory to the agent base if desired, although there is nothing in the agent-based account I have given that forces us to do so. On such a theory, what is right is what God wills or commands, given that God has the perfectly good inner motivations that he has. The laws of morality are those that express these motivations or other inner states of God, but it is the inner states that are good in the primary sense of good.[8] In this way, an agent-based ethics, combined with a traditional philosophy of God's nature, yields a theory that is structurally like Divine Command theory, except it is focused on God's motivations rather than on his will.[9] One advantage of doing so is that it avoids the problems of arbitrariness that plague Divine Command theories. That is because a will is usually thought to require a reason to will what it wills, in virtue of which it is good, whereas it is acceptable to think of motivations such as those of benevolence or love as intrinsically good; no external reason is required. Another advantage is that a theory of value based in divine motivation can be broadened into a general moral theory in which good is based on human motivations, whereas the analogous extension to basing human good on human will is implausible.

4.3. An agent-based approach to the problem of evil

If God is the source of all goodness outside himself, that is because God is internally perfect and the goodness of the objects of his choice derives from the goodness of his own nature. Something is good if and because it is the object of choice of an inherently perfectly good being. This position can be generalized to produce the foundations of a full agent-based ethics. We could say that something is good just because it is the object of choice of an inherently good being, whether that being is divine or human, but the inner goodness of human beings is itself derived from the inner goodness of God. I will not argue for this position here since my aim is not to defend this particular kind of non-teleological virtue ethics for all the purposes of theoretical ethics. For the purposes of this paper, I am making the more restricted claim that the ethics of God's behavior is best understood in an agent-based fashion.

According to this approach, we have to give up any idea that God aims to create in the world something he independently considers to be good. His motivation cannot be explained by saying that he does something because it is good. God does what he does because it is expressive of his nature. God's actions are like those of the artist who creates works of beauty, but hardly can be said to create these works because they are beautiful. He simply creates out of a desire to create, a desire that expresses the inner beauty or aesthetic value of his own inventive imagination. In the same way, God does not create because his creation is good. It is not as if God sees in thought that such a creation would be good and then goes about creating it. The created universe is good because it is the expression of the desire to create of a perfectly good being whose inventiveness is a component of his omniscience and omnipotence.[10]

On this account, how are we to understand the evil in the world? It should be clear from what has been said so far that God would not permit evil for the sake of some good—the good of free will, the good of the world or its creatures, or the good of God himself. There is no independent conception of good for the sake of which some independent conception of evils is to be permitted. To explicate this further, let us consider the analogy of the behavior of parents with their children. A good parent loves her child and wants him to develop into a full person. Gradually giving the child autonomy is necessary to that end, but the parent need not act this way because doing so makes the child morally better, or because the loving relationship she wants to have with her child is good. Still less need she do it because the overall amount of good in the world will increase if she does so.[11] It seems to me that the parent would want this for her child even if the child did not use his autonomy to do good or to be better off, and even if much less good were produced in the world overall. She acts this way because she loves her child and that is the way loving parents act. It is also true that her love is good. But she is not motivated to act this way because her love is good. Goodness does not figure into her motivation at all. She does not think to herself, "I want my child to be happy because happiness is good," or "I do not want my child to suffer because suffering is bad"; much less does she think, "I love my child and it is good that I love him and so it is good that I do what love prompts me to do." To think in such a way is to have what Bernard Williams calls "one thought too many" (Williams, 1981b). It is true that she wants her child to be happy and not to suffer, but not because of the goodness of the one and the badness of the other. And it is also true that her love for her child leads her to do whatever contributes to the development of his personhood whether or not it leads to good. What parent would ever agree to turn her child into a non-person or even less of a person because her child is bad or because her child is worse off for being a full person?

The fact that the parent is so motivated in no way detracts from her goodness. And it indicates that promoting good and preventing evil are not necessarily part of the motivational structure of a good being, even in the human case. Instead, I submit that it is possible, even probable, that a perfectly good being would be willing to permit any amount of evil, not for the sake of some good, but out of love of persons. To love a person logically requires permitting that person to be a person. To allow a person to be a person requires that she be allowed to contribute to the making of her own personhood, or what John Hick (1978) calls soul-making, through her free will. This is justified, not because the existence of free persons is good, nor because love is good, nor for the sake of good in any other way, but simply because loving persons is something good persons do, and loving persons in such a radical way that any evil is permitted for the sake of their personhood is something a perfectly good being would do. Premise (1) of the argument for an inconsistency between the existence of evil and the existence of God is therefore false.

This approach to the problem of evil utilizes the necessity of free will, but not in the usual way since the goodness of free will is not the issue. This approach depends instead on the fact that only a free person is a person, that loving a person entails permitting him to be a person, and that the reason why one person loves another is independent of the goodness of the person loved and even of the goodness of the love itself.

In what I have just said I have attempted to lay out a plausible account of how God's love for human creatures works in a way that is analogous to parental love and have shown how this account rests on an agent-based ethical theory, a type of theory that has independent support in experience and in ethics, as well as in natural theology. But notice that taking an agent-based approach to the problem of evil does not commit us to the particulars of my account. Given the standard Christian position that God is perfect goodness and the source of goodness as applied to everything else, and given an agent-based approach, it follows immediately that whatever God is motivated to bring about is good and whatever God is motivated to do is right. If in addition we accept the traditional view of the creation, according to which everything that occurs in the world is ultimately traceable to some motivation in God, it follows that ultimately everything that goes on in the world can be evaluatively justified because of its derivative connection with the motivations of a perfectly good being. It does not follow from this, of course, that ultimately everything that goes on is good, but only that on balance there is moral justification for the fact that everything that goes on is permitted by the motivational structure of a perfectly good being. We need not add an analysis of what that motivational structure is and how it can intuitively be seen to be good in itself, regardless of its consequences. But I have attempted to fill out the account by using the analogy of the motivation of parental love for two reasons. One is that the problem of evil is such a serious problem for most of us that it helps considerably to have an intuitively plausible model for thinking about it in our ordinary lives. I also want to show that agent-basing is not an ad hoc reaction to a theological problem, but is something that can be and has been used to understand ethical problems in human life.

The existence of agent-based ethical theories undercuts the basis for using the existence of evil as grounds for rejecting the existence of an omnipotent, omniscient, and perfectly good God. A consideration of this kind of theory shows that we cannot simply say that the state of the world is a bad thing according to some non-agent-based theory of justice or the human good, and then conclude that we have evidence against the existence of an omnipotent, omniscient, and perfectly good God. To object fairly, the objector to theism would have to look at the theory of God's justice or goodness that derives from the agent-based approach before claiming that he has a case against God's existence based on the existence of evil in the world. Alternatively, of course, he can attack agent-basing itself once the theory is developed more fully.[12]

4.4. Problems and conjectures

An objector to theism who accepts an agent-based theory could still make the following objection: We have some idea of how persons with good inner traits behave, and no one with good inner traits, or at least no one with perfectly good inner traits, would have wanted to create a world like the one we have. Loving persons do not want to see people suffering, least of all do parents want to see their children suffer. Would they want a child crippled and unhappy as the price, if it were necessary, of their being full persons? The problem of evil can be reformulated in an agent-based fashion as the problem that a perfectly loving God simply would not permit such a world as ours, and the existence of evil is evidence against the claim that there is a God who has the motivations we have identified as good from an agent-based perspective.

To make this objection work, the objector would have to make a persuasive case that the external manifestations of the good motives in question are unlike the ones we know to obtain in the world. If the motivation said to generate the problem is love, then the objector would have to be very clear on the way loving persons act toward those they love, and it would have to be highly plausible that any sort of behavior on the part of a person toward those she loves that permits them to suffer counts against the fact that the person is motivated by love.[13] But in fact we do not always draw such a conclusion, even in the human case. To return to the parent-child analogy, loving parents do not always stop the suffering of their children when it is the consequence of the parental motivation to help their children become full persons. Of course, children often do not understand the parental motivation and become angry or hurt at the parent, and similarly, if there is a God with the attributes described in this paper, we would expect human creatures to be angry or hurt at the existence of human suffering because of a lack of understanding of the divine motivation. This answer, of course, does not do much to make us feel better about suffering, but it indicates that it is presumptuous of us to expect to understand the motivations of a loving God in any but the crudest fashion.

It follows from the argument of this paper that the problem of suffering is more difficult to handle than the problem of evil with which it is sometimes identified. Notice that when the problem is posed in terms of suffering rather than evil, the discussion shifts from a question that is largely conceptual to a question that is largely empirical. One of the primary reasons the problem of evil has the appearance of great force is that premise (1) seems to be something close to a conceptual truth, whereas the analogous premise in the problem of suffering clearly is not. If premise (1) can be denied in the way I have described and replaced with a premise that claims that a perfectly good being would be motivated to eliminate suffering, the argument shifts to a consideration of what good beings are motivated to do or to allow, and that can only be settled by a consideration of their actual behavior, as suggested in the previous paragraph, not by conceptual analysis.

In spite of what I have said, there are problems of evil that cannot be addressed by analogy with the motivations of a loving parent: the suffering of newborn babies who die before ever getting the chance to develop into full persons, the suffering of animals, the suffering of persons that appears to exceed that which a perfectly loving being would permit, even on the loosest interpretation of the motivation of love. In these cases, my response is to fall back on the barebones agent-based answer to the problem of evil without the parental analogy. Under the assumption that there is a perfectly good God whose goodness is understood as the source for all other attributions of goodness and rightness, and whose motivations are ultimately responsible for the world as it is, it follows that all things considered, the world is to be judged positively. The world contains some features that are astonishingly unexpected in a world produced by a perfect being. To observe these features is analogous to observing the radiantly good person described earlier permitting some startling things, including severe suffering or indignity. It is quite possible that we could see such a person permitting these things without losing her radiant nobility and evident goodness in our own eyes. If that happened, we would be puzzled, bewildered, frightened, even angry, but we would not necessarily be forced to retract our judgment of her motivations and her fundamental goodness. I am not denying that there are cases in which a person who once appeared to us as good later changes in our eyes when her behavior begins to look seriously wrong to us. What happens in those cases is that wrongful behavior reflects back on the character of the person; we cease to see her as virtuous and we see her as vicious instead. My point is that this need not happen. She may continue to exude the same goodness as before. Her motives and virtues may be as evident as before; the behavior is simply not what we would expect to see in such a person. What happens in these cases is that the inner goodness of the person is reflected forward onto her behavior and the aims of her motivations, and we may then reconsider our evaluative judgments on the things she does or permits. If we take agent-basing seriously as an ethical theory, such a move can be appropriate and it is particularly appropriate when the agent is God.

A second problem that could be raised by an objector to theism who accepts an agent-based theory is that the account I have given has mistaken the motivation of love for some other motivation, such as that of respect. Western ethics is very heavily influenced by the idea of respect for persons, the central concept in

Kantian ethics, and it is the primary motivation behind the Western tradition of human rights. It might be claimed that the attempt of this paper to trace the state of the world to God's interest in the autonomy necessary for being full persons, and to ground that interest in God's motivation of love, is mistaken because it is not love, but respect, that leads one person to care about the autonomy and full personhood of another. Loving persons are more concerned about the suffering of their loved ones than their autonomy. Respectful persons are more concerned for their autonomy than their suffering. In short, the problem of evil could be reformulated in an agent-based fashion as the problem that we could use a lot more love and a lot less respect from the deity.

This objection makes a couple of important but dubious assumptions that I will let pass. One is that to love a person is to care more for her suffering than for her autonomy. Another is that love is more important than respect. Neither of these assumptions is clearly true. But it is worth remarking that there is an important concept in traditional Aristotelian virtue ethics that the agent-based ethicist can adopt to handle this problem, and that is the concept of *phronesis* or practical wisdom. Even in the case of ordinary human choice, we find that we often need to balance two good motivations that lead in different, even opposing, directions. Agents who are motivated by both fairness and compassion, for example, might not always do what people do who are motivated by fairness but not also by compassion, and conversely. Whether or not it requires a separate virtue like *phronesis* to handle these cases is not my point. Persons advanced in virtue do handle these cases in a way that adequately expresses their combined motivations, and these cases are significant for their importance in calling attention to the dangers of focusing the analysis of moral judgment on a single virtuous motivation to the exclusion of others that overlap the area of judgment in question. Presumably, then, the same point applies to the motivations of the divine agent. Even if God does not always do what he would have done if no other motivation were relevant than love, this is not to deny either that he is motivated by love or that his judgment arises from motivations that are good.

In conclusion, the logical problem of evil rests on the assumption that good beings are motivated to eliminate evil and to produce good. I maintain that a version of virtue ethics that is new, at least in the West, denies this assumption for reasons that have nothing to do with the problem of evil or any theological considerations. There are grounds for accepting an agent-based ethics both in experience and in theoretical ethics. But in addition, I have suggested that the traditional position on the relation between God's nature and goodness and between God's goodness and the goodness of anything besides God makes agent-basing where God is the agent highly desirable for theological reasons. Finally, I wish to propose that if an agent-based ethical theory is combined with the traditional Christian view of the nature of God, we get another advantage not yet mentioned. Recall that the first theoretical advantage of agent-based ethics mentioned in this paper is that it unifies ethical phenomena. The position for which I have argued here allows for an even more extensive unification since it permits a single theory of ethics to account for the ethics of both divine and human behavior and to do so in a way that is straightforwardly faithful to the traditional view on the nature of God. In addition, it has the significant advantage of giving us a new and interesting way out of the problem of evil.[14]

Notes

1. A well-known example is Alvin Plantinga (1974a).
2. See, for example, Marilyn Adams (1986) and (1988).
3. Often only the second clause of the premise is used since it is the motivation to eliminate evil that does the primary work in generating the dilemma, rather than the motivation to produce good.
4. See Michael Slote (1995). Others like Christine Swanton and Philip Pettit have adopted this usage. Julia Annas has used "agent-centered" for something similar, but that terminology risks confusion with the usage by Samuel Scheffler in a totally different context. My own usage changed after writing this paper and I stopped using the term.
5. This paper was written while I was writing a book that applied this style of ethics to a range of concepts in normative epistemology in Zagzebski (1996a).
6. In a note that appeared in the second edition (1864) of *Utilitarianism*, John Stuart Mill makes the evaluation of the motive completely independent of the evaluation of the act. This note was dropped in subsequent editions, but the implausibility of Mill's claims, as well as his failure to give a unitary account of morality that can handle both the motive and the act, is worth noting. The note ends as follows: "The morality of the action depends entirely upon the intention—that is, upon what the agent wills to do. But the motive, that is, the feeling which makes him will so to do, if it makes no difference in the act, makes none in the morality: though it makes a great difference in our moral estimation of the agent, especially if it indicates a good or a bad habitual disposition—a bent of character from which useful, or from which hurtful actions are likely to arise" (Chap. II, n. 3).
7. See Michael Stocker (1976), Larry Blum (1980), and Susan Wolf (1982).
8. It is interesting to compare this theory with that of Robert Adams (1979), in which he adds the stipulation that what is right is what would be commanded by a *loving* God.
9. Michael Slote has suggested to me that we might see this as a theory based more on the New Testament, while traditional Divine Command theory is more naturally interpreted as having its basis in the Hebrew Scriptures. The human analogue of Divine Command theory is the idea that something is good for a child because the parent says so, and young children are expected to accept this as an explanation of morality adequate for their level of understanding. The human analogue of

an agent-based theory says that something is good/acceptable for a child because a loving parent is motivated to command it from the child or to tolerate it. On this view, will is treated as a derivative part of the psyche. Older children are expected to accept this in virtue of their trust in their parents, which is to say, they trust internal properties of their parents, particularly their understanding and loving motivations.

10. James Ross has another way of comparing the creativity of God to that of the artist. He likens God's creative acts to that of an improvising jazz musician who creates beauty out of his own nature without knowing in advance how it will turn out.
11. It could be argued that if any of these reasons were the parent's motivation, she would be treating her child as a means to an end—the end of producing good. If so, premise (1) conflicts with the Kantian Categorical Imperative. I am not taking this approach myself, but it does suggest an alternative line of argument for rejecting premise (1) in the derivation of the alleged inconsistency between the existence of evil and the existence of God.
12. I subsequently proposed a development of this style of theory for the Christian in Zagzebski (2004a).
13. This objection was made to me by John Hick.
14. I presented the general idea on the solution of section III in response to a paper by William Rowe at a conference in Claremont, California, on the work of John Hick in 1989. The exchange was subsequently published in Hewitt (1991).

5
Good Persons, Good Aims, and the Problem of Evil (2017)

5.1. A meta-ethical assumption in the argument from evil

Standard formulations of the argument from evil claim that an omnipotent being who is perfectly good would not permit, or probably would not permit, the vast quantity and severity of evil in the world. These arguments almost always have an implied assumption about the motivational structure of a good being. Examples of the kind of premise that reveals this assumption are the following:

(1a) A good being always eliminates evil as far as it can (Mackie 1955).
(1b) If God is morally perfect, God has the desire to eliminate all evil (Tooley 2013).
(1c) An omniscient, wholly good being would prevent the occurrence of any intense suffering it could, unless it could not do so without thereby losing some greater good or permitting some evil equally bad or worse (Rowe 1979).

Although there are some differences among the preceding premises, they all affirm a connection between being a good person and acting with the aim of eliminating evil.[1] Since the aim of preventing evil is almost always connected with the aim of producing good, an initial formulation of the implied assumption is the following:

(2) A good person aims at producing good and preventing evil.

Tooley's premise (1b) mentions desires rather than aims, but it is clear from his version of the argument that he thinks of a desire to do x as something that is sufficient to get a person to attempt to do x, so I take it that Tooley would accept (2).[2]

Rowe's version specifies intense suffering as an example of the kind of evil a good being would aim to prevent. Perhaps Rowe would be willing to claim that a good being would aim to prevent suffering *whether or not* it comes under the category of evil, and that possibility suggests that suffering and evil have different conceptual connections to the motives of good persons. I believe that the problem of suffering is a distinct and more difficult problem than the problem of evil, but for this paper, I presuppose the most straightforward interpretation of (1c), according to which (1c) refers to suffering *qua* evil. So understood, (1c) implies (2).[3]

Mackie's (1a) goes farther than (2), stating that a good being always *acts* in a way that prevents or eliminates evil as long as it has sufficient power, but presumably Mackie believes that a good being aims at doing what it does, and so Mackie assumes (2). These days few writers on evil would go as far as (1a) because it is commonly recognized by all sides that a good being need not always prevent evils because there can be morally justifiable reasons to permit them. For instance, if there are evils that are outweighed by goods that cannot be obtained without permitting the evils, the permission of those evils is not only compatible with (2), but follows from it. Rowe's version of the premise in (1c) acknowledges that explicitly. A well-known candidate for this category is the proposal that the good of free will outweighs all the evils that are produced through the exercise of free will. There are other possibilities, but in each case, if the proposed morally justifying reason for evil is the fact that some good states of affairs cannot be obtained without permitting evil, then (2) is assumed. Consequently, I see no differences among the arguments of Mackie, Tooley, and Rowe with respect to their assumption of (2). Indeed, skeptical theists responding to the problem of evil typically assume (2) as well.

Thesis (2) might appear innocuous because all it says explicitly is that two properties go together: the property of being a good person, and the property of aiming at producing good states of affairs and eliminating evil states of affairs. A being who has the first property has the second. But (2) raises a number of questions because good persons do much more than aim at producing good and preventing evil. Among other things, good persons attempt to *be* good persons and to *do* good acts, or at least to avoid evil acts, and the connection between being a good person and aiming to produce good and eliminate evil is not obvious. It is even possible that there can be a conflict between being a good person—having a good will and good motives, and aiming to do acts that have good consequences. A good person might aim to perform acts that have a certain character rather than to produce certain consequences, or a good person might act in a way that expresses a quality or state such as love, without aiming at producing good in the outcome. The connections among good persons, good acts, and good aims need to be clarified if we wish to understand what is said in (2).

Let us suppose that (2) is true. That does not tell us anything about why or how the property of being a good person is connected to the property of producing good and eliminating evil. If one property is more basic than the other, (2) does not tell us that. Here are two opposing possibilities, both of which are compatible with (2):

> (2a) A condition for being a good person is that she aims at producing good states of affairs and preventing evil states of affairs.
>
> (2b) A condition for something being a good state of affairs and something else an evil state of affairs is that a good person aims at producing the former and preventing the latter.

The difference between (2a) and (2b) is striking, even though both are compatible with the thesis that a good person aims at bringing about good and preventing evil. According to (2a), aiming to eliminate evil is a more basic property than being a good person. The possession of the property of aiming to eliminate evil is a condition for the possession of the property of being a good person. But according to (2b), a good person aims to produce good and eliminate evil because what *counts* as producing good and eliminating evil is just what good persons aim to do. The property of being a good person is more basic than the property of aiming to eliminate evil.

To bring out the difference, consider this analogy. Moral philosophers of different kinds might affirm the following:

> (3) Virtuous persons act rightly.

But (3) is compatible with two very different views on the relation between virtue and right acting:

> (3a) Virtuous persons are persons who act rightly.
> (3b) Right acts are acts that virtuous persons do.

(3a) makes the possession of the property of being virtuous derivative from the property of performing right acts. A right act is the more basic property. Right acts are determinable in advance of the determination of the virtuous persons. In contrast, (3b) makes the possession of the property of performing right acts derivative from the property of being a virtuous person. Being a virtuous person is the more basic property. The determination of the acts that are right depends upon a prior determination of the virtuous persons.

Similarly, we could affirm (2) because we think (2a) is true. We might think that one of the things that makes a person good is that she aims at eliminating evil states of affairs. Evil states of affairs can be determined in advance, and being a good person depends upon having the right relation to those states of affairs.

Alternatively, we could affirm (2) because we think (2b) is true. We might think that what makes an aim the aim of eliminating evil is that it is an aim to eliminate what good persons aim to eliminate. The goodness of persons is determinable in advance, and what makes a state of affairs evil is its relation to good persons.

(2a) and (2b) are by no means the only ways good personhood and the aim of eliminating evil can be connected in a way that is compatible with (2). The goodness of persons and the goodness or evil of the states of affairs at which persons aim could each be connected with some third thing the goodness of which is more basic than either persons or states of affairs—for instance, good acts. Another possibility is that there is a general correlation between being a good person and having certain aims, with no deep connection between them at all (like the connection Jane Austen thought obtained between being virtuous and living in the country). There are many other possibilities that could explain the putative truth of (2).

It seems to me that typical proponents of the argument from evil, as well as most of its attackers, assume (2) in the sense of (2a). That may not be explicitly stated, but it is indicated by the structure of standard arguments in which the hypothesis under attack is that there is a God who is perfectly good. Assuming that God is omnipotent, the apparent fact that God does not act with the aim of eliminating evil is taken to be grounds for *retracting* the hypothesis that God is perfectly good. In the dialectic of the argument, the evil of certain states of affairs comes first. The goodness of a person depends upon that person aiming to eliminate these states of affairs. So well-known forms of the argument, including the arguments from Mackie, Tooley, and Rowe, proceed roughly as follows:

(4) There are certain evils in the world, the evil of which is determinable independently of the goodness or evil of persons.

(5) A condition for being a perfectly good person is that that person aims at preventing those evils in a way that is compatible with also aiming at producing good.

(6) God apparently does not aim at preventing those evils.

(7) So God is not perfectly good.

(5) immediately entails (2a), but notice that the argument from evil does not get off the ground if (2b) is used instead. With (2b), the apparent fact that a perfectly good God permits the evil states of affairs of this world would not be grounds for retracting the hypothesis that God is good. Rather, it would be grounds for retracting the judgment that those states of affairs are evil. Alternatively, if (2) is interpreted as merely asserting a correlation between the goodness of a being and the goodness of the states of affairs at which that being

aims, then the existence of evil would be taken to be disconfirming evidence of that correlation. On the fourth interpretation mentioned previously, good persons and aims to prevent evils are connected by their connection to something else, such as good acts. With that interpretation, the argument clearly would need to be filled out with additional premises connecting the goodness of acts to good persons, on the one side, and to good aims, on the other.

So far I have argued that standard arguments from evil assume that a good person aims to produce good and eliminate evil, and what they typically mean by that is (2a): A condition for being a good person is that she aims at producing good states of affairs and preventing evil ones. The condition intended in (2a) is most naturally interpreted as a metaphysical condition: a condition for being a good person is that that person aims at producing good states of affairs. Alternatively, the condition in (2a) might be interpreted as epistemic: Our reason for believing that a person is good is that she aims at producing good states of affairs. I will look at the metaphysical interpretation in section 5.2, and the epistemic interpretation in section 5.3. I believe that (2a) is problematic on both interpretations.

5.2. The goodness of persons and their aims: The metaphysical interpretation

5.2.1. The goodness of persons and the Pauline principle

The advocate of the argument from evil presumably knows that theists believe that there are firm grounds for the judgment that God is perfectly good; in fact, there is a tradition that identifies God with Goodness itself. A person (or Trinity of persons) is the exemplar of goodness. So even if (2b) is not true universally, it is much more plausible when the person in question is God. The aims of God could be the standard for what counts as good aims. Nonetheless, the proponent of the argument says that the existence of evil shows that God fails (or probably fails) to satisfy a necessary condition for being good. As I have said, the argument must assume that (2) is true in the sense of (2a). The property of being an evil state of affairs precedes—in a sense to be determined—the goodness of God. That is, whether or not it turns out that God is good, certain states of affairs are evil. A good person is (among other things) a person who aims at eliminating those states of affairs, and if God does not aim at eliminating those states of affairs, then God is not good, but those states of affairs are nonetheless evil.

Let us begin by taking (2a) in its most straightforward sense as a metaphysical claim about the relation between the moral properties of persons and the good or evil of states of affairs. Interpreted this way, the metaphysical thesis implied by (2a) is the following:

(8) The goodness or badness of persons is derivative from the goodness or badness of the states of affairs they aim to bring about or prevent.

According to (8), moral goodness or badness flows backwards from the moral properties of states of affairs to the moral properties of the aims to bring about or to prevent those states of affairs, and from there to the moral properties of the persons who have those aims as follows:

Persons ← aims ← states of affairs.

Consequentialism gives us a familiar model of the way value is transferred in this way. In a consequentialist value structure, the only thing intrinsically good or bad is states of affairs of a certain kind. The moral properties of acts are derivative from the goodness or badness of the states of affairs to which those acts lead. The moral properties of persons are derivative from the moral properties of acts as follows:[4]

Persons ← acts ← states of affairs

I am not suggesting that an adherent of (8) must be a consequentialist. Indeed, (8) makes no reference to acts at all, and there are many views on the morality of acts compatible with (8). But I mention consequentialism because its picture of the way value flows backwards from what is intrinsically good or bad to what is derivatively good or bad is the same as in (8). I think this means that some well-known objections to consequentialism are also objections to (8).

One objection is the traditional Pauline principle: Never do evil that good may come of it. As stated, the principle is obviously vague, but it identifies one of the most historically important problems with consequentialism—that consequentialism demands the performance of vicious acts in certain circumstances, the standard example of which is the killing of innocent persons to save many lives. Acts of that kind are said to be intrinsically evil. They do not derive their moral status from their consequences.

Notice first that it is not necessary to think that the Pauline principle has no exceptions in order to see the problem. If consequentialism *ever* morally requires what a morally good person would not do, there is a problem with consequentialism.

Second, notice that if acts can be evil intrinsically, that constitutes an objection to (8) as well as an objection to consequentialist ethics. Given that

(8) says that the goodness of a person derives from the aim of producing good and eliminating evil, then the goodness of a person can require the aim of killing innocent persons to save other lives. If a good person would not kill or aim to kill an innocent person to save lives, then her goodness cannot always be derived from the aim of producing good and preventing evil states of affairs.

Third, this means that the general meta-ethical issue raised by the Pauline principle extends beyond the issue of whether there are intrinsically evil acts. As I see it, the key insight of the Pauline principle is that the moral properties of acts do not derive (or do not always derive) from the value of states of affairs at which the agent aims. That could be the case because either there are intrinsically good or bad acts, or because the moral properties of acts derive from the moral properties of the persons who perform the acts. In both cases, the moral properties of some acts do not derive from the moral properties of states of affairs. So there are two distinct possibilities:

Possibility A. There are intrinsically good or evil acts, and the moral properties of persons derive from the moral properties of acts. The moral properties of acts and persons do not derive from the goodness or badness of states of affairs:

Persons ← acts ↮ states of affairs,

Possibility B. The moral properties of acts derive from moral properties of persons. Again, the moral properties of acts and persons do not derive from the goodness or badness of states of affairs:

Persons → acts ↮ states of affairs

Let us look at both possibilities since they are both incompatible with (8).

Possibility A is one in which there can be an intrinsically evil act, meaning an act the evil of which does not derive from anything outside of the kind of act that it is. Standard examples are lying and intentionally killing the innocent. Why think that such acts are intrinsically evil? My defense would be this. Suppose that lying is intentionally telling someone a falsehood. The badness of that act cannot derive from the badness of someone's believing a falsehood because even though believing a falsehood is not good, the badness of lying greatly exceeds the badness of someone's believing a falsehood. The badness of lying therefore cannot derive from the badness of the state of affairs at which the act aims. Similarly, intentionally killing an innocent person cannot derive from the badness of the loss of life of an innocent person since the badness of murder greatly exceeds the badness of the loss of innocent life. In these cases, the badness of the act is in the intentions of the agent. The will of the agent in an act of that kind is disordered, and the person derives badness from the badness of her will to perform the act.

I think that the same point can apply to the intrinsic goodness of an act. Consider an act of intentionally giving someone else peace and comfort. The state of affairs of feeling at peace is good, but the value of the act of aiming at giving someone peace greatly exceeds the value of feeling at peace. Again, the value of such an intentional act cannot derive from the value of the state of affairs at which the agent aims. The agent derives goodness from the goodness of her will to perform the act.

In possibility A the moral properties of a person who performs an act may derive from the moral properties of the acts the person performs. The moral properties of some of those acts are intrinsic. It follows that the moral properties of persons do not derive exclusively from the goodness or badness of the states of affairs at which those persons aim. (8) is therefore false.

Let us look next at possibility B. This possibility also arises from the focus on intentions in the Pauline principle, and the insight that the goodness or badness of an intentional act cannot derive from the value of outcomes or the state of affairs at which the act aims. But it does not follow that the value of such an act must be intrinsic. Possibility B focuses on the intuition that there is a close connection between persons and their acts, and in fact, the act as a category is partly defined by what is going on in the mind of the agent.

What the person does unintentionally is not the same kind of act as what she does intentionally, and the difference is in the agent. That difference makes a moral difference even if there is no difference in the outcome. The focus on intentions in acting also leads to the distinction between what one intends and what one merely foresees, and that also leads to a moral difference between the good or evil of what one does intentionally and the good or evil of what one lets happen. For moral theories that focus on the good or bad of outcomes, this distinction is not relevant.

What a person intends to do expresses love, hate, respect, honor, pride, envy, or other personal states that arguably have intrinsic value or disvalue. If so, when a person intentionally kills an innocent person, the badness of the act derives from the fact that such an act expresses the dishonoring of innocent human life, which is a disordered quality of the person. On this picture, the personal quality of dishonoring innocent human life is intrinsically bad, and any act that expresses dishonor of innocent human life is bad derivatively. It is bad because it expresses an intrinsically bad state. This view leads to the same position as the view that there are intrinsically bad acts—namely, that there are acts whose badness does not derive from the badness of the intended outcome. Either way, (8) is false.

It seems to me that the picture of the flow of value given in the diagrams of A and B deserve attention in discussions of the source of the value of acts. Acts can be:

(i) intrinsically good or bad,
(ii) good or bad because of their connection to the states of affairs they aim to bring about,
(iii) good or bad because of the qualities of persons that are expressed in such acts.

An act is the bridge between a person and the world. An intentional act is rooted in the psyche of the agent, and it affects the world through an intentional structure. It is not controversial that there are properties of good or bad throughout the entire structure, but there are many different ways value can flow within that structure, and it is by no means obvious that value does not flow as depicted in the diagrams of A or B.

My view of the Pauline principle, then, is the following:

(i) It need not be an absolute principle to constitute a threat to the view that the only thing intrinsically good or evil is states of affairs.
(ii) It constitutes a threat to more than the consequentialist view that the value of acts derives from the value of consequences. It is also a threat to (8), for if it is implausible to say that the moral properties of acts derive from the value of consequences, it is also implausible to say that the moral properties of persons derive from the value of the states of affairs they aim to bring about.
(iii) One need not insist that there are intrinsically evil acts to see the problem in claiming that the value of acts derives from states of affairs. The value or disvalue of an act could be intrinsic (Possibility A). Alternatively, it could derive from properties of persons rather than outcomes (Possibility B).

If I am right that (8) is presupposed in many arguments from evil, the Pauline principle is a threat to the validity of these arguments. I think that improved arguments from evil should shift their focus from variations of (8) to the claim that a good person would not act in ways that God acts, or would act in ways that God does not act. The fact that there are evil states of affairs in the world is not sufficient to establish such a claim.

5.2.2. Integrity and predicting consequences

I have argued that most standard arguments against theism from the existence of evil presuppose:

(8) The goodness or badness of persons is derivative from the goodness or badness of the states of affairs they aim to bring about or prevent.

I have argued that one set of objections to (8) comes from the Pauline principle. But there is another well-known problem with consequentialism that applies to (8). Bernard Williams argued in his well-known critique of utilitarianism that consequentialism demands of agents that they ignore their self and the story of their lives when doing so has better consequences (Smart and Williams 1973). Personal projects, plans, and values must be overridden when dictated by the utility calculus, assume that one's personal values include many things that are distinctive of the individual person—e.g., taking care of one's children, developing loving relationships with particular individuals, embarking on a career in philosophy, developing one's talent for music, taking up a hobby in gardening or genealogical research. Each of these projects involves an extended commitment of time, resources, and energy that could otherwise be used to maximize good from an impersonal viewpoint. If utilitarianism demands of a person the sacrifice of these deep commitments for the sake of the consequences, then utilitarianism attacks integrity in one of its senses.

Williams formulated this objection as a problem for utilitarianism, but notice that it also applies to (8) because it is an objection to consequentialism as a principle of practical reasoning. The problem is that if the moral status of persons derives from the value of the consequences at which they aim, then it does not matter what a person honors, loves, and cares about as long as she aims to produce good and eliminate evil. But we define ourselves in part by what we care about and how we design our lives around the things we care about. But according to (8), the way we define ourselves is irrelevant to our moral status except insofar as we define ourselves in a way that lines up with the utility calculus. So the Williams objection from integrity is not simply an objection to a certain way of evaluating the morality of acts; it is an objection to a certain way of evaluating the moral status of persons.

The Williams objection applies to the problem of evil because God has a life, a fact that is easy to ignore in an argument about the motives of a good being rather than a good person. Scripture reveals that God has plans, although presumably not all divine plans are revealed to humans. Still, theodicies have been developed that refer to a divine plan for a life of mutual sharing between God and his creatures. For instance, Marilyn Adams (2006) has offered a Christological approach to the problem of evil, in which the story by which Christ defeats the horrors of human life is a component of a narrative of the *divine* life. The stories of individual human lives and the life of the Church are held together by the Christological narrative, and that narrative is a component of God's plan for his own life.[6] In a different way, Eleonore Stump's (2010) extended reflections on biblical narratives reveal the way evil and suffering are components of a larger divine narrative in which God desires union with human persons. The integrity objection to utilitarianism is connected to narrative defenses like theirs because they clearly think of God as a person whose life is designed by God himself. That life includes the desire to merge his life with the lives of creaturely persons who are also designing lives. Why such a person as God would design a life in which his creatures must suffer is a serious problem, but it is not the problem that a good person aims at producing good and preventing evil. To assert, like (8), that a good person must aim solely to produce good outcomes is to fail to understand the structure of a life and what makes it good as judged by the person who designed the life. Similarly, defeating evils in a life is not a matter of producing goods that outweigh the evils. Evils in a life are elements in the organic narrative structure of a life the goodness of which is not an outcome of the process of living. If the integrity objection applies to ordinary human beings, it applies all the more to the Creator, whose design for his life in communion with his creatures cannot be superseded by a demand to calculate the value of the outcome of each divine choice.

In this section I have argued that (2a) can be interpreted as offering a metaphysical condition for the possession of the property of goodness by persons. If interpreted that way, I proposed that (2a) arises from a view of value given by (8), the thesis that the moral properties of persons derive from the goodness or badness of the states of affairs at which persons aim. Two important objections to consequentialism are also objections to (8). One objection is that the prohibition on intentionally killing the innocent requires that the morality of acts does not always derive from the value or disvalue of the states of affairs to which the acts lead. The Pauline principle is a traditional way to express this prohibition, and I argued that that principle need not be understood as absolute, and it need not even require the view that there are intrinsically evil acts to pose a problem for (8). The second objection is that utilitarianism attacks the integrity of persons. This also can be formulated as an objection to (8) because the problem is not just that utilitarianism sometimes requires the agent to put aside her deepest projects and commitments, but that any theory that makes the moral status of persons derivative from the value or disvalue of states of affairs ignores the moral importance of distinctive features of individual persons. Indeed, it ignores what a person is.

5.3. The goodness of persons and their aims: The epistemic interpretation

It is possible that the proponent of (2a) treats it as a statement of an epistemic condition rather than a metaphysical condition. She might think that it is easier to identify evil states of affairs than it is to identify good persons, and a criterion for thinking that some person is good is that that person aims to eliminate what we take to be evil. That interpretation of (2a) makes the evil of states of affairs prior in the order of discovery rather than in the metaphysical order, and she might affirm (2a) in its epistemic interpretation regardless of her position on the metaphysical interpretation of (2). Whether or not aiming at eliminating independently identified evils is a condition for *being* a good person, reasonably believing that some person aims at eliminating independently identified evils may be a condition for reasonably *believing* that that person is good. So understood, (2a) is the following thesis:

(9) A condition for reasonably judging that some person is good is that one reasonably judges that that person aims to produce good and to prevent evil.

If we are more confident of our ability to identify evil states of affairs and people's aims than to identify good persons, it is reasonable to make our identification of good persons conditional upon our prior identification of good and evil states of affairs, and our judgment of whether someone aims to produce or eliminate those states of affairs.

So consider the following set of potential beliefs:

(i) God is a good person.
(ii) X is an evil state of affairs.
(iii) God does not aim to prevent or eliminate X.

The proponent of (9) says that (ii) and (iii) have epistemic priority over (i). One reasonably ought to make a judgment such as (ii) and (iii) in advance of a judgment about God's goodness. Given certain background assumptions, including assumptions about God's knowledge, power, and the other goods that God can produce and evils that God can eliminate, (9) says that judging (ii) and (iii) is grounds for judging the negation of (i), or at least for being skeptical of (i). Belief (i) is treated as epistemically less well grounded than (ii) and (iii) because the grounds for any judgment of God's goodness include judgments like (ii) and (iii).

How do people reasonably form the belief that God is good? Is it because they look at the created world, see that it is mostly good, and see that God aims to eliminate the evils in it? That can be one of the reasons. But they can also know that God is good in other ways: through Scripture and tradition, religious experience, the teaching authority of the Church. These reasons for believing (i) are independent of beliefs about the existence and quantity of evils in the world and beliefs about God's aims. The belief in (i) might be very well grounded, or it might not be. It might be reasonable to be confident in it, or it might not be. But I do not see that the issue of whether (i) is reasonable is settled by making the prior judgments (ii) and (iii).

The adherent of (2b) treated as an epistemic principle will do the reverse and will say that (i) and (iii) have epistemic priority over (ii). Reasonably judging (i) and (iii) is grounds for skepticism regarding (ii). Another possibility is that someone uses (i) and (ii) as grounds for skepticism regarding (iii). Yet another possibility is that a person denies (2) in any form, in which case she may not even detect a tension among the beliefs (i)–(iii).

Most people, however, are probably in none of these positions. They do not use (2a) as an epistemic principle, nor do they use (2b), even though they think that there is a sense in which (2) is true. I think also that for many theists, the judgments (i), (ii), and (iii) are, to some extent, formed independently. Beliefs in (i) may be based on what I have mentioned previously—Scripture, religious experience, and the teaching of religious authority. Likewise, beliefs about the existence and quantity of evils in the world are generally grounded in experiences and natural dispositions that are independent of the belief that God is good. The belief (iii) typically depends upon observations of the world and a number of beliefs about the psychology of a good person that are independent of beliefs (i) and (ii). Given the kinds of grounds these beliefs have, both (2a) and (2b) are questionable as principles of moral epistemology. In any case, I think that (2a) deserves more critical attention. Without that principle, it can turn out that our judgment of a person's goodness is better grounded than our judgment of his aims together with our judgment of what is evil.

5.4. Conclusion

In this paper I have argued that standard versions of the argument from evil assume

(2) Good persons aim to produce good and prevent evil,

where the context of the argument makes it most natural to interpret (2) as

(2a) A condition for being a good person is that she aims at producing good states of affairs and preventing evil ones.

The kind of condition intended in (2a) can be either metaphysical or epistemic. Interpreted metaphysically, the thesis assumed in (2a) is

> (8) The goodness or badness of persons is derivative from the goodness or badness of the states of affairs they aim to bring about or prevent.

Two objections to consequentialist ethics are also objections to (8). First, the Pauline principle that one should not do evil to produce good is both an objection to the view that the moral properties of acts derive from the moral properties of their consequences, and to the view that the moral properties of persons derive from the moral properties of the states of affairs at which persons aim. There may be acts a good person would not do either because of the kind of act that it is (possibility A) or because the act expresses qualities a good person does not have (possibility B). Second, the famous integrity objection by Bernard Williams arises from a view of persons as having the moral right to design lives the goodness of which is not an outcome at which they aim. A good person lives a good life, but a good life is not solely a function of how good a job that person does in aiming to produce the best outcome.

If instead (2a) is interpreted epistemically, the thesis assumed is the following:

> (9) A condition for reasonably judging that some person is good is that one reasonably judges that that person aims to produce good and prevent evil.

(9) is a principle in moral epistemology that makes the judgment

> (i) God is a good person

derivative from the judgments

> (ii) X is an evil state of affairs,

and

> (iii) God does not aim to prevent or eliminate X.

I have not argued that (9) is false, only that it is far from obvious.

Some of the most subtle theodicies reveal problems with (9). Narrative theodicies can weaken (9) by revealing ways in which we find out the goodness of God without reference to God's aims. But in addition, narratives can sometimes reveal divine aims we would not have considered otherwise, and they can reveal goods and evils that we would not have independently identified. For instance, although we might have thought of the good of union with God and the evil of separation from God, we might not have thought of suffering as a sharing in the divine life, and we might not have thought about the difference between eliminating evil and defeating evil without a narrative account of divine and human life.

If I right in this paper, then narrative insights on the nature of a good person and a good life are connected with the denial of (8) and (9), and reveal the weakness of a central assumption in standard arguments from evil.

Notes

1. I say "person" to make it clear that these arguments are not about good beings like stars and flowers, but about beings who act intentionally.
2. That is implied by another one of Tooley's premises: "If evil exists and God exists, then either God doesn't have the power to eliminate all evil, or doesn't know when evil exists, or doesn't have the desire to eliminate all evil." This premise implies that a being with the desire to do x in Tooley's sense would aim at doing x, and would succeed in doing x if he has the requisite power and knowledge.
3. I argued for that claim in Zagzebski (1996a), Chapter 4 of this volume, and in Zagzebski (2004). Good and evil are opposed conceptually, but suffering and good are opposed in a different way, a way that goes to the heart of human experience. When we see horrible suffering, we think, "A loving God would not permit *that!*" In my opinion, it is much easier to handle alleged conceptual incoherence than to respond to the problem of suffering.
4. There is more than one way a consequentialist can evaluate a person's motives and intentions. Motives and intentions can be assessed directly by their consequences, or they can be assessed indirectly by the consequences of the acts to which they lead. For instance, some motives generally have good consequences even though they are not well correlated with the performance of right acts as determined by the consequences of the acts. See Robert Merrihew Adams (1976) for a discussion of the way motives can be evaluated by the utilitarian.

6
Weighing Evils
The C. S. Lewis Approach (2007)

Coauthor Joshua Seachris

6.1. Introduction

The intuition that the vast amount of evil in our world counts against traditional theism in a way that lesser quantities do not is prevalent both in lay circles and in philosophical treatments of the problem of evil. For example, Hume says in the mouth of Demea: "Were a stranger to drop, on a sudden, into this world, I would show him, as a specimen of its ills, a hospital full of diseases, a prison crowded with malefactors and debtors, a field of battle strewed with carcasses, a fleet foundering in the ocean, a nation languishing under tyranny, famine or pestilence" (Hume 1990, 106). Dostoevsky's Ivan Karamazov echoes Demea's intuition. Following depictions of horrendous evils involving small children, Ivan remarks, "Listen to me: I took children only so as to make it more obvious. About all the other human tears that have *soaked the whole earth through*, from crust to core, I don't say a word..." (emphasis added) (Dostoevsky 1992, 243).

Both Demea and Ivan imply that a large quantity of evil is a greater threat to the existence of God than significantly fewer evils would be. Indeed, contemporary philosophers often take it for granted that the problem of evil is worse due to the great quantity of evil in our world. For example, William Rowe says, "In light of our experience and knowledge of the variety and scale of human and animal suffering in our world, the idea that none of this suffering could have been prevented by an omnipotent being without thereby losing a greater good or permitting an evil at least as bad seems an extraordinarily absurd idea, quite beyond our belief (Rowe, 1990, 131). And Daniel Howard-Snyder endorses the position that the quantity of evil magnifies the problem of evil: "... even if there is a reason that would justify God in permitting *some* evil, even a great deal of it, there may be no reason at all that would justify his permitting *so much*..." (Howard-Snyder 1999), 101.[1]

Why would a greater quantity of evil make the existence of God less likely than a lesser quantity? Presumably any quantity of evil is a problem for the existence of an omnipotent and omnibenevolent deity, but contemporary objectors usually admit that some evils (or, at least, some apparent evils) might be such that an omnipotent and omnibenevolent being would have a morally sufficient reason to permit. That is to say, they might not be gratuitous.[2] However, the greater the quantity of evil, the more likely it is that at least some of those evils are gratuitous, and hence, the less likely it is that the God of traditional theism exists.

It is hard to know how to evaluate this argument without at least a rough way to determine the total quantity of evil in a world. Often evil is quantified on the model of the hedonic calculus, the way in which pain is quantified in classical utilitarianism. On this method, there are at least three scales of measure: the severity of the pain, the duration of the pain, and the number of instances of pain. According to this calculus, each scale is commensurate with the others, so the total quantity of pain in the world can be summed up. For example, one person may have a pain twice as severe but equal in duration to the pain of two others, in which case the first person's pain would be $2n$, and the other two persons' pain would be $1n + 1n$, resulting in the same total amount of pain. We will call this approach to quantifying evil the additive approach (AA). Possibly evils other than pains can be quantified by AA, but we will focus on the problem of pain because it has the best chance of being quantifiable in this way.[3] We will return to the problem of separating the problem of pain from other evils and countervailing goods at the end of this paper.

Using AA as the method for measuring quantity of pain, the quantitative argument from pain would go roughly as follows:

Quantitative argument from evil

(1) The quantity of pain in the world should be measured by AA, and on that measure the quantity is enormous.
(2) The greater the total quantity of pain, the more likely it is that some of the pain is gratuitous.
(3) The more likely it is that there is gratuitous pain, the less likely it is that the God of traditional theism exists.
(4) Therefore, it is unlikely that God exists.

In this paper we will examine C. S. Lewis's objection to (1) and will argue that Lewis is right to reject AA, yet there is also a sense in which Lewis underestimates the quantity of pain. But the quantity of pain in that sense does not significantly increase the probability that some pain is gratuitous, so premise (2) of the preceding argument is false in that case. Lewis is therefore right in his implied rejection of the quantitative argument from evil.

6.2. Undermining AA: A cue from Clive

In a collection of his posthumous writings, Wittgenstein says, "The Christian religion is only for the man who needs infinite help, solely, that is, for the man who experiences infinite torment. The whole planet can suffer no greater torment than a single soul" (Wittgenstein 1998, 52). C. S. Lewis also takes the position that the total amount of pain in the world cannot be greater than that experienced by one person, but he offers a different reason:

> We must never make the problem of pain worse than it is by vague talk about the "unimaginable sum of human misery." Suppose that I have a toothache of intensity x, and suppose that you, who are seated beside me, also begin to have a toothache of intensity x. You may, if you choose, say that the total amount of pain in the room is now 2x: search all time and all space and you will not find that composite pain in anyone's consciousness. There is no such thing as a sum of suffering, for no one suffers it. When we have reached the maximum that a single person can suffer, we have, no doubt, reached something very horrible, but we have reached all the suffering there ever can be in the universe. *The addition of a million fellow-sufferers adds no more pain.* [emphasis added] (Lewis, 1996, 103)[4]

Here Lewis seeks to demonstrate the illegitimacy of referring to the "unimaginable sum of human misery," and appealing to such a sum with anti-theistic motives—that this incomprehensible sum jeopardizes God's existence in a way that a much smaller sum does not. The argument is grounded in a claim about the relationship between quantity and the limitations of the conscious experience of pain. Summation of pain makes sense only within the consciousness of a single being, argues Lewis, but no one conscious being can experience the summation of all the pain in the world. In fact, no one being can experience the pain of more than one conscious being. We cannot peer into anyone's consciousness and there discover the aggregate of pain of even two persons, much less all the pain in the universe.[5] In speaking of the "unimaginable sum" of suffering, objectors attempt to refer to an experiential evil that no one actually experiences.

If pain can only be summed within the consciousness of a single individual, Lewis has an argument that there is a maximum amount of pain in the world, and that is the maximum pain a single conscious being can suffer. It does seem reasonable that given the neurological systems of creatures, there is some amount of pain that is the most such a being can suffer at any one time, and given the finitude of life, there is some amount of pain that is the most such a being can suffer during an entire lifetime. It is less plausible to claim that this amount is the maximum amount of pain in the world, and it is also implausible to think that there is *no* sense in which the pain of many creatures is worse than the pain of one. Nonetheless, we think there is something right in Lewis's argument.

Let's look at how Lewis's approach to quantifying pain (LA) contrasts with AA. For convenience, we will call a unit of pain a turp.[6] Suppose *A* and *B* each suffer one turp of pain in some situation *S*. According to AA, we can consider the experiences of *A* and *B* jointly and conclude that

(a) *S* is characterized by two turps—the summation of *A*'s and *B*'s pain. And we might conclude from (a) that
(b) *S* makes the existence of God less likely than a situation in which *A* suffers one turp and *B* does not suffer.

LA, in contrast, sums the pain in *S* as one turp, contra (a), and concludes that *S* is less threatening to the existence of God than the defender of AA acknowledges. Notice that Lewis uses the rejection of the way pain in *S* is quantified by AA as a reason to reject (b).

We think both AA and LA are partly right, but to see the problems of each approach, we need to compare a number of worlds. Assume that the maximum amount of pain a single conscious being can experience is ten thousand turps.[7] And let W1 be a world containing one person suffering one turp of pain.

W2 consists of ten thousand persons each suffering one turp.
W3 consists of a single person suffering ten thousand turps.
W4 consists of a billion people each suffering one turp.
W5 consists of a single person suffering one billion turps.

According to AA, the amount of pain in W2 equals the amount of pain in W3, and the pain in W4 equals the pain in W5. W2 and 3 have ten thousand times as much pain as W1, and W4 and W5 have a billion times as much pain as W1. According to LA, in contrast, the pain in W1, W2, and W4 are equal, and the pain in W3 is the worst possible. World W5 is an impossible world.

We agree with Lewis that W3 is worse than W2, and W5 is impossible, given the assumption that the maximum amount of pain a single individual can experience is well below a billion turps. We think that the position that W3 is worse than W2 is *prima facie* justified, but even if they are equal in quantity of pain, as AA maintains, W3 needs a greater justifying reason for its existence than does W2. This is evident if God's properties include the desire to have a relationship with his creatures, or at least, with each creature capable of having a relationship. Surely in that case God would need a much more serious reason to permit a world in which one of his creatures suffers the greatest amount of pain of which that being is capable, rather than a world in which the same number of turps of pain is distributed over ten thousand creatures. So we think that (i) W2 and W3 are not equal in total quantity of pain, but (ii) even if they are equal, W3 needs a greater justifying reason than W2. Whether W2 and W3 are compared by LA or by AA, Lewis is right in his implied conclusion that W3 is more threatening to the existence of God than W2.

But LA leads to counterintuitive results also. Surely, worlds W1, W2, and W4 are not actually equal in total amount of pain, or at least, the pain in W2 is greater *in some sense* than the pain in W1, and the pain in W4 is greater still. That is implied by the fact that we believe it is praiseworthy for a person to choose to have her hand burned to spare ninety-nine others from such pain. Presumably we think that her pain prevents pain that is *greater* in some sense. Her act is admirable, not only because it is done for others, but because it prevents a greater degree of pain from happening.

This must be the case even on Lewis's assumption that pain can only be summed within the consciousness of a single individual. If the total pain in one person's consciousness is a bad thing, then the total pain in the consciousness of each of a thousand or a billion individuals is each a bad thing, and God needs a reason to permit each of those bad things, even if the consciousness of each individual is taken individually and the aggregate cannot be summed. Another way to put this point is that *there are as many problems of pain as there are sentient beings*. W2 has ten thousand problems of pain and W4 has a billion, whereas W1 has only one. This is the sense in which W1, W2, and W4 are not equal in the problem of pain even if they are equal in total quantity of pain, as Lewis maintains. The suffering in W2 and W4 brings with it an increased burden on God to rectify or justify the suffering. Indeed, he needs ten thousand reasons in W2 and a billion reasons in W4.

6.3. The many problems of pain

How does the fact that there are many problems of pain affect the probability that pain is gratuitous, premise (2) of the quantitative argument from evil as we have stated it? Let's compare W1, W2, and W3. We suggested earlier that it is more difficult to see how God could have a reason to permit W3 than to permit W2 even if the sum of pain is the same in the two worlds. The inference that the pain in W3 is gratuitous is stronger than the parallel inference for W2. We want to argue now that W2 may be no more difficult to justify than W1, or at any rate, not significantly harder to justify, given relevantly similar conditions for the individuals in W2. The inference to the probable gratuitousness of the pain in W2 is comparable to the inference to the probable gratuitousness of the pain in W1.

To see this, consider what we normally say about sufficient justifying reasons that are repeatable in similar situations. If one person has a reason to swallow her bitter-tasting medicine to cure her infection, any person has a reason to take the medicine, given relevantly similar conditions. If one person has a reason to have a cancerous tumor removed despite the pain it will cause, so do ten thousand or a million people with cancerous tumors in similar circumstances. If one person has a reason to ask forgiveness of a person she loves whom she has harmed, so does anybody else in the same situation.

This point is generalizable. Any time a person A has a sufficient justifying reason to permit E in situation S, anybody has a sufficient reason to permit something relevantly similar to E in situations relevantly similar to S. What counts as relevantly similar is disputable, of course, but the principle is both fair and widely accepted. In fact, it is probably universally accepted. In any case, the principle need not be embraced in its full generality for it to be applicable to God's permission of evil. We are appealing to the following more limited principle, which we can call the Principle of Repeatable Reasons (PRR):

> If person A has a sufficient justifying reason to permit E in situation S, then A has a sufficient justifying reason to permit states of affairs relevantly similar to E in situations relevantly similar to S.

We can see the expectation of PRR in the following example. If a worker comes down with the flu, this is a legitimate reason for him to stay home from work. And if sickness is a legitimate reason to stay home from work on this occasion, it retains its legitimacy on other occasions. If he stays home from work a year later because of sickness, his boss cannot rightly say, "You need a *new* reason this time." If sickness is a legitimate reason on one occasion, it is on another occasion, assuming that the conditions are relevantly similar.

The relevance of PRR to God's permission of W2 or even W4 rather than W1 should be clear. If God's reasons to permit one person's pain are relevantly similar to his reasons for permitting another person's pain, W2 and W4 are as justifiable as W1, assuming that the pains of the individuals in W2 and W4 are relevantly similar to those in W1 in relevantly similar circumstances. God does not have to have a collective reason for permitting the pains in W2 or W4. It is sufficient if God has repeatable reasons for permitting the pain of each individual.

PRR will need to be qualified. Sometimes the justifying reason for some state of affairs is not repeatable within a certain range because the reason is a good end that only requires a single instance of a state of affairs of a certain type. For example, suppose a shop owner is losing money and will need to lay off one of her sales workers. Although she has a reason to permit one of her employees to lose his job, it does not follow that she has a reason to permit another to lose his job at the same time. But she would have a reason to permit another employee to lose his job at a later time if she was losing money again at that time, and according to the more general form of PRR, other shop owners in similar circumstances would have a reason to lay off an employee. We do not claim, then, that PRR holds without qualification. But we think its range of application is wide enough to show that premise (2) is significantly flawed.

6.4. Adding pains with countervailing goods

On the view that pain is additive, premise (2) of the preceding quantitative argument from evil has another problem. The probability that a given quantity of pain is gratuitous cannot be separated from other factors that provide the context in which the pain occurs and through which the pain must be understood. To see this, consider a number of worlds in which individuals suffer the pain of a needle prick. Assume that one turp = the pain of one needle prick while being vaccinated.

> Let W6 be a world in which a single person suffers one hundred turps and is successfully inoculated against a fatal but painless disease.
> W7 consists of a single person who suffers one hundred turps and is not successfully inoculated against the fatal but painless disease.
> W8 consists of one thousand persons each suffering one turp and each is successfully inoculated against the fatal but painless disease.
> W9 consists of one thousand persons each suffering one turp and each is not successfully inoculated against the fatal but painless disease.

According to AA, W6 and W7 contain the same amount of pain, as do W8 and W9, and the latter pair are ten times as bad as the former pair. But surely the problem of pain is not equal in W6 and W7, nor is it equal in W8 and W9. Other things equal, W7 is worse than W6 and W9 is worse than W8. W7 needs a greater justifying reason than W6, and W9 needs a greater justifying reason than W8. Furthermore, the pain in W8 is less likely to be gratuitous than the pain in W7 even though the former is considerably worse on the additive approach. And if we were right in the preceding section, W8 may be no harder to justify than W6.

6.5. Conclusion

We have argued that Lewis's point that the pains of multiple individuals are not additive is plausible, and for that reason W3 is worse than W2. But there is still a sense in which a greater number of individuals suffering pain increases the quantity of evil. That is because even on Lewis's assumption that pain is only additive within the consciousness of each individual, there are as many problems of pain as there are suffering individuals. However, a world with multiple individuals suffering pain has a different relation to the probability that the pains are gratuitous than a world with the same total quantity of pain, but where the pain is suffered by a single individual. The pain suffered by a single person needs a justifying reason that can explain the quantity of pain suffered by that individual. Pain suffered by multiple individuals in the same circumstances can often be justified by a reason that explains any one of them. The probability that the pain in W2 or W4 is gratuitous may be no greater than the probability that the pain in W1 is gratuitous, and is far less than the probability that the pain in W3 is gratuitous. W5 cannot have gratuitous pain since it is not a possible world. Furthermore, the probability that a given quantity of pain is gratuitous cannot be calculated apart from the connection between the pain and countervailing goods that are not additive, such as protection from a fatal but painless disease. We conclude that both premises (1) and (2) of the quantitative argument from evil are probably false.

We are not suggesting that the problem of pain is not severe. It follows from our reasoning that a world containing creatures who suffer the maximum amount of pain of which those creatures are capable has problems of pain that threaten the existence of God. There may well be creatures in our world who suffer the maximum amount of pain for some period of their lives, and there needs to be an explanation for their suffering. We may think of Rowe's suffering fawn in the raging forest fire, or twelve-year-old Ashley Jones, who was brutally beaten, raped, and murdered, or the cement truck driver who accidentally ran over his three-year-old daughter while she played in his front yard. These are appalling cases of suffering and evil that bring us almost unbearable emotional anguish and cry out for explanation, but we do not think that adding more suffering creatures to the world significantly reduces the probability that there is a God if the suffering is in similar situations. Given PRR, we think that the reason for one can be applied to others. We therefore need not embrace the claim of Hume, Dostoyevsky, Rowe, Howard-Snyder, and many other philosophers that the quantity of evil suffered by many different individuals makes the problem of evil significantly worse.[8]

Notes

1. Howard-Snyder then delineates the argument from the quantity of evil as follows:
    (1) There is no reason that would justify God in permitting so much evil rather than a lot less.
    (2) If God exists, then there must be such a reason.

(3) So God does not exist (1999, 102).

He then says that the argument from amount is the argument that he finds most troubling (1999, 102–103).

2. Rowe (1990) concedes this: "Intense human or animal suffering is in itself bad, an evil, even though it may sometimes be justified by virtue of being a part of, or leading to, some good which is unobtainable without it.... While remaining an evil in itself, [it] is, nevertheless, an evil which someone might be morally justified in permitting" (127).
3. Using this approach to sum moral evils is much more difficult. Does it make sense to say that one act of injustice or betrayal or deception is twice as bad or forty times as bad as another? Is there a scale of duration for an act of injustice or betrayal, or does that scale apply only to the pain and suffering of its effects?
4. Lewis's comments here are fascinating, but we find them in embryonic form. He leaves them without further explication that might have strengthened his case against AA. It is helpful to remember that Lewis's aim was not to write a technical piece of philosophy, but to address a general audience.
5. Of course, one person A can feel empathic pain for the pain of B, but A's empathic pain is A's pain, not B's.
6. Plantinga uses "turp" (turpitude—an instance of baseness, vileness, or depravity) to designate one unit of evil, whereas we are using it to designate one unit of pain. Clearly, there are objections to the idea that there are units of pain that have application to different sentient beings, and Lewis at least hints that he is sympathetic with those objections, but we are granting the idea for the sake of argument.
7. Of course, we are merely stipulating the numerical value of the maximum amount of pain a single conscious being can experience, but if there is a maximum amount, there will be some number n which is such that it is impossible that there is a world containing an individual experiencing pain greater than n.
8. We are grateful for helpful comments from members of the audience at the Midwest Regional meeting of the Society of Christian Philosophers, Dubuque, Iowa, March 2007.

III
DEATH, HELL, AND RESURRECTION

7
Sleeping Beauty and the Afterlife (2005)

The Christian doctrine of the resurrection of the body is one of the most philosophically vexing of the credal beliefs. When we consider that philosophers have no trouble describing scenarios in which it is problematic whether some person in the near future is me, it is no wonder that the problem of whether I will exist in the far distant future taxes our imaginative and conceptual resources beyond the limit. Nonetheless, many of us like to test the limit. The following story is set in the Middle Ages and freely uses some of the philosophical resources of the time, particularly the work of Aquinas, but most of the arguments and conclusions are not those of any actual medieval philosopher. The scientific knowledge of the protagonists is also premodern (although small bits of matter are called molecules in the narrative). I have designed the story as an extended thought experiment describing something that *could* happen compatible with the following rules: (1) In the story, the bodies of the deceased must come back to life long after death. (2) The story may make no reference to an omnipotent deity or to a supernatural realm or to souls that can exist detached from bodies. (3) The story must alter what we know about the laws of nature as little as possible, compatible with the preceding rules.

7.1. A medieval tale

At the christening of Princess Aurora, a wicked fairy appears and puts a curse on the baby in a fit of pique over not being invited to the festivities. She proclaims that the little girl will one day prick her finger on a spinning wheel and die. The good fairies present have sufficient magical power to alter the curse, but not to eliminate it entirely. They say that she will not die, but she will fall asleep for a hundred years. One might think that the curse and its alteration amount to the same thing, but perhaps not. That is one of the things we will investigate.

The princess's distraught parents destroy all the spinning wheels in the kingdom, but on Aurora's sixteenth birthday, the wicked fairy lures her to the top of a tower in the castle, where the fairy is spinning on a wheel that makes an enchanting sound. Aurora is curious because she has never seen a spinning wheel, and as she approaches, she falls under the spell of the music, dancing closer and closer to the wheel, whereupon she pricks her finger and falls into a deep sleep. Since the good fairies cannot wake her, they cast a sleeping spell on the entire castle. Every living creature falls asleep on the spot. The good fairies then make a tall, dense hedge of sharp thorns grow around the castle so that the inhabitants are undisturbed in their slumber. From time to time, princes from faraway kingdoms hear the legend of the sleeping princess and attempt to get through the hedge, but they all fail. (It is no accident that all of them are guys the princess would not be interested in anyway.) At the end of a hundred years, Prince Charming appears, makes it through the hedge with the aid of the fairies, and awakens Sleeping Beauty with a kiss. At that instant, everyone else awakens and no one realizes that a hundred years have passed. The very same humans and animals who fell asleep a hundred years before continue their lives exactly where they left off.

How do the good fairies accomplish this feat?

Maybe they have sufficient magic to stop all causal processes. Perhaps they freeze the food, the animals, and the humans. To be on the safe side, they probably should put everything in cryonic suspension. The entire castle with all its contents could be enclosed in a giant block of ice. But maybe the fairies do not want to do that, or maybe there is some reason why it will not work. If freezing is not an option, they will have to do something to prevent the food from spoiling, the wood from rotting, the plants and animals from aging and dying. And they will have to do something about the fact that the animals are not taking in food and water. This does not strike me as an easy task. After all, the fairies did not create the world. I assume they are embodied beings themselves. They have magical powers that permit them to rearrange natural phenomena, but their powers are limited by nature—loosely interpreted, of course.[1]

The fairies must either prevent the causal processes of nature from occurring or figure out a way to reverse the effects of those processes. One option might be to continuously replace each individual molecule. That seems tedious, but within the capabilities of a fairy. Assuming the fairies replace all the molecules, does that change the castle or anything in it? I think not, assuming that there is literally no change except a change of molecules. (Whether that is possible is an issue to which we will return.) Nor does it matter if the material particles are replaced gradually or all at once. Some philosophers have the intuition that an object is more likely to survive the replacement of parts if the process is gradual than if the same number of parts were replaced very rapidly. My conjecture is that there are two explanations for this intuition, neither of which has anything to do with the replacement of molecules per se. One is that in the non-magical world a large proportion of the physical parts of a physical object cannot be rapidly replaced without destroying what Aristotle calls the form of the object, whereas a gradual change of physical parts does not compromise the object's form to any significant degree. A car is still the same car while the tires are being changed or the radiator is being changed, and so on, but if the car is taken apart and every part changed, there is no form of a car for a time, and hence, no car. Second, in many thought experiments involving change of parts, the parts replaced have fairly intricate form themselves—for instance, the engine of a car or the keyboard of a computer. In these cases, the thought experiment describes not only a removal and change of the matter of an object, but also a removal and change of the form of some of the parts necessary for the functioning of the whole. I think, then, that the worry is not about the change of matter, but about the change of form that accompanies the change of matter. Of course, Aristotle says that there is no matter without some form, so even a change of one molecule includes some change of form. But I think we do not worry about that when the object is of sufficient size and complexity that a molecular change makes no difference to the form of any functioning parts, although the judgment is obviously difficult to make in many cases. Some objects have only meager form to begin with—say, a rock—and there is a fine line between changing the form of an insignificant part and altering the form of the whole.

In fact, there may be no line at all. Aquinas maintains that an artifact is a collection of substances conjoined by an accidental form. It has no substantial form. Each of its parts retains its own form while it is part of the artifact. So a computer would have only an accidental form and its keyboard would retain its accidental form while functioning as part of the computer, and the substances that are parts of the keyboard would retain their substantial form. In contrast, a living organism has a single substantial form that organizes the substance into a single living body. No part of a substance is a substance while it is a component of a larger whole that is a substance even if it would be a substance when not a component of the whole.[2] A living organism is thus a single substance with one substantial form. In the case of animals and humans, the organism is a living body. The substantial form of a living body is a particular.[3] It is what makes the body live and function as a thing of its kind. It configures the matter of the body in a distinctive way, causes the organs of the body to function in the way they function for that species, and is that in virtue of which the organism lives and grows in characteristic ways. It causes the animal to have the characteristic consciousness of an animal—sensation. If it is human, it causes it, in addition, to have the characteristic conscious powers of humans—reasoning and will (and I think we should add characteristic human emotions). Something is identical to a particular substance S just in case it has the particular substantial form of S.[4] In contrast, because artifacts have no substantial form but are a compilation of parts, each of which retains its form when part of the artifact, they do not have determinate conditions of persistence from one moment of time to the next.[5]

The fairies are well acquainted with the concept of a form. The Daisy Fairy, who has undertaken a study of Aquinas, argues that the project of keeping in existence the living bodies within the castle differs from the project of keeping artifacts in existence. That means, she says, that they should be wary of applying their intuitions about the identity of artifacts to the identity of living organisms. To do so is to use harder cases in an attempt to illuminate easier cases. The rest of the fairies are not sure that the identity of an artifact is any harder to figure out than the identity of an animal, but they agree that the problems differ and that this complicates their task. It may be harder to keep some kinds of objects in existence than others, and they will not always know when they have succeeded. In the case of some kinds of objects, there may not even be a fact of the matter as to whether they have succeeded.

Now suppose that the good fairies are busy and decide at the outset that they will replace all the molecules of the castle and everything it contains once a week. Again, let us assume that they are able to do this without changing anything in the form of the objects in the castle except the form of the molecules themselves. They pluck out each molecule successively and zap a qualitatively identical one in its place almost simultaneously. As far as I can see, that does no damage to the identity of the objects whose molecules the fairies replace. It is still the same castle, same inhabitants, same food on the table, same dog sleeping under the table by the roast beef. In some cases, the molecule replaced may have changed during the week, in which case it must be replaced by a molecule qualitatively identical to the way it was one week before. But presumably, the fairies prefer that the objects do not change very much before they replace their molecules. If so, since some objects change more rapidly than others, and change of molecules threatens the identity of some objects more than others, they settle on a scheme of changing the molecules of the food on the table very frequently, the molecules of living organisms fairly often, the molecules of the table less often, and the molecules of the rocks very infrequently.

There is another way the story could go that I think we should take seriously. Suppose that in the case of living things it turns out not to be possible to replace every molecule without altering the form of the whole. Suppose that while replacing the molecules of the sleeping dog, all seems to be going well until suddenly the dog dies. The fairies do not understand what they did to cause the animal's death and quickly backtrack, replacing the last molecule removed with the original, whereupon the dog revives. They discover that they are able to replace most but not all of a living body's molecules without destroying the body's form, but they are not able to figure out in advance which ones are necessary and which are not. It is not even clear whether there are particular molecules necessary, or only a certain proportion of the original molecules necessary, or whether instead their action in replacing the molecules has some undetectable physical consequence that destroys the organism's form. But let us assume that enough molecules can be replaced to keep the organism alive for a hundred years.

What do the fairies do with the molecules they remove from the castle? Maybe they just add them to their stockpile of molecules—far away, of course. (They do not want Prince Charming running into a pile of molecules on his way to the castle.) Once they have removed the molecules of some object in the castle, such as the king's throne, then, if they have the time and the inclination, they might find it fun to fashion a qualitatively identical throne in some remote place using the same molecules. The Lilac Fairy warns that this would create a problem because if the throne assembled in the remote place is identical with the original throne, then there are two thrones identical to the original, and that is impossible. Most of the fairies decide that their original intuition stands. If they pluck out each molecule of the throne and immediately replace it without changing the form of the throne, the throne that results is the same throne upon which the king has been sitting. The throne assembled in a remote place has a different form (recall that a form is a particular), even though it has (at least most of) the same molecules as the original.

The Rose Fairy observes that some artifacts survive being taken apart and reassembled in a different place, such as a large lamp that was sent from a distant castle, but the Iris Fairy argues that even in such cases, it is doubtful that it is the identity of matter that makes it the same artifact. Rather, we think that the form of some artifacts permits the artifact to be disassembled; the form does not require a constant unity of parts. This leads to further discussion, and at the end, the fairies take the tentative position that what makes an object that exists at one time identical to an object that exists at another time is identity of form, and identity of matter is required only if and when it is not possible to change the matter without changing the form. But they also decide to heed the Daisy Fairy's warning that artifacts may not have determinate persistence conditions, so there may be no answer to the question of which throne is the original throne and which artifacts survive disassembly.

Suppose now that the good fairies are so busy that they do not have time to change the molecules very often. They let the food spoil, the hair and fingernails grow, and the sleeping bodies age a few weeks before they replace the molecules. Then they replace them with newer molecules that make the food wholesome again and the animal bodies exactly as they were at the time the spell was cast. Surely the bodies are the same bodies, the plants are the same plants, the food is the same food. If you doubt this, then we can suppose the fairies use a process that reverses the deterioration process. The natural causal process that began just after the spell was cast is reversed until everything is exactly as it was at the beginning of the Great Sleep. If each object and living thing maintains its identity while it gradually deteriorates, surely it maintains its identity while it reverse-deteriorates.

Suppose, however, that the rosebush by the castle door dies before the fairies can prevent it. The fairies consider this a serious problem because most of them think that that rosebush is now no longer in existence. They agree with the Lily Fairy, who proposes that to be this rosebush is to have a certain life, to be a certain *living* organism. A dead rosebush is not the rosebush that existed on the same spot before it died. The Tulip Fairy adds that if a rosebush is just a living organism of a certain kind, then a dead rosebush is not literally a rosebush at all.[6] Some of the fairies are not sure that they agree with that, but they agree that the dead rosebush is not numerically identical to the rosebush that used to live on that spot. The castle is now missing an item, and if they want everything in and around the castle when Sleeping Beauty awakens to be identical to everything that existed when she fell asleep, they are going to have to bring that very same rosebush back into existence. Is that possible? It is possible, I propose, if it is possible to bring into existence a rosebush that is a continuation of the same life as the previous rosebush. If so, perhaps the task is not much more difficult than it was before the bush died. If the process of reverse-deterioration works while the bush lives, I do not see why it cannot work soon after the bush dies. If the causal process can run backwards, it can do so whether or not the bush dies in the interim. Granted, the death of a living thing results in rapid changes in the configuration of matter (which the fairies say is produced by its substantial form), but in this case, those changes have not progressed very far, so if they are reversible, the bush can live and bloom again.

To say that the numerically identical rosebush exists as the result of such a process commits us to saying that there can be gaps in the existence of a living thing. I am not opposed to such a commitment. In the non-magic world, we do not see reverse causal processes, much less reverse causal processes that reverse the process of going from life to death. But if we did, I think we would say that the rosebush came back to life, not that a new rosebush came into existence. If the rosebush exists when and only when a certain substantial form exists, then there can also be gaps in the existence of a substantial form.

The problem of bringing the rosebush back to life and the case of the reassembled throne may suggest that spatial continuity is more important than temporal continuity. One reason for thinking that the throne that is assembled from the throne molecules in a different place is a different throne is that the throne does not exist in the spaces between the castle and the new location, even if the throne is reassembled so rapidly that there is no temporal gap. On the other hand, a consideration in favor of the judgment that the revivified rosebush is the same rosebush is that it comes back to life in the same place even though there is a temporal gap in its existence. But we must be careful about drawing this conclusion. If identity of substantial form is necessary and sufficient for the identity of a living organism, spatial or temporal continuity is relevant only insofar as such continuity is a condition (or perhaps just an indication) of identity of an object's form. With the rosebush, even though the substantial form is gone once it dies, the dead bush has some form. There is something in that space that is related both to the bush that used to live on that spot and the bush that comes to life. But another reason we would think it is the same bush is that the causal process through which the dead bush goes from death to life simply reverses the process through which the living bush went from life to death. I do not think we can say which of these reasons is the more salient without looking at further cases.

Now let us make the situation harder. Suppose the fairies are so busy that they do not notice that the king has died. This is a real problem because they certainly do not want Sleeping Beauty waking up to find out that her father died on her birthday. The king is a human being and the fairies assume that a human being is an individual human animal, a living human body.[7] Hence, the king is a living human body. This is not to say that the fairies believe the king is a bunch of body cells. To be a living human body is to be informed matter. Because the king is dead, the informed matter that used to exist on the throne is no longer there. The king's corpse is not the king for the same reason that the dead rosebush is not the rosebush. The king no longer exists in the castle where he is supposed to be. In fact, the fairies conclude that he no longer exists at all, just as the rosebush no longer exists once it dies.

Because the powers of the fairies do not extend beyond nature, they have no direct contact with heaven or any realm outside of space and time, nor can they maneuver human souls into the matter of this world. If we use Swinburne's analogy of the soul as a lightbulb and the brain as a socket, they cannot plug the lightbulb into the socket (Swinburne 1986, 310f). So the fairies hope that Swinburne's analogy is inaccurate. If the king has a soul that left his body, they are not going to be able to find it. But maybe their task is not much harder than it was with the dead rosebush. So long as the king's body is mostly intact, if they can rejuvenate the cells of the dead body by replacing them with healthy cells, perhaps he will live again. This might work if we assume that there is a connection between the form of the dead body and the substantial form that exists when the individual cells are revivified, and that assumption is as plausible for the king as for the rosebush. But on the view we are considering, the body that comes alive is the king's body if and only if it is matter informed by the king's substantial form. The Azalea Fairy is skeptical that the plan will work. At death, the king's substantial form is completely gone, and what is left is a corpse with a different form.[8] If that corpse is revivified, by what right can they claim that the newly living body has the same substantial form the king had before death? Revivifying his corpse may not be sufficient to bring *him* back to life.

The fairies discuss this possibility for a while. The Lily Fairy argues that because they agree that the king just *is* his living human body, any way to make his body live again makes *him* live again, although the Azalea Fairy points out that that does not solve the problem because the dispute is over what counts as *his* body. After considerable discussion, the fairies conclude that it is the king who lives again if they can make his body live again, and it is likely that they can make his body live again if they replace the decaying cells before the configured matter of the body has deteriorated very much. As with the rosebush, the considerations in favor of this judgment include the fact that spatial continuity is preserved and the process that makes a king come to life is the same causal process that led to the king's death, only in reverse.

The Lily Fairy proposes that they apply the same identity criterion to a human body as to a rosebush: a living human body at $t2$ is identical to a living human body at $t1$ if and only if the body at $t2$ is a continuation of the same life as the body at $t1$. The fairies agree with this criterion, but the Tulip Fairy points out that that is not very illuminating because the issue they are debating is whether the revivified body of the king is a continuation of the same life as before the king's death. The intuition of most of the fairies is that it is.

Notice that the continuation-of-life criterion does not preclude a gap. A life may include the occasional temporal gap so long as it is the same life before and after the gap. If so, and if the fairies are sufficiently busy, the plants and animals in the castle may die many times and be rejuvenated many times as long as their lives continue after the gap.

Now suppose the fairies are very busy indeed, flying around trying to outwit the Evil Fairy. Suppose they wait 99 years and 364 days. By that time, the bodies are no longer sleeping, they are dead and decomposed, and the derelict castle is in serious disrepair. In this case, it is not merely a question of replacing molecules one by one because it is not just the substantial form of each living thing that has changed. Most of the accidental forms have changed too, although the matter is presumably around somewhere. Is reversing the causal process sufficient to bring back into existence the very same castle, the same rosebush, the same food on the table, the same dog, the same king, queen, and courtiers, and the same Sleeping Beauty? Possibly, but this is the sort of situation most of us find conceptually difficult in the extreme. The fairies agree that the task is hopeless unless they can count on the truth of the principle that it is possible that there are gaps in the existence of an individual living thing. The gaps that are most plausible are short ones, not because there is any metaphysical difference between short and long, but because there is a causal connection between the living thing and the corpse, and it is more plausible to think that the process is reversible as long as some form remains in the corpse. Still, they agree that there is no metaphysical prohibition in principle to there being gaps in the existence of a living thing.

The Lilac Fairy then proposes that they accept the following principle.

Lilac's principle

Necessarily, a replica or duplicate of a human being S is not identical to S.[9]

In support of her proposal, the Lilac Fairy argues that if a person is replicated once, it is possible for her to be replicated twice, but if replication is sufficient for identity and it is possible to be replicated twice, it would be possible that there are two beings identical to the original person. But it is not possible that two persons are identical to one. Hence, a process of replication or duplication does not result in a person identical to the person replicated.[10]

The Tulip Fairy is not convinced. "Of course, two human beings cannot be identical to one," she remarks, "but that does not rule out identity by replication. It just means that at most one person resulting from replication has the substantial form of the original person and is thus identical to the person replicated. Because a substantial form is a particular, there will never be two replicas of a human being with equal and maximally strong claims to identity with the individual human replicated. The human we are looking for is the one with the right substantial form. There can never be more than one, so it does not matter what physical process keeps the form in existence. Replication cannot be ruled out."

The rest of the fairies nod in agreement, but then the Lilac Fairy worries that there are many processes that result in *apparently* equal claimants to identity to some object, and how are they to know which one is the actual continuer of the existence of the original object? Not only replication, but bifurcation has this problem. The road leading to the castle bifurcates a quarter mile from the castle gate. The king's deck of cards fell on the floor one day, and half was recovered by one servant and the other half by another. Not realizing that the other servant had the rest of the cards, each of them secretly added enough cards to the ones he had to make a full deck, thereby resulting in two decks of cards with an apparently equal claim to identity to the original deck. It seems obvious, the Lilac Fairy says, that processes of bifurcation resulting in two strong and apparently equal claimants to the identity of an object do occur.

"But those are artifacts," replies the Daisy Fairy, "and there really *is* a problem of conditions for their persistence because they have no substantial form. Some simple substances, such as worms, divide also, and in those cases, it is most reasonable to say that neither one has the substantial form of the original.[11] But maybe the substantial form of a more complex living thing is more resilient. Possibly it can survive replication or bifurcation."

"But how are we to tell which of two competitors has the right substantial form?" asks Lilac. "It is not enough for us to *be* successful at bringing Sleeping Beauty and all the castle's inhabitants back to life; we want to *know* or at least have good reason to believe that we have been successful."

"I don't think we can tell for sure when we have been successful, but surely we can often tell when we have failed," remarks the Lily Fairy. "The substantial form of a living thing is not a mysterious entity whose presence or absence is undetectable. We observe its effects. The most obvious of these is the way in which a bunch of matter is configured. It is the substantial form that configures it in that way, gives the organism life, and in the case of animals, makes it conscious. The particular bodily configuration and particular consciousness of an individual animal are the result of its particular substantial form. So if we try to bring Sleeping Beauty back to life by a process that results in a very different bodily configuration or a consciousness that is not distinctively hers, we will know that we have failed."

The Daffodil Fairy notices that in less than an hour, a hundred years will have passed since the beginning of the Great Sleep, so they had better act quickly. For lack of a better idea, they use the same procedure they used earlier: they reverse the causal process. They need to rely on the principle that there can be gaps in the existence of a living thing, but they have not had time to discuss whether there can be gaps in the existence of the non-living things in the castle, and some of the fairies worry that they have lost their chance to bring back the numerically identical castle with all its furnishings. But they are willing to let that worry slide because it is the living things in the castle that are most crucial. The Lilac Fairy agrees to the plan because a reverse causal process is not duplicable. They then reverse the process, and to their great joy, Sleeping Beauty, the king, queen, courtiers, and servants, as well as all the plants and animals, come back to life. At least, to all appearances, they are exactly the same, and all the humans in the castle seem to have the right memories and psychological characteristics.

"Well, at least we don't know that we have failed," says the Lily Fairy. "I hope we have succeeded." I think the hope is justified.

Now let us look into the future, after the fairy tale normally ends. The fairies have successfully kept everything in existence for a hundred years by whatever means. Sleeping Beauty wakes up, marries Prince Charming, and they live together happily until their deaths. Meanwhile, the thorn hedge is removed by the fairies, but another one is built around the castle and environs so that the castle with the fields and villages around it is sealed off from the rest of the world. A thousand years go by. (The fairies live a long time.) Eventually, the fairies become curious about Sleeping Beauty's castle and they decide to go and see how her descendants are faring. To their disappointment, they find out that all living things within the thorn hedge have died. No plants, animals, or human beings remain, and the castle itself is a ruin. During the time since the Awakening, not only have all the plants and animals that inhabited the castle during the period of the Great Sleep died, but their bodies have decayed and their molecules have become parts of new substances—new plants, new animals, new human beings—which subsequently died and their molecules recycled through further substances. Eventually, the last living thing died. The fairies are distressed because they would like to see Sleeping Beauty and all the other inhabitants of the castle live again. Is there anything they can do to make that happen?

It is much less clear that reversing the causal process will work this time because many of the molecules that were once components of Sleeping Beauty's living body have at later times been components of the bodies of other living things, including other human beings. In fact, it is possible that all of the molecules that were components of her body at the time of her death were eventually components of the bodies of other living things, even many living things at different times. If the fairies reverse the causal process all the way back to the way it was a thousand years before, at best they will have brought Sleeping Beauty back to life, but they will have done so at the expense of failing to bring back to life her descendants and the descendants of the other living things known to her in the castle on the day of her sixteenth birthday.

After considerable discussion, it turns out that most of the fairies are ambitious enough to want to attempt to bring back to life everyone who ever lived in the castle. The Azalea Fairy maintains that the idea is foolhardy. "Far better to bring a few people back to life than to try to bring back everyone and fail," she says. But the other fairies insist on trying, although they admit that the reverse causal process will not work. The Daisy Fairy (whom you may recall is fond of the work of Aquinas) reports on Aquinas's answer to the problem of what happens on the day of the general resurrection to the body of a cannibal who eats nothing but human flesh: " . . . it is not necessary . . . that whatever has been in man materially rise in him; further, if something is lacking, it can be supplied by the power of God. Therefore, the flesh consumed will rise in him in whom it was first perfected by the rational soul."[12] This suggests, she says, that some of the material particles of the resurrected body are those that the body had during life, but it is not necessary that it have all or even very many of the particles it had at any time during life, and missing particles can be replaced. The Rose Fairy agrees and reminds the other fairies that when they substituted molecules during the Great Sleep, they were assuming that there are few material particles necessary for the identity of a human body. If that is the case, why should they pay so much attention to using a process that ends up with the same body cells as Sleeping Beauty had at the end of her life? If the same molecules were not necessary for the hundred years she was sleeping, why should they be necessary now?

"But how else can we proceed?" asks the Azalea Fairy. "We changed molecules when we knew, or at least had good reason to believe, that we were keeping the substantial form intact. But we have no idea how to get the substantial form back except by reversing the process that destroyed the form in the first place." "Aquinas's comment on cannibals gives me an idea," says the Daffodil Fairy. "Let us begin a reverse causal process, starting by reconfiguring the matter of the most recently deceased animals and plants. Then we proceed backward, adding new molecules to fill in gaps when needed to bring back to life a creature some of whose molecules at the time of its death are now in use by a creature whom we have already brought back to life. We will need to add more and more molecules as we go backward, and of course the molecules making up the plant and animal organisms brought back to life will not be the same as those that made up the plants and animals at the time of their death. We will have to be careful, though, because we discovered that sometimes replacing molecules results in a change of form, but we think we can tell when that happens and we have time to try many different arrangements."

The Lilac Fairy denies that the plan will work. "Any reverse causal process that uses some of the same molecules but not all in reconfiguring the bodies we intend to bring back to life can result in duplication. It is possible that whatever molecules are not used in reconfiguring the body of the last person who died can be put to use in configuring another body just like it. The process proposed by the Daffodil Fairy allows the possibility of more than one contender to identity with the original person. We will not be able to tell which one has the substantial form of the original, if either one of them does."

The fairies are distressed, but then the usually silent Iris Fairy speaks up. "This is the way I see our problem," she says. "We have agreed that identity of substantial form is both necessary and sufficient for the identity of a living organism like Sleeping Beauty. If her substantial form has either ceased to exist permanently or has an independent existence in a realm outside our reach, there is nothing we can do to bring her back into existence. We also know that a certain configuration of matter is not sufficient for her substantial form because we can easily configure more than one parcel of matter in that way, but her substantial form is a particular. We felt confident, or at least hopeful, that a precise reversal of the causal process worked, but why did we think that? It could not have been because we ended up with the same matter. We must have thought there was a connection between the substantial form of a living substance and such a process. But our reason for thinking that was pretty weak. We noted that the substantial form of a living organism persists while it undergoes material changes determined by normal causal processes, and so we conjectured that it would persist while undergoing the same processes in reverse. That made sense while the substantial form was still in existence, but once it had gone out of existence, we had to hope that each substantial form operates in nature in a way that distinguishes it from any other form. That was a big assumption because some philosophers think it is possible for two numerically distinct human beings to be indistinguishable in all their qualitative properties, both properties of their bodies and behavior, and properties of their conscious states and memories."

"I cannot agree with those philosophers," says the Lily Fairy. "At best, two substantial forms are indistinguishable from the outside, but surely they are distinguishable from the inside."

"There is no inside to a plant," remarks the Azalea Fairy.

"True, but the human beings are our primary concern. I think that the following options must be considered:

(1) Like artifacts, human beings have no determinate persistence conditions. In particular, it is possible that for some human being $S1$ who exists at $T1$ and some human being $S2$ who exists at $T2$, there is no fact of the matter whether $S1$ is identical to $S2$.

If (1) is true, there may be no fact of the matter whether we have succeeded in bringing back to life Sleeping Beauty and the other castle inhabitants. We have agreed to reject (1), but it is a possibility we should not forget.

(2) For any human being $S1$ at $T1$ and human being $S2$ at $T2$, there is a fact of the matter whether $S1$ is identical to $S2$, but it may be a fact that is inaccessible to any mortal being, including $S1$ and $S2$."

"Now we can debate what it means to be accessible, and what we are to say about various situations in which we can imagine inaccessible identity conditions," continues Lily, "but I propose that (2) is false. Or more cautiously, we should operate as if it is false because otherwise, we are operating in the dark. If so, the following must be true:

(3) For any human being $S1$ at $T1$ and human being $S2$ at $T2$, if $S1$ is identical to $S2$, that fact is accessible to somebody, either to $S1$ and $S2$ or to a careful observer of $S1$ and $S2$. If $S1$ is not identical to $S2$, that fact is accessible to somebody, either to $S1$ and $S2$, or to a careful observer of $S1$ and $S2$.

If (3) is true, it will never happen that there are two equal and maximally strong competitors to identity to any person S. The presence or absence of S's substantial form is a fact about nature accessible to mortal beings who are themselves part of nature."

"Why do we have to choose between (2) and (3)?" asks the Iris Fairy. "Maybe we can usually tell whether the substantial form of some human $S1$ is identical to the substantial form of some human $S2$, but perhaps there are exceptions. If so, (3) would be true for the most part and (2) would be false for the most part, but we need not go so far as to accept (3) unequivocally."

"Why don't we try the reverse causal process I proposed earlier and see what happens?" asks the Daffodil Fairy.

"But if the identity or non-identity of some $S1$ and $S2$ is accessible only from within their own consciousness, how are we to tell what has happened?" asks the Lilac Fairy. "As a matter of fact, I don't know how they can tell either. It's not as if $S2$ at $T2$ can go back in time to $T1$ and inhabit the consciousness of $S1$ to compare it with her own."

"I think it will be observable from the outside if it is a fact accessible to mortal beings at all," says the Rose Fairy. "But that's not really the point. I think we should stop worrying so much about how we are going to know whether to congratulate ourselves on success and spend more time trying to bring these people back to life." The rest of the fairies agree that it is time to take action.

There are many ways the story can go from this point. Here is one of them. The fairies proceed with the Daffodil Fairy's original plan. They start by reversing the causal process that led to the death and decomposition of the last remaining human being in the castle. When she comes back to life, she is delighted to be alive and seems to be the same person who died years before. They then continue working backward, adding new molecules to fill in gaps when needed to bring back to life a human being some of whose molecules at the time of its death are in use by those whom the fairies have already brought back to life. When they have been working for a while, they decide to experiment. They take half the molecules from the original body of Sleeping Beauty's great-great-granddaughter and make one body with that half and another body with the other half. But a curious thing happens when they both come to life. Only one of them is recognizable to family and friends as the woman she once was. They find the other one puzzling. Sometimes when they try this experiment, neither one seems to be identical to the original. Of course, this might happen most of the time or even all of the time. It could also happen that the fairies have to try thousands of times to bring one human to life who seems to be identical to one long deceased, using many alternative arrangements of molecules. But suppose that no matter how many times the fairies try the experiment, it never happens that there are two strong and equally plausible candidates for identity with the deceased. At most, one of them seems to be the person who once lived. The fairies do not understand why this is the case. But they can succeed in bringing a dead person to life without understanding whether and why they are successful. Their success need not have much to do with having a correct theory of personal identity. In fact, they do not even have to know exactly what physical process is sufficient to bring Sleeping Beauty to life, only that if there is one, and they have the time and the patience to try many alternatives, they might get lucky. Perhaps it would take thousands of years of attempts, maybe even millions, in which case we should hope that the fairies are *very* long-lived.

Accounts of an afterlife only aim at the possible, as they should, but some stretch credibility more than others. Of course, the extent to which an account is far-fetched depends upon one's prior metaphysical positions, and accounts vary in their relative advantages and disadvantages. The partial account of personal identity and the afterlife given in this paper has some advantages over other accounts. The fairies do not have to find all the same molecules in order to bring back to life an individual human body. So they do not have the problem of two distinct persons competing for the same molecules. Nor do the fairies have to resort to making a replica.[13] I assume that the identity of a replica to the thing replicated is at best problematic. The fairies are not bifurcating Sleeping Beauty, a view that is problematic for the same reason as the replica theory.[14] The problems with bifurcation and replication exist as long as it is possible that a process of either kind results in two maximally strong claimants to identity to a person. Thought experiments in which such things happen are so common that we are used to thinking of those scenarios as possible. I am proposing that we do not actually know that any such thing is possible.

Further, the fairies do not face the problem that each person has a soul that could continually change while their bodies remain the same, a well-known complaint against traditional dualism.[15] Finally, the fairies do not have to take an allegedly subsistent individual form in a realm outside of the natural world and somehow inform it in new matter, as in the theory of Aquinas.

This account is intended to be neither materialist nor dualist in their contemporary senses. A substantial form is a particular, but it is not a substance capable of existence independent of the body. It has properties that no material base has, and it is compatible with the tale I have told that a substantial form is an emergent entity, but I have left the story of the origin of the substantial form untold.

7.2. Conclusion

There are two strands of thought about human beings that are in tension with each other and force us to make some hard choices. One is the motive to think of human beings as human organisms, part of the natural world. The other is the motive to think that an individual human being is a *person*, the sort of thing that is distinct from everything else in the world, including every other person, in a very strong sense. If so, a human being has determinate persistence conditions. Furthermore, a human being is not replicable or subject to any process that results in two equal and maximally strong claimants to identity to that human. The second motive is hard to reconcile with the first because duplication and bifurcation in the material world are ubiquitous. It is not surprising, then, that so many philosophers have been attracted to the idea that each human being is distinct because of the possession of a soul that is outside the realm of the laws of nature. It appears, then, that we cannot have it both ways; we have to make a choice.

In this paper, I have suggested that it is possible we do not have to make the choice. Perhaps nature cooperates with the strong distinctness of human beings as described previously. There might be a substantial form that is a non-duplicable particular, but which cannot exist without informing matter. The principle I propose, then, is this: *A particular human S exists when and only when S's substantial form informs some matter.* The narrative of this paper suggests further that a substantial form might be connected to the matter it informs in such a way that it exists when and only when there is a specific combination of molecules conjoined in a certain configuration. Possibly the specific material base that accompanies the substantial form of a human being is itself non-duplicable, but it is repeatable. If it is repeatable, a person can come back to life. If it is non-duplicable, there will never be two maximally strong claimants to identity to the human being who died. If a particular substantial form is tied to a particular material base by the laws of nature, then resurrection is compatible with the laws of nature.[16]

Notes

1. For this reason, it will not do any good for the fairies to emulate Peter van Inwagen's (1992) proposal on death and resurrection, attempting to move the castle and all its contents to some other region where they have better control over the environment, simultaneously replacing the real castle with a castle simulacrum. There is no other place where the fairies can control the castle any better than they can in its original location. And, of course, there is no need for a simulacrum if nobody can get through the hedge.
2. See Eleonore Stump (2003), 40, for an explanation of the forms of artifacts in Aquinas.
3. As Stump interprets Aquinas, what individuates Socrates is a particular substantial form, a view I am using in this paper. But Aquinas also thinks that a substantial form of a human being is *this* substantial form in virtue of the fact that it configures *this* matter (see Stump 2003, 49). I am not using the latter part of Aquinas's view in this paper, nor am I using his position that the substantial form of a human being subsists—continues to exist after death.
4. According to Aquinas, substances and artifacts do not exhaust the class of things. A severed hand is neither a substance nor an artifact. See Stump (2003), 42.
5. According to Eleonore Stump, Aquinas has no principled way to draw the line between a change of matter that is just an alteration in the artifact and a change of matter that changes the identity of the form of the whole so that the original form, and consequently the original artifact, no longer exist. See Stump (2003), 59.
6. Aquinas thinks that when we apply names of the living body and its parts to the dead body and its parts, we use the words equivocally. A dead body is not literally a human body because at death, the substantial form of the body is replaced by a different, non-animating form. See Stump (2003), 194–195.
7. I do not mean to say, of course, that the defining features of personhood are captured by this identity. If there are non-human persons, then human and non-human persons have something in common that has nothing to do with being a human animal. The features that make something a person (e.g., subjectivity, capacity for emotion, thought, and action) probably accompany some feature of being a living human body, but I will mention these features in this paper only in passing.

8. To say that some form remains is not to say that some part of the substantial form remains after death, according to Aquinas, because the substantial form is a particular that is entirely gone. But there is in place of the animating substantial form of the substance a form that configures its matter for a while.
9. I assume that a replica and a duplicate are the same thing, except that I tend to call something a duplicate when that which it duplicates is still in existence. If not, I usually call it a replica. I don't think my usage is unusual, but if it is, my discussion of replicas can be suitably altered.
10. Derek Parfit argues that identity is not what matters to survivorship in Parfit (2003), 115–143, reprinted from Parfit (1984).
11. Aquinas maintains that when a worm divides, two substances result from one. Neither one is identical to the original worm. See Stump (2003), 41.
12. *Summa Contra Gentiles* IV.81.13.
13. A well-known replica account is given by John Hick (1983).
14. See Dean Zimmerman (1999).
15. This complaint appears in many places, but see "The First Night" in John Perry (1978).
16. I thank Ray Elugardo, Monte Cook, Andrew Dole, Andrew Chignell, Brian Leftow, and William Hasker for discussion of the issues of this paper and comments on previous drafts.

8
Religious Luck (1994)

8.1. Introduction

Moral luck is a phenomenon that captured a lot of attention due to a famous exchange of papers by Bernard Williams (1981) and Thomas Nagel (1979).[1] It occurs when a person's degree of moral responsibility for an act or a personal trait goes beyond the degree to which she controls it. If it exists, people are the proper objects of moral evaluation, including praise and blame, reward and punishment, because of something that is partly due to luck. Nagel argued that this is not a mistake in our moral practices; it is a consequence of the right way of looking at morality. We cannot eliminate luck without destroying moral evaluation altogether. Nonetheless, most of us find moral luck repulsive—even, perhaps, incoherent. Surely, it must be the case that each of us has an equal chance at the one thing that matters most: our moral worth. While we must put up with elements of chance and fortune in the other aspects of our lives, how could this happen in morality? In fact, we could make a strong case for the view that a primary distinguishing feature of moral evaluation as opposed to other sorts of evaluation is that it is completely luck-free. And not only is it luck-free, it compensates for the prevalence of luck in the other areas of our lives. There is, then, a kind of ultimate cosmic justice. Nevertheless, Nagel, Williams, Feinberg (1970), and others have persuasively argued that morality is permeated with luck. If they are right, morality is threatened with inconsistency.

In this paper I will focus on the problem of moral luck as described by Nagel and Feinberg, and I will argue that these problems exist for Christian moral practice and Christian moral theories as well. In fact, the problem of luck for the Christian is worsened by several elements not found in secular morality, including the traditional doctrine of grace and the doctrine of an eternal heaven and hell. Historical disputes over these doctrines within Christianity do not go to the heart of the luck problem. At one time, the dispute took the form of the controversy over predestination versus free will. Nowadays it is more usual for the focus to be on the question of whether an eternal hell is consistent with divine justice, mercy, goodness, or love. The problem I am raising, however, is not a problem about free will or the coherence of the divine attributes, but a problem internal to the concepts of moral responsibility, reward, and punishment as understood by the Christian. I will argue that while secular morality has no resources to handle moral luck, Christianity can do so either by eliminating it or by rendering it innocuous. I will consider five ways this might be done, none of which is an option outside of Christian theology, but each of which raises problems of its own.

8.2. The case for moral luck

Bernard Williams and Thomas Nagel support the existence of moral luck and illustrate it with numerous examples. Nagel argues that there are three main sources of moral luck: luck in consequences, luck in circumstances, and luck in constitution, the last of which might more properly be called luck in traits of character. Together they make luck so pervasive that it contaminates virtually every type of moral theory as well as common moral practice.

Consider first luck in consequences. The idea here is that the outcome of a person's act affects his degree of fault even though the way things turn out is to some extent beyond his control. To take one of Nagel's examples:

> If someone has had too much to drink and his car swerves on to the sidewalk, he can count himself morally lucky if there are no pedestrians in his path. If there were, he would be to blame for their deaths, and would probably be prosecuted for manslaughter. But if he hurts no one, although his recklessness is exactly the same, he is guilty of a far less serious legal offense and will certainly reproach himself and be reproached by others much less severely. (Nagel 1979, 29)

Although the example is a legal one, it is clear in the subsequent discussion that Nagel thinks that the degree of *moral* responsibility differs in the two cases even though the degree of control by the agent is the same. Luck in consequences is the category given the most attention by both Williams and Nagel, but it is also the most vulnerable to objection.[2] I will therefore not make any of my claims in this paper depend upon there being luck of this type.

Let us consider, then, the Kantian move of focusing moral assessment exclusively on the internal sphere of intentions or acts of will. What accrues to our discredit is not literally *what* we do, on this approach, but only those mental acts by which we do it. Will this move eliminate the problem of moral luck?

Unfortunately, it will not. For one thing, a person forms intentions only when the occasion arises, but the arising of the occasion is the result of circumstances largely beyond the agent's control. Again, to take one of Nagel's examples:

> Ordinary citizens of Nazi Germany had an opportunity to behave heroically by opposing the regime. They also had an opportunity to behave badly, and most

of them are culpable for having failed the test. But it is a test to which the citizens of other countries were not subjected, with the result that even if they, or some of them, would have behaved as badly as the Germans in like circumstances, they simply did not and therefore are not similarly culpable. (Nagel 1979, 34)

In an earlier paper, Joel Feinberg (1970) made the same point that responsibility for one's inner states can in some circumstances be wholly a matter of luck. He considers the case of Hotspur, the unfortunate slapper of Hemo, an even more unfortunate hemophiliac, who dies as the result of Hotspur's slap.

Imagine that we have photographed the whole episode and are now able to project the film in such very slow motion that we can observe every stage of Hotspur's action and (constructively) even the "inner" anticipatory stages....

At each of these cinematographic stages there is some state of affairs for which we might hold Hotspur responsible. We can also conceive of a third party, call him Witwood, who is in all relevant respects exactly like Hotspur but who, through luck, would have escaped responsibility at each stage, were he in Hotspur's shoes. We can imagine, for example, that had Witwood caused Hemo's mouth to hemorrhage, Hemo's life would have been saved by some new drug; or at an earlier stage, instead of becoming responsible for Hemo's cut mouth, Witwood lands only a glancing blow which does not cut; or again, instead of becoming responsible for the painful impact of hand on face, Witwood swings at a ducking Hemo and misses altogether. Though similar in his intentions and deeds to Hotspur, Witwood escapes responsibility through luck.

The same good fortune is possible at earlier "internal" stages. For example, at the stage when Hotspur would begin to burn with rage, a speck of dust throws Witwood into a sneezing fit, preventing any rage from arising. He can no more be responsible for a feeling he did not have than for a death that did not happen. Similarly, at the point when Hotspur would be right on the verge of forming his intention, Witwood is distracted at just that instant by a loud noise. By the time the noise subsides, Witwood's blood has cooled, and he forms no intention to slap Hemo. Hotspur, then, is responsible—I suppose some would say "morally" responsible—for his intention, whereas Witwood, who but for an accidental intrusion on his attention would have formed the same intention, luckily escapes responsibility. (Feinberg 1970, 34–35)

Since the introduction of Witwood to the analysis of Hotspur is just a colorful way of talking about what Hotspur himself might have done if he had not been unlucky, the objection might be raised that the claim of moral luck in circumstances rests on the questionable view that there are true counterfactuals of freedom of the form: In circumstances C, Hotspur would have done X. But, in fact, the case rests on no such problematic counterfactuals. It is not necessary that the circumstances in which Hotspur would not have struck Hemo are precisely specifiable, even in principle. All that is required is that there are *some* counterfactual circumstances (perhaps with the proviso that these circumstances not be too far removed from the actual ones) in which Hotspur does not strike Hemo, and that it is beyond Hotspur's control that these circumstances do not obtain; and surely that much is true.

The natural response at this point of the story of Hotspur and Witwood is to go back even farther, before the situation arose. As Feinberg describes the case, Hotspur and Witwood have the same character traits relevant to the type of situation described. They are equally irascible or sensitive about personal remarks, and so if we make the primary focus of moral judgment the character traits themselves, Hotspur and Witwood are equally at fault and so Hotspur neither benefits nor suffers from moral luck arising from actual intentions or feelings. Feinberg does not pursue this line, but Nagel considers it briefly with examples of the traits of envy and conceit and claims that they also are not impervious to luck. As Nagel describes these cases, they are most naturally understood as qualities of temperament rather than vices, but considerations on the nature of virtues and vices show them to be heavily affected by luck as well, at least on a classical Aristotelian theory. To Aristotle, traits of character are not inborn, but are habits acquired through imitation of others. The character of the persons to whom one is exposed while young is clearly outside a person's control, yet it is a major factor in the acquisition of moral virtues and vices. So even if the primary moral responsibility of persons is for enduring traits of character rather than for intentions, acts, or their consequences, moral luck still exists.

A thorough examination of the problem of moral luck would have to give careful attention to the development of our concepts of fault and responsibility and the purpose of rewards and punishments, but my conclusion at this stage is that moral luck does exist and it is a flaw in the institution of morality as we know it. While I do not maintain that luck exists in all of Nagel's categories, there is surely luck in whatever it is people are morally evaluated *for*, since all suggestions on what that is are covered by one of Nagel's or Feinberg's categories. The range of luck is wide enough to cover just about every object of moral evaluation in every known theory: consequences, acts, intentions, dispositions, character traits. Even worse, there is no reason to think that a new theory would help since the problem is pervasive in the practice of morality as we know it, not just in its theoretical formulations.

I maintain, then, that moral luck exists, but I also maintain that the Kantian intuition that morality ought to be free of luck is justified. So while we cannot escape moral luck, we ought to devise moral practices and ways of theorizing that minimize it. What Nagel and Feinberg do not say is that the degree of moral luck is less for some forms of moral evaluation than for others. If we extend Feinberg's imaginary exercise and trace a line backwards from the consequences of an act, to the physical act itself, to the intention to perform the act, to the psychic states out of which the intention is formed, to the enduring character traits from which particular psychic states arise, we find that the farther back we go, the less luck there is. That is because each later point of assessment includes all the luck of the previous points as well as some others. There is a cumulative effect in moral luck. So in Feinberg's example of Hotspur, his degree of luck in killing Hemo includes the luck involved in the personal qualities that led him to become violent, aggravated by the degree of luck in the circumstances in which the intention to commit the act was formed, aggravated by the degree of luck in the circumstances in which death follows the act. The class of theories that focus moral evaluation on intentions are therefore preferable to those that focus on consequences in that they allow less room for luck. Even better than intention-based theories are virtue-based theories. At least with respect to the problem of luck, virtue theories have the advantage.

Nagel is rather sanguine about the existence of moral luck. It is something we will have to live with, he says; we really do not have any choice. Morality may be defective, but we're stuck with it. Notice that this is a reasonable response only if we think of morality as having finite significance. While Nagel does not explicitly make such an assumption, it is clear that a major part of the reason he is willing to accept moral luck is that he assumes it is closely tied to human intuitions, purposes, and practices, the defects of which are so obvious that it really should not be any surprise that the defects extend to the ground of moral evaluation itself.

Feinberg's conclusion following his discussion of the case of Hotspur and Witwood is somewhat different from Nagel's, but equally interesting. Moral responsibility is a matter about which we are all confused, Feinberg concludes, and no individual philosopher or school is especially guilty of this confusion. The problem is not only that our degree of responsibility exceeds our degree of control, as Nagel maintains, but that our moral responsibility is indeterminate, even in principle.

8.3. The luck of the Christian

Christian ethics has some of the same problems of luck that face secular ethics. Perhaps Christian moral theorists are less inclined to hold a person responsible for consequences beyond those she can control, and to that extent Christian ethics does not face the most severe of the three types of moral luck identified by Nagel. Still, the range of objects of moral evaluation within Christian moral theories are all things that Nagel and Feinberg have demonstrated to my satisfaction to possess a degree of luck. To the extent that there is luck in one's moral responsibility for one's virtues and vices, the circumstances in which one forms one's intentions, and the resulting acts themselves—to that extent the Christian faces moral luck.[3] As the Christian understands morality, then, we are faced at least with luck in circumstances and in traits of character.

But Christian ethics differs from secular ethics in ways that make the matter of luck especially problematic. In the first place, Christian moral theory replaces the concept of moral wrongdoing by the concept of sin, an offense against God, and the concept of an abstract state of moral worth that may or may not be determinable is replaced by the concept of one's moral state as judged by God. And presumably that *should be* determinable. Furthermore, there is less room for the acceptance of luck in Christian ethics than in ethics as conceived by Nagel since to the Christian, morality is not simply an institution dependent upon the finite concerns of limited and defective humans. What's more, Kantian intuitions are strong in the Christian tradition and it can be plausibly argued that Kant was heavily influenced by Christian sensibilities in devising his idea that moral worth is strictly under our control. In fact, the precursor to Kant's idea exists in St. Augustine's *De Libero Arbitrio*. There Augustine says that we are contented only if we possess the "good will" (*bona voluntas*), which is the only good fully within our power, and of which we cannot be deprived by worldly circumstances (*De Libero Arbitrio*, Bk. I, chap. 12).

To make matters worse, traditional Christianity includes two doctrines that on the face of it magnify the problem of luck to infinity. These are the doctrines of grace and of an eternal heaven and hell.

Consider the doctrine of grace. On all accounts, grace is necessary for salvation and is an unearned gift of God. While accounts of grace within Christianity differ with respect to the question of how much our efforts can affect the reception of grace, no one suggests that it is wholly under our control. There is, then, religious luck. What's more, religious luck magnifies moral luck, at least in the theology of Aquinas, since he says that not only are the greatest of the virtues, Faith, Hope, and Charity, infused by grace, but no merit accrues to our possession of the ordinary "natural" virtues such as kindness, justice, and courage without the action of grace. And Christian Charity is the supreme virtue without which no other trait we possess nor act we perform gives us any merit.

Most serious of all, the reward or punishment to which a life of grace or the lack of it leads is an eternal heaven or hell. This element of Christian teaching multiplies the effects of moral luck and the luck of grace to infinity. I will not speculate here on the nature of eternity; eternal reward or punishment may not be infinite in duration. Nonetheless, it must be the case that an eternal reward is infinitely greater than an earthly reward, and an eternal punishment is infinitely greater than an earthly punishment. A person controls her individual choices and acts and the series of choices and acts that constitute her life only up to a point, yet her reward or punishment is infinite. That means that even in the best case, one in which we can assume that the cumulative luck in a person's life from natural qualities, circumstances, and consequences is fairly small, since an infinite reward or punishment is at stake, the effects of even a small degree of luck become infinite.

Religious luck is not strictly parallel to moral luck, however. Moral luck occurs when the rewards or punishments a person *deserves* are partially a function of matters beyond the person's control. In the case of religious luck, traditional Christian doctrine maintains that everyone deserves the worst punishment, namely, eternal damnation. So religious luck is not luck in what one *deserves*, although it is luck in what one gets after the final judgment, and that at least appears to be reward and punishment. Two people may be in exactly the same position as far as their control is concerned, yet one is saved and the other is damned.[4] So the fact that moral luck is a matter of desert, and religious luck is not, hides a more fundamental similarity. Both moral and religious luck involve an inequality in the way persons are treated by the institution of morality itself.

A more important way that religious luck is disanalogous with moral luck is that most Christian theologians maintain that grace is offered in such abundance that everyone receives more than is sufficient for salvation. In fact, on some accounts, everyone receives many times a sufficiency. That changes the analogy with the cases of moral luck in circumstances. A typical example of the latter is a situation in which two persons, David and Mark, appear at the scene of a burning house. David gets there first and saves a child from the fire. Mark would have done the same thing had he arrived on time, but as it is, David is the moral hero instead. Although Mark did not even have the opportunity to save the child, David both gets and deserves more praise than Mark.

To make this case analogous to the case of religious luck due to the circumstances of grace, its description must be amended. We would have to say that both David and Mark have numerous chances to save a child from a burning house or acts of a similar nature, and all either one of them has to do to receive the big reward is to perform one such act of heroism. David does have more chances than Mark, but provided that Mark has opportunities in abundance, the inequality between him and David loses some of its sting. This suggests that the greater the opportunities for even the least religiously lucky person, the less problematic the inequality between his luck and someone else's appears to us.[5] Nonetheless, the issue of the inequality remains, and that is the heart of the problem of luck as proposed by Nagel.

Historical disputes within Christian theology over predestination versus free will and over the precise nature of Faith and the way grace works were partly disputes about luck, but not in the sense we are considering. All sides agreed that no one earns or deserves grace, and so grace is clearly a matter of luck in the sense that it is gratuitous. Still, there were disputes over the relationship between human effort, will, or action and the reception of grace. There may have been less room for luck in the Catholic position than in the Calvinist position, but all the traditional positions included a substantial degree of luck in the sense we are addressing here, even the Pelagian heresy. It should be clear from Nagel's discussion that the issue is not one about incompatibilist free will. If there is no incompatibilist free will, then our moral acts, choices, and traits of character are wholly a matter of luck. If there *is* incompatibilist free will, then they are only partly a matter of luck. That is because the claim that there is incompatibilist free will is merely the claim that past circumstances do not completely determine the choice that a person makes; no one disputes that past circumstances, including many beyond a person's control, strongly influence a person's choice. No matter which way we go on free will, there is luck. This luck contaminates any account of moral worth, including accounts of grace. If grace is both offered and received without any control by the recipient, then the luck of it is overwhelming and obvious. If the recipient controls either its offer or its acceptance to any extent through a free choice, the luck is still present in abundance, only less obviously so.

As with the doctrine of grace, traditional discussions of heaven and hell have tended to be about different problems from the one I am addressing. Even in contemporary philosophical theology, discussions of hell usually approach it from the point of view of its consistency with other divine attributes: divine justice (Peter Geach [1977], George Schlesinger [1988]; divine goodness (John Hick [1966], Eleonore Stump [1986], Richard Swinburne [1983]; and divine love (Thomas Talbott [1990]). The question that concerns me here is not a problem for the divine attributes, but a problem for the Christian conception of morality. If there is moral luck and that is a flaw in morality, we cannot so blithely say, as Nagel does, that this is just something we will have to live with. The stakes are infinitely greater than those assumed by Nagel.

8.4. What makes luck a problem?

On the face of it, the problem of luck in Christian moral theology is far greater, even infinitely greater, than it is for secular moral practice and theory. But on the face of it, Christian theology, with its doctrines of an omniscient and providential God, also has the resources to handle conceptual difficulties that would be impossible for a theory without such a deity. God can mend problems in moral evaluation that nothing can mend in ordinary moral practice. But before turning to the ways God can alleviate the problem of luck, let us look more closely at exactly what makes luck a problem for moral evaluation. Ironically, the existence of an omniscient God worsens the problem of moral luck in one respect.

There are many kinds of luck. No one denies that we do not all begin life with the same advantages—in natural endowment, in material well-being, in the emotional support of the family, etc., and as life goes on these advantages and disadvantages can change—some due to human choices, some not. It is sometimes argued that a just society should attempt to minimize the effects of luck by such things as aid to persons with physical or mental disabilities or special academic programs for the disadvantaged, or programs aiming at redistributing income. One thing is certain, however; pure luck is much easier to accept morally than inequality that is the result of human choice or social or economic structures over which we have some control. Helmut Schoeck (1966) argues in his classic study on envy that the concept of luck is a socially positive concept which mitigates the envy resulting from material or social differences:

> It is significant that concepts such as luck, chance, opportunity, "hitting the jackpot"—what we generally regard as someone's being undeservingly favoured by circumstances beyond his or our control—are *not* found in all cultures. Indeed, in many languages there is no way of expressing such ideas.
>
> Yet where one of these concepts exists in a society, it plays a crucial part in controlling the problem of envy. Man can come to terms with the evident inequality of the individual human lot, without succumbing to envy that is destructive of both himself and others, only if he can put the responsibility on some impersonal power—blind chance or fortune, which neither he himself nor the man favoured is able to monopolize. "Today it's the other man who is lucky—tomorrow it may be I." We derive the same consolation from the expression "to have bad luck." Thus what is involved is no providential God, whose favours can be won by special zeal in worship or a pure way of life, for this would most surely induce that bitter, consuming envy of the "holier-than-thou" fanatic, so amply corroborated by history—as in the witch trials, for instance. (Schoeck 1966, 284–285)

Once we get past Schoeck's concluding hyperbole, we see that he has suggested an additional problem of luck for the Christian. I have already argued that it is difficult to accept that even a portion of the grounds upon which we are morally evaluated are beyond our control, but what is worse, we are not even able to fall back on the idea of our moral luck as blind chance or the luck of the draw. If there is an omniscient God, it is not accurate to describe that which we do not control as pure luck—something that is nobody's fault. The luck described by Nagel and Feinberg occurs due to impersonal forces that have nothing against you (or *for* you) personally. If Sarah had been born with a more naturally cheerful disposition, she would have found it much easier to acquire the virtues of benevolence. If Mark had arrived at the burning building a few moments earlier, he would have been the one to save the child instead of David. If the young gang member had not been born in poverty to a drug-addicted mother and an absent father, he would not now be in court faced with a string of charges from car theft to murder. In each case there is nobody to blame for the bad luck. It just happened that way. But if there is an omniscient God, and especially if omniscience includes a degree of knowledge of what a person would do or would be likely to do in counterfactual circumstances, it does look as if God is picking on some people.

So moral luck for the Christian is faced with a dual problem. Not only is there the problem identified by Nagel and magnified by the doctrines of grace and eternal reward and punishment, but the element of luck for the Christian is not independent of the knowledge and will of God. God permits it to go on in full awareness of who will be morally lucky and who will be unlucky. There is not even the consolation of luck as impersonal chance.

There is another way to look at luck, however, in which even conscious and calculated luck in some circumstances may seem benign. Brynmor Browne (1992) argues that luck in rewards is not nearly so bad as luck in punishments. It is not as bad if some people are rewarded beyond what they control than for some people to be punished beyond what they control, and that is at least part of the reason that nobody complains about the existence of an eternal heaven, while many people argue that there is something wrong with an eternal hell. It is reasonable to say that no one has been treated unfairly in rewards as long as each person is rewarded at least as much as she deserves. So even if some people are rewarded more than they deserve and the reward is not based on the luck of the draw but is consciously calculated by the reward-giver, then there are no grounds for complaint on the part of those who receive less. Presumably this is the moral of the parable of the workers in the vineyard.

But parallel considerations can be given for the fairness of luck in punishments. Just as there is no unfairness so long as each person is rewarded at least as much as she deserves, we might say that there is no unfairness so long as each person is punished no more than she deserves. In each case it is gratuitous generosity that motivates the giver of rewards and punishments to increase the reward or to decrease the punishment for some. Just as only envy or spite could lead me to complain that others are the recipients of special generosity in receiving rewards, similarly, only envy or spite could lead me to complain that others are the recipients of special generosity in receiving punishments. In both cases, fairness for me is determined by my direct dealings with the laws of morality and their divine sanctions. The fact that someone else gets special consideration should be no concern of mine. On the model of the workers in the vineyard, we can think of my relationship with morality as being like a contract between me, God, and the laws of morality. What happens to other people is irrelevant to me.

This defense of the element of luck even in the case in which luck is not blind forces us to come to terms with the issue of inequality at the heart of the examples of moral and religious luck. There is little doubt that there is something repellent about inequality to the contemporary mind, although it might be argued that this is an obsession arising from modern political theory. But even if contemporary worries about inequality in wealth or opportunity are excessive, it hardly seems excessive to worry about inequality in moral assessment, especially when the consequences are as drastic as infinite reward or punishment. Inequality of treatment by morality and by God are not easily dismissed.

But there is an even more fundamental worry that the defense of religious luck just given overlooks. The problem of moral luck is not fundamentally a problem about the comparison of the moral worth of one person and another, but a comparison of the moral worth of a particular person and that same person under different counterfactual circumstances. The bothersome inequality, then, is between one person and himself in other possible circumstances. To return to Feinberg's example, the problem is not that Hotspur is the unlucky bearer of bad moral luck while Witwood has good moral luck, but that Hotspur *might have been* Witwood. As Witwood is described by Feinberg, he is just Hotspur's alternative self. The issue of envy that we find in the parable of the workers in the vineyard does not arise on this reading of the problem. Hotspur cannot be envious of his alternative self. He is simply distressed that he is not that self and that the fact that he is not is wholly beyond his control. The solution to the Christian problem of moral luck must address the problem that Hotspur and Witwood are the same person and it is only luck that determines that it is Hotspur that is actualized, not Witwood.

8.5. Five ways to deal with religious luck

Suppose that there are true counterfactuals of freedom and that God has Middle Knowledge. That is to say, for each person S, God knows what S would freely choose to do in every possible situation. God would then be in a position to judge S, not just for her actual virtues and vices, and for the acts she in fact performs, and their actual consequences, but for the sum total of everything she would choose to do in every possible circumstance. Of course, some of those circumstances exhibit bad luck, but others exhibit good luck. It is reasonable to think that luck is eliminated if her choices in the totality of possible circumstances are the basis for her moral assessment. Lovers of Middle Knowledge who are haters of moral luck may find this solution attractive. Such a procedure for moral assessment would no doubt have a leveling effect on the moral worth of human beings. After all, there is probably *some* possible circumstance in which almost anybody would do almost anything, whether it be good or bad. Whether this consequence is a good or a bad feature of this solution, I cannot say. A feature of it that many would find seriously defective, however, is that it makes the actual world meaningless as far as moral evaluation is concerned. In fact, there is really no reason to have an actual world at all for such purposes. God could just as well have created the beings he wanted, and then he could have gone straight on to their final judgment, skipping the in-between step of letting a particular world unfold. It must be admitted, then, that this approach is very far removed from our ordinary notions of moral evaluation. But, of course, the defender of this approach can always say that that is because our ordinary notions of moral evaluation are permeated with elements of luck, as Williams and Nagel have shown, and the proper response to this is to say so much the worse for our ordinary notions of moral evaluation. So while I do not think this approach is absurd, it should be admitted that it is radical.

A second solution is to say that a person is morally evaluated for just that element of her character and her acts that she controls. Although Nagel says that when we view ourselves from the outside, that portion of the moral self that we control threatens to shrink into nothing, the argument that there is moral luck does not rest on such a position, and in this paper I have been leaving open the possibility that there is incompatibilist free will. If so, why couldn't our moral evaluation be determined by an omniscient God in proportion to our control?

The problem here is that it is not at all clear that there is any such thing as *the* proportion of our control. Recall Joel Feinberg's conclusion to the discussion of Hotspur and Witwood. There he claims that moral responsibility is indeterminate, not just relative to our epistemic situation, but in itself. The precise determinability of moral responsibility is an illusion, he says; moral responsibility is undecidable *in principle*. While Feinberg's argument may not be given with the care necessary to demonstrate such a dramatic conclusion, it does at least draw our attention to the range of questions that would have to have determinate answers if luck were to be eliminated by this move. Not only would there need to be a determinate degree of causal control a person has over a choice, but there would have to be a determinate degree of control that a person has over the fact that she is in certain actual circumstances rather than in any one of the infinite number of counterfactual circumstances. Further, there would have to be a determinate degree of her control over the fact that she has the virtues and vices that she has. It is highly doubtful that there is any such degree at all. And if not, even an omniscient judge could not base his evaluation on it.

A third solution is suggested by George Schlesinger (1988, chap 7) in a discussion of divine justice. The problem he addresses there is much more narrowly focused than the one I am raising here, but the solution might be applicable.

Schlesinger is concerned about the fact that the religious beliefs requisite for salvation are much easier for some to acquire than others. As he puts it, different individuals have different opportunities to avail themselves of arguments and evidence for the existence of God:

> Suppose I am a non-believer who has remained unconvinced by the various proofs for God's existence I have read or heard. There is, however, a new argument which would appeal to me so much that it would most likely convert me to theism. It so happens that I never get the chance to gain knowledge of the argument and thus persist in my ungodly ways. Is it not grossly unfair that, owing to circumstances beyond my control, I should be deprived of the ultimate felicity I could have shared with the righteous? (1988, 184)

While Schlesinger puts the emphasis on the acceptance of theism based on argument, one need not be an evidentialist to agree that whatever it takes to believe in God is not something that everyone has an equal opportunity to obtain. Those who grow up in a happy religious home obviously have far greater opportunities for salvific Faith than those who grow up in deprived circumstances in which religion is either nonexistent or, perhaps even worse, is associated in their experience with bigotry or hypocrisy. Schlesinger's answer is that "in accordance with the pain is the reward" (1988, 186). "The true amount of virtue embodied in a given individual is not determined by the absolute level of piety he has reached, but by the nature of the hostile circumstances he has had to contend with in order to raise himself to the level he has succeeded in attaining" (1988, 188). So the harder it is for a person to be saved, the greater his reward if he does his part in exhibiting a sincere good will; the easier it is for a person to be saved, the less the reward for making a lesser effort. Some people gamble for higher stakes with a lower chance of success, while others gamble for lower stakes with a higher chance of success.

I have two worries about this solution. In the first place, it is not at all clear that the initial positions of the sincere person in a pagan society and the ordinary person in religiously ideal circumstances are really equal. After all, a real gambler has a choice between going for higher stakes with a lower chance of winning or going for lower stakes with a higher chance of winning. Much of what makes the game fair is that the choice is his. But in the religious case as Schlesinger sees it, it is not up to us to choose the game we play. We do not get to decide initially how much of a risk we want to take. Second, this solution faces the same problem that infects the previous solution. Is it even possible in principle to determine a person's chance for salvation? Is there any such thing as the proportion of his success or failure that is due to efforts completely under his control? What Schlesinger does not mention is that luck in circumstances is only part of the problem. There is also luck in those traits of character that lead some people to make the greater efforts needed for salvation. What Schlesinger calls "a sincere good will" is itself partly a matter of luck.

The fourth solution is to embrace a doctrine of grace according to which grace not only does not aggravate luck, it eliminates it.[6] The idea here is that since God desires everyone to be saved, more grace is given to the morally unlucky. Everyone gets grace, but some get more of it to compensate for their bad moral luck. This does seem to be what a loving parent would do. A mother who loves all her children equally will not necessarily give each child equal attention and help. Those who need it more, get more. On this approach it would not be necessary for God to determine in advance a precise level of grace needed to neutralize the effects of moral luck since God can intervene at any time to provide more than enough grace when needed. The problem of the indeterminacy in moral responsibility or degree of control could therefore be circumvented on this approach.

The problem with this solution is that it does not accord well with our experience. Of course, it might be the case that truly corrupted criminals (such as the principal character in the recent French film *L'Elegant criminel*) really did have more than enough chances to stay on the moral path and again later to reform themselves, but it certainly does not *seem* that way. What's more, an acceptance of this approach might lead to severe harshness in our moral assessment of others. That is, it suggests that the excuses people seem to have for their behavior are not really excuses after all since, unseen by us (and even themselves), they had even more opportunities for grace than most of us, but simply rejected it.

The fifth solution is that while God does not eliminate moral luck, he makes it innocuous through universal salvation. This solution involves severing the moral order from the order of salvation. We have seen that Christian luck includes at least some of the kinds of luck discussed by Nagel and Feinberg, and that it is aggravated by several aspects of Christian teaching. First, Christian luck is not blind, but is known in advance to an omniscient God. Second, there is some degree of inequality in the operation of grace. Third, and most serious of all, the doctrine of an eternal heaven and hell magnifies the extent of moral luck to infinity. What is most problematic in these doctrines is the way the concepts of grace and heaven and hell are connected with the moral institution of rewards and punishments. Suppose, however, that there is no eternal hell. If so, we avoid the worst problem of an infinite degree of luck in punishment, and at the same time, an eternal heaven makes innocuous the effects of all the other sorts of moral and religious luck we have accumulated during our earthly existence, including inequality in the operation of grace. The fact that there is no blind luck and that all of this is known to an omniscient God is an advantage rather than a disadvantage of this solution.

It might appear radical to sever the moral order from the order of salvation, but notice that the Christian is already committed to this in part since Christian theology dissociates what we get from what we deserve in the case of heaven. When the generosity of a reward-giver is extreme enough, it is inappropriate to call his gift a reward. Heaven is not a reward, and so it is not part of the moral order. Hell, however, *is* a punishment since all who go there deserve it. Such a view requires an awkward partial break between morality and ultimate destiny. The fifth solution to the problem of moral luck would make a clean break between the two.

In distinguishing the moral order from the order of salvation, it is not necessary to radically alter our moral intuitions and practices in order to deal with moral luck, the major defect of the first solution. The solution of universal salvation does not take away luck in the moral order; moral luck simply has no bearing on one's ultimate destiny. This means that we can accept morality as a finite institution with finite significance, as Nagel does. If morality requires finite punishments after death, there is nothing in this solution to prevent them from occurring. The point is that whatever the defects of the institution of morality as we know it, that is something we can live with as long as all is made well in eternity. A consequence of this solution is that morality is ultimately not as important as many of us think. In any case, it ought to be cut down to size, the only size it can realistically manage.

This solution will be attractive to those who already maintain for independent reasons that there is no eternal hell. The arguments I know of for this conclusion almost always rest on a consideration of the divine attributes, and the argument is that an eternal hell is inconsistent with divine justice, mercy, goodness, or love. My argument here is concerned only with the problem of moral luck and the fact that the problem can be handled rather well if there is no eternal hell. Independent arguments for the nonexistence of hell might give this solution additional support. It should be admitted, however, that this approach does go against the dominant view in the Christian tradition. It is mostly dependent upon *a priori* philosophical reasoning, but, then, most of the other solutions are *a priori* as well. It is doubtful that the problem of moral luck as I have formulated it in this paper was even considered in the tradition, so it is no surprise that there is little in the tradition of direct relevance to the problem.[7]

8.6. Conclusion

I have argued in this paper that moral luck is a problem and that its existence shows that common views on morality flirt with inconsistency. Some of the sources of moral luck identified by Thomas Nagel and Joel Feinberg are problems for Christian morality as well. Moreover, I have argued that there are several features of Christian doctrine that magnify the problem enormously. I have gone through five solutions to the problem. All of them in one degree or another modify traditional views about grace, heaven and hell, or the grounds for moral evaluation. The only way I know to maintain untouched the traditional doctrines I have referred to in this paper requires the denial that moral luck is a problem even when infinite rewards and punishments are at stake. I believe this view to be deeply counter to modern moral sensibilities, although I have not attempted to defend those sensibilities in this paper, only to call attention to them. Furthermore, all of the solutions have problems of their own. But in spite of this, it seems to me that if the problem of moral luck has a solution at all, it will have to be within a theological structure which goes beyond morality as normally discussed in the secular philosophical literature. Non-religious ethics does not have the resources to handle the problem. For the purposes of this paper, I have considered only those approaches that arise within the Christian tradition. Non-Christian religious solutions, such as reincarnation, should also be considered.[8]

Notes

1. Early versions of both papers were presented at the Aristotelian Society and published in *Proceedings of the Aristotelian Society*, Supplemental Vol. 50 (1976), 115–135.
2. Judith Jarvis Thomson (1989) claims that the argument that there is luck in consequences plays upon an ambiguity in the notion of blame. In the sense of blame that reflects discredit on a person, there is no luck in consequences. The two negligent drunk drivers are equally at fault. But there is also a sense of blame in which we say a person is to blame *for* an undesirable state of affairs, such as a person's death. In this sense, the driver who actually kills someone is clearly to blame, while the one who does not is not.
3. Philip L. Quinn (1989) argues that a different sort of moral luck exists for the Christian, and that is the moral dilemma. A person faces a moral dilemma when no matter what she chooses, she does the wrong thing. It is therefore a type of moral trap. Quinn argues that Shusaku Endo's novel *Silence* depicts a person faced with a situation in which the two great commandments—the command to love God with our whole heart, and the command to love our neighbor as ourselves—require conflicting acts. If Quinn is right that the Jesuit missionary Sebastian Rodrigues faces a moral dilemma in Endo's novel, then that is another way in which moral luck arises for the Christian, but in this paper I will limit my discussion to the categories of moral luck identified by Nagel and Feinberg.
4. One way this could happen is if they sin together and one is killed right after she repents, but the other is killed immediately after the sin but before repenting. If one's eternal destiny is determined by one's state at death, the former would receive eternal

reward and the other eternal punishment. I thank an anonymous referee for this suggestion.
5. This disanalogy between grace and moral luck in rewards was pointed out to me by Thomas D. Sullivan.
6. This solution was suggested to me by Kenneth Rudnick, S.J.
7. A sixth solution was suggested to me by Stephen T. Davis. Suppose that God gives us the opportunity to make a luck-free choice in eternity and eternally rewards or punishes us on the basis of such a choice. Notice the similarity between Davis's suggestion and the Myth of Ur at the end of Plato's *Republic*.
8. Earlier versions of this paper were presented at the meeting of the Midwest region of the Society of Christian Philosophers (SCP) at the University of St. Thomas, St. Paul, Minnesota, October 1992, and at the meeting of the Pacific region of the SCP January, 1993. I thank the participants at both conferences for their helpful comments, especially Thomas D. Sullivan.

IV
GOD AND MORALITY

9
The Virtues of God and the Foundations of Ethics (1998)

> Nothing will be called good except in so far as it has a certain likeness of the divine goodness.
> —Aquinas SCG I. 40. 326

9.1. The foundations of virtue ethics

A moral theory is an abstract structure that aims to simplify, systematize, and justify our moral practices and beliefs. The shape of the structure itself is typically either foundationalist or coherentist, although well-known problems with both these structures within epistemology may lead some ethicists to seek an alternative. A more radical approach is to give up the very *idea* of a moral theory, and virtue ethicists have been among the most prominent of the anti-theorists.[1] Contemporary virtue ethics, then, is often portrayed as not only an alternative to act-based theories, but as an alternative to theory itself.

Virtue ethicists tend to be skeptical about foundationalist moral theory. Aretaic theories deriving from Aristotle or Aquinas make the foundational moral concept *eudaimonia*, or human flourishing, where *eudaimonia* is derivative from or dependent upon the allegedly non-moral concept of human nature.[2] But many contemporary ethicists have despaired of ever giving a clear and plausible account of *eudaimonia*, much less one that has universal applicability, and the concept of nature has been attacked throughout the modern era on the grounds that it depends upon an outdated biology. Nonetheless, the concept of human nature has survived,[3] and even *eudaimonia* has survived, although typically without the pretense of being foundational in the sense I mean here.[4] So skepticism about the ability of virtue ethics to even get started has kept many a contemporary philosopher away from it. And virtue theorists themselves are prone to this skepticism. So when virtue ethics entered a renaissance in the last decades of the twentieth century, it did so without most of the theoretical trappings of modern theories.

I am convinced that if virtue ethics is ever to be the equal rival of deontological and consequentialist ethics, it should have a theoretical form, one that addresses such basic issues as whether moral properties are grounded in nonmoral properties, whether moral judgments have a truth value, where morality gets its authority, how the moral properties of persons, acts, and states of affairs are related to each other, and many others.[5] I would not deny that it is desirable to have forms of virtue ethics that ignore these theoretical issues, and we probably cannot do both at the same time. But I believe that the human need to theorize is a powerful one. We want to understand the moral world as well as the natural world and, indeed, to understand the relation between the two. For Christians there is also the need to understand the relation between the moral world and the supernatural world. The reliance of the moral world on God puts constraints on the way we answer the deep questions just mentioned, although, as far as I can tell, belief in the Christian God puts no special constraint on whether the theory is deontological, consequentialist, aretaic, or some alternative, nor on whether the structure of the theory is foundationalist, coherentist, or some alternative. But Christian philosophers have traditionally agreed that in some sense God is the foundation of moral value, and that makes the search for a foundationalist structure a natural one, even though I see no reason to think that a belief in moral foundationalism is a requirement of Christianity.

In this paper I want to exhibit one way to structure a virtue ethics with a theological foundation; in fact, the theological foundation is an extension of virtue theory to God. It is, then, a divine virtue theory. Previously, I outlined a strong form of virtue ethics I call motivation-based.[6] This theory makes all moral concepts derivative from the concept of a good motive, the most basic component of a virtue, where what I mean by a motive is an emotion that initiates and directs action toward an end. In outlining that theory, I left unanswered the important question of what makes a motive a good one. In this paper I will give motivation-based virtue theory a theological foundation by making the motivations of one person in particular the ultimate foundation of all moral value, and that person is God. I call the theory Divine Motivation (DM) theory.

DM theory has the following structure: The motivational states of God are ontologically and explanatorily the basis for all moral properties. God's motives are perfectly good, and human motives are good insofar as they are similar to the divine motives as those motives would be expressed in finite and embodied beings. Like motivation-based virtue theory, all moral properties, including the moral properties of persons, acts, and states of affairs, are grounded in their relation to good motives, but they are more specifically grounded in their relation to the motives of a perfect being whose nature is the metaphysical foundation of all value. The theory is structurally parallel to Divine Command (DC) theory, but it has many advantages over that theory while avoiding the disadvantages.

9.2. The theory without the theological foundation: Motivation-based virtue theory

In any foundationalist moral theory there is something that is good in the most basic way. If the goodness of something is really foundational, it cannot be justified or explained by the goodness of something else, and it is usually claimed that it *needs* no justification or explanation. Theorists almost always hedge this claim, however, and try to think of some way of justifying what the theory says cannot be justified, as Mill does in attempting to justify the goodness of pleasure in Chapter 4 of *Utilitarianism*. Even Aristotle (who may not be intending to present a foundationalist structure anyway) appeals to common belief in justifying his claim that *eudaimonia* is the ultimate good in Book I of the *Nicomachean Ethics*. Kant uses a transcendental argument to defend the primacy of the Categorical Imperative. And Sidgwick reaches his allegedly self-evident moral principles from reflection upon moral intuition in *Methods of Ethics*.

What I mean by a pure virtue theory is one in which the concept of a good human trait (a virtue) is logically prior to the concept of a right act, and in the strongest form, the concept of a virtue is also prior to the concept of a good state of affairs. The theory I will outline here is an instance of the strongest form of pure virtue theory, making all evaluative concepts logically dependent upon the concept of a virtue—more specifically, on the most basic component of a virtue, a motivation. In this section I will outline the structure of a motivation-based virtue theory only briefly since my principal interest in this paper is to show how a theological foundation can be given for this theory that should be attractive to the Christian philosopher. That task will be left for sections 9.3–9.5.

I propose that moral properties presuppose the existence of persons. They are either properties of persons or their acts, or they are derivative from the properties of persons, e.g., the properties of personal creations—social institutions, practices, laws, etc.[7] It is common in ethics to think of the will as the center of the moral self, and for this reason, moral properties are often thought to be most fundamentally properties of the will. The primacy of the will as the bearer of moral value emerged gradually throughout the medieval period, reaching its clearest expression in that period in the work of Duns Scotus, and, of course, reaching its zenith in the modern period in Kant's famous claim that there is nothing good without qualification but a good will. My proposal is to retain the focus of moral evaluation on the person, but to shift it away from the will, both when we are talking about God and when we are talking about human beings, and to focus instead on emotion.

I suggest that moral properties in the primary sense attach to emotions. Emotions are good or bad in themselves; they do not derive their goodness or badness from their relation to anything else that is good or bad. In particular, they are not good or bad in virtue of their relationship to the states of affairs that are their intentional objects, or the states of affairs that produce them. For example, it is bad to take delight in the misfortune of others or to enjoy the sight of animals in pain, even when these emotions never motivate the agent to act on them. And the badness of these emotions is not derivative from the badness of the pain of animals or the misfortune of others. I will not give an account of the state of emotion here, but it suffices for the purposes of this paper to say that an emotion has a cognitive component as well as a feeling component. The cognitive component may or may not be as fully formed as a belief or a judgment, although it always involves taking or supposing or imagining some portion of the world to be a certain way—e.g., threatening, exciting, boring, pitiful, contemptible.[8] The feeling component accompanies seeing something as threatening, exciting, contemptible. The agent feels threatened by something seen as threatening, feels excited by something seen as exciting, feels contemptuous of something seen as contemptible, and so on.

The cognitive aspect of emotion suggests that emotions have intentional objects, which is to say, a person is afraid *of* something, is angry *at* someone, is excited *about* something, loves someone, and so on, and some writers have taken the intentionality of emotion to be a characteristic that distinguishes emotions from similar psychic states such as moods or pure feelings. I am inclined to accept this position, although it is not critical for the thesis of this paper.

A motive is an emotion that initiates, sustains, and directs action toward an end. Not all motives are emotions since some motives are almost purely physiological, such as the motives of hunger, thirst, or fatigue, and for this reason these states are sometimes called "drives." But the motives that have foundational ethical significance are emotions. It is also possible that not all emotions are motivating since some emotions may be purely passive, which is why emotions were formerly called "passions." Examples of passive emotions might include joy, sadness, tranquility, and the enjoyment of beauty. But even these emotions probably can motivate in certain circumstances. It is usual to *call* an emotion a motive only when it actually operates to motivate on a particular occasion. But when an emotion that sometimes motivates does not operate to motivate at a particular time, it retains its motivational potential. So not all motives are emotions, but the morally significant ones are emotions, and most, if not all, emotions are or can be motives. That is, they have potential motivational force.

Motives tend to be persistent and become dispositions, at which point they become components of enduring traits of character—virtues or vices. Each virtue has a motivational component which is the disposition to have an action-guiding emotion characteristic of the individual virtue. The virtuous person is disposed to perform acts motivated by such an emotion. So a person with the virtue of benevolence is disposed to act in ways motivated by the emotion of benevolence;

a person with the virtue of courage is disposed to act in ways motivated by the distinctive emotion underlying the behavior of those who face danger when they judge it to be necessary to obtain a greater good; a person with the virtue of justice is disposed to act in ways expressing an attitude of equal respect for the humanity of others, and so on.[9]

A virtue also has a success component which is a component of reliability in reaching the end of the motivational component of the virtue. Some virtuous motives aim at *producing* a state of affairs of a certain kind. The state of affairs may either be internal to the agent or external to the agent. Other virtuous motives aim to express the emotion of the agent. Temperance is an example of a virtue whose motivational component aims at producing a state within the agent, whereas fairness is a virtue whose motivational component aims at producing a state of affairs external to the agent. Empathy and gratitude are examples of virtues whose motivational components aim at expressing the agent's emotional state. Successfully achieving the end of a virtuous motive, then, sometimes amounts to bringing about a state of affairs distinct from the motivating emotion, and sometimes success is achieved by merely expressing the emotion itself.

Some human motivations are good, and others are bad. Good human motivations are components of virtues; bad human motivations are components of vices. If a human motive is a good one, reliable success in achieving its end is also a good thing. The goodness of the virtuous end is derivative from the goodness of the motive, not the other way around. The combination of a good human motivation with reliable success in reaching its end is a good human trait—a virtue. A vice is the combination of a bad human motivation and reliable success in reaching the end of the bad motivation.

The evaluative properties of acts are derivative from the evaluative properties of persons. Roughly, a right (permissible) act is an act a virtuous person might do. That is, it is not the case that she would not do it. A wrong act is an act a virtuous person characteristically would not do. Vicious persons characteristically perform wrong acts, but so do persons who are neither vicious nor virtuous, and virtuous persons also may perform wrong acts, but uncharacteristically. A moral duty is an act a virtuous person characteristically would feel compelled to do. She would see the act as the only option and would feel guilty if she did not do it.[10] A virtuous act is one that expresses the motivational component of the virtue. For example, a compassionate act is one that expresses the motivation of compassion. It is an act in which the agent is motivated by compassion and acts with the intention of reaching the motivational end of compassion—the alleviation of the suffering of someone else. In the case of certain virtues, most especially justice, acts expressing the virtue are all moral duties. In the case of other virtues (e.g., compassion, kindness, mercy) many acts express the virtue but are not moral duties.

The moral properties of states of affairs can also be defined in terms of good and bad motivations. Roughly, a good state of affairs is one that is the end of a good motive. A bad state of affairs is one that is the end of a bad motive.[11] The goodness and badness of motives are more fundamental than the goodness and badness of states of affairs. This is a generalization of the point that all moral value derives from a personal being, God. (Of course, non-moral value does also, but the subject of this paper is moral value.) My conjecture is that the nature of moral value is such that it must derive from persons and more particularly, from the motivational states of persons. This view on the relation between the value of a motive and the value of the state of affairs at which it aims reverses the more usual view that the motive to bring about a bad state of affairs such as pain in others is bad because pain is a bad thing. Instead, my suggestion is that pain is a bad thing in the *morally* relevant sense because of the badness of the motive to bring it about. That motive is an emotional state that is bad in a sense that does not derive from the badness of anything other than other motives of a good being.

In motivation-based virtue theory, there is a logical connection between the two senses of good—the admirable and the desirable, with the latter deriving from the former. Similarly, there is a logical connection between two senses of bad—the despicable or contemptible, and the undesirable.[12] Intuitively the distinction between the two senses of good and bad can be important since we think there is a fundamental difference between the sense in which injustice is bad and the sense in which pain is bad, or the sense in which compassion is good and the sense in which tranquility is good. And this difference is not simply the difference between moral and non-moral good and bad because those things that are good or bad in the sense of desirable/undesirable can have moral significance. If so, it would be very peculiar if the two senses of good and bad just distinguished were unconnected, and I am proposing that they are not. The good in the most fundamental sense of good is the admirable, and the bad in the most fundamental sense of bad is the despicable. The good in the sense of desirable is defined in terms of what is desired by admirable people, while the bad in the sense of undesirable is what admirable people desire to prevent or to eliminate.

In motivation-based virtue theory, motives are good or bad in the most fundamental sense of good or bad. But what makes a motive good? One way we might answer this question is to borrow a suggestion from Plato in the *Republic,* where Socrates states that a good (just) person is one whose soul is in harmony. The idea would be that motives (emotions) are good when they integrate into a harmonious whole. This suggestion is worth pursuing, but the answer I want to give here is a theological one. Moral value is constituted by a harmony with the divine, not just a harmony within the soul. Human motives are good insofar as they are like God's motives. Since motives are emotions, that means that God must have emotions, a controversial position in Christian theology, although I will argue that the theory can stand without the claim that the states in God that are the counterparts of human emotions are also emotions. In any case, human virtues are modeled on the virtues of God. In humans, virtues are finite representations of the traits of a perfect God. Since the gap between God and ourselves is infinite, it may seem to be hopelessly impractical, even if theologically and metaphysically desirable, to model our moral traits on God in this way. But we have Christ incarnate as our archetype. What I will propose in what follows is a way to give the traditional Christian idea of ethics as the imitation of Christ a theoretical structure.

9.3. The virtues of God

There are many accounts of virtue in the history of ethics, but all accounts agree that virtues are excellences; they are good personal traits. If we assume that the goodness of God is the metaphysical ground of all value, it is natural to ask whether God has virtues. It may seem that the answer is no, and in good Thomistic fashion I will start with the objections to the thesis before proceeding to argue that God does have virtues, and that the divine virtues include both a motivational component and a success component, as described in section 9.2. More importantly, the divine virtues are not simply pale imitations of the more robust and richly nuanced traits of embodied and encultured beings. The relationship between divine and human virtues is, in fact, the reverse: Human virtues are pale imitations of the divine virtues. Admittedly we cannot really grasp perfection and we tend to find imperfection more interesting, perhaps because it admits of more variety than perfection and we find that thinking about perfection is too demanding a task since our experience is limited to the imperfect. Nonetheless, I believe that God is the only being who is virtuous in a pure and unqualified sense. As Aquinas says, all moral properties are attributed primarily to God and only analogously to humans. I believe that this includes the virtues and the primary component of virtue, a motivation.

In giving the following objections, I will work with the high metaphysical view of God's nature that was developed in the medieval period and has its most subtle and penetrating expression in the thought of Aquinas. I will, however, propose a modification of that view since I submit that God has emotions.

> *Objection 1*: God cannot have a virtue if a virtue includes a motivational component and a motive is an emotional state since God has no emotions. God cannot have emotions because (i) emotions involve the sense appetite and

require a body, but God has no body or sensory appetite, and (ii) emotions are passions, ways of being acted upon, and that implies imperfection, but God is perfect and, hence, impassible.

Objection 2: Virtues are habits that involve overcoming contrary temptations and they take time to develop, so they only make sense when attributed to imperfect beings who undergo change. But God does not *develop* his traits and has no contrary temptations; he is perfect and unchangeable.

Objection 3: Virtues are traditionally explained teleologically by reference to the natural end of a thing of a certain kind, an end that is not already actualized. This means that virtue presupposes potency. The virtues are goods for a thing as a member of a natural kind, but God is not lacking anything and has no potency, nor does God belong to a natural kind. Furthermore, it is hard to see how anything could be good *for* God.

Objection 4: Virtues in their richer and more interesting forms are socially and culturally conditioned. Honesty in parts of Asia is very different from honesty in the United States, even when we consider only the later twentieth century. Cultural differences are even greater when we look at other historical periods. The practical usefulness of the concept of virtue depends upon our learning these richer, culture-dependent concepts. But it is hard to see how the virtues of God could serve such a practical purpose, even under the assumption that God does have virtues. We learn virtues by learning social practices, not by learning theology.

I answer that: Virtues are the good traits of moral agents. The more perfect the moral agent, the more perfect the virtues. God is both a moral agent and a perfect being. Therefore, God has perfectly good moral traits—perfect virtues. Like all moral agents, God has motives, where motives are both explanations of and justifications for an agent's acts. In humans, motives become dispositions, but if God has no dispositions, then God's motives are always in *act*, and God is always acting upon them. Since God is the perfect agent, God's motives are the perfect motives. God's love is the perfect motive of love; God's compassion is the perfect motive of compassion; God's mercy is the perfect motive of mercy, and so on. Since compassion, love, mercy, etc., are emotions, God's compassion, love, mercy, etc., are perfect emotions. I am not suggesting that it necessarily follows from the fact that God acts from compassion, and that the state of compassion in humans is an emotion, that God has emotions. I do think that having emotions is part of what makes a being a moral agent. But the minimum I want to insist upon in this paper is that God's virtues, like our virtues, include a component of motivation—a state that is act-directing, as well as reliable success in bringing about the aim of the motive. God's motives are perfect, and his success is perfect as well. God is, therefore, not just reliable, he is perfectly reliable. A divine virtue, then, is the combination of a perfect motive with perfect success in bringing about the end of the motive.[13]

Reply to objection 1: An emotion is a state of consciousness of a certain kind. I have suggested that that state includes a cognitive aspect whereby the emotion's intentional object is understood or construed to be a certain way distinctive of the virtue. But an emotion is also an affective state; it has a certain "feel." The fact that God has no body precludes God from having emotions only if the possession of a body is a necessary condition for the states of consciousness in question, and that, of course, is denied by the Cartesian view on the relation between mind and body. Furthermore, even if Aquinas is right that sensory experience necessarily requires a body, it is not obvious that emotions necessarily have a sensory component if we mean by "sensory" a state that is of the same kind as states of consciousness that arise from the five senses or that are localized, such as the sensation of pain. But suppose we grant the objection. Suppose we agree with Aquinas that God has no passions (*passiones*) since these belong to the sensory appetite and the sensory appetite requires a body. Aquinas agrees that God does have *affectiones* since the latter admits of two kinds, sensory and intellective. God has intellective appetites which belong to the will. In this category are included states that we call emotions, states such as love and joy. We see, then, that there are two words that refer to affective states in Aquinas: *passiones* and *affectiones*. *Passiones* may be translated as "passion" or "emotion," whereas Norman Kretzmann suggests "attitudes" as the translation for *affectiones*.[14] As Kretzmann translates Aquinas, then, God has certain "attitudes" of love and joy, but these states are not emotions since Kretzmann maintains that Aquinas maintains that God has no emotions. But a case could be made for translating *affectiones* as "emotions" if it is true that even in us, states of emotion are not necessarily sensory. If some of our emotions are, or could be, intellective *affections*, that would mean that the sensory aspect of an emotion is not essential to a state's being one of emotion. If so, a state could not be denied the categorization of an emotion on the grounds that it is not a sensory state. Thus, even if God has no sensory states, it would not follow that he has no emotions.

Objection 1 gives a second reason for thinking that God cannot have emotions, and that is that emotions are passions, ways of being acted upon, and thereby imply lack of perfection. I will not here address the issue of whether emotions are necessarily passive, but I do want to raise the question of whether emotion is an intrinsically defective state, a state that only makes sense when attributed to defective beings. I do not see that there is anything about emotion per se that implies imperfection, although there is no doubt that there are particular emotions that do have such an implication—e.g., fear, hope, jealousy, envy, hatred, bitterness. I hesitate to say that sadness implies a defect since sadness need not require any lack in the agent who has the emotion since it is a response to defects outside of the agent. It is important that the issue of whether the agent who has a certain emotion is defective does not correspond to the distinction that is sometimes made between positive and negative emotions. Some negative emotions such as sadness may imply no defect, whereas some positive emotions such as hope probably do imply a defect. That would mean that while God does have emotions, he does not have the range of emotions that human beings have.

I have already said that it is not necessary to accept that God has emotions for the argument of this paper in spite of what I have said in this reply. Even if God does not have emotions, God nonetheless has states that are the counterparts of the states that in us are emotions. God has emotions in at least the same sense that God has beliefs. God's emotions may not be just like ours, but God's cognitive states are not just like ours either. What is of particular importance for DM theory is not so much that God's emotions are similar to ours in the way they feel, but that the divine states that are the counterparts of human emotions are motivations. That much should not be controversial. Since God is a moral agent, God acts from motives, and among those motives are compassion, forgiveness, and love.

Reply to objection 2: As Norman Kretzmann has pointed out to me, while Aquinas says that virtue is a habit, *habitus* to Aquinas means fundamentally the same thing as "having." The dispositional aspect of a *habitus* is important in his account of human virtues and vices because of our temporality and imperfection, but the idea of a disposition or habit is not essential to a *habitus* as Aquinas means it, and it does not prevent God from having qualities that in us would be habits or dispositions. For example, knowledge is a *habitus* and most human knowledge is dispositional. But the fact that God has no dispositions does not prevent God from having knowledge, nor does it prevent God's knowledge from being a *habitus* since God's knowledge is the eternal *having* of all truths. Similarly, even though a virtue such as compassion is a *habitus* which in us requires development over time, culminating in a disposition distinctive of the virtue of compassion, that does not prevent God from having compassion, nor does it prevent compassion in God from being a *habitus*. God eternally has the emotion of compassion, not just as a disposition, but as an eternal motive-in-act.

Reply to objection 3: If a natural kind is a species, then God is not a natural kind, although God does have a nature and God *is* a certain kind of thing, namely, Absolutely Perfect Being, or Necessarily Existent Being. Each of the traditional arguments for the existence of God identifies a kind of thing that must be God, a kind of thing that, it must be argued, can have only one member. The divine virtues express the perfections of the kind *God*. There is no potency in God, but we can see that there is nothing inconsistent in the claim that a being with no potency has virtues since if, *per impossibile*, a human being reached full actualization of her potential with respect to some virtue, say, compassion, we certainly would not on that account deny that she is compassionate. The way in which a virtue is acquired is not essential to the virtue itself, although it may be essential to beings with a human nature to acquire virtue in a certain way. That means that there is nothing good *for* God if that means an extrinsic good that God needs for actualization, but there is still a sense in which God's virtues are good for him since even in the human case we do not cease claiming that what is good for us is good for us once it is attained. It is good for a human to have knowledge even when the knowledge is possessed; it is good for a knife to be sharp even when it *is* sharp. And it is good for God to be perfectly just, merciful, etc.[15]

Reply to objection 4: This is not an objection to the claim that God has virtues, nor even to the theoretical usefulness of understanding human moral properties in terms of God's virtues, but to the practical relevance of the claim for moral education and training. An answer to this objection would require a demonstration of the way the idea of a virtuous God can be integrated into the biblical doctrine of *imitatio Dei*. That issue will be addressed in the next section.

9.4. Divine Motivation theory

Motivation-based virtue theory is a very general form of pure virtue ethics in which motivational states are the most basic bearers of moral value and the moral properties of persons, acts, and states of affairs are defined in terms of the goodness and badness of motives. I outlined the way to give these definitions in section 9.2. DM theory makes the motives of one being in particular the primary bearer of moral value, and that is God. The complete theory can still make the goodness of human motives the primary bearer of moral value in a universe of human persons, human acts, and the states of affairs encountered by human beings. But the goodness of human motives needs to be explained since we humans are quite clearly imperfect in our nature and the goodness of our motives is never pure.

God has such virtues as justice, benevolence, mercy, forgiveness, kindness, love, compassion, loyalty, generosity, trustworthiness, integrity, and wisdom. God does not have courage, temperance, chastity, piety, nor perhaps humility, nor does he have faith or hope. Each of the virtues in the latter group involve handling emotions that are distinctive of limited and embodied creatures like ourselves. Sexual feelings make no sense when applied to a disembodied being, and since God does not have to deal with fear, the awareness of inferiority to a superior being, the sense of powerlessness, or the need for faith in God, which is to say, himself, it does not make sense to say that God has the virtues in this category. That means that God's virtues correspond to only some of the traits we consider human virtues. Of course, it does not follow that God's virtues are limited to these traits. It would be presumptuous of us to think that all divine virtues are perfections of human traits. If there are angels, God's virtues no doubt include perfections of angelic virtues, and if there are any other moral creatures in existence, God's virtues would include the perfections of the virtues of those beings as well. This position is expressed by Aquinas as follows:

> For just as God's being is universally perfect, in some way or other containing within itself the perfection of all beings, so also must his goodness in some way or other contain within itself the goodness of all things. Now a virtue is a goodness belonging to a virtuous person, for "it is in accordance with it that one is called good, and what one does is called good" [NE 1106a22–4]. Therefore, in its own way the divine goodness must contain all virtues. (SCG I. 92.768)[16]

But how are we to understand what it means for God to "contain" all the virtues, even those I have already agreed God does not have—virtues like chastity, humility, and courage? And how can the virtues that God does have give us any practical guidance in the moral life? The answer, I suggest, is that we humans ought to think of DM theory in conjunction with the doctrines of the Trinity and the Incarnation. The arguments in natural theology about the nature of God do not pertain to Christ, the Incarnate Son of God. Christ did have the virtues of chastity, humility, and courage, as well as all the other virtues humans ought to develop, so the virtues of Christ were "contained" in the nature of God in the way that Christ is contained in God according to the doctrines of the Trinity and the Incarnation. That means that these important Christian doctrines have a special place in the metaphysics of Christian morals. The Incarnation also helps us to resolve the practical problem of how we learn to be moral since we are called to develop the virtues by the imitation of Christ.

The idea that humans should become as much like God as is humanly possible is the basis of the primary ethical doctrine of the Hebrew Bible, that of *imitatio Dei*.[17] "Thee shall be holy, for I the Lord your God am holy" (Lev. 19:2) To become like God is to follow God's commands: "The Lord will establish you for a holy people unto Himself, as He has sworn unto you; if you shall keep the commandments of the Lord your God, and walk in His ways" (Deut. 28:9). The focus of Christian ethics, in contrast, is less on following divine commands than on imitating the virtues of Christ, and the focus of the New Testament is primarily on the motivational component of these virtues. We see Jesus in a variety of human circumstances that produce recognizable human emotions, including temptation, weariness, anxiety, sadness, and anger. Jesus makes very few commands, but when he does, his injunctions generally call us to have motivations (emotion-dispositions) that I claim are the basic components of virtues, as in the Beatitudes and the two great commandments of love. The New Testament does not typically call us to will, but to be motivated in a virtuous way, so St. Paul says, "Owe no one anything but to love one another" (Romans 13:8). The Golden Rule appeals to a motive, not to a volition. We imagine how we would want to be treated and imaginatively project our own wants onto others. This leads us to have an emotional response to other persons that motivates our treatment of them. Our motive for loving and forgiving is not that we are to follow God's commands, but that God himself loves and forgives. And we see that there is no limit on the forgiveness of injuries because it corresponds to God's forgiveness of us, not because it will win over the offender or because God wills it (Matt. 18:21ff). The same point applies to the call, "Be perfect even as your heavenly father is perfect" (Matt. 5:48).

Many Christian ethicists have worked on basing ethics on the imitation of Christ. Much of this work uses the narrative approach to ethics, and my purpose is not to duplicate it, but to show how this approach can be combined with the theoretical structure I have outlined here to produce a theory that is both theoretically powerful and practically useful. In addition to narrative ethics, many Christian ethicists have produced careful and subtle elucidations of the individual virtues based on Scripture and the Christian tradition of veneration of the saints. Here also I neither intend nor am able to duplicate this work, which has been done very well by others, but to show how the philosopher's theoretical urge can be formulated in a way that combines naturally with these other approaches to Christian ethics.

9.5. Advantages of Divine Motivation theory over Divine Command theory

DM theory is structurally parallel to DC theory in that DM theory makes moral properties derivative from God's motives, whereas DC theory makes moral properties derivative from God's will. In this section I will briefly compare the two theories to show how DM theory avoids the well-known problems of DC theory and has some decided advantages.

DC theory makes the divine will the source of moral value. Roughly, good states of affairs are what God wills to exist; bad states of affairs are what God wills not to exist. The focus of the theory, however, is generally on the rightness and wrongness of human acts. An act is morally required (a duty) just in case God commands us to do it; an act is morally wrong just in case God forbids us to do it. Since a divine command is the expression of God's will with respect to human and other creaturely acts, the divine will is the fundamental source of the moral properties of acts as well as of states of affairs.

The nature of the relation between God's commands and moral requirements is an important issue for DC theorists. To say that "x is morally required" just *means* "*x* is commanded by God" is too strong since that has the consequence that to say "*x* is right because God commands it" is a mere tautology; it is just to say "*x* is commanded by God because *x* is commanded by God." On the other hand, to say that God's commands and moral requirements are extensionally equivalent is too weak. That is compatible with the lack of any metaphysical connection whatever between the existence of moral properties and God's will. DC theory, then, aims at something in between identity of meaning and mere extensional equivalence. It should turn out that God's will *makes* what's good to be good and what's right to be right. States of affairs are good/bad and acts are right/wrong *because of* the will of God. God's will is the metaphysical ground of all moral properties. This is also the sense in which God's motives ground moral value in DM theory.

An important objection to DC theory goes back to Plato's *Euthyphro*, where Socrates asks, "Is what is holy holy because the gods approve it, or do they approve it because it is holy?" (10a). As applied to DC theory, this question produces a famous dilemma: If God wills the good because it is good, then goodness is independent of God's will and the latter does not explain the former. On the other hand, if something is good because God wills it, then it looks as if the divine will is arbitrary. God is not constrained by any moral reason from willing anything whatever, and it is hard to see how any non-moral reason could be the right sort of reason to determine God's choice of what to make good or bad. The apparent consequence is that good/bad and right/wrong are determined by an arbitrary divine will. God could have commanded cruelty or hatred, and if he had done so, cruel and hateful acts would have been right, even duties. This is not only an unacceptable consequence for our sense of the essentiality of the moral properties of acts of certain kinds, but it also makes it hard to see how it can be true that God himself is good in any important, substantive sense of good.

Robert Adams (1979) has attempted to address this problem by modifying DC theory to say that the property of rightness is the property of being commanded by a *loving* God. This permits Adams to allow that God could command cruelty for its own sake, but if God did so he would not love us, says Adams, and if that were the case, he argues, morality would break down. Morality is dependent upon divine commands, but they are dependent upon the commands of a deity with a certain nature. If God's nature were not loving, morality would fall apart.

But even if Adams's proposal succeeds at answering the objection it is designed to address, it seems to me that it is unsatisfactory because it is ad hoc. There is no intrinsic connection between a command and the property of being loving, so to tie morality to the commands of a loving God is to tie it to two distinct properties of God. In DM theory, however, there is no need to solve the problem of whether God could make it right that we brutalize the innocent by making any such modification to the theory since being loving is one of God's essential motives. The right thing for humans to do is to act on motives that imitate the divine motives. Brutalizing the innocent is not an act that expresses a motive that imitates the divine motives. Hence, it is impossible for brutalizing the innocent to be right as long as (i) it is impossible for such an act to be an expression of a motive that is like the motives of God, and (ii) it is impossible for God to have different motives. (ii) follows from the highly plausible assumption that God's motives are part of his nature.

DC theory also can argue that God's will is part of his nature, and Eleonore Stump and Norman Kretzmann (1985) have used the Thomistic doctrine of divine simplicity, which has the consequence that God's will is identical with his nature, to solve both the arbitrariness problem and the problem that God could command something like cruelty.[18] This solution is not ad hoc, but it requires argument to make the needed connection between the divine will and the divine nature. That is because a will is logically separable from its possessor in a way that motives are not. In fact, the feature of a will that led to the theory of the existence of a will in the first place—namely, its freedom—is the very feature that seems to have that consequence. In contrast, God's love, mercy, justice, compassion, etc., make God what he is. There is no need to overcome by argument a prior expectation that God's motives are dissociated from his nature as in the case of God's commands. The arbitrariness problem may or may not be answerable in a DC theory, but the problem does not even arise in DM theory. That is because a will needs a reason, but a motive *is* a reason. The will, according to Aquinas, always chooses "under the aspect of good," which means that reasons are not inherent in the will itself. In contrast, motives provide not only the impetus to action, but the reason *for* the action. If we know that God acts from a motive of love, there is no need to look for a further reason for the act. On the other hand, a divine command requires a reason, and if the reason is or includes fundamental divine motivational states such as love, it follows that even DC theory needs to refer to God's motives to avoid the consequence that moral properties are arbitrary and God himself is not good. Such a move makes divine motives more basic than the divine will, even in DC theory.

Aside from DC's difficulty with these objections, DM theory has an important theoretical advantage. DM theory gives us a unitary theory of all evaluative properties, divine as well as human, whereas DC theory does not. DC theory is most naturally interpreted as an ethics of law, a divine deontological theory, wherein the content of the law is promulgated by divine commands. God's own goodness and the rightness of God's own acts, however, are not connected to divine commands. In contrast, DM theory makes the features of the divine nature in virtue of which God is morally good the foundation for the moral goodness of those same features in creatures. Both divine and human goodness are explained in terms of good motives, and the goodness of human motives is derived from the goodness of the divine motives. DM theory, then, is a virtue theory that applies to both divine and human moral properties.

We have already seen another feature of DM theory that gives it an advantage over DC theory, and that is that DM theory shows the importance of Christology for ethics, whereas DC theory does not. DC theory ignores the doctrines of the Trinity and the Incarnation, focusing on the will of the Creator-God as the source of moral value. It is, in effect, an Old Testament theory. The features of Christian ethics that derive from the life of Christ do not appear in the theory, at least not in any straightforward way. The fact that DM theory integrates these features into the theory makes it theologically preferable, as well as easier to apply.

Elsewhere (Zagzebski 1996b, 1997) I have argued that DM theory, like DC theory, has the resources to solve some important puzzles in natural theology: the paradoxes of perfect goodness and the logical problem of evil. I will not review these arguments here, but if they work, they point to an advantage that both DM and DC theory have over other theories. If DM theory also has the advantages over DC theory I have mentioned here, that suggests that a strong case could be made for DM theory. I will undertake a full defense of the theory in a longer project.[19]

Notes

1. Bernard Williams (1985) argues that we ought to jettison moral theorizing because it takes away the knowledge needed in ordinary moral practice. Ethical theorizing has been rejected for other reasons as well. See S. G. Clarke and E. Simpson (1989) for a collection of papers on anti-theory in ethics. (As I edit this paper in 2021, I am struck by the degree to which anti-theory has faded from moral discourse.)
2. But Julia Annas (1993, 441) argues that in ancient ethics there is no such thing as a substantial notion of the natural that is not dependent upon holding certain moral theses to be true.
3. See, for example, Leroy S. Rouner (1997).
4. See Annas (1993). For a good collection of essays on happiness in ethics, see Stephen Engstrom and Jennifer Whiting (1996).
5. Some of these questions are usually considered meta-ethical. I do not believe in the independence of meta-ethics from normative ethics. I think that a complete ethical theory, whether or not it is a virtue theory, should include answers to these questions.
6. Previous to this paper, I outlined motivation-based virtue theory in Zagzebski (1996a), Part II.
7. Cf. Dietrich von Hildebrand's claim that moral values necessarily presuppose a person in von Hildebrand (1953), 169.

8. Compare Robert C. Roberts' (1998) definition of an emotion as a "concern-based construal." I agree with Roberts that some aspect of the world is construed to be such-and-such in an emotional state. I add the suggestion that the such-and-such is a concept of the type listed earlier. These concepts are or include what Bernard Williams calls thick ethical concepts, but I will not discuss this part of my theory of emotion here. I pursue that question in Zagzebski (2003).
9. One of the problems in discussing motives is that our vocabulary about emotions and virtues is rather limited. Sometimes we have no word for an emotion that is a component of a particular virtue or vice when we have a word for the virtue or vice itself. This is probably the case with courage and cowardice, fairness and unfairness. On the other hand, sometimes the word for the virtue or vice is borrowed from the word for the component emotion. This is probably the case with benevolence, compassion, cruelty, kindness, and many others.
10. The definition of duty that I proposed in Zagzebski (1996a) and in this paper in its original form defined duty as what a virtuous person (a *phronimos*) would do. I decided that the definition had to be strengthened in Zagzebski (2017b), where a definition of duty close to the one I have given here appears on page 196.
11. A bad state of affairs can also be defined as one that a good motive would attempt to prevent or to eliminate, and a good state of affairs can be defined as one that a bad motive would attempt to prevent or to eliminate. I use this way of defining good and bad states of affairs in Zagzebski 1996b and in Zagzebski 2017a, reprinted as chapters 4 and 6 of this collection.
12. "Undesirable" is probably too weak a word to apply to what we think is truly repulsive, but I know of no more appropriate word.
13. This raises questions about what counts as perfect success. Is it the highest possible number of successes? That would lead to paradoxes. I think we can at least say that it is impossible for God to try and fail. God's perfect compassion means at least that whenever he attempts to act compassionately, he succeeds in his aim.
14. See Norman Kretzmann (1997) for a detailed commentary on Aquinas's natural theology. The translation to which I refer appears in chapter 8.
15. I thank Norman Kretzmann for suggesting this line of reply to the objection that nothing is good for God.
16. Translation by Norman Kretzmann, quoted in Kretzmann (1997), 251.
17. For a description of the *imitatio Dei* in the Hebrew Scriptures, see Menachem Kellner (1991), 84.
18. See also Stump and Kretzmann (1988) for the same view.
19. I subsequently explained and defended Divine Motivation Theory in a book-length project (Zagzebski 2004a), and later presented the general secular form of a theory of this kind in Zagzebski (2017b).

10
The Incarnation and Virtue Ethics (2002)

10.1. Can there be a distinctively Christian Ethical theory?

Christian ethics purports to center on the life of Christ, but little of it actually does so. Perhaps the approach that comes the closest in recent years is narrative ethics.[1] This technique is easily adapted to the use of the Gospels as vehicles of moral instruction, but it has usually been offered as an alternative to theory. In my view, ethical theory serves an important purpose and it is premature to reject it. Nonetheless, it is difficult to harmonize any kind of theory with a Christocentric ethics. That is because theories are systems of concepts, not descriptions of persons or stories about them. Christian thinkers no doubt agree that Jesus Christ was paradigmatically good, but when this belief is incorporated into a theory, it too often amounts to nothing more than secular ethics plus an example. Even when Christian philosophers promote an explicitly theistic theory, they have traditionally adopted either a form of Divine Command theory or a form of Natural Law theory. In both theories the incarnation is at best peripheral and neither is distinctively Christian. Both are simply monotheistic.[2]

If the incarnation had a moral purpose other than the atonement, one would expect it to be given a central place in Christian ethics, and indeed, in Christian ethical theory. But it appears that we are caught in a dilemma. If a Christian ethical theory is really Christian, it is not really a theory; if a Christian ethical theory is really a theory, it is not really Christian.

In this chapter I shall propose a formal framework for an ethical theory that makes the incarnation central to the theory and the imitation of Christ the basic normative idea. The formal framework may be called exemplarism. I will then give a sketch of a particular form of exemplarist virtue theory that I call Divine Motivation theory.

Before proceeding further, there are two matters that need to be addressed, at least briefly. First, why not embrace a form of narrative ethics that eschews theory? Second, why think that the incarnation had a moral purpose other than atonement for the Fall? And even if it did, why think that that purpose should be given a central place in Christian ethics?

To begin, it should be admitted that while most human beings care about living an ethical life, the theorizing urge is far from universal. A theory is an abstract structure that aims to simplify and systematize a complex area of life or field of inquiry. Ethical theory attempts to impose order on the moral life, but moral phenomena are so complicated and diverse and have so many different purposes, that the price we pay for the order we get from theory is bound to be a certain amount of distortion. Our moral beliefs and practices are simply not as rational and coherent as we would like to think, and any attempt to pretend otherwise is bound to miss some important subtleties in our practices. For example, Bernard Williams (1981a) and Thomas Nagel (1979) have illustrated the ways in which we both tolerate and do not tolerate moral luck.[3] Some moral intuitions move us to attempt to eliminate luck from the moral realm, but a theory that eliminates luck entirely will be incompatible with important intuitions undergirding our practices. Equally important is the work of moral particularists who argue that what the abstraction necessary for theory leaves behind is often what is most important. What makes one individual person or set of circumstances different from any other can sometimes make a moral difference. When that difference is abstracted, we lose what we might better have preserved. The cost of theoretical purity may therefore be a certain degree of error, and the loss of a certain kind of subtlety. It is very hard to retain that subtlety without stories. That is the advantage of narrative ethics.

There is no doubt, then, that theory has its limitations, but it also has some impressive advantages. Theory compensates for the finitude of the human mind. We are not capable of comprehending the whole of reality, and we are not even capable of comprehending very much at any one time. Abstraction sacrifices detail for the sake of giving us greater scope. Theory leaves behind the richness of detail, but it reveals structures that the details cover up. It is not necessary to understand these structures to be a morally good person; the purpose of theory is not moral training. Rather, the philosophical theorist's aim is to satisfy an intellectual desire, the desire to understand. Understanding is greater the more extensive the grasp. What we aim to achieve in ethical understanding is the grasp of the whole of value and everything related to it. But we can never achieve that state if all we have to work with is stories. There is a reason why metaphysics was invented, and philosophical ethics was invented for the same reason. We want a map of ethical reality.

Theory is valuable, but I believe that a moral theory that is Christian in any important way must refer to the person of Jesus Christ and the stories about his life, particularly as they are found in the Gospels. And the reference to Christ ought to be an essential aspect of the theory. Christ is not just the instantiation of a set of virtues and his life an illustration of a set of general principles. If that were the case, someone else could have filled the role instead. This raises the second preliminary issue mentioned earlier. Should Christians think of the incarnation as a central event in human moral awakening, or was its purpose limited to the atonement for sin?

For Anselm, the incarnation was a drastic move in response to human sin. It was not part of the original divine plan, and its primary purpose was the atonement. In the thirteenth century Robert Grosseteste rejected Anselm's view, contending that God would have become incarnate even if the human race had not fallen. The incarnation would have perfected the human race and all creation because it would have been a manifestation of divine goodness, wisdom, and power.[4] Notice that the aims Grosseteste identifies are not moral ones. God would have become incarnate for the sake of the order and excellence of the universe, not for the purpose of being a moral exemplar. (Presumably the latter purpose is not as lofty as metaphysical order.) Bonaventure was sympathetic with both positions and declared both to be defensible, but decided that it was more consonant with piety to regard the incarnation mainly as a remedy for sin.[5]

Aquinas concurred.[6] However, Scotus enthusiastically adopted the view that God would have become incarnate even if Adam had not sinned. The hypostatic union is a proximate means for enlarging the trinitarian community of co-lovers, and this was settled by God prior (in the explanatory order) to the Fall and God's foreknowledge of the Fall. Scotus's reason for rejecting the Anselmian/Thomistic position is particularly interesting. If the incarnation were motivated only by the sin of Adam, he said, then the best thing God does in creation would be motivated by the worst thing creatures do, and that would be irrational.[7]

In the Hebrew Bible it is clear that humans are made in the image of the one God, and the basic moral doctrine is the *imitatio Dei*, to become as much like God as is humanly possible. "You shall be holy, for I the Lord your God am holy" (Lev. 19: 2). In the Hebrew Scriptures we do not become like God by modeling ourselves on him, which we cannot do, but by following his commandments. The incarnation shifts the ethical direction. Christ is the Word made flesh, the perfect revelation of the Father, which means that to the Christian, God is most perfectly revealed in a person, not in a set of commandments or any written or spoken words, although Jesus says he comes to fulfill the law, not to destroy it (Matt. 5:17). Through him we have access to the Father and come to share in the divine nature (Eph. 1:9). In the Letter to the Philippians, Paul says, "In your minds you must be the same as Christ Jesus" (2:5). Throughout the New Testament the motive for imitation is that what we are imitating is the love that we have already received. Love is naturally imitative. "We love because he first loved us" (1 John 4:18).

In the second century, Irenaeus tells us how the image of God is shown through the incarnation, so that the *imitatio Dei* of the Hebrew Scriptures is dramatically deepened:

> The truth of this was shown when the Word of God became man, assimilating Himself, so that, by His resemblance to the Son, man might become precious

to the Father. For in times past it was *said* that man was made in the image of God, but not *shown*, because the Word, in whose image man was made, was still invisible. That is why man lost the likeness so easily. But when the Word of God was made flesh, He confirmed both things: He showed the true image, when He Himself became what His image was; and He restored and made fast the likeness, making man like the invisible Father through the visible Word. (*Adversus Haereses* 5. 16.2)[8]

Irenaeus may have been the first Christian theologian to propose a moral purpose for the incarnation in addition to the atonement:

> There was no other way by which we could learn the things of God than for our Teacher, who is the Word, to become man. No other could have revealed to us the secrets of the Father, none but the Father's very own Word. "For who (else) has known the mind of the Lord, or who has been His counsellor?" (cf. Rom. 11: 34). Again, there was no other way for us to learn than to see our Teacher and hear His voice with our own ears. It is by becoming imitators of His actions and doers of His words that we have communion with Him. It is from Him who has been perfect from before all creation that we, so lately made, receive fulfilment. (*Adversus Haereses* 5. 1. 1)[9]

Near the other end of the spectrum of Christian history, Dietrich Bonhoeffer (1995) argues that our primary task is to recognize that we are reconciled with God. We need a metamorphosis, a complete inward transmutation of our previous form, a "renewing of mind" (Rom. 12:2), a "walking as children of light" (Eph. 5:8). This metamorphosis of man can only be the overcoming of the form of the fallen man, Adam, and conformation with the form of the new man, Christ (42). Bonhoeffer writes:

> The will of God, therefore, is not an idea, still demanding to become real; it is itself a reality already in the self-revelation of God in Jesus Christ.... After Christ has appeared, ethics can have but one purpose, namely, the achievement of participation in the reality of the fulfilled will of God. But this participation, too, is possible only in virtue of the fact that I myself am already included in the fulfilment of the will of God in Christ, which means that I am reconciled with God. (1995, 209)

Bonhoeffer does not speak of the "imitation" of Christ, but of "conforming" to Christ since Christ is the one who initiates our metamorphosis. This difference is important, but for my purpose here it suffices to notice that Bonhoeffer's view shares the fundamental point of the imitation literature: The Christian's primary moral aim is to be like a certain person.

I find it reasonable to conclude that the purpose of the incarnation was not only to atone for the sin of Adam and Eve, but it was also to give us a perfect moral exemplar. It is arguable whether there would have been an incarnation in the absence of the Fall, but even if there would not have been, it does not follow that the purpose of the actual incarnation was limited to the atonement. Furthermore, even if the revelation of the perfect human in God incarnate was not part of the *purpose* of the incarnation, it nonetheless did have that effect, and the effect is powerful and significant. The imitation of Christ is therefore not just an accidental feature of Christian piety, but is central to the Christian's attempt to live a moral life.

10.2. Exemplarism

There are not many ways to go about defining something when we do not pretend to know what it really is. However, there is one way of doing so that has become important in contemporary philosophy of language. In fact, a similar technique was arguably used by Aristotle. In the 1970s, Saul Kripke (1980), Hilary Putnam (1975), and others proposed a way of defining natural kind terms that became known as the theory of direct reference. Leaving aside differences among the versions of the theory, the idea was that a natural kind such as *water* or *gold* or *human* should be defined as whatever is the same kind of thing or stuff as some indexically identified instance. For example, they proposed that gold is, roughly, whatever is the same element as *that*, water is whatever is the same liquid as *that*, a human is whatever is a member of the same species as *that*, and so on. In each case the demonstrative term "that" refers to an entity to which the person doing the defining refers directly, typically by pointing. Subsequently, the theory was applied to terms other than natural kind terms, including terms for theoretical entities.

One of the main reasons for proposing definitions like this was that Kripke and Putnam believed that often we do not know the nature of the thing we are defining, and yet we know how to construct a definition that links up with its nature. Some of us may not know the nature of gold, and for millennia nobody knew its nature, but that did not prevent people from defining "gold" in a way that fixed the reference of the term and continued to do so after its nature was discovered. In fact, when we say that the nature of gold was "discovered," that implies that modern speakers are knowledgeable about the nature of the same stuff of which pre-modern speakers were ignorant. The theory of direct reference permits the referent of the word "gold" to remain invariant after it was discovered what makes gold what it is. If "gold" did not refer to the same thing both before and after such a discovery, it is hard to see how we could claim that there is *something* about which the discovery was made.

This proposal began a revolution in semantics because it meant that competent speakers of the language can use terms to successfully refer to the right things without going through a descriptive meaning. Gold is not whatever satisfies a certain description, nor is water. A natural kind term is associated with a descriptive *stereotype*, according to Putnam, but the stereotype is not part of the meaning of the term, and it can be mistaken. It is important that the stereotype be revisable, whereas the referent of the terms remains invariant. An important consequence of this theory is that it is not necessary that speakers associate descriptions with natural kind terms, and it is even possible that they succeed in referring to water and gold when they associate the wrong descriptions with terms like "water" and "gold."[10] What is required instead is that they be related by a chain of communication to the actual stuff: water and gold.[11] It is not even necessary that every speaker be able to identify water and gold reliably themselves as long as some speakers in the community can do so and the other speakers rely on the judgment of the experts. This point led to an important feature of Putnam's version of the theory: the division of linguistic labor. According to Putnam, non-specialists can successfully refer to the kind in question because they are part of a linguistic community some of whose members can reliably pick out instances of the kind. Obviously, this is not as important for a kind like water, but for kinds like diamond and uranium it is crucial.

The theory of direct reference assumes that nature can be carved at the joints (to use Putnam's phrase), which means that nature must *have* joints at which it can be carved. The theory also assumes that human minds are naturally suited to notice the joints of nature, and when we make a demonstrative reference to a natural kind in the preceding definitions of natural kind terms, it is to those kinds that we intend to refer. This is important because reference is in principle indeterminate with respect to indefinitely many objects. For instance, our pointing gesture could be variously construed as referring to the surface of the water, the water plus the glass, the water and a portion of the air above it, the water at this moment only, and so on. Demonstrative reference to a natural kind is successful provided that it is natural for speakers to have the idea of a natural kind and to intend to refer to such a kind, and for others in the linguistic community to understand the intention and to interpret the ostensive reference appropriately.

A widely discussed consequence of the theory of direct reference is that there can be necessary, *a posteriori* truths. Kripke argued that since the reference of "water" is fixed by ostension, scientists can then discover the nature of water empirically. Since the nature of water is essential to it, it follows that certain necessary truths such as "water is H_2O" are known *a posteriori*. The process would proceed roughly as follows: (1) We know *a priori* that the deep structure of water is essential to it. (2) We discover *a posteriori* that the deep structure of water is its chemical constitution, H_2O. We conclude (3) it is essential to anything that is water that it is H_2O. We know (3) *a posteriori* because we cannot know (3) without empirical observation. If that is right, it means that the connection philosophers had accepted for centuries between the modal status of propositions and the way in which we know them is mistaken.

Let us now look carefully at the way Aristotle defined *phronesis*, or practical wisdom. I think we find a remarkably similar demonstrative procedure, but without the well-developed semantics of the theory of direct reference. Aristotle has quite a bit to say about what the virtue of *phronesis* consists in, but he clearly is not confident that he can give a full account of it. And what is more important for my purposes here, he apparently thinks that that is not a problem because we can pick out persons who are practically wise in advance of investigating the nature of *phronesis*. Although Aristotle does not say so explicitly, he seems to agree that the *phronimos* is a person *like that*, where we can make a demonstrative reference to a paradigmatically good person. That is, we can pick out paradigmatic instances of good persons in advance of our theorizing.[12]

I suggest that Aristotle was basically right about this. Just as competent speakers of English can successfully refer to water or gold and make assertions about it whether or not they know any chemistry, so can competent speakers successfully talk about practically wise persons. They can do this even though they can neither describe the properties in virtue of which somebody is a *phronimos* or even reliably identify the *phronimoi* in their community. But like "water," the term *phronesis* (or the English "practical wisdom") is something that each speaker associates with paradigm instances. The *phronimos* is a person *like that*, just as water is a substance *like that*.

If I am right about this, the traditional charge against Aristotle that his definition of *phronesis* is circular is misplaced. I suspect that Aristotle was attempting a way of defining *phronesis* directly, parallel to the way of defining "water" in the theory of direct reference. Perhaps Aristotle did not actually have this in mind, but he might have. At least, it seems to me to be consistent with Aristotle's exposition of *phronesis*, and, in any case, this interpretation aids his theory.

Like the use of direct reference in defining natural kind terms, the use of direct reference in defining "good person" or "practically wise person" makes certain assumptions. It assumes that what is good is natural, not conventional, and that our minds are equipped to notice the division of persons and things into good and bad. Like the stereotypes of natural kinds, there are no doubt also stereotypes of good persons that are subject to revision. There is also probably some room for a division of linguistic labor in that some people are better at identifying good persons than others (although it is unlikely that people will be as quick to defer to the "experts" on moral matters as they are on scientific matters).

Let us now return to the issue of what a moral theory is and how it should be constructed. A moral theory is a system of concepts. Some concepts in the theory are defined in terms of others. But unless we are willing to accept conceptual circularity, some concept or concepts will either be undefined or will refer to something outside the domain. Most moral philosophers have done the latter. The basic evaluative concept in their theory is defined in terms of something non-evaluative, typically human nature, rationality, or the will of God. The alternative I am suggesting is to anchor moral concepts in an exemplar. Good persons are persons like that, just as gold is stuff like that. The function of an exemplar is to fix the reference of the term "good person" or "practically wise person" without the use of any concepts, whether descriptive or non-descriptive. The exemplar therefore allows the series of conceptual definitions to get started. The circle of conceptual definitions of the most important concepts in a moral theory—*virtue, right act, duty, good outcome*, etc.—is broken by an indexical reference to a paradigmatically good person.

Making the exemplar a person has an even more important advantage than its aid to theory. If all the concepts in a formal ethical theory are rooted in a person, then narratives and descriptions of that person are morally significant. It is an open question what it is about the person that makes him or her good. When we say that water is whatever is the same liquid as the stuff in this glass, we are implicitly leaving open the question of what properties of the stuff in this glass are essential to its being water. For the same reason, when we say that a good person is a person like that, and we directly refer to St. Francis of Assisi, or to Mahatma Gandhi, or to Jesus Christ, we are implicitly leaving open the question of what properties of St. Francis, Gandhi, or Christ are essential to their goodness. Perhaps there are non-evaluative descriptions of these persons that are sufficient to determine their moral goodness; perhaps not. Perhaps their goodness is not determined by any descriptive properties we know how to apply, and we need to resort to narratives.[13] Perhaps the distinction between evaluative and non-evaluative properties is itself problematic.[14] The exemplarist approach has the advantage that none of these matters need to be settled at the outset. We need to observe the exemplar carefully to find out what the relevant properties are. Since narratives can be considered detailed and temporally extended observations of persons,[15] exemplarism gives narrative an important place within the theory itself. If I am right, then, we do not need to choose between theory and narrative ethics. This view commits me to the position that ethics is not purely *a priori*, but that is a reasonable view in any case. At least, I see no reason to think that ethics is any more *a priori* than the metaphysics of natural kinds. I find it fascinating to consider the possibility that if propositions such as "water is H_2O" are necessary *a posteriori*, there are also necessary *a posteriori* truths in ethics and that some of them are discovered in a way that parallels the discovery of the nature of water. Perhaps narratives serve a purpose in ethics analogous to scientific observation about natural kinds. Narratives might reveal necessary features of value by uncovering the deep properties of a good person.

10.3. Exemplarist virtue theory and the imitation of Christ

Ethical theory is concerned with at least three general objects of moral evaluation and the relations among them: acts (right, wrong, duty), persons (virtues and vices), and states of affairs (good and bad).[16] Usually one of these categories is taken as basic and the others evaluated in terms of the basic one. For example, some theorists maintain that persons have traits of character like kindness or unkindness because of their propensity to perform acts of a certain description. These theories make the moral properties of acts more basic than the moral properties of persons. Some of them also make the evaluation of acts more basic than that of states of affairs; others do not. So they may define the concepts of a right and wrong act in terms of the goodness and badness of the states of affairs those acts bring about (consequence-based), or they may instead treat the concepts of act evaluation as basic (act-based). Both kinds of theory differ from the type of theory according to which acts have moral properties in virtue of the fact that they are the sort of act that good or bad persons do. This kind of theory makes the moral properties of persons more basic than the moral properties of acts. That is what I mean by a virtue theory. In the most radical form of virtue theory, all moral properties derive from the property of being a good person or having a good personal trait, including the moral properties of states of affairs. There are, of course, many ways to structure a theory of this kind.[17]

In introducing exemplarism in the last section, I assumed that the moral exemplar is a person, but that is not actually required by the logic of exemplarism. If the only purpose of an exemplar is to break the circle of concepts in a moral theory, that can be done in any number of ways. If the theory is not foundationalist in structure and has no basic concept, then the circle can in principle be broken anywhere. If the theory does have a basic concept, as in the kinds of theory mentioned in the preceding paragraph, then the basic concept is the one that we would want to define by ostensive reference to an exemplar. An act-based or consequence-based theory could in principle use the exemplarist procedure I have described, but if we want the exemplarist approach to give a theoretical basis for the Christian idea of the imitation of Christ, the exemplar should be a person and the resulting theory will be a form of virtue theory.

There is another reason why we would want the exemplar to be a person apart from theological considerations. It is an advantage of a theory if it is practically useful. For that purpose, we need to take into consideration the facts of human behavioral learning. There is significant evidence in developmental psychology that human infants are born to learn through imitation and that the imitation mechanism is innate. It is critical during development and remains an important aspect of social interaction throughout life, and most behavior is acquired in this way. (Bandura 1971, 1986). Moreover, there is evidence that humans model not only overt behavior, but the attitudes and emotional reactions of others. These features of human learning make it desirable that the paradigmatic instance used in exemplarist moral theory be a person who can be imitated. Humans naturally imitate other persons, particularly admired other persons. There is plenty of evidence, then, that the Christian idea of the imitation of Christ is based on good behavioral psychology.

In an exemplarist virtue theory, all three of the categories of moral evaluation mentioned previously—personal traits, acts, and the states of affairs brought about by acts—would be defined by reference to the exemplar or exemplars identified by the theory. Good and bad traits of character are defined in terms of the traits of character of the exemplar. The moral properties of acts are defined in terms of the actual or hypothetical acts of the exemplar. Good and bad outcomes are defined in terms of the states of affairs the exemplar aims to bring about or to prevent. Clearly, this is a very general schema and it can be adapted to a number of different approaches to virtue ethics.

Traditional Aristotelian virtue ethics makes the concept of virtue dependent upon the more basic concept of *eudaimonia*—happiness or flourishing. *Eudaimonia* is in turn dependent upon the idea of human nature, understood as teleological. It is well known that one of the stumbling blocks to the acceptance of virtue ethics among modern philosophers is the worry that we will never get agreement on what constitutes *eudaimonia*, as well as doubts that human nature is teleological, and even radical doubts that there is any such thing as human nature at all. Exemplarist virtue theory has an advantage since it is not teleological in structure and does not refer to either *eudaimonia* or human nature. It is consistent with exemplarism that *what makes* an exemplar good is that he or she has traits that are constitutive of *eudaimonia* or that lead to the fulfillment of human nature, but the theory does not require that that be the case. To return to the analogue of natural kinds, we have discovered that what makes something water is that it is H_2O, but that has been settled by scientific investigation, not by the way "water" is defined. Similarly, it may turn out that what makes the exemplar good are certain descriptive properties or the fact that he or she leads a life of a certain kind or the fact that he or she fulfills the potentialities of human nature, but that need not be settled in advance of the construction of the theory. We need not refer to any of these features of the exemplar in defining "good person."

The particular form of exemplarist virtue theory that I have developed is what I call Divine Motivation theory. This theory is a form of a non-teleological virtue theory I call motivation-based, but it has a foundation in God's motives.

The main idea of motivation-based virtue theory is to derive all moral concepts from the concept of a good motive, where what I mean by a motive is an emotional state that initiates and directs action toward an end. A virtue is defined as an enduring trait consisting of a good motive-disposition and reliable success in reaching the end (if any) of the good motive. Moral properties of acts (right, wrong, duty) in a set of circumstances are defined in terms of what virtuous persons would characteristically do, would characteristically not do, or might do in relevantly similar circumstances. Good outcomes are defined in terms of the aims of good motives. The theory is exemplarist because the basic concept in the theory, that of a good motive, is defined via reference to the motives of a paradigmatically good person.

The structure of motivation-based virtue theory is quite general and it can have religious or secular forms, depending upon the identity of the paradigms. Divine Motivation theory is the Christian form of motivation-based virtue theory. It is motivation-based virtue theory with a foundation in God's motives. God is the paradigmatically good person in the theory. Value in all forms derives from God's motives. The paradigmatically good person is God. Value in all forms derives from God's motives. God's motives are perfectly good, and human motives are good insofar as they are like the divine motives as those motives would be expressed in finite and embodied beings.[18] Motive-dispositions are constituents of virtues. God's virtues are paradigmatically good personal traits. Human virtues are those traits that imitate God's virtues as they would be expressed by human beings in human circumstances. The goodness of a state of affairs is derivative from the goodness of the divine motive, not the other way around. So outcomes get their moral value by their relation to good and bad motivations. For example, a state of affairs is a merciful one or a compassionate one or a just one, because the divine motives that are constituents of mercy, compassion, and justice respectively aim at bringing them about. Finally, acts get their moral value from the acts that would, would not, or might be done by God in the relevant circumstances.

What can it mean to say that a human virtue is a trait God would have if he were human? What can it mean to say that a wrong act is an act God would never do if he were human and were in relevantly similar circumstances? What can it mean to say that a good state of affairs is one God would be motivated to bring about? We cannot expect a procedure for determining the answers to these questions, but we have a revelation of value in the incarnation. The life of Christ is a narrative that illuminates a point of view from which we can see a number of exemplary acts, and especially exemplary motives and the virtues of which they are constituents. The message of the Sermon on the Mount is a call to us to do the same, to transform our motives into a life of love and compassion.

Many Christian theologians and ethicists have written penetrating discussions of the Gospel narratives for the ethical viewpoint they reveal. I will not try to add anything to that work. My purpose here is to show that an ethics centered in Gospel narratives can be given a viable theoretical foundation that would be desirable even apart from the needs of Christian ethics. An exemplarist virtue theory is the only form of ethical theory I can think of that harmonizes well with an ethic of the imitation of Christ. The ultimate ground of moral value for all human motives, traits, acts, and aims is the motives, traits, acts, and aims of Christ. Divine Motivation theory requires the doctrine of the incarnation because the theory needs both a human exemplar to whom we can refer in moral discourse, and a divine metaphysical ground for value. The theory needs a God-man to serve both roles.

In the previous section I raised the possibility that we could find out necessary truths about the nature of good persons empirically for the same reason that we can find out necessary truths about the nature of water and gold empirically. In Divine Motivation theory (and in exemplarist virtue theory in general) the motivational structure of a good person is parallel to the chemical structure of water. It is a necessary truth that the motivational structure of a good person is the motivational structure of Christ, just as it is a necessary truth that the chemical structure of water is H_2O. Clearly, however, there are disanalogies between water and a good person that make my theory more complicated than a theory of natural kinds, since motivational structure is much more complex than chemical structure, and we permit many variations in the motivational structure of a good person, whereas we permit no variation at all in the chemical structure of water. That means that to imitate Christ is not to aim to be an exact copy of Christ. Another reason why imitation is not copying is that Jesus had a distinctive mission that the rest of us do not have. But each of us does have a mission, and each of us should try to be as faithful to it as Jesus was to his.

There are many ways to imitate Christ, and that is why there are so many different kinds of saints. Some saints exemplify one moral trait in an extraordinary degree, such as Mother Teresa. Others excel because of the overall quality of their character. They possess the full complement of virtues in a uniformly admirable life. These saints may not stand out for any particular admirable quality, but they are morally worthy in the whole of their lives. Others, such as St. Thomas More or Oskar Schindler, are exemplary because of a single noble decision. Which saints a person should imitate is probably determined partly by his or her life circumstances and partly by his or her individual personality. Of course, there are also exemplars in other religions, such as the Buddhist *arahant*, the Confucian sage, and the Jewish *tzaddik*.[19] I will not attempt here a discussion of moral pluralism and its challenge to Christian ethics, which is a problem no matter what kind of theory the Christian chooses, but it is worth pointing out that exemplarist virtue theory can have either an inclusivist or an exclusivist form. There is nothing in the structure of the theory itself that requires one rather than the other.

In traditional Christian philosophy it is taken for granted that in a very important sense God is the foundation of all value. God is good and everything that is good or bad is good or bad because of something about God. Acts derive their rightness or wrongness from God. This has most often been interpreted to mean that something is right or wrong because God commands it or forbids it. Divine Command theory has a very long history in Western ethics. In fact, its only serious rival among those who think ethics should have a theological foundation is Natural Law theory. But from what has already been said about the structure of a moral theory, I think we can see that both Divine Command theory and Natural Law theory presuppose something about ethical theory that is arguable: they assume that an ethical theory is a way of systematizing rules or principles for human action that have a law-like form. Both are act-based, not virtue-based theories. To return to the observations of Bonhoeffer, the will of God is not an idea waiting to become real; an ethic of law is that of the Old Testament. The law is fulfilled in the incarnation, and after Christ ethics has the purpose of achieving participation in the reality of the fulfilled will of God. That leads to an ethic of imitation rather than of law. This is not to deny the place of law in Christian virtue ethics. Divine commands have a place in Divine Motivation theory parallel to the place of laws and principles in any form of pure virtue theory: they are derivative. One of the things we see in imitating Christ is that Jesus was obedient to the Father; Jesus followed his Father's commandments. But the moral life of Jesus was not exhausted by the following of divine commands. He taught that the entire moral law can be summed up in the two great commandments of love—to love God with our whole hearts and to love our neighbor as ourselves, but even here the law is subsumed under the motive of love, and I think that that is significant.

10.4. The self versus the exemplar

Human beings have an innate propensity for imitation, but that does not mean imitation has been unchallenged as a method for learning the most important human behavior. Even if we can identify the morally best persons, some of us hesitate to model ourselves on them. The complaint is not that we do not want to be good and even as good as we can be, but that we want to be ourselves. In modern philosophy being oneself usually means making one's own decisions, making up one's own mind about what to do, perhaps even making up one's own mind about the kind of person one wants to be. That might mean consulting reason, but even then, it is one's own reason that one wants to consult. Iris Murdoch reminds us how riveting Kant is when he says that even when confronted with Christ, a man still consults his own reason:

> How recognizable, how familiar to us, is the man so beautifully portrayed in the *Grundlegung*, who confronted even with Christ turns away to consider the judgement of his own conscience and to hear the voice of his own reason. Stripped of the exiguous metaphysical background which Kant was prepared to allow him, this man is with us still, free, independent, lonely, powerful, rational, responsible, brave, the hero of so many novels and books of moral philosophy. (Murdoch, 1970, 101)

Is the man who consults his own reason when confronted with Christ a hero or an anti-hero? Dostoevsky's Grand Inquisitor is just such a man.[20] Murdoch believes that the center of this way of looking at ethics is the notion of the will as the creator of value. When a society that once embraced Divine Command theory gives up belief in God, values collapse into the human will. I am proposing the reverse move: keep God in value theory, but give up the idea that values are rooted in a will. Nonetheless, I want it to be clear that I know what the alternative is—and how attractive it is in its own way. But that way has been tried, and Murdoch's assessment of its subsequent history may temper our enthusiasm. Here is the continuation of the passage just quoted:

> The raison d'être of this attractive but misleading creature is not far to seek. He is the offspring of the age of science, confidently rational and yet increasingly aware of his alienation from the material universe which his discoveries reveal; and since he is not a Hegelian (Kant, not Hegel, has provided Western ethics with its dominating image), his alienation is without cure. He is the ideal citizen of the liberal state, a warning held up to tyrants. He has the virtue which the age requires and admires, courage. It is not such a very long step from Kant to Nietzsche, and from Nietzsche to existentialism and the Anglo-Saxon ethical doctrines which in some ways closely resemble it. In fact, Kant's man had already received a glorious incarnation nearly a century earlier in the work of Milton: his proper name is Lucifer.

I suggest we heed Murdoch's warning. Perhaps she overstates the consequences of adopting the Kantian imperative of making the will the center of value. But better to be like Christ than Lucifer.

Notes

1. For an overview of the use of narrative ethics in religious philosophy, see Robert C. Roberts (1997).
2. Theologians have also been criticized for failing to make their moral theologies Christocentric. Edward Vacek (1994, xvii) points out that James Gustafson has passionately and rightly criticized theologians for their failure to provide a theocentric ethic, yet his own critics argue that he does not provide a sufficiently Christian understanding of God.
3. In my paper "Religious Luck" (Chapter 8 of this volume), I argue that some Christian doctrines magnify the problem of moral luck, whereas others make it easier to handle. One of the attractions of Kant is his clear attempt to eliminate luck in the moral realm. Many Christian philosophers have found Kantian ethics appealing partly for this reason, yet John Hare (1996) has argued that a Kantian view of the moral demand, combined with a Christian view of human moral ineptitude, produces a gap that is irreparable without Christian doctrines of grace and salvation.
4. See discussion of these views by Marilyn McCord Adams (1999, 24).
5. Adams (1999), 27.
6. Aquinas, ST 3a 1. 3. Quoted in Adams (1999), 51.
7. Adams (1999), 69–70.
8. Quoted in H. U. von Balthasar (1990), 56.
9. Von Balthasar (1990), 57.
10. On one version of the theory, natural kind terms have no meaning; they are purely denotative (like John Stuart Mill's theory of proper names). On another version of the theory, natural kind terms have a meaning, but meanings are not in the head. That is, they are not something a speaker grasps and through which she finds the referent. See Putnam (1975).
11. In some versions of the theory, the chain is thought to be causal, originating with Kripke's proposal on the reference of proper names in *Naming and Necessity*. But the idea that the use of a term by many speakers is causally connected was not part of the original theory and in fact was not endorsed by Kripke.
12. Aristotle treats the *phronimos* as a person to whom others would go for advice, and those persons are identified through the community. Since Aristotle thinks that the virtue of *phronesis* is both a necessary and sufficient condition for having the moral virtues, the truly phronetic person will always be paradigmatically good as well as paradigmatically practically wise.
13. "Resort" may be an unfair word because it suggests that narratives are something we appeal to as a last resort, and I do not mean to imply that. But I do think that narratives are harder to handle than descriptions. There is a good reason why our language developed thick descriptive terms like "courageous," "compassionate," and "haughty." It saves a lot of time.
14. I argue for this in Zagzebski (2003).
15. The narrative of internal consciousness is a modern invention, and one we could not expect to get out of Gospel narratives. The latter are closer to third-person observations.

16. John Rawls (1974–1975) proposes something similar to this as a way of classifying ethical theories. Gary Watson (1990) pursues the idea in the attempt to show what virtue theory would have to be like in order to be a distinctively different kind of theory. I examine Watson's argument in *Divine Motivation Theory* (2004a), chapter 1.
17. I examine some alternatives in *Divine Motivation Theory* (2004a), chapter. 1. In *Virtues of the Mind* (1996a) I outline two forms of pure virtue theory, one happiness-based, the other motivation-based.
18. In my view a motive is an emotional state and God has emotions. But Divine Motivation theory does not require accepting the controversial position that God has emotions. It suffices to say that God's motives are related to human emotions analogously. God has emotions in the same sense in which he has beliefs. I explore the issue of God's emotions and virtues in "The Virtues of God and the Foundations of Ethics," Chapter 9 of this volume.
19. See Robert M. Adams (1984) for a defense of the category of saints.
20. I thank Eberhard Hermann for reminding me how the Grand Inquisitor fits Kant's description of the autonomous man in the passage mentioned in the preceding quotation.

V
OMNISUBJECTIVITY

11
The Attribute of Omnisubjectivity
(2013, 2016)

11.1. Introduction

One of the most important events in the history of philosophy was the modern discovery of subjectivity. What I mean by subjectivity is consciousness as it is experienced by the individual subject. Beginning with Descartes, there arose the idea that philosophical problems of all kinds look interestingly different if we start from the viewpoint of the individual subject rather than from an alleged objective viewpoint outside any person's consciousness. But subjectivity raises its own problems. One is the issue of how one person's conscious experiences can be grasped by someone else. There are ways to investigate a conscious experience from an outside perspective, or at least, there are ways to describe it, as I am beginning to do now. But what is distinctive about subjectivity is that it is consciousness from the inside perspective. Since the subject's point of view is intrinsic to it, no one else can grasp it without "seeing through their eyes," as we sometimes say.

I will argue that the existence of subjectivity requires an addition to the traditional attributes of God. I call the attribute *omnisubjectivity*. It is the property of consciously grasping with perfect accuracy and completeness every conscious state of every conscious creature from that creature's first-person perspective—the perspective of *I*. I will use the analogy of empathy to defend the possibility of omnisubjectivity. I will argue that given the existence of conscious beings in the universe, omnisubjectivity is entailed by such traditional attributes as omniscience and omnipresence, and it is implied by traditional practices of prayer, but as far as I know, it is not explicitly addressed in theological writing on prayer and contemplation. In fact, I do not know of anyone else who has discussed this attribute.[1] I will conclude by using the idea of one person's grasp of another person's subjectivity to give a possible explanation of the differences in the consciousness of the Persons of the Trinity.

11.2. Omniscience and subjectivity

Subjectivity can be understood in a number of different ways. In one of its senses, it is the feature of consciousness that allows us to say that there is such a thing as *what it is like* to have a conscious experience of a certain kind—what it is like to see the color red, what it is like to taste chocolate, what it is like to sense like a bat, what it is like to feel fear, and so on. Thomas Nagel (1974) gets the credit for calling our attention to subjectivity in this sense in his well-known essay, "What Is It like to Be a Bat?" This sense of subjectivity raises the problem of how a being can know what it is like to have conscious experiences that it cannot have. It would seem that only a bat can know what it is like to be a bat. A person blind from birth cannot know what it is like to see color. In fact, we can go farther and say that even creatures who *can* see color do not know what it is like to see color if they have never seen color. That was one of the points of Frank Jackson's (1986) famous thought experiment about Mary. In that story we imagine that Mary has lived all her life in a black-and-white room and has never seen a single colored object. All her education comes from black and white videos and books. Yet we also imagine that Mary knows everything there is to know about the physical world. There is no physical fact she does not know. But Jackson concludes that she does not know everything there is to know because when she leaves her black-and-white room and sees in color for the first time, she finds out something she did not know before. She finds out *what it is like* to see in color. Knowing what it is like to see in color is something that cannot be known descriptively. She knew complete descriptions of colored objects and human perception before. So even though Mary always was human, and hence was the kind of being who can see in color, she did not previously know what it is like to see in color because she had not yet experienced seeing color.[2]

The existence of subjectivity raises a further possibility. Maybe nobody but me sees exactly what I see when I see a red object at a particular time. Maybe nobody but me tastes exactly what I taste when I take a bite of a chocolate torte. Maybe nobody but me is in a state exactly like the state I am in when I feel anxious about a deadline. If so, how can anybody else know what it is like to have my conscious experiences? Even if they have felt something similar to the anxiety I feel, they do not know exactly what it is like *for me* to feel the anxiety I feel unless they have felt something identical to my feeling. And of course, the same point applies to any conscious state. Talking about an imaginary person who has never seen color is just a dramatic way to make the point that a person must have been in a conscious state of a certain kind in order to know what it is like to be in such a state. What you feel when you feel anxious or cheerful or indignant or serene might be similar to feelings I have had, but if there are any differences, I cannot know exactly what it is like to have your feelings, and you cannot know exactly what it is like to have mine.

I am sure you can see how this problem applies to God. How can a divine being know what it is like to be one of his creatures? No traditional Christian denies that God knows all the objective facts about his creation. God knows of every true proposition that it is true, and of every false proposition that it is false, and he knows it with the greatest possible clarity and precision. The problem is that knowing all the facts about his creatures is not enough to know everything there is to know about his creatures because there is more to know about them than the facts. Having conscious states is a feature of conscious beings, perhaps the most important feature. If God knows everything, he must know the subjective part of his creation as well as the objective facts. He must know what it is like to see in color. But like Mary, it seems that he cannot know what it is like to see in color unless he sees in color or has seen color in the past.[3] Likewise, he cannot know what it is like to taste chocolate, feel anxiety, and so on, unless he himself has had the conscious experience of tasting chocolate, feeling anxiety, and all the rest of the conscious states experienced by creatures. Even worse, if there are differences between different creatures in their sensations of color or their emotions or moods or other conscious states, it seems that God cannot know with complete accuracy what it is like to be in the conscious states of his creatures without having had conscious states exactly like those of each one of his creatures.

Some philosophers will respond that this is not a problem for God's *knowledge* because knowledge is directed at propositions, and so long as God grasps the truth value of all propositions, God is omniscient. There is nothing left to be known. This response does not solve the problem; it merely requires that it be reformulated. I do not insist that what God would lack if he lacked a grasp of what it is like to have the conscious experiences of his creatures is knowledge. The crucial point is that he would lack something, and what he would lack is cognitive. He would not fully cognitively grasp everything that happens in his creation. Each of us cognitively grasps what it is like to be in the conscious states we are in right now, and those states are parts of the created world. If God does not grasp those states and grasp them as well as we do, God is not cognitively perfect. As Aquinas says, "Even the Philosopher considered it absurd that anything cognized by us should be uncognized by God" (ST Ia.14.11). Hence, if God is cognitively perfect, he must grasp what it is like to be his creatures and to have each and every one of their experiences. I will argue that the attribute of omnisubjectivity solves this problem.

There is another reason that subjectivity may make it impossible for one person to know the consciousness of another, even if the qualitative aspects of their sensations and emotions are the same. Some philosophers maintain that a proposition expressed by the indexical "I" is not equivalent to any proposition expressed by a sentence without the indexical. If Mary knows *I am reading a book*, the proposition she knows is not identical to the proposition Sam knows when he knows the proposition *Mary is reading a book*. If that is correct, it creates a problem for God's omniscience because it appears that there are propositions knowable only by a single person. If nobody but Mary can know what she knows, then omniscience is impossible.[4]

I do not have a position on the issue whether Mary and Sam know the same proposition when their beliefs are directed toward the same state of affairs. But clearly, there is *something* different about Mary's belief state that distinguishes it from Sam's belief state.[5] Mary's perspective on the fact that she is reading a book is first personal, whereas Sam's perspective and the perspective of everybody but Mary is third personal. The state Mary is in when she believes *I am reading a book* on a certain occasion is a state only Mary can have. It seems, then, that only Mary can grasp what it is like to be in that state. I will argue that omnisubjectivity solves this problem as well.

11.3. Omnipresence

Another traditional attribute of God is omnipresence, or the property of being everywhere. Omnipresence has never received the attention of such attributes as omniscience and omnipotence, and what little attention it gets usually focuses on the puzzle of how an immaterial being can be present at all points of space. That puzzle is not my current concern, but the solution to the puzzle is interesting because it has an implication that nobody talks about, as far as I know.

Anselm's solution to the puzzle of omnipresence requires denying that being present at a point in space is to be extended in space or contained by some portion of space, the way a chair is contained by the room in which it is located and spread out on the floor beneath it, each part of the chair taking up a different portion of space. God has no parts and does not take up space, and God is not subject to spatiotemporal laws. God is wholly present in each part of the created world. But that means that there is nothing special about God's presence in spatial beings as opposed to non-spatial beings. Anselm accepts that implication explicitly when he says: "The supreme nature exists in everything that exists, just as much as it exists in every place. It is not contained, but contains all, by permeating all. This we know. Why not say, then, that it is 'everywhere' (meaning in everything that exists) rather than 'in every place'" (*Monologion* 23).

Aquinas reduces the omnipresence of God to other attributes.[6] He says that God is in all things in three ways: by his power, since all things are subject to his power; by his presence, since "all things are bare and open to his eyes"; and by his essence, because he is present to all as the cause of their being (ST I, q 8, a 3). Notice that Aquinas's explanation of the way in which God as a pure spirit is present at each point of space interprets omnipresence in a way that eliminates any reference to space per se. Omnipresence applies to all things in the created world, whether material or immaterial, whether spatial or non-spatial. The solution to the puzzle of how an immaterial, non-spatial God can be present at all points of space has the same consequence for Aquinas as for Anselm. Omnipresence applies to the non-spatial part of the creation as well as to the spatial world.

It seems to me that it is as reasonable to think that God is in every non-physical place as to believe that God is in every physical place. If God cannot be "in" a physical place the way a coffee cup is in the cupboard, any sense in which God *can* be in a physical place would apply to non-physical parts of the creation. Of the three senses that Aquinas mentions, one is particularly important for my topic. Aquinas says that to God, all things are "bare and open to his eyes." Presumably, what he has in mind is presence in the sense of intimate acquaintance. There is no aspect of the created world about which God does not have intimate acquaintance, not simply propositional knowledge. I propose that that must include each of your thoughts and feelings. This sense of omnipresence requires that God not only knows *that* you are anxious, but that God is *present in* your anxiety. Since your anxiety is part of the created world, God is present in it in the same way he is present in each spatial object. I think that the presence of God in a conscious being is important as a condition for its being the case that God and that being are present to each other in the sense of presence that is a component of intimate love. I believe that omnisubjectivity is a requirement of omnipresence in this sense, but before I get to that, I want to look at another issue that is much more personal than the implications of divine attributes: the practice of prayer.

11.4. The practices of prayer

There is very little scholarly work on prayer by philosophers, and the little I know of usually focuses on issues about petitionary prayer. For instance, if God does not change, prayer cannot make him change, and if God is providential, there seems to be no need to pray anyway. But I am not focusing on any issues about petitionary prayer in particular. The issue I want to raise is how we understand what is going on between us and God when we pray any kind of prayer. It could be a prayer of praise, of thanksgiving, of contrition, a request, or just a coming together with God.

In Catholic theology, prayer is traditionally defined as raising one's mind and heart to God.[7] What is interesting to me about this definition is that it focuses on the human side of prayer and is curiously silent about the recipient. Does God hear our prayers? Most people who pray do not think of prayer as a form of talking to themselves. They will say that their prayers are directed to God, and they believe, or at least hope, that God hears their prayers. But it is hard to get clear on how God hears them. In communal prayer at Mass or a worship service, people pray out loud, but it is very unlikely that they think of God as hovering above them in the room. Obviously, they do not think that they need to pray loudly to make sure God hears them. In fact, many prayers are not vocalized. The words are only in the head, yet we still think of that as prayer. If God can hear prayers, surely, he can hear the words that are unspoken. As the psalmist says, "Before a word slips from my tongue, Lord, you know what I will say" (Psalm 139).

But consider also the practices of prayer that do not involve words, not even unspoken words. Many meditative practices begin with images before the mind, and in more advanced states of contemplation the images disappear, and the person feels herself or himself to be in the presence of God with neither words nor images. Is God aware of that person's state? Well, why not? It seems to me that that is no more difficult to imagine than to imagine God hearing the unspoken words mentioned by the psalmist. In both cases, God would have to be "in our head" to be aware of our mental state. But if he can be aware of words we are thinking, why not images we are having and feelings we are feeling?

What exactly is the connection between your own psychic state when you are praying with or without words, and God's psychic state? One possibility is that your conscious space is occupied by two persons, or two conscious selves. It is hard to get that to make sense because often a self is defined as the being who possesses a certain conscious space. A psychic state is individuated by its bearer. Only one being can be thinking the thought you are having right now, and that being is you. If someone else had that thought, it would not be *that* thought, although, of course, it could be like your thought in content. If you feel an itch, you are the being who has the itch. Nobody but you can have that individual itch. If you make a choice, you are the one making the choice. There cannot be any other being making that choice. If more than one being had those states, that would mean that there are two of you, and that is impossible.

We can, however, imagine two persons leading parallel lives, having exactly the same conscious states in the sense of qualitatively identical states. We can imagine that the entire series of *A*'s conscious states is exactly the same as the entire series of *B*'s conscious states. It is a little hard for this to make sense when it comes to *A* and *B* making the same free choice, but we can let that pass. It does seem possible that they make exactly the same choices, think exactly the same thoughts, have exactly the same sensations and feelings, and so on. In this scenario *A* and *B* do not occupy the same conscious space. They occupy two distinct conscious spaces that happen to be qualitatively identical. *A* and *B* need not have anything to do with each other. Neither one is present in the other's consciousness or is even aware of the other's consciousness, so this model does not help us understand how God can hear your prayers as well as you hear them yourself.

There is also the radical model in which you are a part of God, or at least, your entire conscious life is a part of God's conscious life.[8] This model is interesting, but I find it unsatisfactory for two reasons. First, the price of avoiding the impossible situation of two distinct persons occupying the same conscious space is that you are not a distinct person. One conscious self (God) has another conscious self (you) as a part. The self you thought you were is not a distinct self. Since this means that we must radically reinterpret what a conscious self is, this view does not answer our question. We want to know how God—another person— can hear our prayers, the prayers of distinct persons. If I am simply a part of God, I lose much of the point of *addressing* God as a distinct person.

Second, the view that our consciousness is a part of God's consciousness has the consequence that when you make a decision, God makes the decision, even when the decision is sinful. God literally feels your pain and your fear, and God thinks your thoughts and makes your choices. This position will not work on anything close to the traditional view of God, although there are interesting departures from the tradition, such as the view of Charles Hartshorne (1982), who argues that God is able to feel the feelings of all creatures because the world makes up God's body.[9] I appreciate Hartshorne's sensitivity to the problem that an omniscient being must know what it is like to experience what each creature experiences, but I am aiming for another model, one that does not require that you are a part of God, and which does not require that God literally feels your feelings and makes your choices, and which also explains how God understands your prayers as well as you do.

11.5. The model of total empathy

The model I will use is human empathy. This is the closest model I can think of, but it must be acknowledged at the outset that it has an important feature that is necessary for human consciousness, but which does not apply to God. In human empathy, the grasp of another's consciousness is indirect. On the classical view of God, God's knowledge is direct, unmediated by concepts, percepts, memory, the structure of language, logical inference, or any of the other cognitive aids we use in order to know the world around us. And it surely cannot be mediated by imagining what it would be like for *him* to be in our place. The model of empathy is not a perfect model of direct awareness of another's conscious state, but I think that it is a good place to start.

I assume that empathy is a way of acquiring an emotion like that of another person. When Michael empathizes with Elizabeth's grief, Michael becomes conscious of Elizabeth's grief and acquires an emotion like that of Elizabeth by going through a process of taking on her perspective—imagining what it would be like to be Elizabeth in her situation as she sees it—e.g., to have lost her loved one, and to have her personal history with that person. Michael's grief is not identical to the grief Elizabeth has because human empathy is never a perfect copy, but more importantly, Michael's emotion is consciously representational, whereas Elizabeth's emotion is not. Elizabeth's emotion comes first and has nothing to do with Michael. Michael's emotion comes in response to hers, and loses its point if he discovers that she does not have the emotion he thought she had. His psychic state includes his attempt at copying Elizabeth's emotion "as if" from her first-person perspective, but it also includes his own ego. So he does not himself grieve over the death of Elizabeth's father when he empathizes with her, but he imaginatively adopts a state of grieving as if he were Elizabeth.

I assume that this experience of empathy is common, but it is not important for my purpose that I have identified the features of every instance of human empathy. I am starting with an experience that I think everyone has had. I want us then to imagine expanding that experience to apply to the transference of other psychic states from one person to another, and I will use that as a model for the transference of all psychic states from a human to God.

Suppose you imaginatively project yourself into another person's perspective and attempt to copy other conscious states she has in the same way you attempt to copy her emotion when you empathize with her. We can do that with intimate friends. We can often do that when we are reading a novel. As we imaginatively project ourselves into the character's point of view, we imagine having his or her thoughts, beliefs, feelings, desires, sensations, and emotions, making choices, and acting and experiencing various responses from others, as these states are described by the novelist. Our ability to do all of that is limited by both the novelist's skill at description, and by the fact that we have to depend upon our previous experience to use those descriptions in imagining what it is like to be the character in the novel. My conjecture is that novelists usually are fairly successful at conveying visual scenes because they can depend upon the readers' past experience of seeing virtually all colors and shapes and most elements of nature, which aid readers in imagining something visual. But it is harder for the writer to convey sounds and smells and tastes. If the writer says the character smells cinnamon, perhaps most readers can bring the fragrance to mind, but if the writer says the character smells Chinese Five Spice, many readers will not know what to imagine. The same point applies to tastes and sounds, and it certainly applies to emotions, which is the reason the young have so much trouble understanding stories in which complex emotions play a central role.[10] Conveying the character's thoughts, beliefs, and decisions is easier because those kinds of states are verbally mediated even within the character's own mind, and since the novelist makes the character mentally verbalize, the reader can imagine the character's experience of thinking, believing, and deciding from the character's viewpoint. What we do when we imagine being the character and taking on the character's beliefs and decisions in this way is analogous to empathizing with her feelings. Since we never forget we are doing this in imagination, there is no problem of confusing who we are with who the character is. We are always aware that the character's beliefs are not our own beliefs; the character's sensations are not our own sensations; the character's decisions are not our own decisions. But we have an imaginative identification with the character that permits us to empathize—very imperfectly—with many different psychic states of the character, and thus to grasp—again very imperfectly—what it is like to be such a character.

We can expand this model even farther. What I will call total empathy is empathizing with every one of a person's conscious states throughout that person's entire life—every thought, belief, sensation, mood, desire, and choice, as well as every emotion. What I call perfect total empathy is a complete and accurate copy of all of a person's conscious states. If *A* has perfect total empathy with *B*, then whenever *B* is in a conscious state *C*, *A* acquires a state that is a perfectly accurate copy of *C*, and *A* is aware that her conscious state is a copy of *C*. *A* is in this way able to grasp what it is like for *B* to be in state *C*. Because *A* is in an empathic state, *A*'s awareness of her ego is included in her empathic state, so an empathic state always includes something not included in the state of the person with whom she is empathizing. In addition, since she is always aware that her empathic copy is a copy, her empathic copy of *B*'s awareness of being *B* is not an awareness of being *B*. Nobody can be aware of being *B* except *B*.

Finally, imagine total perfect empathy that is direct, rather than acquired the way humans acquire empathy with other persons. Imagine empathy by direct perception, or something analogous to perception. Apart from the traditional conception of God as a being who knows everything directly, it seems to me that if empathy is perfectly accurate, it would *have* to be direct. I propose that God has direct, total, perfect empathy with all conscious beings who have ever lived or ever will live. That is the property I call omnisubjectivity. It is not mediated by anything analogous to a novelist's attempt to convey conscious states of an imaginary character to the reader, nor is it inferred from behavior, as in our experience of persons in daily life. Since it is not inferred, it does not require a similarity of past experience between God and creatures in order for God to understand the experience. There is no imaginary projection from the outside. What we do by imagining, God does by directly grasping someone's conscious state. Since your state is from your first-person point of view, God grasps it as if it were from your first-person point of view, but in an empathic way, never forgetting that he is not you. Also, like empathy, you may be unaware that there is someone empathizing with you. The empathizer's consciousness does not necessarily affect what is going on in your own consciousness, although it can, and I will return to that briefly at the end of the paper.

I think that the model of omnisubjectivity as direct, total, perfect empathy shows that omnisubjectivity is coherent. At least, I do not see anything that rules out its possibility. It does not rely upon the view that two distinct selves literally have the same conscious state. You and God are not confused or merged, and you are not a part of God. If omnisubjectivity is direct, total, perfect empathy, it is the most intimate acquaintance possible compatible with a separation of selves.

I propose that omnisubjectivity resolves the puzzles I mentioned about the attributes of omniscience and omnipresence. If an omniscient being is a being who knows everything there is to know, that being must know what it is like to have every conscious experience anyone has ever had, and since each conscious experience is distinguished by the way it is experienced from the perspective of the subject, then an omniscient being must know what it is like to have the experience from the perspective of the subject. God is not omniscient unless he is omnisubjective. The puzzle about omniscience is solved as long as (a) omnisubjectivity is possible, and (b) an omnisubjective being knows what it is like to have each conscious state, and knows it as well as the subject who is in that state.

Omnisubjectivity also permits God to know the difference between Mary's belief that she is reading a book, expressed as "I am reading a book," and Sam's belief about the same state of affairs, expressed as "Mary is reading a book." They each have a distinct point of view on the same state of affairs, whether or not they believe different propositions, and an omnisubjective God grasps both Mary's belief state and Sam's belief state, and the difference between them.

Omnisubjectivity recognizes that there is something to be known through living a conscious life that cannot be known in any other way. What we learn through living a conscious life is not a list of facts. There is something about lived experience that cannot be summed up by facts about the world that are gleaned from that experience. I am suggesting, then, that God lives through the conscious experience of each being who possesses consciousness. He knows everything you know or understand from living your life, and similarly for every other conscious being. He knows what it is like to be you, what it is like to be your dog, and what it is like to be each and every creature that has ever lived and had conscious awareness.

If I am right about that, omnisubjectivity is implied by the traditional solution to the puzzle of how an immaterial God can be present at all points of space. As I have said, the traditional answer to the puzzle is that an immaterial being is not present in space the way a material being is located in space or extended over some portion of space. Instead, to say God is omnipresent is to say at least this much: God is present to everything that exists, and he is present to everything that is going on in the sense of being immediately and directly acquainted with it. It is "bare and open before his eyes," as Aquinas says, and that applies as much to the non-physical part of creation as to the physical part. If omnipresence means that everything is immediately and directly grasped by

God, then surely that includes not only objects located in space, but conscious experiences that are not located in space. If God is truly everywhere, God must be omnisubjective, and if God is omnisubjective, we see the importance of the doctrine of omnipresence.

This brings me to the implications of prayer. What I have said about practices of prayer so far does not require the full attribute of omnisubjectivity because it does not require that God is intimately acquainted with the first-person perspective of beings who do not pray. But it requires at least the attribute of assuming the first-person perspective of all human beings who have ever lived and have ever prayed, or will ever live and will ever pray. However, I think that our practices of prayer do not assume that God becomes aware of our conscious life only at the moment of the prayer. How could we address God in prayer unless God was already aware of what was happening in our consciousness? If I'm right about that, prayer is a practice of us noticing God more than of God noticing us. If so, our practices assume that God is directly acquainted with the conscious states of any being who can pray, whether or not that being actually prays. That would require the attribute of grasping the conscious states of all human beings from their own perspective. We might call that attribute "omni-homo-subjectivity." It would not apply to non-human conscious animals, animals who cannot pray. But if you accept such an attribute, it is but a small step to accepting the full attribute of omnisubjectivity. Surely a being who has the power to enter into the consciousness of a human also has the power to enter into the consciousness of all creatures with consciousness. If he can do it for one, he can do it for all of them. I have already argued that an omniscient and omnipresent God *should* be omnisubjective, and I have argued in this section that he *can* be omnisubjective. I am claiming now that we already treat God as having an attribute close to omnisubjectivity in our practices of prayer.

11.6. Omniscience and counterfactual subjectivity

Does God have total empathy with psychic states that do not exist in the actual world, but exist in other possible worlds? For instance, suppose Mary never leaves her black-and-white room during her entire life. Does God know what it *would be like* for Mary to see color? What if Mary was never born. Would God know what it would be like if Mary came into existence, spent much of her life in a black-and-white room, and then saw color for the first time? My description of the way God grasps the subjective states of conscious beings implies that God grasps what it is like to see red by direct apprehension of the consciousness of beings who see red. But if there is no actual being who sees red, maybe there is nothing for God to grasp.

I have always found it puzzling that the only thing distinguishing the actual world from other possible worlds is that the former has the crucial but mysterious property of actuality, a property unlike any descriptive property. In my first omnisubjectivity paper (Zagzebski 2008), I offered the conjecture that a merely possible but non-actual being has no subjectivity. There is no such thing as what it would be like to be a conscious being who will never exist. There is nothing that is what the world would look like to such a being. A merely possible conscious being can have general properties such as liking chocolate, but there is no such thing as what this particular piece of chocolate would taste like to that being. This point is related to the idea that fictional characters do not have the specificity of actual beings. My conjecture, then, was that the subjectivity of the beings in the actual world is something that no other possible world has. That has the interesting consequence that omnisubjectivity explains (in part) what an omniscient being knows when he knows that this world is actual.

On the other hand, it can be argued that God ought to grasp counterfactual subjective experiences for the same reason he ought to grasp actual subjective experiences. Although ordinary omniscience applies only to the actual world, my argument about the connection between omniscience and omnisubjectivity did not depend upon the definition of omniscience, but instead, focused on cognitive perfection. If God grasps what it is like for Mary to see red, he has a more extensive grasp of his creation than if he merely knows the propositional fact that Mary sees red. But then it seems that God would be even more cognitively perfect if he grasped what it would be like for Mary to have any conscious state she could have, and what it would be like for any possible conscious being to have any conscious state possible for that being. If some other possible world containing conscious beings were actual, that world would contain first-person subjective experiences. Lacking a grasp of those experiences as they would be experienced by individual beings in that world is a failure to fully grasp that world, and hence, it is a failure to grasp the ways the actual world could have turned out. That does not seem worthy of a cognitively perfect being. But of course, that is assuming that there *is* such a thing as what it would have been like for a being to have a possible but non-actual subjective experience, and that is not obvious.

It could also be argued that the ability to grasp counterfactual conscious states from a first-person perspective is a necessary condition for ideal governance of the world. If God does not know what it would be like for conscious beings to have their experiences, how can God know what to create? I do not deny that a deity who knows a complete description of the facts in any possible world has plenty of information, but if am right in my earlier argument, he would not know everything there is to know about a world unless his omnisubjectivity extends to a complete grasp of the first-person conscious states of all conscious beings in that world. He would not know what it *would be like* if that world were actual, and that means he would not be able to compare what it would be like if one world were actual rather than another.[11] He would not know which world he prefers if some of the most important features of a world (arguably, all of the important features) are outside his conscious grasp.

Even without counterfactual omnisubjectivity, God could know the amount of good and evil in a world, assuming that there are facts about quantity and severity of good and evil in all worlds. Without being omnisubjective of other worlds, God could also know facts about the subjective states of possible creatures, e.g., that Mary in world $w1$ likes chocolate ice cream better than pistachio, that Sam in $w2$ dislikes loud noise, and so on. But he could not know what it would be like for Sam if Sam existed and listened to noise, nor would he appreciate the difference between Mary's experience of chocolate and her experience of pistachio. Lacking such a grasp, he also could not know what it would be like for him to create such a world and to have an empathic awareness of it. This not only puts serious limitations on a creator God, but it also limits his knowledge of his own counterfactual self.

There are other practical problems that ensue if God's omnisubjectivity does not extend to other worlds. God's interaction with the world does not end with the creation. God might intervene in temporal events, and God presumably acts in ways that involve reward and punishment, either during a person's lifetime or at the end of it. If God does not know in advance what it would be like for persons to have subjective experiences, including experiences of joy and suffering, how can he have a plan for rewarding or punishing those persons?

I think, then, that there are strong arguments in favor of the position that God's omnisubjectivity extends to a total grasp of all possible conscious states of all possible conscious creatures from their first-person perspective. However, I have also said that there may be reasons to think that there is nothing to know about the subjectivity of possible but non-actual beings, and if so, it is no limitation on God if he cannot do the impossible. I also think that it is not clear whether our determination of what is possible should be made independent of what we believe, upon reflection, to be properties of a perfect being. If the idea of perfection entails properties that seem to be impossible on another line of reasoning, it is not obvious to me that the other line of reasoning wins.

I am now undecided about whether the property of omnisubjectivity includes the grasp of possible but non-actual conscious states, including states of possible but non-actual creatures. The lines of reasoning I have given in favor of counterfactual omnisubjectivity are strong but not overwhelming. The reason for rejecting it that I find most powerful is that doing so permits us to see the significant difference in the metaphysical status of the actual world compared to other possible worlds. What is the difference between reality and the infinitely many worlds that could have been real but are not? What makes this world *actual*? It is usually assumed that the *only* difference between the actual world and other possible worlds is just that this one is actual. Actuality is a primitive notion that is supposed to be sufficiently understood by the difference between what is and what might have been. But on the hypothesis I am considering, there is more *in* the actual world than in other possible worlds. Subjective consciousness adds something to the actual world that is missing in merely possible worlds. There is a total objective description of every possible world, and in that way all possible worlds are on a par. But the actual world includes the feature of subjectivity, and that makes God's grasp of it extend much farther than his grasp of the merely possible. In the actual world there is more to grasp. At least, that is the hypothesis and I am undecided about it. Thinking about the attribute of omnisubjectivity forces us to reconsider the place of the actual world in the realm of possible worlds, but in what follows I will be neutral on whether omnisubjectivity includes the grasp of counterfactual subjective states.

11.7. Timelessness, immutability, impassibility

I have defended omnisubjectivity partly by arguing that it is entailed by omniscience and omnipresence. I take for granted the importance of omniscience in the Christian tradition, and I assume that omnipresence has a long tradition as well. But omnisubjectivity arguably conflicts with some of the other traditional attributes, particularly timelessness, immutability, and impassibility. These attributes have not fared particularly well in recent history. Nonetheless, they are part of a long tradition, and they are clearly found in Aquinas.

Let me start with the problem that omnisubjectivity appears to be incompatible with immutability and timelessness. Many philosophers and theologians are willing to deny these attributes for reasons that have nothing to do with my proposal here. But since many people still endorse them, and since I have not given up on them myself, I would like to say briefly why I think that omnisubjectivity poses no special problem for immutability and timelessness.

Everyone agrees that God grasps the sequence of temporal events. At a minimum, God is present at each moment of time in the same way Aquinas says he is present at each point of space: he has direct, intimate acquaintance with everything going on at each moment of time. Omnisubjectivity adds intimate acquaintance with each conscious experience from the first-person viewpoint of the subject. Does this raise any greater problem for a timeless and immutable God than the problem of intimate acquaintance with other temporal events?

Possibly it does. An omnisubjective being knows what it is like to experience time. He knows what it is like to anticipate an event, to wait, to hope for something in the future, and to be relieved when something unpleasant is over. Each of those states involves a temporal point of view. Furthermore, he must also know what it is like to go through a temporally extended process, whether it is a short process like brushing your teeth, or a long process like remodeling your house. It is an essential part of all those states that they involve temporal duration and change. But it is hard to see how a being can know what it is like to experience temporal duration and change without experiencing temporal duration and change.

I agree that since an omnisubjective being knows what it is like to experience temporal duration, he must have direct acquaintance with the experience of temporal sequence, but it does not obviously follow that he must exist in time. There are models of the way a timeless being could grasp temporal duration in the literature.[12] My own suggestion is that a timeless being can know what it is like to experience temporal duration the same way he knows what it is like to smell roses. He does not smell the roses himself, but he permeates the consciousness of a being who smells roses. Similarly, even if he is not in time, he permeates the consciousness of beings who experience temporal duration, and empathically grasps what temporal duration is like.

But this might not yet be a satisfactory answer because we might think that a being outside of time is prevented from consciously entering into the experience of temporal duration. For instance, to really "get" what it is like to wait, and wait, and wait, getting more bored with each passing second, one must experience the passage of time as boring, and one cannot do that without experiencing the passage of time. But I think this conclusion is too hasty, and I suggest that we look again at the way we empathize with the experience of a character in a novel. Rarely do we imagine the character's experience in real time. Usually our conscious representation of the character's experience is temporally compressed. We experience in a few seconds a copy of what the character goes through in several minutes or hours. Sometimes it can be the reverse. Our empathic experience can take longer than the experience of the character, as when the novelist intentionally stretches out the description of an event that would take only a few seconds. Alternatively, the reader might be the one who stretches it out. I sometimes find myself slowing down and taking more time to absorb the experience than necessary, perhaps because the situation is too frightening or too exciting. My point here is that the empathic copy of an experience need not have the same temporal duration as the experience it copies, and in fact, typically does not. I also think that a temporally compressed copy of an experience need not be inferior because of the temporal compression. I have already said that human empathy is defective, but I do not see any reason to think that it is defective because of temporal compression. If I am right about that, we can imagine a being whose empathy with someone's experience is compressed to a single moment. God grasps in a flash what it feels like to go through a temporally extended experience of boredom, or of eager anticipation, waiting, and joy; or of dread, followed by pain and then relief.

I think, then, that empathizing with the experience of temporal duration is no more difficult for God to do than empathizing with smelling roses, feeling fear, and choosing to sin. If it is possible to empathize with feeling fear without feeling fear, and, in fact, being the kind of being who cannot feel fear, then it seems to me it is possible to empathize with the experience of the passage of time without experiencing the passage of time, and being a being who cannot experience the passage of time. I am not going to deny that some people will find the attribute of omnisubjectivity impossible, and they will deny that God can empathize with human conscious states in the way I have described, but I do not see any additional problem with empathizing with the human experience of temporality. Of course, those people who think God is temporal will not worry about this issue anyway, but I want to say that those who think God is timeless and immutable should find no greater problem in the idea that God can empathize with the subjective experience of temporality than with the idea that God can empathize with other human experiences.

The traditional attribute of impassibility is different. Impassibility is the divine property of being unmoved by anything outside of himself. Traditionally this was interpreted to mean that God does not suffer or feel emotions since emotions were understood as "passions," or ways of being affected by something external, and it was thought to be an imperfection to be affected by anything external. I have argued in another place (Zagzebski 1998, Chapter 9 of this volume) that even if God does not have passions, God could still have a number of psychic states that we call emotions, but that is not what I want to say here. It follows from my argument that God knows what it is like to suffer and to feel pain, to feel fear, and all the other emotions. God has perfect empathy with all those states exactly as they are felt by his creatures. Possibly it could be argued that direct, perfect empathy with a sensation of pain is not a pain, and likewise for a feeling of fear or of terror. But even if that is so, perfect empathy with pain is surely ruled out by impassibility, as is empathy with every other sensation or emotion, whether positive or negative. A perfectly empathic being is affected by what is outside of him, even if his empathic states are not literally sensations and emotions. I think, then, that omnisubjectivity is incompatible with impassibility. That forces me to think about which of the two attributes comes closer to expressing what is included in perfection and the implications of prayer and worship. I have already said that I think that omnisubjectivity is a requirement of several other components of traditional ways of thinking about God and encountering God in prayer. So if omnisubjectivity is incompatible with impassibility, I conclude that God is not impassible.

11.8. The moral objection

Omnisubjectivity would be a problem if (a) some conscious states are immoral, and (b) even the empathic grasp of such states in the consciousness of a perfectly empathic being is immoral. I will not deny that some conscious states are immoral. If an act is morally wrong, surely the conscious decision to perform the act is wrong, and probably also the intention to perform it. Motivational states and certain emotions might be wrong as well—e.g., hate, envy, bitterness, jealousy. There are probably also morally wrong beliefs, such as the belief that some person does not deserve to be treated as a full person. There are so many examples, it does not matter if I am mistaken about some of them. Clearly, there are morally wrong conscious states.

But if a state is wrong, is it wrong to accurately grasp it in one's own mind? Once again, think about reading a novel. If a character is vicious, is there anything wrong with empathizing with that character's vicious feelings, beliefs, or decisions? Surely there is nothing wrong with empathizing with the character's decision or belief since a representation of a decision is not a decision, and the representation of a belief is not a belief. One can fully grasp a belief from the character's viewpoint without having the belief, and likewise for a decision.

But what about empathizing with a sensation or an emotion? As I have already suggested, the conscious state of grasping a sensation is something very much like a sensation, and similarly for an emotion. One cannot grasp what it is like to see red without seeing red in imagination, and seeing red in imagination is very much like seeing red. The difference is that when we humans imagine, we usually do not imagine as vividly as an actual sensation, but that is because of a defect in our imagination. If we could imagine red perfectly, wouldn't the sensation of red pop into our minds? I am not saying we would be confused about whether the imaginary sensation is an actual sensation. We would probably have a way to tell the difference—for instance, because we know we intentionally brought it to mind, rather than to have it inflicted on us by turning our heads. My point is not that we could not tell the difference. I am only suggesting that a copy of a red sensation is phenomenally very much like a red sensation. Even though the items in our imagination tend to be weaker than the items they copy, a perfect empathizer would not have to rely upon imagination, and the empathic state would not be weaker than the state of the creature. If there are morally bad sensations, an omnisubjective being would have a morally bad sensation. Or so it seems.

The problem is aggravated when we look at copies of emotions. Possibly there are no morally bad sensations, but emotions are a harder kind of case. Suppose a person feels hatred or fury or envy. Maybe someone takes pleasure in the pain of another. Wouldn't it be morally wrong for a perfectly empathic being to adopt those states empathically in his own consciousness?

I think the answer is no, but to explain why I think that, I want to return to reading a novel or watching a movie. The most evil person I have ever seen depicted in any form—biography, novel, or film—is the character of Daniel Plainview, played by Daniel Day-Lewis in Paul Thomas Anderson's movie, *There Will Be Blood*.[13] Assuming you can tolerate watching this movie and can bring yourself to empathize with Daniel Plainview, you project yourself into the consciousness of a person who fears love and humiliates people who love him, who has no appreciation of the value of other persons, who enjoys inflicting pain, is treacherous, prideful, greedy, and more. When you do that, you grasp the world and Plainview's reactions to the world through his eyes, but you also respond to those attitudes and feelings as yourself. If you have a negative reaction to cruelty and greed and hate, you will have a negative reaction to your empathic copy of those psychic states. You "get" what it feels like to be hateful and greedy, but that does not make you hateful and greedy or even more likely to be hateful and greedy. In fact, it probably makes you less likely to be hateful and greedy. Since Plainview enjoys hurting people, empathizing with him will permit you to get what it feels like to enjoy hurting people, and I imagine you will feel revulsion for that feeling also. Of course, it can happen that empathizing with another person in the real or fictional world leads you to change your reaction to certain psychic states. You might even come to judge that someone's feelings are not bad after all. Such a judgment is either correct or incorrect. If it is correct, it is no objection to the morality of empathizing with him. If it is incorrect, that is because you, the empathizer, have made a mistake in your reaction to the psychic state with which you are empathizing, but that is no objection to the empathic state. It is a problem with the reaction that you have as the empathizer. Since God does not make mistakes in his responses to states with which he empathizes, there is no danger that empathizing with a hateful person is a taint on God's character, any more than it must be a taint on your character if you empathize with Plainview in *There Will Be Blood*. In fact, I think a case can be made that God must empathize perfectly with a person's conscious states in order to judge the person with complete accuracy and fairness.[14]

This answer will not satisfy someone who insists that there are intrinsically immoral emotions, and the conscious representation of an intrinsically immoral emotion is itself intrinsically immoral. If the conscious grasp of the immoral emotion is direct, that might be even worse. On this view, God would be contaminated by his own creatures if he really grasped what it is like to have their bad feelings. God can only know these things in the abstract. According to this view, God can know *that* someone is hateful, but God cannot grasp what it feels like to be hateful without jeopardizing his own goodness. A perfectly good God must be shielded from too intimate a contact with certain human experiences.

I find the idea that God would be less than fully perfect, and hence less than divine, if he had too close a contact with the created world peculiar and quite implausible, but I doubt that this issue can be settled without a closer look at other Christian doctrines pertaining to the relationship between God and human beings, such as the doctrines of grace, providence, and sanctification, and I will only raise a couple of questions about the implications of these doctrines. For instance, given that a person in a state of grace shares in the divine life (I Cor. 1:9), does that sharing go both ways? I am inclined to think that it does because intimate sharing between two persons always goes both ways. Sanctification may involve a breaking down of the barriers between human life and divine life, so that when a human being shares in the divine life, God also shares in our own lives. Sharing between humans can reach the level of deep intersubjective exchanges of experience. We get a glimpse into what it is like to be another person, and we would expect no less from God. We might also want to know what the perfection of intersubjectivity would be like. I think that the model for sharing of lives among persons is the Trinity, and I propose that it is the perfection of intersubjectivity.

11.9. The Trinity

According to the doctrine of the Trinity, there are three divine Persons, but one divine nature. I interpret the doctrine to mean more than that the three Persons share a nature in the way you and I share a nature. If that was all there was to the doctrine, there would be no mystery to it, and the correct answer to the question "How many Gods are there?" would be "three." But I assume that there is one God, one divine being. I think also that there is only one divine substance, although I am not going to try to adjudicate controversies about the concepts of "being" and "substance." I do, however, want to say something about the concept of a person since it is a concept that connects omnisubjectivity with the Trinity.

I said at the beginning of this paper that I believe there is something unique about persons. I do not know whether the uniqueness is qualitative, meaning that each person has a different *kind* of experience than anyone else. To make this point another way, I do not know whether chocolate has a different kind of taste to one person than to another, whether each person's fear has some qualitative difference from any other person's fear, whether your thought that Oklahoma is a state in the middle of the United States has a different conceptual content than my thought that Oklahoma is a state in the middle of the United States. But I do think that there is *something* different in my consciousness that makes it impossible to duplicate and that is intrinsically connected to what makes me the person that I am. If the difference between my conscious states and your conscious states were merely qualitative, there would be nothing in principle preventing the duplication of my conscious states. But if there is something unique about each person, and if each person is essentially tied to her conscious states, then the difference between one person and another cannot be limited to a qualitative difference between the conscious states of one person and another. But what could it mean for there to be a non-qualitative difference between the conscious states of one person and another? In this paper, I have adopted the idea that one person necessarily differs from another in what we vaguely call "point of view." This perceptual term is misleading because a person is not just the bearer of a particular view on the world. A person is also a self, and the way a self is understood by another self is necessarily different from the way a self understands herself; there is something superior or more fundamental about the way a self relates to herself than the way someone on the outside relates to her. When I say a person has a point of view that is necessarily unique, I mean to include the uniqueness of selfhood as well as uniqueness in viewpoint on what is outside the agent.

I have argued that God is not omniscient nor omnipresent unless God is in some sense "in" the mind of each conscious being, able to grasp what that being grasps in as perfect a way as is possible, compatible with a distinction in persons. I think this point applies to the Persons of the Trinity. Intrinsic to the personhood of the Father, Son, and Holy Spirit is a distinction in point of view and a different relation to himself than to the other persons of the Trinity. The point of view of the Father is necessarily distinct from the point of view of the Son and from the point of view of the Holy Spirit because, on my hypothesis, such a difference is intrinsic to the distinction in personhood. The sense of the Father's sense of self is different from the Son's and Holy Spirit's sense of self.

But if each Person of the Trinity is omnisubjective, each perfectly grasps the point of view and sense of self of each other member of the Trinity, but does so in the way I have described, in which the omnisubjective person A grasps the conscious states of person B "as if" from B's viewpoint, but never forgetting that A is himself. As I mentioned in describing empathy, when A empathizes with B, there is more in the consciousness of A than in the consciousness of B because A has her own ego in her consciousness as well as a simulacrum of the ego of B. On this model, the Father perfectly grasps the Son's experience of suffering as if from the Son's point of view, but the Father is aware of being the Father grasping the Son's conscious state, and that is not identical to the Son's grasp of his own state. But the Son is also omnisubjective. So the Son grasps all of the Father's conscious states from the Father's point of view, which means that the Son grasps the Father's grasp of the Son's conscious states. The same point applies, of course, to the Holy Spirit. I propose that each member of the Trinity is perfectly omnisubjective of each other member of the Trinity. The Trinity is a model of the most perfect understanding possible among persons, the most perfect understanding possible within a community of persons. The union of consciousness among the Persons of the Trinity is perfect, and that is compatible with a difference in the point of view of each member of the Trinity and a different sense of self, the center of consciousness. What unifies them is not that they think the same thing and will the same thing, but their perfect grasp of each other. That grasp makes possible something else—perfect love among the three Persons. We cannot love what we cannot grasp. Love is premised on understanding the other, and the fuller the understanding, the greater the possibility for love. The Trinity gives us a model of love between perfect persons that is generated from perfect comprehension of the other. Similarly, I am proposing that God's love for each of us is generated from a preceding act of total, unmediated intellectual comprehension of us. God knows everything we know about ourselves through living our life, in addition to knowing all the things we do not know about ourselves. I am suggesting that in addition to the reasons for omnisubjectivity I have already described, omnisubjectivity is a condition for the perfect love God has for us.

11.10. Conclusion

I like the attribute of omnisubjectivity because it is the most personal of divine attributes, and yet it is just as much a high metaphysical property as omniscience, omnipotence, and perfect goodness. It is an attribute we would expect in a perfect being, but it is not vulnerable to attack on the grounds that it belongs to the so-called God of the philosophers, who does not seem to be a person at all. The traditional "omni" attributes have often been criticized as a holdover from Greek philosophy, insufficiently grounded in the biblical message of a loving God who has continuous personal relationships with his people. In my view, omnisubjectivity ties omniscience and omnipresence to the personhood of God. It is the attribute of being omniscient and omnipresent in the most personal way. An omnisubjective God is the most intimately loving because he is the most intimately knowing. If there is an omnisubjective God, each of us has the comfort of knowing that, no matter what is going in, we are never truly alone. That knowledge allows some people to acquire a knowledge of God and a depth of love for him that would be impossible if there were not an omnisubjective God present to them. Perhaps mystics are those persons who become aware of God's awareness of them, as we sometimes can do when someone is empathizing with us and we are able to detect the sharing of our emotion. That awareness brings us into the conscious life of the empathizer, and that can affect the way we think of our own experience and its significance. More importantly, it brings us into unity with the empathizer. We feel understood, accepted, sustained, and loved.

We can understand and love others because we ourselves have been understood and loved in the way of perfect intimacy.

Notes

1. I first proposed that God has the attribute of omnisubjectivity in Zagzebski (2008). That paper argued that omnisubjectivity is entailed by omniscience. This chapter incorporates some of the arguments of that paper and gives additional reasons for the attribute and some implications. It is a compilation of Zagzebski (2013) and (2016), with some additions.
2. Jackson uses the story for a different purpose. He argues that since physicalism entails the thesis that if you know all the physical facts, you know everything there is to know, the fact that Mary learns something new when she leaves her black-and-white room shows that physicalism is false. Jackson has recanted that position in Jackson (2003).
3. I assume that somebody can know what something is like if he or she had the experience in the past and is able to remember it. If Mary leaves her black-and-white room, enters the colored world, and then goes back to the black-and-white room, she knows what it is like to see color even though she is not currently seeing color. That does not help the problem for God's knowledge because it is just as hard to imagine that God saw color in the past as in the present. Similarly, the problem of knowing what it is like to be a bat or a fish or a human is not a problem with God's current consciousness. It is the problem that the kind of consciousness required seems to be impossible for God.
4. Patrick Grim (1979) argues for this conclusion. I discuss Grim's position in Zagzebski (2008).
5. John Perry (1979) argues that when I know a proposition expressed in the first person and someone else knows a proposition about the same state of affairs expressed in the third person, the object of our respective epistemic states is the same. We do know the same thing. However, we are in different belief states. The difference is real, and the problem I am raising is that God ought to grasp that difference, whether or not the two persons grasp different propositions.
6. I thank Marilyn Adams for help in distinguishing the way Anselm and Aquinas handle the attribute of omnipresence. Aquinas's account is reductive, whereas Anselm's is not. Scotus and Ockham also reject a reductive account of omnipresence. These differences are not critical for my point about the way omnipresence affects God's cognitive presence in all of creation.
7. See *Catechism of the Catholic Church*, 2nd edition (1995), 2559, 2590. The wording of the definition is taken from St. John Damascene in the eighth century.
8. It is interesting that Frege thinks of this model in "The Thought: A Logical Inquiry," in the course of discussing the problem of comparing two subjective experiences. He begins by saying that if the word "red" signifies an impression within my own consciousness, it is impossible to compare my sense impression with that of someone else:

> It is so much of the essence of each of my ideas to be the content of my consciousness, that every idea of another person is, just as such, distinct from

mine. But might it not be possible that my ideas, the entire content of my consciousness, might be at the same time the content of a more embracing, perhaps divine, consciousness? Only if I were myself part of the divine consciousness. But then would they really be my ideas, would I be their bearer? This oversteps the limits of human understanding to such an extent that one must leave its possibility out of account. In any case it is impossible for us as men to compare another person's ideas with our own. I pick the strawberry, I hold it between my fingers. Now my companion sees it too, this very same strawberry; but each of us has his own idea. No other person has my idea, but many people can see the same thing. No other person has my pain. Someone can have sympathy for me but still my pain always belongs to me and his sympathy to him. He does not have my pain and I do not have his sympathy. (Frege, 1956, 299–301).

I thank Chad McIntosh for calling my attention to this passage.
9. Hartshorne asks some of the same questions about omniscience with which I began this paper. ". . . [W]hat does it mean to know what sorrow is, but never to have sorrowed, never to have felt the quality of suffering. I find nothing in my experience that gives meaning to this set of words" (1982, 55).
10. Movies have an advantage over novels in that they can play the music the character hears, but movies do not as yet convey smells and tastes to the audience. I think that a movie is not as good a model of empathy as a novel because the viewer of a movie is clearly watching the character, not getting into the character's head. In addition, the viewer is not imagining the music as the character hears it; she is actually hearing it herself.
11. I thank Chad McIntosh and Timothy Miller for making this point independently and for prodding me to think about the issues raised in this section.
12. One way has been defended by Eleonore Stump and Norman Kretzmann (1981) in their description of divine eternity as atemporal duration. In his book on eternity, Brian Leftow (1991) denies that if a being x knows a changing thing as changing, then x undergoes change, and he offers two models to support his view (342–348). Although Leftow does not discuss a property like omnisubjectivity, his second model is one in which God is aware of our awareness, and he says it would apply to knowing colors and what it is like to be a bat.
13. This character is loosely based on the character of James Arnold Ross, the father in Upton Sinclair's novel *Oil*. The father in *Oil* is not the main character of the novel, and he is not as bad as the Daniel Day-Lewis character in the movie. The latter is unremittingly horrible, whereas the former has some redeeming features.
14. I thank Terry Cross for making this point in conversation at Lee University, where he is Dean of the School of Religion.

VI

THE RATIONALITY OF RELIGIOUS BELIEF

12
The Epistemology of Religion
The Need for Engagement (2004)

12.1. Introduction

A curious feature of current American religious epistemology is the lack of engagement between religious believers and their skeptical interlocutors. Unlike most other areas of philosophy, those writing in religious epistemology do not see themselves as part of the same epistemic community, using common concepts and working together to answer the same questions. By far the largest part of the discourse is defensive. This is particularly noticeable in the writings of Alvin Plantinga, whose work is partly defense against specific attacks, and is partly addressed to Christians, arising from Christian convictions. A close look at Plantinga's most recent book, *Warranted Christian Belief*, shows that even though much of it appears to engage the typical arguments of non-believing philosophers, very little of it actually does so.

There are at least three features of philosophical culture that explain the lack of engagement within religious epistemology. First, religion has a very different place in academic philosophy than it has in the wider culture. Religious philosophers often feel under attack by other philosophers in a different way than, say, free will libertarians feel under attack by determinists. The response has been a huge body of defensive literature. This defensiveness is striking when seen from the perspective of the culture outside of the academy, which in most parts of the United States is strongly religious and unthreatened by philosophical atheism.[1] In my experience, students often find religious epistemology peculiar since much of it is concerned with answering a kind of attack they never thought deserved so much attention. Religious epistemology is even at odds with some of the scholarship in areas of the humanities outside of philosophy, where the prevailing attitude tends to be culturally inclusive, and the Age of Atheism is identified with the Enlightenment, an age that has been in disrepute for most of the period in which Plantinga was writing. From both inside and outside the academy, then, many people find the dominant arguments in religious epistemology puzzling. Many theists find the defensiveness odd, while reasonable critics who do not frame their questions as belligerent attacks, but who put themselves in the same epistemic community as religious believers, are ignored.

A second feature of philosophical culture responsible for this problem is that engagement within American epistemology is difficult anyway. When epistemologists use words like "rationality," "justification," and probably even "knowledge," it is not clear that they are all talking about the same thing. This also is partly a legacy of the Enlightenment, which taught us to distinguish between first-person and third-person perspectives. That eventually led to an unresolved split between epistemic evaluation from the first person or internal perspective, and evaluation from the external perspective or the perspective of a being who sees the agent's mind and her environment. In Plantinga's latest book, the former is very narrow and the latter is very wide. I will argue that this also has led to a lack of engagement between Plantinga and his interlocutors.

Third, Anglo-American philosophy has not yet fully emerged from the radical empiricism that dominated the mid-twentieth century. Hilary Putnam (2004) discusses this phenomenon in his book, *The Collapse of the Fact-Value Dichotomy*. Putnam argues that the fact/value dichotomy was associated with a fact/logic dichotomy, where *fact* generally meant *empirical fact*. The fact/logic dichotomy created problems for an understanding of both value and metaphysics. The result was that some metaphysics was put into the category of logic (e.g., the topology of time); some metaphysics was put into science; some was abandoned by philosophical discourse. It seems to me that religious metaphysics has been put in this last category. It is no longer considered meaningless, but like any high-level metaphysics, there is no method to deal with it. Nonetheless, philosophers do metaphysics more and more, and there is less and less reason to declare religious metaphysics especially problematic.

Alvin Plantinga's first book on warrant (1993a) was an important contribution to the debate about justification and warrant that dominated epistemology in the 1980s, and his second book (1993b) presented an important original theory of warrant that showed how belief in God can be warranted and can constitute knowledge. In the third book of the trilogy, *Warranted Christian Belief* (2000b), Plantinga responds to a particular kind of attack on the rationality of Christian belief in a way that leaves out both a more typical philosophical critic and even many Christian believers. There he distinguishes two kinds of rationality. What he means by internal rationality is too easy to achieve, whereas what he means by external rationality, closely associated with warrant, is almost completely a matter of luck when applied to Christian belief, leaving very little for religious epistemologists to discuss. Neither of his two senses of rationality coincides with what many philosophers mean by rationality, and neither contributes to the question many of them are asking: "What should *we* think about these questions?"—where they are looking for guidance in the epistemic behavior of philosophers on all sides.

My position is that it is our business to be good epistemic agents. What that involves and when it is satisfied is something all philosophers can and should discuss no matter what their personal beliefs. We may not be able to give an exhaustive account of the properties that constitute good epistemic agency, and we cannot always distinguish the good agents from the bad agents, but we can recognize enough good ones and enough bad ones to give us dependable models. This is one way in which the conditions for being a good epistemic agent are social: our models are other agents. Emulating exemplary agents is the most natural and straightforward way to achieve our goal of being good epistemic agents ourselves. But being a good epistemic agent is no easier than being a good moral agent. I want to argue that it is much harder than being internally rational in Plantinga's sense, and it is nothing like being externally rational in his sense.

12.2. Plantinga's Warranted Christian Belief

In *Warranted Christian Belief* (2000b), Plantinga proposes a prototype for distinctively Christian beliefs that he calls the Aquinas/Calvin model (A/C model), consisting of a set of propositions that are core Christian doctrines. He then extends the model by adding a proposition about how the believer comes to believe the doctrines in the set (Chapter 8). According to the extended model, human beings come to believe that Jesus is God and other important Christian doctrines through the instigation of the Holy Spirit on the occasion of their coming in contact with the doctrine, for example, upon hearing the Gospel proclaimed. The model specifies that Christian belief does not come by way of normal human faculties. Plantinga says:

> These beliefs do not come to the Christian by way of memory, perception, reason, testimony or credulity, moral intuition, the *sensus divinitatis*, or any other of the cognitive faculties with which we human beings were originally created; they come instead by way of the work of the Holy Spirit, who convinces us of, causes us to believe these great truths of the gospel. These beliefs don't come by way of the normal operation of our natural faculties; they are a supernatural gift. (2000b, 245)

These beliefs are basic, and since they occur according to the divine design plan, they are properly basic. Plantinga argues that they are justified and internally rational and, if true, they are externally rational and warranted. He concludes that if belief in Christian doctrines operates as described in the model, these beliefs are justified, rational in two senses, and warranted.

Let me begin with what Plantinga calls internal rationality. In introducing this kind of rationality, he says:

> We can initially characterize internal rationality as a matter of proper function of all belief-producing processes "downstream from experience"... (110) There is more that internal rationality requires; we can deal with it briefly. A person is internally rational only if her beliefs are coherent, or at any rate are sufficiently coherent to satisfy proper function.... Further, an internally rational person will draw the right inferences when the occasion arises.... Still further, given the beliefs she has, she will make the right decisions with respect to her courses of action—that is, the decisions required by proper function.... And finally, if she is internally rational, she will do what proper function requires with respect to such things as preferring to believe what is true, looking for further evidence when that is appropriate, and in general being epistemically responsible. (2000b, 112)

Plantinga devotes a single paragraph to the question of whether distinctively Christian belief is internally rational for the Christian. He says:

> Internal rationality... has a dual aspect: on the one hand, it requires proper function in the part of the cognitive system that lies "downstream from experience"; on the other, it requires more generally that you have done your best or anyway well enough with respect to the formation of the belief in question. You have considered how it fits in with your other beliefs, engaged in the requisite seeking for defeaters, considered the objections that you have encountered, compared notes with the right people, and so on. Clearly, on the model *(and even apart from the model)*, someone who accepts the Christian beliefs in question can easily meet these conditions. (2000b, 255) (emphasis added)

Assuming that internal proper function includes doing our epistemic duty, internal rationality is connected with justification. Plantinga says:

> This requirement of internal rationality may seem to overlap with justification. It does, if in fact there are intellectual duties prescribing the behavior required by rationality. Even if there are no such duties, however, internal rationality still requires the behavior in question. (2000b, 255, note 26)

When applying the issue of justification to Christian belief, Plantinga says:

> Justification needn't detain us for long. There should be little doubt that Christian belief can be and probably is (deontologically) *justified*, and justified

even for one well acquainted with Enlightenment and postmodern demurrers. If your belief is a result of the inward instigation of the Holy Spirit, it may seem obviously true, even after reflection on the various sorts of objections that have been offered. (2000b, 252).

Plantinga's conditions for internal rationality are somewhat vague, but he treats them in such a way that it appears that not only is it easy for the Christian to be justified and internally rational in her beliefs, it is easy *in general* for a person to be justified and internally rational in her beliefs. It is easy enough that voodoo beliefs, for example, can satisfy it. With respect to the justification of voodoo beliefs, Plantinga says, "obviously the voodooists could be within their intellectual rights in thinking what they do think (if only by virtue of cognitive malfunction)" (2000b, 346). And he says the question of whether they can be internally rational is also easy:

> A belief is internally rational ... if, given your experience (including doxastic experience) at the time in question, it is compatible with proper function that you accept the belief in question. That could certainly be so for the voodooists. Perhaps they have always been taught that these voodoo beliefs are true, and all alleged contrary evidence is cleverly explained away by the priests; or perhaps they are all in the grip of some cognitive malfunction upstream from experience, one that skews their doxastic experience. (2000b, 346)

Of course, Plantinga assumes that voodoo beliefs are false, and since he thinks beliefs formed by properly functioning faculties in the appropriate environment are generally true, there is no doubt malfunction somewhere in the formation of voodoo beliefs, either in their epistemic community, or in the environment. Wildly false beliefs can be internally rational and justified because of dysfunction somewhere prior to the experience upon which the belief is based. Presumably these beliefs also fail to be externally rational, but Plantinga does not mention that in his discussion of the internal rationality and justification of voodoo beliefs. He chooses to focus on how easily the voodooists can be internally rational and justified. But if that is the case, neither internal rationality nor justification is much of a prize.

One could object that it is harder than Plantinga thinks to satisfy his own conditions for justification or internal rationality. It is not at all clear that someone who reflects upon objections to his belief and still finds his belief obviously true has done enough to satisfy his epistemic duty, and it is even less clear that it is easy to be epistemically responsible in the way needed for what he calls internal rationality. But perhaps Plantinga is simply stipulating that internal rationality in the sense he is using is a state whose satisfaction conditions are permissive. Either way, Plantinga fails to engage his interlocutors. Many epistemologists have devoted considerable attention to the conditions for justification and epistemic responsibility, conditions that it is not easy to satisfy, and some have then questioned whether various religious beliefs satisfy these conditions. By offering conditions for justification and internal rationality that are easily satisfied and then dealing with the issue of whether Christian beliefs satisfy them in a few lines, Plantinga has either failed to appreciate how difficult many philosophers think it is to satisfy those conditions, or alternatively, he has invented new notions of justification and internal rationality, in which case he has failed to engage the notions of justification, epistemic responsibility, and rationality as used by his interlocutors. Either way, there is a mismatch between what Plantinga is talking about and what his objectors are talking about.

To see why I find this problematic, let us return to voodoo beliefs. Suppose there are some philosophers among the voodooists. Like us, they have a sense of belonging to a worldwide community of philosophers past and present, and they regularly communicate with philosophers who are not voodooists. The latter understandably point out to the former that voodoo belief is not justified or rational. "You shouldn't believe in voodoo," they say. Now surely it would be disingenuous of the voodooists if they replied that they can easily be both justified and internally rational since they have done the things Plantinga describes. They have considered the non-voodooist belief as a potential defeater for their voodoo beliefs, but upon reflection, they find that voodoo beliefs still seem obviously true. Voodoo beliefs cohere with their other beliefs, and there is no reason to think that they suffer from a malfunction in the way they respond to experience. That experience is, after all, an experience of having been taught voodoo as part of a culture that goes back as far as their historical memory. I would imagine that the non-voodooist philosophers would reply that that is all very well, but their objection did not depend upon any particular understanding of justification or rationality, and that anyway, "internal rationality" is not *their* term; the bottom line is that the voodooists should not believe in voodooism. It would be fair for the voodooists to reply, "Why not?" and it would also be fair for them to ask the non-voodooists to be clearer about the kind of wrongdoing of which they are accused. Are they supposed to be violating an epistemic duty? Are they being epistemically irresponsible? Are they epistemically vicious in some way? Or is the problem simply that the non-voodooists are convinced the beliefs are false? But if the voodooist and non-voodooist philosophers perceive themselves to be partners in an epistemic community, they will think of all their arguments and objections to each other as components of a joint project which each of them serves in his own way. This is what I find lacking in contemporary discussions of the justification and rationality of religious belief.

THE EPISTEMOLOGY OF RELIGION   219

Let us now look at the second pair of properties of positive epistemic status discussed by Plantinga: external rationality and warrant. These two are also closely connected. In introducing external rationality, Plantinga says:

> And now that we have internal rationality in hand, external rationality is easy to explain. It requires, first, proper function with respect to the formation of the sensuous experience on which perceptual belief is based. And it consists second in the formation of the right kind of doxastic experience—that is, the sort of doxastic experience required by proper function. (2000b, 112)

Plantinga says that external rationality is also the first condition of warrant (2000b, 257). In addition to external rationality, warrant requires that the cognitive environment is that for which the faculties and processes were designed, that they are processes designed to produce true beliefs, and warrant in the degree necessary for knowledge requires that the beliefs in question are, in fact, true.

Plantinga argues that if the extended Aquinas/Calvin model is true, belief in the propositions in the model is externally rational and warranted. The argument is straightforward:

> First, when these beliefs are accepted by faith and result from the internal instigation of the Holy Spirit [the epistemological extension of the model], they are produced by cognitive processes working properly; they are not produced by way of some cognitive malfunction. Faith, the whole process that produces them, is specifically designed by God himself to produce this very effect—just as vision, say, is designed by God to produce a certain kind of perceptual beliefs. When it does produce this effect, therefore, it is working properly; thus, the beliefs in question satisfy the external rationality condition, which is also the first condition of warrant. (2000b, 257)

Plantinga goes on to show that the other conditions for warrant are also satisfied if the model is true. The beliefs are produced in the Christian by the Holy Spirit according to a design plan aimed at truth in an environment for which they were designed and, of course, they are successful in reaching the truth as long as the model is true.

Notice next that if beliefs in the propositions in the model are basic, they are externally rational and warranted *only if* the model with its epistemological extension is true. For according to the model, the Holy Spirit causes Christians to believe the doctrines in the model in a way that is not due to natural faculties, but which is part of the design plan after the Fall. If the Holy Spirit actually operates according to the model, belief in the doctrines of the model is externally rational. If the Holy Spirit does not operate that way, but someone believe the doctrines in the model in the basic way, her beliefs would be produced neither by natural faculties nor by a supernatural process that is part of the design plan. The beliefs would therefore be basic but not properly basic. Therefore, if the model is true, belief in the doctrines in the model is externally rational and warranted. If the epistemological extension of the model is false, belief that the model is true is neither externally rational nor warranted. Apparently, Plantinga agrees with this conclusion.[2]

Plantinga's position, then, is that Christian beliefs are externally rational and warranted if and only if they are true. This position permits him to show that one sort of critic of Christian belief can be answered—the critic who maintains that while Christian beliefs might be true, the Christian is not rational or warranted in holding them. But by tying the external rationality and warrant of Christian belief to the truth of a very specific epistemic claim about the way the Holy Spirit operates, Plantinga makes it even more difficult to answer the more typical critic, one who does not already believe the model. This would include many traditional Christians who base their Christian beliefs on some combination of experience, testimony, and reason. The thesis that Christian beliefs are typically basic beliefs that are warranted if and only if the Holy Spirit operates in a certain way leaves very little for the Plantinga-style Christian to discuss with non-Christian philosophers and even many Christian philosophers.

The problem, then, is that neither internal rationality nor external rationality and warrant in Plantinga's sense engage the interlocutor who sees the issue of the rationality of Christian belief as something for the Christian and the non-Christian to investigate together. Internal rationality is too narrow. It refers only to the operation of the believer's mind "downstream from experience," where the requirements of proper function in that segment are apparently not very demanding. In contrast, external rationality is so wide, it includes the design of the world and human faculties as God intended it. The non-Christian interlocutor is not asking the Christian to address the rationality of Christian beliefs from *that* perspective since the two of them do not occupy it, nor is he asking the Christian to defend the rationality of Christian beliefs downstream from the believer's experience, a position which the non-believer does not occupy either. If the non-Christian philosopher is doing what philosophers usually do in addressing philosophical questions, he is asking the Christian to discuss the rationality of Christian beliefs from a perspective they both occupy, the one they occupy when they are exploring together important philosophical questions. I am not suggesting that the Christian philosopher should occupy this standpoint all the time. Philosophers sometimes have personal reasons for taking particular positions on philosophical issues, and there is nothing wrong with that. But as philosophers we participate in the communal project of searching for the truth together. How we go about that depends upon which group of philosophers we are working with at any given time. When we share beliefs that can be used in this search, of course, it is important to take that into account. When we do not, we need to approach the communal project in a different way. The value of such a joint project is closely related to the value of philosophy. I take for granted that that is a good thing.

Suppose, however, that I am wrong about the communal nature of philosophy. It is still the case that a broad epistemic community, one that extends beyond our immediate culture, imposes norms on our beliefs. Consider the racial bigot or the suicide terrorist. He might satisfy Plantinga's conditions for both justification and internal rationality with respect to racially bigoted beliefs. He might have done everything Plantinga describes in defending the internal rationality of Christian beliefs. He might have considered how his beliefs fit in with his other beliefs. He might have consulted the people he considers the right people. He might have reflected on the opinions of others who believe he is wrong and still feels certain of his beliefs, responding to criticisms of his view in an angry tirade on Facebook. Has he fulfilled his epistemic duty? Is he epistemically responsible? If the answer is no to either of those questions, Plantinga's conditions for justification or internal rationality are not sufficient for epistemic duty and responsibility. But as I mentioned earlier, even if Plantinga has proposed a new notion of internal rationality whose conditions are satisfied by the racial bigot, there is another sense of rationality that is harder to satisfy and which such a person is missing. Elsewhere I have called this "rationality in the second person" (Zagzebski, 2001, Chapter 14 of this volume; and Zagzebski 2004a, Chapter 9).

The second-person perspective is a middle-level perspective, neither so wide as to encompass all truths, including truths about what God does, nor so narrow as to be contained within the perspective of a single person, a perspective that may be radically out of line with reality, metaphysical or moral. What is important about the middle-level perspective for both moral and epistemic appraisal is that we think that individuals *do* have the ability to assume it—within limits, of course. Other persons are checks on our own rationality and virtue, and we have a responsibility to see ourselves as others see us, at least part of the time. Often when we face criticism from others, the criticism threatens the rationality or justification or virtue of our beliefs or acts whether or not we are doing our best to conduct ourselves properly, and whether or not our beliefs are true. Plantinga has succeeded in showing that the truth of a certain kind of proposition virtually ensures the external rationality and warrant of Christian beliefs in his sense, but that is not the sense for which we are being criticized. Nor is doing our best by our own lights enough to be epistemically good in the sense that is the target of the criticism. Different writers call the intended state justification, rationality, warrant, intellectual virtue, or something else. I do not think it matters what it is called. The point is that it is good to be good epistemic agents and bad not to be. What it takes to be a good epistemic agent is captured by none of the states Plantinga has identified.

12.3. Good epistemic agency

It is no accident that Plantinga divides rationality into two distinct kinds, internal and external, since as he understands them, they are not only distinct, but independent. The conditions for internal rationality in Plantinga's sense are not well correlated with his conditions for external rationality or warrant. The fact that a person is functioning properly internally says nothing at all about whether her experiences are appropriate to the environment and whether her epistemic community is trustworthy, or whether her internally rational and justified beliefs are likely to be true. The ease with which voodoo beliefs and other wildly false beliefs can be internally rational and justified according to Plantinga illustrates this point. There is a wide gap between internal rationality in his sense and truth. It seems to me, however, that the main reason we think rationality is important is that we assume the world is constructed in such a way that a person who does what she is supposed to do internally is well placed to get the truth. There is no guarantee, of course, but evil demons and streaks of bad luck aside, a person who is epistemically virtuous or functioning properly is probably also going to get true beliefs, and she gets true beliefs partly *because* she is virtuous and functioning well internally. I think this means that there is a loose but unitary notion of rationality according to which rationality refers both to behavior that satisfies certain descriptions—behaving well epistemically, and behavior that is truth-conducive. The notion of rationality can serve this dual role as long as the descriptive behavior to which it refers is more or less the same behavior as that which is truth-conducive. So what we mean by rational behavior is behavior that falls under a certain description, a description of what rational persons do (and, I would add, epistemically virtuous persons do even better). They understand and appreciate the evidence, are epistemically thorough, careful, and responsive in characteristic ways to opponents; they are open-minded, good at drawing logical inferences, and so on. But "rational" is also a normative term; it refers to behavior that is good. So rationality is a unitary concept only because we assume that the behavior I have just described is a good thing, and it is a good thing in part because we assume that that behavior is conducive to true belief.

Of course, the connection between internally rational behavior and truth requires a cooperative environment, including a reliable epistemic community, but since there are feedback mechanisms between the environment or community and the epistemic agent, the agent can generally count on a reasonably close connection between the behavior I have described and dependably getting true beliefs. Part of good internal functioning is being a member of an epistemic community whose members are responsible to each other. Any epistemic mismatch between the agent and her community normally means that she is not functioning well *internally*. Responsibility to a community is therefore a part of proper internal functioning, and it is because of the agent's relationship to an epistemic community that the connection between internal rationality and true belief is usually fairly close. Of course, whole communities can be mistaken, as in the case of voodoo beliefs, and that is why an epistemic agent needs to be responsible to more than one epistemic community.

Plantinga's account of rationality and warrant breaks this connection. Being internally rational has virtually nothing to do with getting the truth in the case of Christian beliefs, nor would the connection be gained by strengthening his requirements for internal rationality. Even if he were more demanding about the conditions for internal rationality, that would go no distance at all toward causing the agent to get the truth or even to increase the probability that she will get the truth. Getting the truth about Christian beliefs according to his model occurs quite literally by an act of God. Nothing the agent does by way of epistemic justification or internal rationality, even with requirements of social responsibility added, puts the agent in a dependable position for getting true belief. It is not even clear why we would care about being internally rational in our religious beliefs since internal rationality has no value as a means to truth and does not even have a value as a component of the design plan in this instance. Proper functioning in this case means bypassing normal functioning, the functioning that we usually call rational, and it certainly bypasses the behavior we usually call virtuous. Given that rationality is a normative concept, it is not even clear why the internally rational Christian believer in Plantinga's sense is rational in any sense.

But isn't it possible that there is some domain of human knowledge in which an agent can get the truth in a way that has nothing to do with his internal epistemic functioning? Yes, of course, and if that happened, it would be a big stroke of epistemic luck. The Holy Spirit might operate the way Plantinga describes. But I doubt that the typical objector disagrees with Plantinga on that. Someone might get the truth by a process that has nothing to do with being a good epistemic agent, just as someone might produce the ends of moral action by a process that has nothing to do with being a good moral agent. God could intervene in the causal consequences of the actions of some group of people and make them successful in bringing about certain moral ends—e.g., the welfare of others, even when there is no connection between the morally proper functioning of those persons and welfare. But there is a difference between the epistemic case and its moral analogue. We have ways of finding out whether welfare is produced independently of good internal moral functioning. We cannot do that in Plantinga's epistemic scenario. It is not as if we can run a check on the truth of religious beliefs to find out whether and when getting the truth is disconnected from good internal epistemic functioning. As a matter of fact, I think this point applies to all beliefs, not just religious beliefs, although my argument in this paper does not depend upon the general point. For some kinds of belief, we think that their truth is confirmed when a predicted future experience occurs, but even that is not a determination of the truth of a belief independent of proper internal functioning. The best we can do in any area of belief is to rely on the social norms developed over millennia of human experience in observing the epistemic agents who are most successful, but success cannot be determined independent of those norms.

Predictive success is one way in which epistemic agents can be successful, but there are others. Some agents are recognized for their understanding or wisdom, or what Aristotle calls *phronesis*. I have argued in other work that these people are recognizable in advance of identifying the properties in virtue of which they have practical wisdom. Not only is imitating epistemic exemplars the best way to dependably get true beliefs as well as beliefs that have epistemic value other than truth, but we do not even have the ability to identify exceptions to the connection between good epistemic behavior and gaining the truth apart from using the standard for good epistemic behavior. As I have said, whole communities can be wrong, but there is nothing we can do except to continue to use our internal standards, including standards arising from membership in epistemic communities whose members both support and correct each other. An important reason why we assume a connection between good internal epistemic behavior and truth, then, is that we really have no choice.

I argued earlier that Plantinga's defense of the rationality and other desirable epistemic properties of Christian belief does not come from a standpoint common to him and the philosophers to whom he is responding. That standpoint arises from the fact that philosophers form an epistemic community, and I have further argued that such communities constitute an important link between the individual's efforts and success at getting the truth. In fact, we cannot even tell whether the individual has succeeded in getting the truth apart from being a good epistemic agent, which means good internal functioning in consort with that of the various epistemic communities of which we are a part. The best we can do to become a good epistemic agent is to become a person who is as much like epistemic exemplars as possible. The traits of such agents are the intellectual virtues. Many of the intellectual virtues have a strong social dimension. That is what we would expect if I am right that good internal epistemic functioning does not dependably lead us successfully to epistemic ends such as true belief and understanding without an elaborate social network that interacts with our epistemic behavior. Epistemic communities exist because their existence is the best way for everyone to be successful at epistemic ends. The virtues that lead individuals successfully to epistemic ends include many traits that involve social interaction and cooperation—virtues such as open-mindedness, intellectual fairness and humility, trust in the trustworthy, and being trustworthy oneself.

Most of these traits coincide with neither internal nor external rationality in Plantinga's sense, nor with the two together, nor do they coincide with warrant, or any combination of warrant, justification, internal rationality, or external rationality. One obvious difference is that the properties Plantinga discusses are primarily properties of a belief or a set of beliefs, not traits of persons, but in addition, epistemic virtues cut across the internal/external distinction. They include features of the consciousness of the believer, features of her community, and the relationship between the believer and her community, and some of them include the feature of epistemic success. All of these are traits we expect, or at least hope to see, in other members of our epistemic community, as well as in ourselves. These traits bind an epistemic community together. The lack of these virtues in individuals in a community is a problem for the entire community, not just for the individual.

Consider the related virtues of epistemic trustworthiness, credibility, and authoritativeness. A trustworthy person is one who deserves trust, which means at a minimum that she is a reliable truth-teller. A trustworthy person must not only have whatever virtues it takes to reliably acquire true rather than false beliefs, she must also be a reliable communicator. She must be motivated to communicate clearly and accurately and she must be successful at doing so. This virtue bridges internal and external rationality and warrant in Plantinga's sense. No one is trustworthy unless she generally has warranted beliefs, and she also must function well at each stage in the formation and communication of her beliefs. But it is possible for a person to have a set of beliefs that have all of the evaluative properties identified by Plantinga and not be trustworthy. The most obvious way this can happen is when some individual belief or set of beliefs has all of the properties Plantinga discusses, but most of the agent's other beliefs do not. If a person is not epistemically trustworthy, other persons should not trust her even if in some particular case her belief is justified, internally and externally rational, and warranted. Everyone in the community loses epistemically when that happens. The rest of the community loses by losing the true belief the agent possesses; she loses, since by losing their trust, she loses the epistemic advantages they could give her.[3]

It is also possible that most of an agent's beliefs are justified, internally and externally rational, and warranted, but she fails to be trustworthy because she lacks the ability to be a clear and accurate communicator, or because she has that ability but is not motivated to use it because she is not sufficiently respectful of the value of giving others epistemic advantages. But even if she *is* trustworthy, that is not sufficient to make her a valuable member of an epistemic community. It is possible to be trustworthy, but to lack the related virtues of credibility and authoritativeness. A credible person is a believable one. A person is not credible unless she not only deserves to be believed, but *is* believed by others in her epistemic community. When the virtues of trustworthiness and credibility come apart, the consequences can be tragic, as we see in the Greek legend of Cassandra. Recall that Apollo gives her the gift of prophecy as part of a scheme to seduce her. When she rebuffs him, he makes it happen that while she continues to see the future, nobody believes her. The epistemic effect on others of Cassandra's curse is serious—her warning that the Trojan horse is a trick goes unheeded, with disastrous results, but it arguably has even worse epistemic effects on her because she is unable to benefit from epistemic relationships.[4] To be a valuable member of an epistemic community, one needs to be both trustworthy and credible.

Now let us return to Plantinga's Aquinas/Calvin model of Christian belief. Since the Christian can have beliefs that are justified, internally and externally rational, and warranted without being trustworthy, or can be trustworthy without being credible, it is not enough for the Christian as a member of an epistemic community that includes non-Christians to have beliefs with the properties Plantinga discusses. There is nothing in the model with its epistemological extension that requires that the Christian believer is trustworthy since she might otherwise be very untrustworthy, nor is there anything in it that requires that she is credible. But there is nothing in the model that precludes her trustworthiness and credibility either. She may generally be a trustworthy and credible person. But the model Plantinga describes imposes a form of epistemic isolation on the Christian. Like the mythical Cassandra, she is isolated from those without the supernatural gift, although thankfully there are others who believe in the way described in the model, so her isolation is not as severe as Cassandra's. Like Cassandra, she is trustworthy in those beliefs produced by the gift, but she is in danger of imitating Cassandra in lacking credibility. Of course, the Christian who believes as described in the model does not entirely lack credibility since other Christians believe her, whether or not they believe by the process described in the model. But I seriously doubt that anybody believes on her authority or because of her trustworthiness. The mythical analogy to Plantinga's model would be a scenario in which Apollo gives the gift of prophecy to a number of individuals who then form a community. Let us call them the Seers. Imagine also that Apollo does not curse them by making others disbelieve them, but the Seers' grounds for believing have no social dimension. If others believe what they believe, it is for independent reasons. Of course, there is nothing preventing the Seers from discussing these independent reasons with the non-Seers, but the Seers cannot contribute to the social project of helping the non-Seers come to know the future through the Seers' epistemic advantages. Even though the Seers can be justified, internally and externally rational, and warranted, as Plantinga understands these properties, that is useless to the non-Seers. What is epistemically good about the Seers is not shareable.

This is what I find troublesome about the strategy of Plantinga's book on warranted Christian belief. Even if the entire argument goes through, it is socially useless. Its value is solely that of defense against a very specific kind of attack. There are forms of defense that can be used to further the common project of working out the answer to a philosophical problem with opponents. Plantinga's defense is not of that sort. For those of us who think many religious doctrines are metaphysical theses that ought to be openly discussed and evaluated in competition with other metaphysical theses, the defensive tack is not helpful. Plantinga's approach does not overcome epistemic isolation, but it is designed to retain it. I believe God made us social beings who are good epistemic agents when we have the intellectual virtues, many of which have the social features I have described. These virtues put us in the best position to get truth and other epistemic goods such as understanding. It is possible that some true beliefs can be given to us directly by God, but if that happens, I see no reason to think that God would subvert his own creation by requiring the agent to remove herself from the community of philosophical inquirers. As we see in the story of Cassandra, epistemic isolation is not a blessing, but a curse. We should strive to overcome it.

Notes

1. In a curious reversal of philosophical culture, the religious tone of American culture is currently strong enough that some atheists feel under attack by theists. In an op-ed piece in the *New York Times*, July 12, 2003, Daniel Dennett says it is time to "sound the alarm," and he asks atheists to "come out of the closet." His adversarial spirit is unmistakably expressed in his preferred term for an atheist—a "bright," suggesting, of course, that theists are "dims."
2. In a book symposium on *Warranted Christian Belief* in *Philosophical Books*, April 2002, I argued that while Plantinga gives considerable attention to arguing that if his model of Christian doctrine is true, it is rational and warranted to believe the doctrines in the model, he is committed to the position that these beliefs are rational and warranted *only if* the model is true. In response to me Plantinga says, "I thought it pretty obvious (Plantinga 2000b, 112) that Christian belief can be rational; the interesting question is whether it can have *warrant*. I argued that (probably) Christian belief is warranted if and only if it is true." I am not sure that Plantinga has explicitly made the same claim about external rationality as about warrant. But if the proposition about the way the Holy Spirit operates is false, presumably something has gone wrong in the segment of the belief-forming process upstream from experience since he makes it clear that beliefs in the model are rational downstream from the experience, and that means that

the belief would not be externally rational in his sense. But if I am wrong about that, nothing much changes in this paper since I am primarily claiming that the truth of the extended model is not sufficient for the kind of epistemic goodness the objector is interested in. I am not focusing on the claim that it is not necessary.
3. If instead they *do* trust her even though she is not trustworthy, they lose because even though they get the truth in this case, they also get a lot of falsehoods from her.
4. Of course, the effects on Cassandra of her curse go well beyond the epistemic. She is completely miserable.

13
First-Person and Third-Person Reasons and Religious Epistemology (2011)

13.1. The distinction between first-person and third-person reasons

13.1.1. Two kinds of epistemic reasons

I assume that believing *p* is a state in which I have settled for myself whether *p*. An epistemic reason to believe *p* is a state in virtue of which it is reasonable to think some proposition *p* is true. It is something on the basis of which I can settle for myself whether *p* insofar as my goal is truth, not benefit or some other practical or moral aim. I want to argue that there are two kinds of epistemic reasons, one irreducibly first personal, the other third personal, and that attending to the distinction illuminates a host of philosophical problems, including several that have special importance for philosophy of religion.

What I mean by *theoretical reasons* for believing *p* are facts that are logically or probabilistically connected to the truth of *p*. They are facts (or propositions) about states of the world or experiences which, taken together, give a cumulative case for or against the fact that *p* (or the truth of *p*).[1] They are not intrinsically connected to believing. We call them reasons because a reasonable person who comes to believe them and grasps their logical relations to *p* will see them as reasons for *p*. They can be shared with others—laid out on the table, so they are third personal. They are relevant from anyone's point of view. In fact, they do not require a point of view to be reasons. The connections between theoretical reasons and what they are reasons for are among the facts of the universe. Theoretical reasons aggregate and can be used in Bayesian calculations. What we call evidence is most naturally put in the category of theoretical reasons, although the notion of evidence is multiply ambiguous.[2] But when I mention evidence in this paper, I will mean facts that are in the category of theoretical reasons.

In contrast, what I call *deliberative reasons* have an essential connection to *me* and only to *me* in my deliberations about whether *p*. Deliberative reasons connect *me* to getting the truth of *p*, whereas theoretical reasons connect facts about the world with the truth of *p*. Deliberative reasons do not simply provide me a weightier reason for *p* than they provide others. They are not reasons for other persons at all. They are irreducibly first personal.

To see the distinction I have in mind, consider experience as a reason for belief. If you have an experience, the *fact* that you have it is a theoretical reason for believing a variety of propositions. You can tell me about your experience, and if I believe what you tell me, I can then refer to the fact that you had the experience as a reason to believe whatever it supports. You and I can both refer to the fact that you had the experience as a reason to believe something, and so can anybody else who is aware of the fact that you had the experience. The fact that the experience occurred is therefore a theoretical reason. It is on the table for all to consider, and everyone can consider its logical and probabilistic connections to other facts about the world.

However, you are in a different position than I am with respect to your experience because you not only grasp the fact that you had the experience; in addition, you and you alone *had* the experience. That experience affects many of your reasoning processes, emotional responses, and the way you come to have or give up certain beliefs directly, and that is quite proper. In contrast, the fact that you had the experience is something you and I and many other people can come to believe. My way of describing the contrast is that your experience gives you a deliberative reason to form certain beliefs, whereas the fact that the experience occurred gives anybody a theoretical reason to form certain beliefs.[3] Anybody can form the belief that you had the experience, thereby accessing that fact, but nobody but you can have your experience.

Another type of deliberative reason is what are loosely called intuitions in one of its senses. I will not attempt an account of intuition, but what I have in mind is, very roughly, something internal to the mind that responds with an answer to a question, often as a response to a concrete case. For example, if a fat man is stuck in the mouth of a cave, is it morally permissible to blow him out of the cave to save yourself and the other spelunkers from drowning in the rising tide? My intuition might be no, but perhaps yours is yes. I have no position on the strength of an intuition of this kind as a reason to believe what the intuition supports. Maybe it is strong, maybe it is not. But insofar as it is a reason at all, it is a deliberative reason. My intuitions are mine alone, and they give me but not you a particular kind of reason for certain beliefs. But again, the fact that I have an intuition can be put out on the table. I can tell you that my intuition is such and such, and that then becomes a theoretical reason supporting some position. So the fact that most people think that Gettier cases are not cases of knowledge is a reason for anyone to reject a theory that has the consequence that the believer knows in a Gettier situation, but your own intuition about such cases is a reason for you alone to draw certain conclusions. Intuitions, then, are like experiences. The intuition and the experience provide the agent with first-person reasons to believe something, but the fact that the experience occurred or that the intuition is what it is can be treated as evidence, as a theoretical reason for the truth of some proposition.

I propose that there is another important deliberative reason that is more basic for us than any theoretical reasons we can identify. We can see the need for such a reason by reflecting on the need for a link between third-person reasons and something in myself. Theoretical reasons do not operate as reasons for me to believe anything until I take them on board, but *my taking* a certain set of theoretical reasons for p as reasons to believe p is not sufficient in itself to make it likely that p is true. That is because my taking a set of theoretical reasons to be reasons to believe p is irrelevant to the actual connection between those reasons and p unless I have taken them properly—properly identified the facts, figured out the correct logical and probabilistic relations between those facts and p, have appreciated the significance of individual facts, and have not left anything out. But my reasons to believe *that* depend upon the more basic belief that my faculties are trustworthy. And that raises the question of what reasons I have to believe that my faculties are trustworthy. It has been pointed out by others that any such reasons are circular. I have no way of telling that my faculties in general get me to the truth without using those faculties.

A reasonable response to the phenomenon of epistemic circularity is epistemic self-trust.[4] I am not arguing here that no other response is reasonable (although it is my position that no other response is *as* reasonable), but I am claiming that it is reasonable to trust my faculties. Trust includes believing that my faculties are generally trustworthy, and dispelling doubts about their trustworthiness or holding such doubts at bay. Given that doubt is partly affective, it takes an affective state to dispel it, and so I propose that self-trust includes an affective component, a component of feeling trusting. It is because of self-trust—a state that is partly affective—that I take the theoretical reasons I identify to point to the truth of some proposition p, and as long as self-trust is reasonable, I am reasonable in doing so.

I said earlier that a reason to believe p is a state in virtue of which it is reasonable to think some proposition p is true. If so, self-trust is a reason because it is in virtue of self-trust that I believe that what I take to be theoretical reasons for believing p are truth-indicators, and that is a reasonable thing to do. Self-trust *is* a reason, but a reason of a distinctively first-personal kind. It is a second-order reason because it is a reason to believe that I have properly identified reasons for a belief, whether theoretical or deliberative. The way self-trust gives me a deliberative reason to think I am properly connected to theoretical reasons shows that there are deliberative reasons that are more basic for me than any theoretical reasons I can identify. Of course, they are not more basic than theoretical reasons, which are facts of the universe, but they are more basic than my use of any theoretical reasons in deliberations about what the truth is.

I have said that deliberative reasons can be first-order reasons like experience or intuition, or second-order reasons like self-trust. I want to argue next that trust in myself, which is a deliberative reason, can give me a reason to trust others, another deliberative reason. A deliberative reason can be a reason to have other deliberative reasons.

How does self-trust give me a reason to trust others? My position is that if, in believing in a way I trust, I come to believe that others have the same faculties I trust in myself, then given the *a priori* principle that I ought to treat like cases alike, I have a reason to trust their faculties. If I reasonably trust their faculties, I have a reason to believe the deliverances of their faculties. Trust in someone else gives me a deliberative reason to believe some proposition p because my reason is based on their similarity to *me* and my trust in myself.[5]

If I am right that trust is partly an affective state, and if I am also right that trust can give me a reason to believe p, then a state that is partly affective can give me a reason to believe p. This is an epistemic reason, not a practical or moral reason. I think that there are probably other affective states that are deliberative reasons for belief. One is the emotion of admiration. I may epistemically admire someone and trust the admiration upon reflection. Admiration for a person can give me a reason to think that she has the truth in some domain that includes p, and it can give me a reason to try to imitate her in a way that includes coming to believe p. In that case, my admiration for her is a deliberative reason to believe p. There are no doubt theoretical reasons to admire her, but those are not the reasons for believing p.[6]

Deliberative reasons to believe p because of trust or admiration for another person are not necessarily reasons to think that the other person has theoretical reasons for p. Of course, it often happens that a person who has the truth whether p also has theoretical reasons to believe p, but my reason to think someone has the truth whether p is not the same as a reason to think that she has theoretical reasons to believe p. Even if she has theoretical reasons for p, that is not what I have reason to believe. Deliberative reasons like trust and admiration are higher order reasons to think that I or someone else has the truth whether p, and therefore has reason to believe p, but their reason may be deliberative rather than theoretical.

I have mentioned a number of kinds of deliberative reasons: an experience, an intuition, trust in myself, trust in others, admiration. The first two have a third-person analogue that is a theoretical reason. The fact that someone had an experience, and the fact that someone has an intuition, can be treated by anybody as theoretical reasons to believe p. Trust and admiration are different. The fact that you trust something or admire someone is not a theoretical reason. It is not the kind of reason that can be put out on the table for all to consider in favor of the truth of some proposition. It may, however, be a deliberative reason for someone who trusts what you trust.

13.1.2. The contrast between theoretical and deliberative reasons

There are important differences between theoretical and deliberative reasons that put them in distinct categories. First, deliberative reasons do not increase my theoretical reasons, and theoretical reasons do not increase my deliberative reasons. That follows from the first-person character of deliberative reasons and the third-person character of theoretical reasons. That is because nobody has figured out how to put the first-person and third-person points of view together. My deliberative reasons are not facts of the universe that affect the theoretical case for p, and I can understand that even if *I* am the one giving the theoretical case. Suppose I am giving the case for the proposition that driving while talking on a mobile phone is dangerous. I would point to studies by reliable researchers that show that people who talk on the phone while driving have reduced peripheral vision, slower response time, and a higher accident rate than people who do not, but I would not add that I trust the people who did the studies and I know that they believe its conclusion. (Studies of that sort rarely even mention the personal conclusion drawn by the researchers.) The fact that people I trust believe what they believe or have certain epistemic qualities does not make the relationship between the data in the studies and the conclusion stronger. To refer to it when giving the evidence linking mobile phone use and auto safety is beside the point. If driving while on the phone is dangerous, it does not matter what anybody anywhere thinks about it. Of course, I might cite my experience driving while on the phone as a reason for me to believe it is unsafe, and you could cite the fact that I had that experience when giving your theoretical reasons for the same conclusion. But when you cite the fact that I had the experience as a theoretical reason for believing that talking on the phone while driving is unsafe, you are not referring to the same thing to which I refer when I cite my experience.

Both theoretical and deliberative reasons are kinds of reasons to think some proposition is true, but I put them together in a way that is unique to me since I am the only one who has my deliberative reasons. Together they can increase or decrease my confidence that p. So, if I believe p based on theoretical reasons and then find out that you believe p, too, that increases my confidence that p. Adding a deliberative reason to my theoretical reasons increases my confidence. But while it is true that finding out that you believe p increases my confidence in myself in the way I come to believe p, and therefore increases my confidence in p, it is not additional theoretical evidence for p. If we were listing the facts of the universe that indicate the dangers of driving while on the phone, we would not list the names of the people who believe that it is dangerous.

Reasons do not aggregate in the other direction either. I might believe p on the basis of deliberative reasons—say, I epistemically trust you and you believe p.

Then I get a piece of evidence that p and that increases my confidence that p. In that case it might appear that the theoretical reason increases the force of my deliberative reason; it increases my trust in you. But that also is a mistake. Getting a piece of evidence for p does not support my trust in you when you believe p. It shows that your conclusion is more likely to be correct, and so I am more confident in p, but even if I get heaps of evidence for p, that should not increase my confidence that you are trustworthy in the way you came to your belief p. I could get evidence that you are trustworthy, but that is not part of the theoretical case for p. It is part of the theoretical case that you are trustworthy.

I am not claiming that the beliefs of others cannot be treated as evidence. I could get evidence that you are reliable in some domain and evidence that you have a belief in that domain. That would give me a theoretical reason to have the belief. It could be put out on the table as inductive evidence for the truth of the belief. That is not the same as the trust I have in you that can give me a deliberative reason to believe what you believe or what you tell me. I have described trust as a state that is partly epistemic and partly affective, and trust in others arises because it is a commitment of my attitude toward myself. A judgment of reliability is a third-person judgment that involves nothing about personal relations or agency. In a judgment of reliability, a person is treated no differently than a thermometer or a calculator.

Theoretical reasons aggregate with each other since they are third personal. Deliberative reasons can affect other deliberative reasons, but your deliberative reasons do not aggregate with mine. Nonetheless, your deliberative reasons can affect mine. If I trust you and you tell me that you trust someone else or some authoritative body, I might take that as a reason to trust that person or body. But if I do not trust you and you tell me you trust yourself or someone else, your trust is irrelevant to me. Your deliberative reasons are relevant to me only insofar as they connect with *my* deliberative reasons.

There is another interesting difference between theoretical reasons and deliberative reasons. I have no control over the relation between theoretical reasons for p and p, but I exercise executive control over the way deliberative reasons are reasons for p. There is no automatic connection, a connection that could be computed by somebody else, between my experience, my trust in someone, or my intuition, and a belief that p. I make the connection. It is because of my deliberative reasons that what I believe is up to me.[7] I am not suggesting that deliberative reasons are voluntary, but my agency is involved in deliberative reasons, whereas it is irrelevant to theoretical reasons. By the nature of deliberative reasons, they connect me and the exercise of my reflective faculties with the aim I have in exercising those faculties in the domain of belief. For present purposes, I am assuming the aim is truth, although we can also have deliberative reasons to think that our faculties connect us to other epistemic ends such as understanding.

To summarize what I have said so far:

- Theoretical reasons are third personal, deliberative reasons are first personal.
- Theoretical reasons have no essential connection to belief; deliberative reasons are essentially connected to my deliberations about what to believe.
- Theoretical and deliberative reasons do not aggregate. Deliberative reasons for me to believe p do not increase the theoretical case for p. Theoretical reasons for p do not increase my deliberative reasons for believing p.
- There are deliberative reasons that are always more basic than any theoretical reasons I can identify.
- I have no control over theoretical reasons, whereas deliberative reasons are reasons for me as a particular self and my agency is, or at least can be, involved.

Both theoretical and deliberative reasons are reasons, and they are truth-directed. They are epistemic, not practical. Theoretical reasons are facts that support the truth of the proposition p. Deliberative reasons are reasons that support my believing p insofar as my aim is truth. They are reasons that support *my* believing p rather than your believing p. Both deliberative reasons and the theoretical reasons I identify increase my confidence in my belief p.

The distinction I am proposing is not the same as the distinction between first-order and second-order epistemic reasons. There are both first-order and second-order theoretical reasons and first-order and second-order deliberative reasons. As I have said, the fact that an experience occurred is a first-order theoretical reason for various beliefs; the experience is a first-order deliberative reason. The fact that a certain person is reliable is a second-order theoretical reason to believe what she believes; my epistemic trust in that person is a second-order deliberative reason.

The distinction between agent-relative and agent-neutral reasons in ethics is closer to the distinction I am drawing here.[8] There are different ways to characterize agent-relative reasons, but sometimes an agent-relative reason is treated as a reason other persons can have, but it has a different force for the agent than for others. For example, everyone has a reason to prevent murders, but the agent has a special reason not to commit a murder herself. In contrast, what I mean by a deliberative reason is a reason only a single person can have.[9]

Another difference is that agent-relative reasons are generally treated as reasons that, while applying in a special way to a particular agent, are reasons for that agent because of some general principle. In this way of looking at reasons, agent-relative reasons are recognizable by persons other than the agent as reasons for that agent independent of the agent's deliberations. So, for example, my agent-relative reason not to commit a murder is not dependent upon my view of the matter. Everyone knows in advance that I have such a reason, and it is not up to me whether that reason applies to me. In contrast, I have proposed that deliberative reasons are connected with the agent's agency, and whether something is a deliberative reason for her in some situation is up to her, at least in the sense that directing her conscious use of reasons is up to her. That is a substantive claim about deliberative reasons that might not affect the way the distinction is made, so perhaps the terminology of agent-relative and agent-neutral epistemic reasons is an appropriate usage for the distinction I have described in this paper. I have no objections to using that terminology, provided that the differences between my way of characterizing the two kinds of reasons and its usage by other authors is recognized.

13.2. Applying the distinction to problems in religious epistemology

13.2.1. Religious experience

The distinction between theoretical and deliberative reasons makes it easier to understand a number of epistemic phenomena. First, it explains *the puzzle of how experience can be a reason for belief*, the enduring problem of the foundation of empirical knowledge. The problem is that the relation between my experience and a proposition I come to believe based on that experience is different in kind from the relation between one of my beliefs and another. There is no way to solve this problem by turning experiences into facts or propositional beliefs in an attempt to make all reasons theoretical. The fact that I have a certain sensory experience of seeing yellow gives me a theoretical reason to believe there is something yellow there, but my grasp of the fact that I have the experience of seeing yellow must itself be justified by the experience of seeing yellow. The foundation of empirical knowledge is experience; it is not a propositional belief, much less some neutral fact about the universe, but something of an entirely different kind. The relation between an instance of that kind and a propositional belief differs qualitatively from the relation between one propositional belief and another.

The distinction between two kinds of epistemic reasons can be used to explain this difference. An experience is a deliberative reason for the person who has the experience to form certain beliefs. Those beliefs then give her theoretical reasons to form certain other beliefs when she grasps the relation between those reasons and what they are reasons for. Since we know that the link between experience and belief has to be different in kind from the link between one belief and another, we seek an explanation for the difference, and the difference between first-person and third-person reasons gives us such an explanation.

This is important for the rationality of religious belief based on religious experience. A religious experience gives the subject an irreducibly first-person reason for belief, one that differs qualitatively from the relation between the fact that the experience occurred and a belief it supports, a relation to which anyone has access, in principle. The distinction between the two kinds of reasons is particularly important for religious experience because religious experience may be uncommon within a population, and that makes it difficult for many people to access the fact that a religious experience has occurred. It is not unreasonable for someone to be skeptical about the evidential support given to a religious belief by the fact that someone else had a religious experience if experiences of that kind are qualitatively different from any experiences that person has had. We usually think that a religious experience is a stronger reason for religious belief for the person who has the experience than for other persons, but I think it is important to recognize a qualitative difference, not merely a difference in degree. In my opinion, discussion of religious experience as grounds for religious belief is aided by focusing on the way deliberative reasons operate in a rational person. The process is very different when the only relevant reasons are theoretical.

13.2.2. Testimony

The distinction between the two kinds of reasons also makes it easier to understand the *practice of testimony*, which can be interpreted either as giving the recipient a theoretical reason for a belief or as giving her a deliberative reason. Most of the literature on testimony treats it as giving the recipient a theoretical reason. According to the reductionist model, the recipient makes an inductive inference from the evidence that a testifier is reliable in the relevant domain and that she has testified that *p*, to the conclusion that *p*. Anything can be treated as evidence, and there is nothing preventing a person from making such an inference. When she does so, she has a third-person reason to believe what another person says. Many so-called non-reductionists also see testimony as giving the subject evidence for belief, only they think the evidence is direct rather than inferential.[10] In these evidence models, the testifier is treated the same way we treat a computer or a clock. The testifier gives anybody in similar circumstances a reason to believe the testimony.

Given what I have said, I cannot consistently treat other persons as simply sources of evidence for me. It is because of trust in myself that I must trust them. When I trust someone else and they believe in a way I trust, I have a deliberative reason to believe the same thing. The person I trust may tell me what she believes in a way that expresses an intention that I believe it, too. When she does so, she is asking me for trust, and if I grant it, I come to believe what she tells me on her word. There is a relationship between the testifier and myself in which each of us plays a role. The testifier assures me, the recipient, that p is true and that she has taken the responsibility to make the belief justified (or in my preferred terminology, epistemically conscientious). I rely upon her for the conscientious formation of the belief and defer to her if challenged.[11] Since telling involves an interpersonal relationship on this model, there is a sense in which belief on testimony is within the control of the recipient. The evidence view of testimony cannot explain that. The evidential view makes it a mystery how asking for trust and granting it can provide a *reason* for anybody to believe something. It does not seem to be in the right category to be a reason for belief.[12] But we can see why the evidence view of testimony exists. It is the view a person is forced to have if the only epistemic reasons she recognizes are theoretical.

The interpretation of the practice of testimony is important for religious epistemology because divine revelation is testimony from God. On the evidence model of testimony, divine testimony gives the recipient either direct or inferential evidence for the content of the testimony. So belief on revelation can be interpreted as based on an inference that the source of some putative revelation is divine and hence reliable, the position of John Locke.[13] Alternatively, divine testimony can be interpreted as direct evidence for the content of the testimony. Anti-reductionists about testimony typically follow Thomas Reid, who thought of belief on testimony as directly justified in the way he thought perceptual beliefs are directly justified by perceptual experience. On this model, the recipient of divine testimony has direct evidence for the truth of the testimony. Notice that the adherent of this approach agrees with Locke that a revelatory event is evidence for the recipient. The difference is that this view makes the evidence non-inferential, whereas Locke makes it inferential.

The distinction between theoretical and deliberative reasons allows us to consider a third position. Suppose that central cases of testimony give the recipient deliberative rather than theoretical reasons for belief. The ground of belief in revelation is trust in God, which gives me a deliberative reason to believe what God tells me. When God tells me that p, God takes responsibility for the truth of p for me and for all other intended recipients of his revelation. God intends that I believe him, and he acknowledges that we who are the recipients place epistemic trust in him by believing him. Our responsibility is to trust appropriately. It is God's responsibility to make the belief true.

There are a number of different ways trust can be an appropriate deliberative reason to believe testimony from God. Some people's trust is grounded in other deliberative reasons such as religious experience or the admiration they have for the Scriptural message. My view is that trust in another person is justified by my conscientious judgment that trusting that person will survive my own conscientious self-reflection.[14] Believing a person who is currently speaking to me or who has written a book or sent me an email is not very mysterious, but believing God requires a theory of revelation to explain how communication between God and me can succeed. My point here is not to give a theory of revelation, but to point out that a theory of revelation should respect the way in which testimony operates between two persons. If testimony involves a personal request for trust and a granting of trust, that element must be a component of an account of divine revelation.

13.2.3. Reasonable disagreement

The distinction between theoretical and deliberative reasons also helps us in framing the topic of *reasonable disagreement*. Suppose I believe p and you believe not p. We get together and compare our evidence, so now we have all the same evidence. Our evidence can include the facts that we have each had certain experiences. We now are aware of the same theoretical reasons for and against p. A problem arises when, in addition to the evidence on the table, I know that you believe not p and I trust you in the way you acquired your belief not p. I now seem to have a weaker case for p than I had before.

This situation is not especially problematic if we think of the conflict as arising within one's theoretical reasons. Theoretical reasons may or may not include facts about people's beliefs. Let us suppose first that they do. The issue in that case is that one reliable person who happens to be me believes p, but another reliable person who happens to be you believes not p. This conflict is no different than the conflict that arises when neither of the persons with conflicting beliefs is myself. It is the common problem of a clash in evidence, and it is presumably resolved by awaiting more evidence. In any case, there is no *special* problem when the disagreement between myself and another is interpreted as this sort of conflict within theoretical reasons.

There is another way the person who sees the problem as a conflict within theoretical reasons can look at the situation. They might exclude from the evidence the fact that the believers have the beliefs they have. The idea here is that persons are simply conduits for communicating evidence to each other. Once the evidence is on the table, it does not matter what anybody believes. What someone believes is a fact about what they do with the evidence; it is not evidence. It might appear that we are forced to draw this conclusion because we do not treat our own belief as evidence. If I am considering the case for and against p, once I start to believe p, I do not think that then I have additional evidence for p. My believing p does not increase my theoretical case for p. But if *my* believing p has no effect on the case for p, *your* believing p should have no effect either. What people believe is not part of the theoretical reasons for belief. On this approach, disagreement is not a problem.

We see, then, that if the only reasons for belief are theoretical, disagreement is a problem of evidence pointing in conflicting directions. This is not mysterious or surprising, and it can be interpreted as no problem at all. But reasonable people do experience their disagreement with other reasonable people as a problem, and it is necessary to explain that. Suppose I believe p and I have certain theoretical reasons upon which I base my belief. As I have argued, my confidence in p is not determined solely by those reasons because those reasons by themselves are not sufficient to justify me in believing p in a non-circular way. I must also trust that my faculties have properly handled the evidence, which means not only that I have figured out the correct logical and probabilistic relations between the evidence and p, but that I appreciate the significance of individual pieces of evidence, and that I have not left anything out. I need to trust that I have used my faculties well and have the relevant intellectual virtues. But given that my confidence in my belief p depends upon the preceding elements, and given that my trust in myself commits me to trust others who are relevantly like myself, the fact that someone else who is relevantly like me believes not p gives me a reason to trust her belief not p and to distrust my belief p. The problem of reasonable disagreement is therefore a problem that arises among my deliberative reasons.

When we consider deliberative reasons for belief, that gives us a different response to the argument that your belief should not count as evidence for me unless mine does also. If a belief is formed in a way I trust, that *does* give me a deliberative reason to believe it. The surprising conclusion is that if *I* form a belief p in a way I trust, that gives me a deliberative reason to (continue to) believe p, just as *your* believing not p in a way I trust gives me a deliberative reason to believe not p. The objector who claims that your belief does not give me a reason to believe anything unless mine does also is correct. There is a symmetry between your belief and mine as reasons for belief. Neither belief gives me a theoretical reason to believe. Both beliefs give me a deliberative reason to believe. The problem of disagreement arises when I trust both myself and someone else who has a conflicting belief.

Religious disagreement was recognized as a problem for religious belief well before the topic of reasonable disagreement got attention from epistemologists. What people did *not* do was to reason as follows: "I and my co-religionists are reliable people and we believe p. The believers in these other religions are also reliable people and they believe not p." If that was what they were thinking, the conflict in their evidence would not have been very interesting, as I have said. But people also did not take the second approach to disagreement within theoretical reasons mentioned earlier. That is, they did not say that the conflicting beliefs of other people are irrelevant because beliefs are not evidence. They were presumably worried about something else. Many people found that their experiences of close association with persons in other religious communities led them to place a substantial amount of trust in those persons, and consequently in their beliefs. They interpreted their trust in those others as giving them a *reason* to believe what the others believed, a reason that conflicted with the reasons they already had to believe in their own religion due to trust in themselves. It is very difficult to explain why this kind of experience leads to a clash of reasons for belief unless we are talking about deliberative reasons.

13.2.4. Believing on authority

The difference between theoretical and deliberative reasons also explains the primary feature of *acting or believing on authority*. According to Joseph Raz (1986), the distinguishing feature of authoritative directives is that they give the subject a preemptive reason to obey the authority, where a preemptive reason is a reason that replaces the subject's other reasons for and against performing the act. For instance, if I stop at a red light on the authority of the law, the fact that the law requires me to stop is my reason for stopping, a reason that replaces any other reasons I have for and against stopping at the light. I will not argue here that acting on authority in this way can be justified. My point is only that acting on authority is something people do, and what they are doing is to treat their reasons for acting as the authority dictates in a certain way, one in which the authority's directive becomes *the* reason for the act, replacing other reasons. But it is very hard to see how one reason can replace another when both reasons are theoretical. In order to permit one reason to replace others, I, the subject, must take the authority's directive as having a certain force for me. I am free to take it as authoritative or not. I therefore exercise the executive function of an agent when I act on authority. My reason to do so must therefore be deliberative.

I argue that the same point applies to believing on authority as to acting on authority. My position is that the belief or testimony of another person whom I conscientiously take to be more trustworthy than myself in some domain can give me a preemptive reason to believe what the authority believes or testifies.[15] The distinction between theoretical and deliberative reasons makes it easier to see how this can happen. The fact that the authority has a belief *p* preempts my theoretical reasons for and against *p*. But preemption seems strange if all epistemic reasons are theoretical.

The rationality of taking religious beliefs on authority gets very little attention in religious epistemology and I have attempted to make that change (Zagzebski 2012, Chapter 9). I believe that it can be reasonable to take a religious belief preemptively out of trust in a religious authority. My reason to take a belief on authority is deliberative. It depends upon a certain connection between the authority and myself, and I exercise the control of an agent when I do so.

The erosion of trust in authority in modern life includes the loss of *reasons* to believe or act as the authority directs. Religious communities have much to contribute to our understanding of building and rebuilding the relationships that give persons deliberative reasons to trust authority. In fact, religious communities may be the most important kind of community in which trust in persons with whom one lacks a direct relationship still exists. I propose that an investigation of the reasons why members of religious communities accept authority in their community will lead nowhere if we expect the reasons to be theoretical, but it will be enlightening if we attend to deliberative reasons.

13.2.5. Conversion

Finally, I want to say that *conversion* cannot be explained except by deliberative reasons. Rarely does anyone convert to a religion because of theoretical reasons she did not previously have, but conversion is sometimes the reasonable thing to do. Trust or admiration for another person or for a tradition or for the sacred texts of a religion is typically the reason for conversion, not just the cause. The fact that conversion can be reasonable is very difficult to explain without reference to deliberative reasons. Of course, someone who maintains that the only kind of epistemic reasons are theoretical will deny that it is ever rational to change one's epistemic stance toward a proposition—whether to believe, disbelieve, or withhold belief when one's apprehension and evaluation of the theoretical reasons do not change. However, my purpose is not to convince anyone of the rationality of conversion. I mention conversion as an example of a phenomenon of change of belief that many people do find rational, which deserves more attention in the literature, and which I conjecture cannot be explained except by reference to deliberative reasons.[16]

13.3. Conclusion

In this paper I have proposed that distinguishing first-person from third-person epistemic reasons permits us to get a better understanding of some important problems in epistemology in general and religious epistemology in particular. The problems I have mentioned have something in common. They reveal the way the human self operates in the attempt to get the truth. The nature of the self and its executive power to manage itself is a difficult problem, and it is unsurprising that epistemologists often prefer to bracket it off from the problems of direct interest to epistemology. But if I am right, we cannot do that without distorting the relationship between epistemic reasons and what they are reasons for. What *I* reasonably take to be reasons to believe some proposition *p* is not identical to the neutral facts that any reasonable person would take to be reasons supporting *p*. But as a reasonable person I must figure out how to combine theoretical and deliberative reasons in my epistemic psychology in a way that gives me a determinate answer to the question whether *p*. It is particularly important that we do not ignore the distinction between the two kinds of reasons in the domain of religious belief since religious belief is a particular person's answer to her own religious questions, yet its content is also the property of all reasonable persons in their common attempt to find the truth.

Notes

1. In this paper I do not distinguish facts from true propositions. If there is a difference, the argument of this paper can be easily amended.
2. For an excellent survey of the different senses of evidence, see Thomas Kelly's (2016) entry, "Evidence," in the *Stanford Encyclopedia of Philosophy* (http://plato.stanford.edu/entries).
3. My use of the terms "theoretical" and "deliberative" is not essential to the contrast I am making, but the terms call attention to a difference in function that I find helpful. Theoretical reasons can also be called third-person reasons and deliberative reasons can be called first-person reasons.
4. See Richard Foley (2001) and William Alston (2005).
5. I defend the argument of this paragraph in detail in Zagzebski (2012), chapter 3. That book was based on my 2010 Wilde lectures and my 2011 Kaminski lectures.
6. The fact that there are theoretical reasons to admire someone in the domain of her believing *p* is not sufficient to give me a theoretical reason to believe *p* because reasons are not transitive. If *A* is a reason for *B* and *B* is a reason for *C*, it does not follow that *A* is a reason for *C*. If *A* is a set of theoretical reasons to admire Sarah, and admiring Sarah is a reason to imitate her in believing *p*, it does not follow that theoretical reason *A* gives me reason to believe *p*.
7. For a different kind of defense of the position that what I believe is "up to me," see Richard Moran (2001).
8. Thomas Nagel (1986) is generally credited with introducing a form of this distinction, where he distinguished subjective and objective reasons for action. Derek Parfit (1984) introduced the terms "agent-relative" and "agent-neutral" reasons, and Nagel subsequently adopted this usage. For an overview of different approaches to this distinction and their respective merits, see Michael Ridge (2017), "Reasons for Action: Agent-Neutral vs. Agent-Relative," *Stanford Encyclopedia of Philosophy* (http://plato.stanford.edu/entries).

9. Derek Parfit (1984) refers to this difference as the difference between Nagel's distinction and his own very similar distinction. Parfit says: "Nagel's subjective reasons are reasons only for the agent. I call these agent-relative. When I call some reason agent-relative, I am not claiming that this reason cannot be a reason for other agents. All that I am claiming is that it may not be" (143). In this respect my distinction is more like Nagel's than Parfit's.
10. This is a point made by Benjamin McMyler (2011, chapters 2 and 3). McMyler argues that testimony gives the recipient a second-person reason to believe what is testified. I have no objection to calling trust in others a second-person epistemic reason for belief. Trust in *you* as a reason to believe something includes an irreducible reference to *me*. The important point for my argument here is that trust in others is clearly distinguishable from theoretical reasons, and it has the properties of first-person, deliberative reasons. I now believe that second-person reasons form an interesting class of reasons, distinct from both first-person and third-person reasons (see Zagzebski 2021, chapter 6).
11. This model is close to the assurance model of testimony of Richard Moran (2006).
12. As Richard Moran (2006) says, it seems as if my recognizing the speaker's intention ought to be pointless. It does not add to my evidence as interpreter to learn that in addition to his believing *p*, the speaker also has the intention that I should believe *p*. Moran mentions Paul Grice's much earlier use of that point (15).
13. See Locke, "Of Faith and Reason, and Their Distinct Provinces," in Locke (1996), Bk IV, Ch. 18, Sec. 7. See also Locke's posthumously published essay, "A Discourse of Miracles." (2002).
14. I defend this idea as the ground for epistemic trust and belief on the authority of individuals and communities in Zagzebski (2012), chapter 3.
15. I argue for this view in Zagzebski (2012), chapter 5.
16. For a classic historical account of the rise of conversion as a phenomenon in the West, see A. D. Nock (1998). Nock argues that in the ancient world, people could be converted to philosophies such as Pythagoreanism, Platonism, Epircureanism, and Stoicism, but not to the ancient Greek or Roman religions. Conversion became important with the rise of Christianity because Christianity included answers to the ultimate questions posed by philosophers, yet it was also in competition with pagan religion since it required people to make a choice.

14
Religious Diversity and Social Responsibility (2001)

Let us imagine a person, let us call her Susan, who has many religious beliefs, some of which are very important to her. Let us also suppose that it is important to Susan to be responsible in what she believes as well as in what she does. But Susan is not sure she understands what is involved in responsible belief and to whom she is responsible. She is not even sure that it makes sense to speak of responsibility in the realm of belief because responsibility is a social notion and it might be thought that one's believing is one's own private business. Susan will probably be willing to concede that she is responsible to *herself*, but is she also responsible to others, and if so, to which others? Does she owe anything to believers in other religions? It is usual in modern liberal society to think that we do not owe other people very much, and we owe the least to people who are not part of our own culture. Certainly, it is widely agreed that we ought to treat persons of other cultures and other faiths with tolerance—and those who wish to go farther say that we also ought to treat them with respect, but how can we owe them anything with regard to our personal beliefs? How can it be the business of anybody else what Susan believes?

At one extreme, then, is the common view that it really doesn't matter to others what you believe; it only matters what you do. Your responsibility to others ends at your overt behavior. At the other extreme, W. K. Clifford became famous for his position that responsibility for belief, any belief, is the same as responsibility for acts. It is moral responsibility. I think both viewpoints are mistaken, but Clifford is closer to being right. Where he went astray, I think, is in his specific account of the conditions under which a belief is responsibly held—that it must be based on sufficient evidence. Evidentialism has received a lot of attention because it is the sort of position that many philosophers love to hate. I think it is fair to say that evidentialism has been decisively refuted, but that does not mean that we do not have responsibility to others for our beliefs.

It is a truism that we share the same nature and the same rationality with all other human beings; a much more substantial claim is that all humans form one community. That is affirmed by the Vatican II "Declaration on the relation of the Church to non-Christian religions." When we reflect upon what it means to form one human community, I think we'll be led to the conclusion that it commits us to treating all other humans as in some sense partners with us in pursuing our common human goals, one of which is the goal of reaching the truth. If that is right, then we have responsibilities to the other members of that community. Curiously, the religious skeptic Clifford was the most prominent advocate of the view that we are responsible to others for our beliefs in a robust moral sense of responsibility grounded in our social obligations. I think his position was basically correct, but I think that what makes it correct is something that Clifford did not believe—that we form a human community because we are all called by God to the same end.

Let us look carefully at Susan's situation. As I've said, we are supposing that Susan has many religious beliefs, some of which are not shared by a substantial number of people in the world. Of course, Susan's religious beliefs are not the only beliefs she has that are not shared by others, and the fact that others do not believe something she believes is not in itself problematic. Often the reason that others do not believe what she believes is that they do not have access to the same information. We do not think that that is a problem because all it takes to reach agreement is an exchange of information. But some of Susan's beliefs directly contradict the beliefs of others, and the disagreement cannot be resolved no matter how much information is exchanged. Like Susan, most of us discover that many of our most important moral beliefs are those about which it is the hardest to get agreement. Beliefs about abortion would be in that category, as well as a great many religious beliefs. That fact bothers us because human beings have an urge to get agreement. I would propose that the urge to get agreement arises from our rational nature and from the fact that we form a human community cooperating in the search for truth. Disagreement bothers us, and disagreement that seems to be irresolvable bothers us even more. In my opinion, we are right to be bothered. Being bothered is the rational response to irresolvable disagreement. But what follows from being bothered? What do we do next?

Let us suppose that Susan has reflected about her participation in the community of human beings and believes that we are all partners in the search for truth. She is bothered by the fact that many people have beliefs incompatible with her own and that the disagreement does not seem to be resolvable. Suppose that Susan is a Christian and she believes that Jesus Christ is the Son of God. She believes that since it is true that Jesus Christ is the son of God, people who believe otherwise believe something false. She also observes that many of those people persist in their belief even when some Christians attempt to convince them otherwise.

Now if Susan is a careful and responsible believer, what is the ground of her worry about the fact that people of other religions have beliefs opposed to her own? We might say that since Susan thinks that she has the truth, she cannot be faulted for not caring about the truth since she thinks she has it. And she cannot be faulted for not caring about the common search for truth since we are assuming that she believes that she cannot convince those who believe differently that they are mistaken. She can *try* to participate in the communal project of finding religious truth together, but she cannot be expected to do the impossible. She is in what Alvin Plantinga calls condition C: She is fully aware of the existence of other religions whose beliefs conflict with her own, she knows that some of their adherents are no less devout than she is, and she knows of no arguments that would convince them of the falsehood of their conflicting beliefs. Plantinga maintains that if she is unmoved by lack of success in convincing others of the truth of the proposition that Jesus Christ is the son of God, she is no more guilty of intellectual wrongdoing than a person who is unmoved by the fact that there are others who disagree with his position that racial bigotry is wrong (Plantinga, 2000a). He goes on to argue that a person who believes that she should not hold the beliefs of a particular religion because of the diversity of religious beliefs is guilty of self-referential inconsistency for she believes the following:

(RD) If S knows that others do not believe p and that she is in condition C with respect to p, then S should not believe p. (2000a, 176)

But RD is itself a proposition about which there is diversity of belief and S is in condition C with respect to that proposition. It follows that if Susan thinks that religious diversity makes her own beliefs improper, she is guilty of inconsistency.

It seems to me that this argument does not give due consideration to the position Susan is worried about. RD is a second-order belief, a belief about beliefs. It is a belief people have proposed after reflecting upon their first-order beliefs and attempting to arrive at criteria for the rational response to diversity in a community of people who are attempting to coordinate their knowledge and experiences for the common goal of getting the truth about any particular issue. This point does not prove that RD is true, of course, but given that it has been widely adopted by rational people in a community of truth-seekers, it deserves careful consideration and respect. In fact, since RD is a policy one adopts in the attempt to make one's beliefs rational, it is not even clear that it is a belief at all in the sense Plantinga uses in his argument for self-referential inconsistency. But if Plantinga is right, RD is false and it should not deter Susan from believing that her religious beliefs are true and those of other religions are false. She should be an exclusivist about religious truth.

Let us define exclusivism about truth as the position that the beliefs of one religion, my own, are true, and the beliefs of all other religions are false insofar as they conflict with mine. Notice that exclusivism about truth is not the same as the more extreme position of exclusivism about salvation, the old dictum "Outside the Church there is no salvation." That position has become much less common in recent decades. Recall that Karl Rahner called sincere practitioners of other faiths "anonymous Christians." According to Rahner, devout Hindus, Buddhists, Muslims, and others can still be saved, so even though he was an exclusivist about truth, he was an inclusivist about salvation. Yet even in his theory of salvation Rahner makes Christianity primary because he says that all are saved through Christ, a point emphasized in the Vatican declaration *"Dominus Iesus."*

The Dalai Lama (1999) says in his book *Ethics for the New Millennium* that he thinks of religion as medicine for the human spirit. Different medicines are efficacious for persons in different cultures and conditions. But when it comes to the truth of the metaphysical claims of the various religions, there we simply have to part company, he says, and treat that as the internal business of each religion. We each think of our own religion as the sole mediator of truth, yet we should recognize that other religions can be salvific (1999, 226–227). I interpret that to mean that the Dalai Lama also is an exclusivist about truth but an inclusivist about salvation.

Detaching exclusivism about truth from exclusivism about salvation might seem to remove some of its sting. But exclusivism about truth has been attacked on other grounds. Wilfred Cantwell Smith declares:

> Except at the cost of insensitivity or delinquency, it is morally not possible to go out into the world and say to devout, intelligent, fellow human beings: "... we believe that we know God and we are right; you believe that you know God, and you are totally wrong." (quoted by Plantinga 2000a, 176)

It seems to me that Smith's objection to exclusivism about truth is not fair because the exclusivist is surely not committed to announcing the superiority of her own religion in any manner at all, much less in an insensitive manner. The issue is whether she would be right if she had exclusivist thoughts and if she would be in any way irresponsible if she had such thoughts.

What about exclusivism about rationality? Exclusivism about rationality is much stronger than exclusivism about truth. I suspect that the most common position among people who have thought about this issue and who have tried to be as fair minded as possible is a combination of exclusivism about truth and inclusivism about rationality: Our beliefs are true and the beliefs of other religions are false insofar as they are incompatible with ours, but their beliefs are still rational. This seems reasonable when we reflect upon our common humanity and the fact that if we had been born in their culture, we would probably believe the same as they do. But there is a problem in combining these two positions. Here is the reason: We are all in trouble if there is not a close connection between rationality and truth. In fact, what makes it a good thing for humans to be rational is that it puts us in the best position to get the truth. But suppose there are nine religions, each teaching a different and incompatible doctrine on the origin of the universe. At most one of these doctrines can be true. But are they all rational? Surely, we must say yes since, as we have already said, believers in all the major religions are endowed with rationality by our common human nature. In fact, there do not seem to be any significant differences in intelligence, sensitivity to religious experience, intellectual and moral virtue, or processes of belief formation among adherents of the major religions. But if we say that all nine of these beliefs about the origin of the universe are rational, then clearly rationality in this case does not make it likely that a person gets the truth—less than one chance in nine, and so we cannot maintain that what makes rationality a good thing is that it makes it likely that we're going to get the truth. It appears, then, that combining exclusivism about truth with inclusivism about rationality forces us to conclude either that rationality is not really such a good thing, or if it is a good thing, its goodness cannot come from its close connection to truth. I call this the problem of the gap.

Of course, the gap is not a general problem. There *are* classes of belief where we think that there is a close connection between rationality and truth, but those beliefs do not help solve the problem of religious diversity because they are beliefs about which we can realistically expect agreement. And there are probably some religious beliefs in this category—for example, the belief that compassion is good is an almost universal belief, a point stressed by the Dalai Lama. If we move to a sufficiently high level of generality, we can find agreement about some of the most fundamental religious beliefs—for instance, there is something wrong with the human condition, that when we are in contact with ultimate reality there is the possibility for both profound moral improvement and a higher level of consciousness. But belief at the level necessary for agreement is very thin, and unless Susan is content to ignore all but such thin beliefs, the fact that her religious beliefs conflict with the beliefs of others remains a problem.

It is not going to help Susan to weaken her commitment to her belief that Jesus Christ is the son of God, or her belief that the universe was created by God, or any of her other beliefs that conflict with the beliefs of many other religions. No matter what she does, she faces a problem in her understanding of rationality. If she retains her beliefs because she judges that they are rational, and she also judges that the conflicting beliefs of other religions are rational, she cannot maintain that the rationality of each such belief makes it more likely to be true. On the other hand, if she gives up these beliefs on the grounds that they are not rational, she is forced to say that she herself as well as all the other religious believers in the world are not rational. And since most of these beliefs are important to their adherents, it means that many of the most important beliefs of all these people are not rational. But having religious beliefs itself is a trait of our common human nature, so it seems very unlikely that that same nature would require us to give them up. The only other option is to maintain that her beliefs are rational but those of others are not—to retreat to exclusivism about rationality, and that, as we've seen, is a position that forces us to ignore the universality of rationality and universal membership in a truth-seeking community.

At this point it looks as if Susan is caught in a trap. She wants to be responsible in the way she believes, and she thinks that that involves trying to have true beliefs, and that her efforts should be part of a communal project. She thinks that being rational is the best *way* to get true beliefs; to be a responsible believer is to believe in a way that we call rational. But if believers in other religions are no less rational than she is, they are in as good a position to get the truth as she is. But if all of them are rational, rationality does not seem to put anybody in the best position to get the truth. Therefore, even though it might be the case that she has the truth and believers in other religions do not, she cannot think of herself as being responsible in trying to get the truth due to her rationality since rationality in this category of belief is not truth conducive. It therefore cannot help *her* any more than it helps the Hindus. How, then, is she being responsible?

Alvin Plantinga seems to accept this consequence. Susan is helped in her attempt to get religious truth, not because she is rational or responsible, but because she has a special gift from God. Plantinga thinks Christians can defend exclusivism by falling back on a belief that explains why Christians are privileged. The Holy Spirit has given the gift of faith in God (as understood by Christianity) to some people and not others. It is a Christian belief that Christians are right and others wrong, and those who are wrong are wrong because they lack a special gift of God. The Christian's epistemic position differs from that of others. Plantinga is right that faith is experienced as a gift. But notice that practitioners of other religions are in the same situation as Susan from their perspective. They may even have a story about why they are right and Susan is wrong. In the BBC video series *The Long Search*, Ronald Eyre asks a Buddhist woman whether she thinks he must have done something wrong in a former life since he was born a Christian in England. She looks embarrassed and then says yes, he must have. It appears, then, that both the Christian and the Buddhist can make use of explanations internal to their respective religions to explain the fact of religious diversity and to block the inference that diversity takes away the rationality of their own beliefs. The Buddhist woman's story is that non-Buddhists brought their fate upon themselves by their actions in a former life. Plantinga's story is that the Holy Spirit freely gives grace to some and not others. Susan is just fine, according to Plantinga, because she is lucky. It is not Susan's rationality or responsibility that gets her the truth; it is luck. I agree that truth *might* come as the result of luck, but responsibility cannot. An exclusivist must find a way to connect responsibility to the human community with the gift of faith.

Let us suppose that Susan has viewed the video of the interview with the Buddhist woman and she is disturbed because she realizes that her first-person perspective is no different from that of the other woman. Plantinga tells her the difference is due to luck. The Buddhist woman thinks the difference is due to something that happened in a past life. How should Susan think about this? Of course, Susan knows there *is* a lot of luck in life, but she is not convinced that her search for religious truth is solely a matter of luck. And she finds the Buddhist woman's explanation even less helpful. Given that she and the Buddhist woman are part of the same human community with a common goal, they ought to be able to help each other to get the truth—if they ever met and were able to communicate. To be told that their differences arise from either a past mistake of which there is no memory or an unbidden gift of God does not help them in that part of their lives that they share—their reflective rational inquiry as members of the human community. So, Susan is not yet convinced that she can be an exclusivist about religious truth and still be responsible.

Plantinga's position makes no attempt to rise above the first-person perspective. As Plantinga understands it, rationality does not require critical detachment from one's own consciousness. He mentions very briefly that a person should think the matter over and consider the objections, but of course, if a close-minded or intellectually unfair person thinks a matter over and considers objections, she is not going to change anything in either her beliefs or her attitude toward the beliefs of others. Our problem is often not a lack of desire for truth, but a lack of perspective on ourselves—a lack of critical detachment.

Suppose that Susan agrees that an important part of human rationality is the power of critical detachment. The same power that makes her stop and think that maybe her acts are not right can be turned on her beliefs. Even though she thinks her beliefs are true (otherwise they wouldn't be beliefs), she can subject them to scrutiny and question them. The habit of critical self-reflection leads us to question all sorts of things. In fact, as soon as we are old enough to know that there are bad reasons as well as good reasons for having a belief, we can no longer be complacent about our own beliefs. Even while thinking p is true, human beings are capable of looking at themselves from without, from a detached perspective. Many philosophers have questioned the extent to which such a perspective is possible, but it is obvious that it *is* possible to a very great extent. A deeper question is the extent to which we should trust it. Suppose, then, that Susan is moving from the first-person perspective to the third-person perspective. An initial third-person perspective that tempts some people is relativism.

One problem with relativism is that it leaves out the observer. The relativist almost always forgets to put herself in the relativistic picture, but when she does, the situation gets even worse because then she treats every culture, including her own, as a phenomenon. The result is that she believes nothing and belongs nowhere. I suspect that this is one of the reasons there are so many atheists in religious studies departments. They think that they cannot look at religion objectively if they participate in it. Some of them believe there is truth in a relativistic sense, but in that sense "truth" is not a weighty word.

A more influential third-person perspective is that of John Hick (2000, 2004) who has promoted a position about the comparative value of the major world religions he calls pluralism. Hick maintains that all the major religions are salvific in that they all offer a path to radically transform human persons from self-centeredness to reality-centeredness, a life centered in ultimate reality. Each religion has something analogous to Christian saints who are the models for this transformation. The fruit of this transformation is a life of love and compassion, and Hick proposes that since we have evidence that all the great religions are productive of a life of love and compassion, we should conclude that they all offer genuine paths to salvation. Hick thinks that the metaphysical conclusion we ought to draw from this is that the salvific ground in ultimate reality is the same in all religions. Hick then uses Immanuel Kant's distinction between the noumenal and phenomenal worlds to explain how such a multiplicity of religions can all be in touch with the same ultimate reality. His idea is that we cannot experience God as he is in himself directly any more than we can experience the world of things-in-themselves according to Kant. All we can do is experience God through the experiential and conceptual forms that each culture has developed. Each religion is a different phenomenal manifestation of the one ultimate reality. And like Kant, Hick maintains that phenomenal reality is as real as it is going to get for us; it is not an illusion. It is the only way we humans can experience the world.

An important difference between Hick and Kant is that whereas Kant believes that the phenomenal world is the same for all humans because it is the world as it has to be in order to be experienced by us, Hick cannot make the parallel claim about religious phenomenal worlds since he maintains there is more than one. But he *can* say that ultimate reality cannot be experienced except through cultural forms, so each religion is a different lens through which ultimate reality is experienced. We are not equipped with a particular religious lens by nature the way we are equipped with Kant's conceptual categories, but we need to have one lens or another. The Muslim world, the Hindu world, the Buddhist world, and the Christian world are all phenomenally real worlds on a par with the reality of trees, houses, and animals in Kantian metaphysics. Should Susan become a pluralist like Hick?

This is obviously a question that cannot be answered without a lot more investigation of the details. But we are at least in a position to say that Hick's pluralism inherits all the metaphysical problems of the Kantian noumenal/phenomenal distinction, and, in addition, Hick does not have Kant's advantage of claiming that there is one phenomenal world that is the only world we humans can experience. Furthermore, Hick has to bend the distinction in some ways to make it religiously more acceptable. The Kantian noumenal world is unknowable, untouchable—we cannot even say anything about it except to give a transcendental argument that we expect it to exist. But Hick wants to say quite a bit about noumenal religious reality. Religious believers *are* in touch with it because it is the ground of their salvation; we *can* say that there is a relationship between the noumenal ground and each religion in that each religion is a manifestation of that noumenal ground. Noumenal reality unifies the different religions of the world in a way that does not come up for Kant since Kant does not discuss alternate phenomenal worlds that need to be unified.

Further, if Hick truly means that each phenomenal world is a real one, then, as George Mavrodes (2000) has argued, he is a polytheist. Perhaps the charge of polytheism is not quite accurate because Hick is a phenomenal polytheist and a noumenal mono-something (not "theist" because he is not willing to call the ultimate reality "God"). But on the noumenal level Hick is committed to the most negative of negative theologies: We cannot say that the ultimate reality is personal or impersonal, one or many, God or being itself. Hick's position appears to be a combination of polytheism and negative theology, neither of which is very attractive.

In spite of these problems, Hick's pluralism does have one important advantage that might tempt Susan to accept it, and that is that it solves the dilemma about the gap between rationality and truth. If Susan accepts pluralism, she does not have to choose between denying that believers in other religions are rational and maintaining that they are rational, but there is no probabilistic connection between rationality and truth in this category of beliefs. The great world religions *are* true and their adherents are rational. Furthermore, they are true in a sense that does not trivialize truth the way relativism does. This is a very important advantage that pluralism has over exclusivism. Still, even if Susan can get past the problems with Hick's metaphysics, she may be worried that his pluralism threatens religious commitment. Christians who become convinced that Christianity is not truer than Hinduism are bound to interpret that as weakening the connection they thought obtained between Christian doctrine and the truth.

At this point Susan's options are not looking very good. She can remain entrenched in the first-person perspective of the engaged believer, or she can attempt to detach herself from her most cherished beliefs and assume some form of the third-person perspective; or perhaps, like David Hume, she can switch back and forth between the two, sometimes acting as critical observer and sometimes as engaged believer, the way Hume did when he put his work aside and played backgammon. I believe this leads us into very deep waters with implications for much more than religious belief. The Enlightenment thinkers were right that what we discover when we attempt the standpoint of the detached observer is valuable. The first-person perspective is not good enough because it does not do justice to our highest human faculties. But those who have rejected Enlightenment philosophy and fled back to the standpoint of traditions are right that there is something fundamentally missing in the mentality of the detached observer.

Thomas Nagel (1986) argues that a host of philosophical problems will be irresolvable until someone figures out how to rise above the perennial conflict between subjective and objective viewpoints. What Nagel means by the subjective point of view is what I have been calling the first-person perspective. It is the perspective from inside one's own head. It is narrow and limited and frequently wrong. But it is also one's own and it is what defines the self. The objective point of view is the third-person perspective. As Nagel sees it, there are degrees of objectivity understood as degrees of distance from the self. Let me illustrate with a simple example. The subjective perspective on a war is the perspective of a patriotic supporter of one's own country who may have friends and relatives fighting in the war. A more objective perspective would see the enemy as no different from one's countrymen. A still more objective perspective on the war would see it from the global and historical standpoint as a phenomenon with long-term social and environmental costs (and possibly also some gains). As the distance from the self increases, the scope of one's vision increases, and the importance of one's self diminishes. But if one goes far enough in this direction one loses first one's culture, and ultimately one's very identity. Even though the objective standpoint on religious diversity and social responsibility is valuable, we cannot move to that perspective without losing what is valuable in the subjective perspective. There is nothing wrong with being a self, and the self has a distinctive point of view. Yet to remain in that perspective is to have a much smaller vision. Nagel says he does not see any way around the problem.

I believe that Nagel is right about this and that the problem applies to perspectives on the self as well as to perspectives on anything else. Neither the first-person nor the third-person perspective on the self can be fully trusted. When we see ourselves only from the inside, we get a distorted view and we are not likely to improve ourselves. But to look at ourselves in the third person is to see ourselves as an object, as just one person among others. I want to suggest another perspective that I believe arises from our participation in the human community, and that arises naturally within the grammar of ordinary language. I call it the second-person perspective, the perspective of seeing ourselves as others see us who engage with us directly and address us as "you." To see ourselves in the second person is to see ourselves as friends see us, those who see us neither as "I" nor as "he" or "she," but as "you." To see how the move from the first- to the third- to the second-person perspective may work, let us recall the famous story of David and Nathan. Plantinga uses this story as well in his defense of exclusivism, but I want to use it for a different purpose.

King David got Bathsheba pregnant and desired to marry her, but she was the wife of Uriah, one of David's officers, so he arranged to have Uriah killed. The Lord sent the prophet Nathan to David, and Nathan told David a story:

> "Judge this case for me! In a certain town there were two men, one rich, the other poor. The rich man had flocks and herds in great numbers. But the poor man had nothing at all except one little ewe lamb that he had bought. He nourished her, and she grew up with him and his children. She shared the little food he had and drank from his cup and slept in his bosom. She was like a daughter to him. Now, the rich man received a visitor, but he would not take from his own flocks and herds to prepare a meal for the wayfarer who had come to him. Instead he took the poor man's ewe lamb and made a meal of it for his visitor." David grew very angry with that man and said to Nathan: "As the Lord lives, the man who has done this merits death! He shall restore the ewe lamb fourfold because he has done this and has had no pity." Then Nathan said to David, "You are that man!" (2 Sam. 12:1-6)

David sees what he has done and repents.

There are many important lessons in this story, but I want to focus on David's perspective on himself, which changes twice. Before Nathan speaks to him, David has no sense of detachment on himself or his desires and actions. It is not simply that he is selfish in the sense of caring about himself at the expense of others, but that he does not see himself accurately because he makes no effort to see himself from the outside. His view of himself is simply that of the subject of various desires and beliefs. But clearly David is capable of self-reflection. When Nathan comes to him and tells him the parable of the rich man who takes the poor man's lamb, David immediately sees himself as that man. He sees himself in the third person as the man in the story. But Nathan does not rely on the parable alone to open David's eyes. He ends the story in the second person, and addresses David directly: "*You* are that man." He continues by addressing David in God's place. "Thus says the Lord God of Israel: 'I anointed you king of Israel. I rescued you from the hand of Saul. I gave you your lord's house and lord's wives for your own. I gave you the house of Israel and of Judah. And if this were not enough, I could count up for you still more. Why have you spurned the Lord and done evil in his sight?'" (2 Sam. 12:7-9).

David respects Nathan and he believes that God is addressing him through the prophet. Through Nathan he is able to rise above his narrow, first-person perspective and to see himself, not from the point of view of the detached, third-person observer, but from the perspective of the second person. When we see ourselves the way other persons see us, particularly wise and sympathetic other persons, we have an advantage over both of the other perspectives. The second person respects our individual selfhood, but it does not have the limitations of the subjective standpoint. One of the epistemic advantages of human communities is that we learn to see ourselves through interaction with others, particularly with friends. Like the third-person perspective, the second-person perspective admits of degrees because the communities to which we belong connect us to more and more distant others. The community of members of the Church is a close community; the community of religious believers all over the world is much larger, with more distant boundaries. Our responsibilities to the former are no doubt greater than our responsibilities to the latter. But my purpose in this paper is not to discuss our responsibilities to the Church or to other Christians, but to talk about our responsibilities to followers of other religions. How should we think of our responsibilities to that community?

If we take the second-person perspective seriously, and we believe that we form a community with people of other faiths, there are some principles of rational membership in that community that follow. One is what I call the *Culture-Sensitivity principle: Persons should treat the members of other cultures and religions as though they are* prima facie *as rational as themselves.*

It follows from the universality of rationality that there is a deep sense in which the rationality of all human beings is the same since it is what makes us human. Of course, this does not mean that every belief is just as rational as every other, but that is because we have independent reason to think that some beliefs are more rational than others. My point is only that the beliefs of others are *prima facie* as rational as ours, not that they are as rational all things considered. The Culture-Sensitivity principle says that in the absence of good reasons to think the contrary, we should assume the rational equality of every culture's distinctive beliefs, and that it is a principle of rational community to treat them that way. Of course, we will not all agree on what counts as good reasons to think that another culture's beliefs are not as rational as our own, and I do not think it is important that we do agree on that. But one kind of reason is ruled out by the Culture-Sensitivity principle: We are violating that principle if we take the fact that our beliefs are ours and their beliefs are theirs as sufficient to lead us to think that ours are more rational than theirs.

The second-person perspective leads to another principle that I call the *Rational-Recognition principle: If a belief is rational, its rationality is recognizable (in principle) by rational persons in other cultures engaged in sympathetic contact with each other.*

This principle is obviously vague and needs considerable refinement. I am certainly not suggesting that every rational person is able to recognize the rationality of every rational belief of every other person even when they are sympathetic and motivated to understand. But I do mean that the rationality of even culturally specific beliefs is recognizable from the outside—perhaps not by every person on the outside, but certainly by those persons ideally situated. Furthermore, our common membership in the human community gives us a responsibility to those on the outside to attempt to see the rationality of their culture-specific beliefs and to help them see the rationality of our own. This is also a check on the rationality of our own beliefs.

The ability to engage with persons of other religions as members of the same community probably requires more than ordinary human wisdom and experience. I believe that a key virtue in doing so is the Aristotelian virtue of *phronesis*, or practical wisdom. All cultures have persons with *phronesis*; they are persons with good judgment. They are the people who help to shape the direction of the community, to critique it, and to lead the community in reaching consensus. Inter-religious dialogue is more likely to be successful when it is practiced by such persons. I think that their judgment of the rationality of the beliefs of other cultures should be taken very seriously by those cultures. In our own case, it is important to see ourselves as practically wise persons see us when they are in direct contact with us and address us as "you," as Nathan did in addressing David. So, a refinement of the Rational-Recognition principle is as follows: *If a belief is rational, its rationality is recognizable (in principle) by persons with practical wisdom in other cultures who are engaged in sympathetic contact with persons who hold the belief.*

Let us return to Susan's problem. If Susan adopts the principles I have proposed, it is doubtful that she can be an exclusivist about rationality. It seems likely that other religions will turn out to be rational on the whole since I think that there is evidence that plenty of people with practical wisdom see these religions as rational. But what about Susan's central problem, whether to accept exclusivism about truth? Is she being responsible in continuing to believe that only one religion is really true and it is her own once she recognizes that from the third-person perspective she and the Buddhist woman are on a par? What will she find out if she adopts the second-person perspective and gives special weight to the judgment of persons with practical wisdom?

I think that the first thing she will see is that persons of practical wisdom do *not* counsel giving up one's own religious beliefs; in fact, many of them have religious beliefs themselves and continue to hold them in full knowledge of religious diversity. We see that many wise persons are exclusivists about truth, so there is nothing contrary to rationality or wisdom in exclusivism about truth per se. To give up commitment to one's religion and to retreat into skepticism about all religions is to give up a major part of one's identity and that is not the outcome of adopting the second-person perspective.

But what about the problem of the gap between rationality and truth? I find that to be the most difficult problem in the general theory of rationality. However, one thing to notice is that the fact that all the major religions are rational on the whole does not entail the rationality of each particular belief such as a belief about the origin of the universe. The Dalai Lama says that such metaphysical beliefs are the "internal business" of each religion, but I disagree. I think that all such beliefs should be subjected to the scrutiny of practically wise persons both inside and outside their religious communities. We owe each other that much as members of the human community. I doubt that practically wise persons will judge all such beliefs to be rational, at least not equally rational. Some may be better supported by evidence external to any religion, such as scientific evidence; some may be better supported than others even within the metaphysical system of their own religion; some may be better supported philosophically. That makes it unlikely that all nine beliefs about the origin of the universe that we were imagining earlier will turn out to be rational. Still, it is likely that more than one of them is rational, in which case, there is still a gap between rationality and truth. The gap is as wide as is permitted by the divergence in the beliefs of practically wise persons. Future convergence of belief among practically wise persons in different cultures would narrow the gap, but we have no guarantee that that will happen.

Second, the problem of the gap is easier to handle once we recognize that rationality may put us in the best position to get the truth even when the connection is not probabilistic. That is, even though we are more likely to get the truth if our beliefs are rational rather than irrational, it does not follow that a rational belief is such that the probability that it is true is very high. We know this phenomenon from other areas of belief, such as those based on medical research. Assuming that the research is done correctly, it is rational to believe the results, and we are more likely to get the truth if we do so, rather than to use irrational methods for forming beliefs about the same issue, yet we also know that subsequent research often shows the results to be false. In other words, the best method we have for getting the truth may not yield results with a high probability of being true. Similarly, many religious beliefs may be rational in that they are more likely to be true than beliefs formed irrationally, and yet still have less than a 50 percent chance of being true. What Susan should think about that, I believe, is that while rationality does put us in the best position to get the truth, we should not expect a high probabilistic connection between rationality and truths about the transcendent world. This leaves room for Susan to accept the gift of faith as a complement to her rational nature, but it does not relieve her of the responsibilities of sympathetic engagement with the entire human community.

It is difficult to combine commitment to our own faith with the openness to others that the second-person perspective involves, but I think that that perspective is our best hope for achieving a critical look at ourselves without losing the beliefs that define ourselves. It is interesting that although the first-person and third-person perspectives have received considerable attention ever since the Enlightenment and its aftermath highlighted the conflict between them, the second-person perspective has been largely ignored. I believe that rationality in the second person is a community achievement that has the promise of resolving many of the problems inherent in the desire to have a unified grasp of reality, one that does justice to the importance of each individual self in a world whose structure goes well beyond what any one person can grasp on their own.

VII

RATIONAL RELIGIOUS BELIEF, SELF-TRUST, AND AUTHORITY

15
A Modern Defense of Religious Authority (2016)

15.1. The modern rejection of authority

It has often been observed that one characteristic of the modern world is the utter rejection of authority, or at least, the rejection of authority insofar as that is possible without leading to societal collapse. The need for political authority is grudgingly accepted to avert social disaster, but the fact that there is no moral authority is generally thought to be too obvious to require argument. For example, Patrick Hurley (2008) claims in his college textbook on logic that the appeal to authority for a moral judgment is an example of the *ad verecundiam* fallacy: "If someone were to argue that abortion is immoral because a certain philosopher or religious leader has said so, the argument would be weak regardless of the authority's qualifications. Many questions in these areas are so hotly contested that there is no conventional wisdom an authority can depend upon" (133). Not only does Hurley think it is obvious that there is no moral authority in disputed domains, but his reason for thinking so is just that those domains are disputed. He does not consider the possibility that someone could actually *have* the authority to give moral prescriptions.

The rejection of authority extends to most domains of belief, not only moral beliefs. The ascendance of modern science is usually credited with convincing people of the untrustworthiness of traditional sources of belief, including, of course, the teachings of the Church. The prestige of science has made scientific experts the closest thing we have to authorities over belief, and if there is any vestige of authority left in the epistemic realm—the realm of belief—then it is science. But although people will often accept the word of experts in an esoteric scientific field, scientific experts are not authorities in any robust sense. It is entirely up to the individual person whether she chooses to believe an expert. There is no question of commanding belief, and no duty to obey.

Are there any *good* reasons for rejecting authority in belief and morals? I think there are two interesting and influential reasons. One comes from John Locke (2009), who argued that nobody may command belief because it is impossible to obey it. "It is absurd that things should be enjoined by laws which are not in men's power to perform. And to believe this or that to be true does not depend upon our will" (24). If authority is the right to command, there is no authority over beliefs.

Locke's claim that belief is not under the control of the will has a measure of truth that has led to an extensive debate in epistemology, but I do not see that it is any harder to believe on command than to believe what ordinary people tell me. It depends upon the circumstances. Suppose my friend Ann says to me, "She will never marry him." Surely it is possible for me to believe her, and if I have good reason to think she is reliable and sincere, I can also be justified in doing so. We all believe plenty of things we are told, often with good reason. But imagine the same situation except that Ann chooses her words a little differently. Instead of saying to me, "She will never marry him," she might say, "Believe me, she will never marry him." She could even make the command mode stronger by saying, "She will never marry him. You *must* believe that." In each case I know that Ann intends for me to believe what she says, and I know that she believes it herself. Whatever reasons I have to think that Ann is privy to inside information on our friend's marital intentions can be the same in each case. I may not like the tone of the last case, but I see no reason to think that I am unable to follow the command. If I can accept Ann's testimony about this particular matter, why would I find myself unable to do so once she turns her testimony into an explicit imperative? The real issue is not whether I can believe on command, but whether I ought to.

There is a second reason why authority over beliefs has been widely rejected in the modern period, and this reason has tremendous significance for almost every area of human life. Authority is thought to be incompatible with autonomy. The idea of autonomy as used in contemporary discourse comes from Kant and philosophers leading up to Kant's work, but the idea has permeated our culture in ways that confuse it with such distinct ideas as the Stoic notion of selfsufficiency, the existentialist idea of authenticity, the idea of integrity, and especially the idea of independence. But in its most basic form what we call "autonomy" is the view that the ultimate authority over the self is the self, and it is this sense of autonomy that appears to conflict with authority. It led Robert Paul Wolff (1998) to his famous argument that the conflict between authority and autonomy makes anarchism the only acceptable political arrangement, and it led to the common view that the final word on whether a person lives or dies is the word of that person herself. What is particularly interesting about autonomy in this sense is that it not only makes the attempted exercise of authority a moral wrong, but it also makes it a moral wrong for the subject to accept it. If a person acts or believes on authority, she is not acting as a self-governing person should act. She is allegedly injuring her own personhood. One's autonomy can be violated by oneself as well as by other persons. The apparent conflict between authority and autonomy is therefore very serious. According to this argument, an autonomous person not only has the right to reject external authority, but has an obligation to do so. It is not surprising, then, that autonomy has a bad reputation among traditionalists. Probably everyone who grew up in a country that values democracy will say that the authority of the political state derives from the consent of the governed, but there are different answers to the question, "Why does it matter if the governed give consent?" If you ask for the source of authority in general, a traditional Catholic may refer to God's governance of the world, or the natural law. If you then ask him why he believes in religious authority, such as the teaching authority of the Church, he will say that Christ founded the Church. If the issue is the authority of Scripture, he will say it was revealed by God. If he is Muslim, he will say that Sharia law was revealed by God. There are many other justifications for authority that could be mentioned, of course, but in almost every case, the defender of authority accepts the position that authority is incompatible with autonomy. The difference between the anarchist like Wolff and the traditionalist is that the former values autonomy and the latter values authority. They agree that you cannot have both.

It is understandable that the traditional adherent of one of the major religions is skeptical about autonomy because the authority structures of the major religions predate the invention of autonomy, and many interpreters think that the idea of autonomy arose as a conscious rejection of those very authorities. That view is probably false, but the motives of historical persons are no longer the issue. The perception that authority and autonomy are strongly at odds, if not downright inconsistent, has had a dramatic effect on the perception of the justification of believing religious teachings. From the perspective of many defenders of autonomy who accept no religion, members of religious communities are unjustified in accepting authority in their community. From a perspective inside the community, authority is justified by reference to other beliefs that arise from within the community, such as "Christ founded the Church." This is not necessarily problematic. There is nothing wrong with being part of a tradition from which one takes various beliefs justified by that same tradition. But accepting the alleged incompatibility between authority and autonomy in effect allows many supporters of autonomy to dismiss the authority structures of religious communities without due regard to the actual implications of autonomy. Historical and cultural divisions make it difficult for a traditional religious community to meet the challenge posed by the modern defenders of autonomy on the latter's own terms, but I think that that can be done and that it should be done.

I propose that what we need to do is to look at how Robert Paul Wolff's challenge was met in the political domain. Given the premise that the ultimate authority over the self is the self, political authority was defended in an influential argument by Joseph Raz three decades ago, an argument that has become classic in the annals of political liberalism. What I will argue here is that a simple generalization of Raz's argument generates an exactly parallel defense of moral authority and religious authority. My conclusion is that if political authority is compatible with autonomy, so is religious and moral authority.

15.2. Using autonomy to justify authority

Joseph Raz's (1986) book, *The Morality of Freedom*, became a landmark in the tradition of political liberalism. In that book and later work, Raz showed how the authority of the political state can be defended from the premise that each person is the ultimate authority over himself. The early influence of Wolff's anarchism disappeared, and Raz is still one of the most influential writers on the philosophy of law in the English language.

Raz proposes some theses about authority in general before moving to the practical domain and in particular, the political domain. One is a thesis about what it *means* to act on authority. This is the *preemption thesis*. It says that to act on authority one must take an authoritative directive as one's reason for doing the act, replacing one's other reasons for and against doing the act. For instance, you may have many reasons for and against stopping at a red light. In favor of stopping, let us imagine that it appears safer to do so, you do not want to get a traffic citation, and the law says so. In favor of not stopping, we may suppose that you are in a hurry and there is a reasonably high probability that you can do it safely and without getting caught. If you put all these reasons together, giving each a certain weight, and then decide that all things considered, you will stop, you are not acting on authority. You are acting on authority only if the fact that the law says to stop is *the* reason you stop. Authority is fundamentally the normative power to give others preemptive reasons.

The preemption thesis says nothing about whether or not you *should* act on authority. For that we need a second thesis, what Raz calls the *Normal Justification thesis*. This thesis says that the normal way to show that one person has authority over another is to show that the alleged subject is more likely to act for her own ends if she accepts the directives of the alleged authority and tries to follow them, rather than to try to act for those ends directly (1986, 53). In other words, given that each self-directing person has reasons for which she acts, it is rational to act on those reasons the best way she can. Sometimes the best way she can is to adopt an indirect strategy: do what authority *A* says to do. If she can act on her own reasons better by doing what *A* says to do rather than by acting independently, acting on authority is what self-direction tells her to do. It is an efficient means to her own ends. By acting on the authority's directive preemptively, she is letting the authority stand in for her in reaching her ends. Acting on authority is therefore not only compatible with autonomy under these conditions, but follows from it.

The task of Raz is to justify a system of laws on the basis of the Normal Justification principle. I have no opinion about whether such a project succeeds. But what I want to do is to call attention to the generality of Raz's thesis justifying authority. Rationally self-directing persons have many ends, some of which are more successfully reached by acting at the direction of someone else, whether it is a political authority or an authority in some other domain. We have lots of ends that are practical, and so the justification of authority thesis can be used to justify taking someone as an authority about many things that have nothing to do with the law—one's health, one's computer, the best way to plant one's garden. We also have lots of ends that are epistemic. We want to find out the truth in many domains, and we have reason to think that there are persons whose authority in these domains can be justified by a specification of Raz's Normal Justification thesis. I propose a justification thesis applied to beliefs as follows:

Justification Thesis for Epistemic Authority
The epistemic authority of another person is justified for me by my conscientious judgment that I am more likely to form a true belief and avoid a false belief if I believe what the authority tells me than if I try to figure out what to believe myself.

Under the assumption that authority for a self-directing person is justified using the Razian framework, authority over beliefs for a self-directing person would be justified by this principle. If I am an intellectually realistic person, I will admit that there are many other people who are more likely to know the truth about some matter than I am myself. When that happens and I am aware of it, it is a demand of my own self-governance to take their word for it and to believe what they tell me because they tell me. The general principle here is that as long as I judge that their process of figuring out the truth using their experience, skills, background knowledge, and judgment is better than mine, I should let them stand in for me in determining whether a proposition in the relevant domain is true. I am serving my own ends by deferring to them in this way, and they are serving my ends by the process they use in coming to tell me that some proposition is true.

There are a number of issues that need to be resolved before it is reasonable for me to believe what someone else tells me preemptively in a particular case. For instance, maybe I have reason to believe that the putative authority is more likely to get the truth than I am, but the authority is only slightly more likely to do so. If I have already formed a belief on the matter for good reason, I can easily be less sure of the authority's superiority to me than if I have not yet formed a belief. It would probably be unwise to defer to the authority in such a situation. This is not a qualification of the justification thesis. It is an acknowledgment of the difficulty in being confident that another person really is superior to oneself in the relevant respect.

Another kind of problem arises when there are competing authorities, both of whom are more likely to get the truth than I, but who disagree with each other, and I am not in a position to judge which one is more authoritative. The reasonable thing to do in such a case might be to defer judgment, or to make a judgment based on other reasons for belief that I have not mentioned, such as believing in a way that is more likely to survive my future reflection. I have not said what aspects of myself I should reflect upon in deciding how to evaluate competing authorities, nor have I said that the end of truth trumps all other ends. But one of the purposes of reflection is to govern oneself in such a way that one reaches one's ends, ends that themselves survive further reflection. After I do as much reflection as is necessary, it can happen that someone satisfies the Justification of Epistemic Authority thesis for me, even when there are competing "authorities."

Both Raz's Normal Justification thesis and my Justification Thesis for Epistemic Authority may need supplementation with other principles to give us a determinate answer about what to do or to believe in a particular case. In fact, the path from Raz's Normal Justification thesis to the conclusion that I ought to take a particular law as authoritative is even more complicated than the path from my Epistemic Authority thesis to the conclusion that I ought to take a certain belief on authority. But it is revealing that many theorists find Raz's thesis successful as a defense of political authority. Likewise, it seems to me that adherents of the value of autonomy ought to take seriously the epistemic parallel I have proposed.

15.3. Moral authority

Are there some domains of belief that are off-limits to authority? As I mentioned at the beginning of this essay, it is widely believed that there is no authority in the realm of morality. To think otherwise supposedly fails to acknowledge what a self-governing person should do. But can we consistently justify taking a belief about a scientific matter on the word of an authority, but not a moral belief? Is there any reason why we should defer to an authority about our computer problem, but not defer to an authority about a moral problem?

One reason immediately comes to mind. Many people believe that there are no moral truths, or they believe that there are moral truths, but only because they are socially constructed. In either case, wouldn't that mean that there cannot be authority over the truth of such beliefs?

Actually, it would not. As long as I aim to make my moral beliefs true in whatever way they can be true, and I judge that I am more likely to get beliefs true in that sense if I accept the testimony of some other person than if I try to figure it out myself, I am justified in taking a moral belief on her testimony even if moral beliefs are not true in the same sense as scientific and other so-called factual beliefs. In fact, I do not even have to think that moral beliefs can be true in any sense. As long as I believe that some moral beliefs are better than others, I can be justified in taking a moral belief on authority when I judge that that person's moral belief is likely to be better than mine in that sense. "Better" can mean better defended, or better at aiding the community in its goal of peaceful coexistence, or better at giving me a belief that I will continue to hold ten years from now, or better in some other way. Provided that I conscientiously judge that some other person's moral belief is likely to be better than mine in whatever sense you want, I am justified in taking that person as an authority with regard to that belief by a simple modification of the justification principle.

Another reason for rejecting moral authority is that it seems to conflict with the right of each person to follow the voice of conscience within her. In fact, it is part of the Catholic moral tradition that a person is obliged to follow her conscience. Much has been written about the conscience, and it has sometimes been treated as a distinct source of moral knowledge, like Socrates's *daimonion*, a voice within him that prevented him from acting wrongly. But conscience can be opposed to authority only if conscience is a power by which I judge independently what is right and wrong in some case. Pope St. John Paul II criticizes this view in *Veritatis Splendor*:

> The individual conscience is accorded a status of a supreme tribunal of moral judgment, which hands down categorical and infallible decisions about good and evil. To the affirmation that one has a duty to follow one's conscience is unduly added the affirmation that one's moral judgment is true merely by the fact that it has its origin in the conscience. But in this way the inescapable claims of truth disappear, yielding in their place to a criterion of sincerity, authenticity, and "being at peace with oneself," so much so that some have come to adopt a radically subjectivist conception of moral judgment. (§32)

Clearly, that cannot be the sense of conscience that has final authority. But there is another sense of conscience that arguably does have final authority: conscience as your best judgment of the truth in some case, all things considered. In this sense of conscience, your best judgment cannot conflict with authority when it is your own judgment that tells you that the authority is more likely to get the truth than you are yourself. Conscience interpreted as one's best judgment does not conflict with authority where authority is defended by the Justification of Epistemic Authority thesis applied to moral beliefs.

There are some disadvantages to taking a moral belief on authority for the self-directing person that should be acknowledged. I have argued that believing on authority can be justified even when the belief has moral content, but we cannot get moral understanding by the testimony of an authority. If a moral authority tells me that abortion is wrong, and I believe it because I conscientiously judge that the authority is more likely to get the truth about the morality of abortion than I am, I am justified in having the belief, but I am not going to understand why abortion is wrong just because the authority said so. This is undoubtedly the reason papal encyclicals and other documents by religious authorities are typically accompanied by extensive argument. Some people (not many) may read the whole document and come to accept the belief advocated in the document on the basis of the reasons given. In such a case, the person is not believing on authority alone, but is letting the authority guide her direct evaluation of the reasons. I would not deny that she is in a better epistemic position than the person who accepts the immorality of some practice on the teaching authority of the Church alone, but my purpose here is not to deny that importance of understanding for a self-governing person, but to make the narrower point that adherents of the modern value of autonomy who think that autonomy conflicts with taking beliefs on authority are making a mistake. Even when the belief is about a moral matter, a person who takes the belief on authority can be justified in the same way political authority is justified in the tradition of political liberalism.

15.4. Religious authority

A person with moral authority in the sense I have been discussing is any person who is more likely to get the truth about some moral matter than some other person. One's grandmother can be a moral authority in this sense. Because the guiding premise has been the modern assumption of individual autonomy, authority needs to be justified by reference to an individual person's reasons for acting or believing. Since that person is in a different state from all other persons in the world, the persons who are authoritative for her will often differ from the persons who are authoritative for someone else. But some persons are authoritative for large groups of people who are bonded together, in part, because of common acceptance of beliefs that are transmitted over generations by an authoritative structure that is recognized in the community as the primary vehicle for that transmission. When authoritative beliefs are transmitted to large numbers of people over many generations, long after any particular person in authority has died, the question is no longer limited to which particular person to accept as an authority, but also what structure of authority is best designed to transmit authoritative teachings long into the future. It is no surprise, then, that moral authorities are often embedded in traditions.

My position is that authority within a religious community can be defended by extension of the same general principle for the justification of authority we have been using. Religious authorities are often both epistemic and practical. A religious community's epistemic authority is justified for me by my conscientious judgment that I am more likely to believe the truth if I believe what we, the community, believe than if I try to figure it out in a way that is independent of the community. The community's practical authority is justified for me by my conscientious judgment that I am more likely to live and die well and ultimately reach salvation by following the directives of the community than if I attempt to reach those ends on my own.

There are some important differences between the Church or religious community and the political state that affects the way authority is justified from the point of view of the individual member or subject. I think it is significant that modern political thought is motivated more by fear of bad authority than by desire for good authority. For historical reasons, it is now considered more important to devise a justification of authority that prevents tyranny than to give the bearer of authority the function of assisting the subjects in pursuing their individual and collective good. That means restricting authority as much as possible, compatible with having a tolerably smooth-functioning society. The contours of authority as proposed by Raz justify the authority of the state by reference to the state's ability to aid the subjects in the pursuit of ends they all have in advance of being subjects of the state. The ends that the state helps the subjects attain are very limited, so while the state has a high degree of authority over the subjects in the relevant domains, the authority of the state does not extend to a very large part of the subjects' lives.

In contrast, communities of all sorts are composed of persons who have something in common that persons outside the community do not share. Communities also have communal ends, which are not the same as the ends of the individuals in advance of joining the community. But by becoming part of a community, individuals assume the ends of the community. Certain communities can become an extended self and its members refer to it as "we," signaling that they identify with the community and its ends. Authority in a community is justified at least in part by reference to the communal ends, not only the ends the subjects have in advance of community membership. When the community is a religious body such as a church, authority is justified partly by reference to individual ends, such as personal salvation, and partly by the ends of the Church as a communal body, such as ministering to the spiritual and bodily needs of persons outside the Church. The range of authority of a religious body can therefore be much more extensive than the range of authority of the state.

The authority of a religious community can be more extensive in another way. The religious community teaches me some of my individual ends. The concept of salvation is something we learn through a community, and we adopt it as an end through membership in the community. In fact, it is not necessary to be a member of a religious community in order to adopt salvation as an end, but the usual way to take a religious end as one's personal end is through membership in a religious community. That means that if we are going to use the Razian approach to justifying authority, we would have to say that in many cases, the authority of the religious community is justified by reference to ends that one adopts on the authority of that same community. How can authority be defended by the demands of individual autonomy in such a case?

I think that the answer requires taking a careful look at what a conscientiously self-governing person does. Defenders of autonomy clearly believe that a self-governing person has ends, but nobody thinks that a self-governing person's ends must be fixed in advance of undertaking the process of self-governance. While governing ourselves with whatever ends we have by nature, we gradually learn to modify those ends. Some ends disappear and new ones are added as we follow the prescriptions dictated by our rational nature. Raz defends political authority on the grounds that acceptance of authority can be defended by the demands of rational self-governance. I am arguing that when authority is defended by rational self-governance, it can also be a demand of rational self-governance to accept a modification or addition to one's ends on the word of the authority. In this way, altering one's ends on authority is entailed by autonomy. There is no reason to think that moral and religious authority are excluded from this line of defense.

Contemporary defenders of autonomy and traditional defenders of authority generally assume that they have so little in common as to make it hopeless to attempt a dialogue on the defensibility of any kind of authority, whether epistemic, moral, religious, or political. But they do have one thing in common. Both sides generally agree that they are hopelessly divided. I think they are mistaken. Under the assumption of the value of autonomy, traditional forms of authority can be defended. If adherents of autonomy have objections to religious or moral authority, it cannot be on the grounds that such authority conflicts with autonomy. There are many ways in which the structures of authority and the exercise of authority can be criticized, of course, but the deepest attack is mistaken.

16
Epistemic Self-Trust and the *Consensus Gentium* Argument (2011)

16.1. Introduction

In this paper I want to explore the reasonableness of religious belief as a consequence of the reasonableness of self-trust. I will argue that the natural desire for truth makes epistemic self-trust a requirement, and consistent epistemic self-trust commits us to epistemic trust in others. One of the implications of this argument is that trust in the self supports the traditional *consensus gentium* argument for the existence of God. The fact that so many people in so many cultures in so many ages of the world have believed in a deity gives each of us a defeasible reason to believe in God that arises from a rational demand of the self. But the commitment to trust in others also shows why religious disagreement poses a particular threat to our own beliefs in matters of religion.

16.2. The need for self-trust

My starting point is the assumption that human beings have natural desires, desires that are part of every pre-reflective self. The idea that there are natural desires occurs repeatedly in both Western and non-Western philosophy, and it is presumed in many fields of study, although some scholars attempt to reduce them to a few basic ones such as the desire to obtain pleasure and avoid pain. I will not make any claims about the scope of natural desires, but I want to focus on a particular desire, the desire for truth, because I think it enjoys a certain primacy in the map of our desires, and if the desire is reasonable, there are some interesting consequences. If the desire for truth is natural, then virtually everyone has the desire, but I do not deny that there may be some exceptions. It is possible that the Pyrrhonian skeptics succeeded in giving it up, but even they recognized that skepticism is not the natural way to be since they thought that they had to go through therapy to get there. So, with a few possible exceptions, I think it is fair to say that everyone desires truth.

We do not need to assume anything controversial about truth to make this assumption about the natural desire for truth. My point is compatible with a deflationary view of truth according to which the word "true" adds nothing to what can be stated without it. So according to some philosophers, if I want to know whether "Hostas prefer shade" is true, that is just to say that I want to know whether hostas prefer shade. We can express my question without the word "true." But that affects only the wording of my point, not its substance. It means that the natural desire for truth is the desire to have my questions answered. I want to know who or what something is, or whether something is the case, or how something works. When I say there is a natural desire for truth, I just mean that it is natural to ask questions and to want answers to them.

Sometimes I do not even know enough to know what question to ask. The desire to be shown the question to ask as well as its answer is also part of what I mean by the desire for truth. What I am calling the desire for truth is the satisfaction of the questioning urge. My claim that there is such a natural desire for truth does not depend upon the position that the word "true" cannot be eliminated from our discourse, nor does it depend upon the idea that there is a single object—truth—which is the aim of the questioning urge.

In addition to the natural desire for truth, I think there is a natural belief that the natural desire for truth is satisfiable. I live my life as if I can get answers to my questions, so I think that the desire for truth can be, and often is, satisfied. I trust my faculties and my environment sufficiently to think that I believe many truths, and I rely upon those faculties and those truths in the normal conduct of my life. The faculties I use in forming beliefs may operate on the environment directly, or they may operate on the testimony of others. It is not only natural to rely upon my own faculties, it is also natural to believe what other people tell me. So, the natural trust with which I start includes trust in the relation between my faculties and my environment, and trust in the faculties of many other people. Philosophers raise the question whether it is reasonable to have trust in this general, basic way, but it is clear that trust is the starting point. It is a component of the pre-reflective self.

I do not know how common it is to reflect upon one's desire for truth or one's belief that the desire is satisfiable, but philosophers reflect upon everything. That might be what is most characteristic of philosophy. It is interesting to investigate what happens to a disciplined self-reflective being who reflects upon the belief that truth is attainable. Does she gain or lose confidence in it? Does she decide that the belief is justified? What does that do to her trust in herself and others?

A number of philosophers have observed that there is no non-circular way to determine that the natural desire for truth is satisfiable, or to put the claim in the preferred idiom, there is no non-circular way to tell that our belief-forming faculties are reliable as a whole. For instance, Richard Foley (2001) argues that there is no answer to the radical skeptic, and since the project of strong foundationalism failed, there is no non-circular guarantee that our epistemic faculties and procedures are suited to discover truths. We can do everything epistemically that we are supposed to do, including following the evidence scrupulously, and we have no assurances that the results will give us the truth or even make it probable that we will get the truth. We therefore need self-trust in our epistemic faculties taken as a whole, together with our pre-reflective opinions. Self-trust is necessary, and since it is a state to which we are led by a process of rational self-criticism, it is also rational.

For Foley, self-trust is a state to which we must move when we reflect upon the skeptical hypotheses and the failure of responses to them, particularly the failure of foundationalism. He implies that trust is a state to which we retreat because we do not have adequate justification, or as he sometimes puts it, a "guarantee" of the reliability of our faculties and opinions taken as a whole.

William Alston (1986) offers a more detailed and subtle argument for a related conclusion about circularity in his paper "Epistemic Circularity," repeating part of the argument of that paper with modifications in his book *Beyond Justification* (2005). Alston argues that as long as the issue is the reliability of broad sources of belief, the attempt to establish the reliability of beliefs deriving from that source will inevitably take us back to the source from which we started (2005, 209–210). Full reflective justification for any belief is impossible (2005, 344). An interesting difference between Alston and Foley is that Alston does not think that the problem of epistemic circularity is necessarily tied to the threat of skepticism. He says that the specter of skepticism is a "dramatic" way to put the issue, "but it is not necessary for a calm, fully mature consideration of the problem" (2005, 216).[1] I think that this is an important point. A person who aims to be fully reflectively justified in her beliefs need not be a person who is afraid that the alternative to full reflective justification is skepticism. She may just be a person who takes reflective self-consciousness as far as she can. She is doing what every self-reflective being does, only she is doing it more thoroughly. In making the attempt to go as far as she can in disciplined self-consciousness, she notices that she runs up against the problem of epistemic circularity. But she need not be motivated by fear of skepticism.

Like Foley, Alston concludes that self-trust is inescapable, and like Foley, Alston thinks of self-trust as the outcome of a sophisticated line of argument. We are forced into it by careful reflection on the human epistemic condition. If we could be fully reflectively justified in our beliefs, presumably we would not need to "take" our faculties to be reliable and our beliefs to be credible. We would not need self-trust because we would have something in principle better, but impossible to achieve.

My approach to the need for self-trust is somewhat different. I have suggested that there is a natural desire for truth and a natural belief that the desire is satisfied. This belief is pre-reflective. Before we reflect upon the justification of our beliefs or the reliability of our faculties, we already trust ourselves and our environment, including other people. Trust is the condition of the pre-reflective self; it is not just for intellectually sophisticated persons who have reflected on skepticism and epistemic circularity and who conclude that we cannot be fully reflectively justified in our beliefs. Trust is the state from which we begin, and we may ask ourselves whether we can escape it. Alston's arguments indicate that the answer will always be no.

What would happen if, *per impossibile*, we could escape epistemic circularity? What if someone thinks upon reflection that strong foundationalism succeeds, or that there is some other answer to skepticism, or some other way to achieve full reflective justification? Will they need less trust in their faculties than the person who thinks there is no answer to the skeptic?

That depends upon what trust is. Foley implies that trust is a fall-back state to which we retreat when we lack the proof we really want, and Alston seems to have a similar view, although he says very little about the state of trust. This way of looking at trust makes a lot of sense in certain contexts. For instance, people often say that they trust their mates when they lack proof of fidelity. But trust in your spouse need not be a state to which you retreat when you lack the proof you would prefer to have. If you had proof, would you have less trust? In such a case you would not have to "fall back" on trust, but it seems to me that typically, you would still have the *disposition* of trust because the point of trust is that it does not depend upon proof, not that it requires the lack of proof. Similarly, I think that trust in one's epistemic faculties does not depend upon the outcome of philosophical arguments. If we could escape epistemic circularity by getting a guarantee that our faculties get us the truth, that would be like the case in which you have proof of your spouse's fidelity. I don't see that trust would disappear. The difference is that epistemic circularity makes self-trust essential, whereas it would be non-essential but still natural if we were able to escape the epistemic circle.

Is there any difference between the pre-reflective state of self-trust and the self-trust we have after reflection on epistemic circularity? Again, that depends upon the necessary conditions for trust. I think that trust has two components that can be separated. First, when I trust x I treat x as trustworthy—deserving of trust. Second, I believe that x is trustworthy.[2] If the trust in question is epistemic trust in myself, that means that I both treat my epistemic faculties and beliefs as trustworthy, and I believe that they are trustworthy. If I rely upon my faculties, as I necessarily do, I am treating them as if they are trustworthy, but it is possible for a person to respond to the problem of epistemic circularity by treating her faculties as trustworthy without believing they are trustworthy. Such a person would have one of the components of self-trust but not the other.

For the purposes of this paper I will not claim that this response is unreasonable, but will merely mention my reason for thinking that it is reasonable to believe ourselves to be trustworthy. To treat something as deserving of trust without believing it deserves trust creates dissonance in the self that becomes noticeable once we start reflecting. When I become aware of self-trust, I am pressured within myself to either stop trusting myself or to believe that I am trustworthy. It is possible to accept the dissonance or to not notice it, so I do not insist that it is impossible to live a normal life without believing that our epistemic faculties are trustworthy. But the self-reflective person at some point will become aware of the dissonance if she does not believe her faculties are trustworthy, and will then have to decide whether to accept the natural belief that her natural desire for truth is satisfiable or else live with dissonance. I propose that it is reasonable to resolve the dissonance by not only trusting our faculties, but also believing that they are trustworthy. I will return to the issue of what it means to be reasonable.

The awareness of epistemic circularity is not the deepest reason why we need epistemic self-trust. Epistemic circularity is relevant to the natural desire for truth only if we make certain assumptions about the nature of mind and the universe, and if we make those assumptions, we need to trust them. We observe the problem of epistemic circularity when we want truth—our questions answered—and we notice that the process of attempting to answer those questions can never be completed. But this would not be a problem unless (1) there is a connection between truth and what we do when we attempt to answer our questions, and (2) what we attempt to do can never be completed. The discovery of epistemic circularity is the discovery of (2), but what about (1)? The assumption that there is a connection between getting truth and what we do when we attempt to answer our questions is the deeper reason for self-trust.

To see why, suppose we resisted or gave up the desire to complete the task of finding reasons, and thus found epistemic circularity non-threatening. Then we would be forced to face the fact that the problem is not just that we cannot *complete* the search for reasons, but that we have to trust that there is *any* connection between reasons and truth. If the process of getting reasons were completed, then we would have the reasons we seek, but we would still need to trust that reasons are the sorts of things that give us the answers to our questions, that connect us to truth. And why do we trust reasons? Because looking for reasons for our beliefs is what a self-reflective person does when she is trying hard to get the truth. We trust reasons in virtue of our trust in the connection between trying to get the truth and succeeding.

The situation would be unchanged if we accepted a strong form of foundationalism. What foundationalism gives us is the completion of the search for reasons, but we would still need trust in whatever power in us produced the foundational beliefs in an attempt to answer our questions, and whatever it is in us that gives us the foundational cognitive structure. We trust reasons at all only because we trust ourselves when we are making the effort to get truth. So even if we were "fully reflectively justified" in our beliefs, we would still need self-trust.

Let us call the quality of trying hard to get the truth *epistemic conscientiousness*. I think of this quality as the self-reflective parallel to the natural desire for truth. It is not just a vague, unspecified, and possibly unconscious desire, but a conscious desire accompanied by the attempt to satisfy it with all of one's available powers. I have argued that we need trust that there is a connection between the natural desire for truth and the satisfaction of that desire using the faculties that any person has, reflective or pre-reflective, but once a person becomes reflective, she will think that her trustworthiness is greater if she makes a greater effort, summoning her powers in a fully conscious and careful way, and exercising them to the best of her ability. What I am calling conscientiousness is the state or disposition to do that.[3] We trust that there is a connection between trying and succeeding, and the reflective person thinks that there is a closer connection between trying hard and succeeding. But it would not be reasonable to trust conscientiousness unless it was already reasonable to place a basic trust in the faculties we are using when we are conscientious. I would not be trustworthy when I am trying hard in using my faculties unless my faculties were already generally trustworthy. It would not be reasonable to trust myself when I am conscientious and for the reason that I am conscientious unless it was already reasonable for me to trust my faculties in a very basic way.

I assume that conscientiousness comes in degrees. Trying a little is natural and requires no special self-reflection. It is probably an automatic accompaniment to the natural desire for truth. But trying hard requires considerable self-awareness and self-monitoring. There are certain things we do when we monitor our beliefs. One of the things we do (but not the only thing) is to expect ourselves to have reasons for our beliefs. A conscientious person might not expect reasons for every belief, but having reasons is something conscientious persons expect of themselves, and we trust the connection between reasons and truth because we have a more basic trust in ourselves when we are being conscientious, and we trust the connection between conscientiousness and the possession of reasons.

The same point applies to trust in evidence, which I assume is closely related to reasons for belief. We do not have evidence that evidence leads to truth. We might think that we have evidence that evidence leads to truth, but what we mean is that we have evidence that evidence leads to more evidence, enough that at some point we say that the matter is settled. In any case, why should we pay attention to the evidence that evidence leads to truth unless we trust evidence? And what do we trust it for? To get to truth. We trust the evidence that evidence leads to truth, and we trust it because looking for evidence that something is true is what self-reflective persons who want the truth do, and we trust that. Like our trust in reasons, our trust in evidence is dependent upon our trust in ourselves when we are being conscientious. We have evidence that evidence leads to more and more evidence. We trust the connection between evidence and truth because of a more basic trust in the relation between conscientiousness and truth.

Is trusting ourselves epistemically reasonable? I have argued for two levels of epistemic self-trust—one a basic trust in our faculties, and the other a particular trust in ourselves when we self-consciously exercise those faculties to the best of our ability, which is to say, when we are epistemically conscientious. We have reasons for thinking that our faculties give us truth, but the reasons are circular. We also have circular reasons for thinking that conscientiousness leads to truth. In both cases we lack non-circular reasons, but we lack non-circular reasons for any of our beliefs, so we do not lack something we can get. The belief that our faculties are trustworthy in getting truth is one of the components of epistemic self-trust, and so one of the components of epistemic self-trust is reasonable. The other component is an attitude, a way of treating our faculties. We treat them as trustworthy. That is reasonable also, assuming the principle: If it is reasonable to believe x is trustworthy, it is reasonable to treat x as trustworthy. There is a parallel argument for the reasonableness of trusting ourselves when we are conscientious.

If we are reasonable in trusting ourselves when we are conscientious, we have another ground for the reasonableness of basic trust in our faculties. We would not be trustworthy when we are conscientious unless our faculties were already basically trustworthy. So the following principle gives us the conclusion that it is reasonable to have a basic trust in our faculties: If it is reasonable to trust x and x would not be trustworthy unless y is trustworthy, it is reasonable to trust y.

To summarize this section, we have a natural belief that our natural desire for truth is satisfiable, and a natural trust in the faculties and processes in ourselves that produce beliefs. There is no rational way to escape this natural self-trust, given the fact that the search for reasons for our beliefs leads to epistemic circularity, and the more basic fact that we have no way to tell that there is any connection at all between reasons and truth without trust in ourselves when we are conscientious. That means that a self-reflective person trusts herself in advance of reasons to trust herself, but she trusts herself more when she is conscientious and for the reason that she is conscientious. She trusts reasons and evidence because of her trust in herself when she is conscientious.

16.3. The need for trust in others

Natural epistemic trust in ourselves is inescapable, but what about the natural trust in other persons? Many philosophers think that it is not only escapable, but that epistemic self-reliance represents an intellectual ideal. Trusting only our own faculties and not those of others is a quality Elizabeth Fricker (2006) calls intellectual autonomy. Almost everyone, including Fricker, agrees that if we did not depend upon others, we would have far less knowledge because we would have far fewer beliefs, but it does seem possible not to rely upon others, whereas it is impossible not to rely upon ourselves. I will argue next that if we trust ourselves epistemically, we cannot consistently fail to trust others epistemically.

Since I have no non-circular reason for thinking I am trustworthy as a whole, I have no non-circular reason to think that as a whole I am more trustworthy than other people are as a whole. By using powers that I trust, I come to believe that other human beings have the same natural desire for truth and the same general powers and capacities that I have. If I believe that I am generally trustworthy and I accept the principle that I should treat like cases alike, I am rationally committed to thinking that they are generally trustworthy also. I should regard them as generally trustworthy in advance of evidence of their trustworthiness, just as I think of myself as trustworthy in advance of the evidence. Since as a conscientious person I trust evidence, I may see that on the evidence some person is not epistemically trustworthy, or not trustworthy in some respect, and if so, my general trust in that person would be defeated. But insofar as I have a general trust in the connection between my natural faculties and desire for truth and success in reaching truth, then I should have trust in the same connection in other people. So long as I see no relevant difference between others and myself, then if I trust myself, I should trust them too.

When I am conscientious I acquire many beliefs about other people. Many other people appear to me to be just as conscientious as I am when I am as conscientious as I can be. At least, many of them are just as conscientious as I am in certain respects or with respect to certain beliefs. Because I place special trust in myself when I am conscientious, I commit myself to trusting the conscientiously formed beliefs I have about both the general epistemic similarity of other persons to myself, and their conscientiousness. Because I trust myself when I am conscientious and for the reason that I am conscientious, I must trust others whose conscientiousness I discover when I am being conscientious. I have said that one of the things I do when I am conscientious (but not the only thing I do) is to look for reasons or evidence for my beliefs. I do have plenty of evidence that other people are as conscientious as I am with respect to numerous beliefs. I also have evidence that some people are more conscientious than I am, and, of course, I have evidence that some people are less so.

My commitment to trust my conscientiously formed beliefs about other people means that I cannot consistently expect evidence of the reliability of another person before thinking of them as epistemically trustworthy. Insofar as I believe myself to be trustworthy when I am conscientious, and I conscientiously believe that many other people are at least as conscientious as I am in certain respects, I must think of them as epistemically trustworthy in those respects. I am committed to that by the principle that I should think of like cases alike. I have said that a conscientious person trusts evidence in virtue of her trust in conscientiousness, and so a conscientious person might expect evidence of another person's conscientiousness before trusting them. But I want to make two points about that. First, having evidence of another person's conscientiousness is not the same as having evidence of her reliability. We do have evidence that conscientiousness is reliably truth-conducive, so if we have evidence that someone is conscientious, we have indirect evidence that she is reliable. But the more important point from the last section is that we trust evidence in virtue of the fact that we trust conscientiousness, not vice versa, so our trust in the evidence that someone else is conscientious derives from our trust in our own conscientiousness. I have left open the possibility that a conscientious person believes conscientiously without evidence in some cases. If so, she can conscientiously believe that another person is conscientious without evidence of the other's conscientiousness.

So far, I have argued that I am committed to thinking of other persons as epistemically trustworthy if I think of myself as epistemically trustworthy, but my trust in myself is basic. I must have a general trust in myself and my faculties if I trust the natural desire for truth, and since I am reasonable in believing that other people have the same faculties and the same natural desire, I am reasonable in trusting them and their faculties for the same reason I trust my own. But my trust in others depends upon my beliefs that they are like me and that I should treat them like me. My trust in myself does not depend upon those beliefs.

Trust in my own conscientiousness is more basic than my trust in the conscientiousness of others. My own conscientiousness is probably something that is transparent to my mind, or at least, it is something I can discover through introspection. I would not deny that self-deception is possible, but in general, I know how hard I am trying. In contrast, my reason to believe other people are conscientious depends upon observation of those people and inferences about their inner efforts from their external behavior. So, my grounds for believing other people are conscientious is less direct than my grounds for believing that I am conscientious. Nonetheless, it is often reasonable for me to believe that other people are conscientious because it is a belief I form when I am being conscientious. Given that I conscientiously believe they are conscientious, then if I am rationally required to accept the principle that I should treat like cases alike, I am rationally required to trust them for the same reason I trust myself.

Somebody might agree that the paths from self-trust to trust in others succeed in showing that I am committed to thinking of all other people as generally trustworthy, and many other people as just as trustworthy as myself. But it can be argued that it does not follow that I am committed to actually trusting any of these people. I have no obligation to trust everyone I believe to be trustworthy. If I prefer to trust myself and not others, or to trust myself more than others, why shouldn't I do that? Can I reasonably refuse to trust others epistemically?

I think that I cannot do so if I care about truth. If I do not trust others, I must ignore my own evidence that other people are trustworthy. I must ignore the beliefs to which I am led when I am conscientious, when I form beliefs out of a concern for truth. The only way to do that is to care about my own faculties and their outputs more than the truth; to care about my own evidence, not because it leads to the truth, but because it is mine; to care about my own conscientious beliefs, not because I am conscientious and care about truth, but because they are my beliefs. I must regard myself as trustworthy, not because of my conscientiousness or even because of my human faculties, but because I am myself. And that is very implausible. The same problem arises whenever I trust myself more than others when my evidence or the conscientious use of my faculties indicates that they are as reliable or as conscientious as I am. To the extent that I trust myself more than I trust them, my reason is not epistemic. I must be valuing my own faculties more than the truth. That is ethical egoism in the realm of the intellect.

Assuming I do not want to be an ethical egoist, I am rationally committed to not only thinking of others as trustworthy, but to actually trusting them on the same grounds as I trust myself. I must have the same attitude of general defeasible trust in all others that I have toward myself, and I must acknowledge that the level of trust that I have in myself when I am conscientious applies to many other people. I am therefore committed to a weak form of epistemic universalism.

16.4. The *consensus gentium* argument

I have argued that general trust in myself commits me to the position that there is a defeasible presumption in favor of the beliefs of any other person, absent any particular reason I have for trusting or not trusting the person, and absent any reason I may have in advance for believing or disbelieving the proposition she believes. But virtually every real-life case of finding out in a way we trust that somebody has a certain belief includes information about the believer that potentially defeats the credibility of the belief. What's more, the content of the belief may be something to which I might assign a low prior probability, given other things I believe, or other psychic states I trust, such as emotions or attitudes. But let us try to imagine a pure case, one in which there is no information that affects the credibility of the belief. Suppose, for instance, that I find out that somebody somewhere of whom I know nothing believes that Poland was invaded by the Tartars in 1279, and suppose that my background knowledge of Poland and the Tartars is so vague that I have no reason to believe or disbelieve it in advance, and suppose that neither believing nor disbelieving that Poland was invaded by the Tartars would have any effect on anything else I trust. I submit that I have a reason to believe that Poland was invaded by the Tartars in 1279.

Of course, there are no pure cases of this kind. I cannot find out that someone believes a proposition without finding out many other things about the believer of the proposition, and in almost every case the content of the proposition has some bearing on my other beliefs or my emotions or attitudes, which I may trust to one degree or another. So in practice my defeasible reason for believing that Poland was invaded by the Tartars might be defeated easily, either because I have evidence that the believer is untrustworthy, or because I already have a belief I trust that conflicts with the belief about the Tartars, or because the belief would produce dissonance with some non-belief state that I trust. Nonetheless, it is worth noting that once I become aware of the fact that somebody believes that Poland was invaded by the Tartars and I trust my belief that somebody has that belief, I have a defeasible reason to believe it myself. I have argued in favor of weak universalism, but I am not claiming that having a defeasible reason to believe *p* means that I have sufficient reason to adopt the belief *p*. Nonetheless, the belief of another person counts in favor of the belief. It is a mark in favor of its credibility.

Suppose now that I find out that large numbers of people have the same belief. Maybe I learn that thousands of people believe that Poland was invaded by the Tartars, and again, we need to imagine that I lack any other information about those people or the content of the belief. It seems to me that the large number of believers strengthens my defeasible reason for sharing their belief. The degree of trust I should have in their belief increases. Of course, it might turn out that most of these people acquired their belief from one or a few other people, and in fact, most beliefs that are shared by large numbers of people are spread through the community by testimony. So, we should at least say that other things equal, a belief independently acquired by large numbers of people is more trustworthy than the belief of one or a few.

However, the importance of independence should not be exaggerated. If twenty people believe the outcome of one person's addition of a list of numbers on the testimony of one who added up the figures, their belief does not count as much as it would if each of them had independently added the figures, but it seems to me that it counts more than the case in which only one person has the belief. That is because the fact that twenty people have the belief is evidence that nineteen people regard the source from which they acquired the belief as trustworthy, and that gives me a defeasible reason to treat the source as trustworthy also. I have a defeasible reason to trust persons who are trusted by persons I trust. If many millions of people share a belief, that gives me a greater defeasible reason to trust the belief than if only one or a few persons believe it, even if the beliefs were not acquired independently. Nonetheless, independence of belief greatly increases the trustworthiness of the belief.

I have argued that trust in agreement by large numbers of other people is rationally required by self-trust. It is common to treat widespread agreement as a defeasible reason to adopt or maintain a belief, aside from the argument I have given, so there is common consent that common consent gives us a reason for belief. This is a ground for belief that is usually unconscious, and even philosophers who are otherwise very careful about identifying and defending their grounds for making an assertion sometimes refer to common agreement without defense.[4] I have offered a defense that arises from consistently applying the attitude of trust in my general epistemic faculties that is both pre-reflective and found upon reflection to be rationally inescapable. I owe the same attitude to anyone else who has the faculties I trust in myself, which is to say all other human beings.

The belief that common consent gives us a reason to adopt a belief has a long history. Perhaps the most famous case of a *consensus gentium* argument is used to defend the belief in God. We find such an argument in Cicero's (1998) dialogue, *On the Nature of the Gods*. Cicero writes:

> [T]his belief of ours is not based on any prescription, custom, or law, but it abides as the strong, unanimous conviction of the whole world. We must therefore come to the realization that gods must exist because we have an implanted, or rather an innate, awareness of them. Now when all people naturally agree on something, that belief must be true; so we are to acknowledge that gods exist ... this is agreed by virtually everyone—not just philosophers, but also the unlearned.... (Book I, 44)

Cicero observes that belief in a deity or deities is virtually universal. Today it is not universal, if it ever was, but it is certainly widespread. In any case, the argument from consent does not require universality of belief. Lack of universality is a problem only to the extent that there are not only large numbers of people who believe in God, but there are also many people who disbelieve in God. Clearly, if the numbers of people who believe in some proposition count, so do the numbers of people who disbelieve that same proposition.

The issue of independence is relevant to Cicero's argument. If millions of people believe in God because they all acquired the belief by testimony from a small number of sources, the vast number of believers does not count as much as the same number of beliefs acquired independently. Most people who believe in God come to believe in the early part of their lives by testimony from their parents and other trusted adults. It is doubtful that the beliefs children get from adults have much more credibility than the beliefs of the adults alone, and I think we should discount the number of children's beliefs as relevant to the *consensus gentium* argument. However, I would not discount the number of theistic beliefs of adults who originally acquired their belief on testimony since there is a defeasible reason to trust their trust in the lack of defeaters for their belief. In any case, there are many millions of beliefs in God that *are* independently acquired. I think we should conclude that the epistemic presumption is in favor of the belief. The fact that another person believes in God gives each of us a defeasible reason to believe. The fact that many millions believe increases the reason, and the fact that many of those millions acquired their belief independently increases the reason further. It is an implication of self-trust that the fact that so many people all over the world at all times have believed in a deity gives each of us a *prima facie* reason to believe in a deity ourselves, a reason that exceeds the reason we would have for believing in God if we were aware of only one or a few believers. Of course, it also follows that the fact that there are many disbelievers counts in favor of disbelief.

Summarizing what I have said, the fact that consistent self-trust leads to trust in others produces a form of the traditional *consensus gentium* argument which we can formulate as follows:

Consensus gentium argument from self-trust

1. Every person must have a general attitude of self-trust in her epistemic faculties as a whole. This trust is both natural and shown to be inescapable by philosophical reflection (from section 16.2).
2. The general attitude of epistemic self-trust commits us to a general attitude of epistemic trust in the faculties of all other human beings (from section 16.3).
3. Therefore, the fact that someone else has a belief gives me a *prima facie* reason to believe it myself.
4. Other things equal, the fact that many people have a certain belief increases my *prima facie* reason to believe it, and my reason is stronger when the beliefs are acquired independently (from section 16.4).
5. The fact that other people believe in God is a *prima facie* reason to believe that God exists, and the fact that many millions of people constituting a strong supermajority believe (and have believed in prior ages) that God exists increases my *prima facie* reason to believe in God myself. Discounting for dependence, there are still many millions of people who independently believe or have believed in past ages in the existence of God.

A parallel argument can be given for atheism since the fact that there are many people who disbelieve in God gives me a *prima facie* reason to disbelieve in God. If there are many more people who believe than disbelieve, the *prima facie* reason for belief is stronger than for disbelief.

The argument I have given here is not the same as traditional *consensus gentium* arguments such as the one I quoted from Cicero. That argument has usually been interpreted as an argument to the best explanation. The idea is that there is a certain datum that needs to be explained: the fact that so many people in so many parts of the world believe in God. The question is then posed whether the best explanation for that datum is the truth of the belief. Various explanations of the datum are weighed against each other from the standpoint of a neutral arbiter. The arbiter could be a person from another planet. No connection is assumed between the arbiter's trust in the way she goes about evaluating alternative explanations for the datum and the arbiter's trust in the beliefs of the persons evaluated. I hope it is clear that the argument I am proposing is not of this kind. My argument links trust in the beliefs of others with self-trust. Trust in the self commits us to granting *prima facie* credibility to the belief of another, and it is reasonable for trust in the credibility of the belief to be greater when the belief is widespread.

The reason for belief in God that we get from the beliefs of other people can be defeated. In particular, it can be defeated by the discovery of lack of conscientiousness on the part of a believer. Given the important place of conscientiousness in self-trust, the argument can be strengthened or weakened, depending upon my conscientious judgment that the people who believe in God are or are not conscientious in their belief. For almost all theistic believers in human history, I have no reason to think that they were especially conscientious or especially unconscientious. I am aware of many extremely conscientious persons who believe in God, but also many whose belief is no more conscientious than baseball players' superstitions. I am also aware of many conscientious persons who disbelieve in God, but the number of conscientious believers seems to me to be significantly greater than the number of conscientious non-believers.

Is there any reason to think that belief in God is over-represented among those who are the least conscientious? Hume notoriously claimed that belief in miracles is more common among "ignorant and barbarous" peoples (Hume 2000, 90). Similarly, some intellectually sophisticated atheists claim that atheism is dominant among intellectually sophisticated persons in Western countries.[5] So some people must think that they can identify a property that defeats the belief that the possessors of the property are trustworthy, although it is unlikely that they think that the property defeats the belief that the possessors of the property are conscientious.

The argument I have given here does not claim that there are no defeaters. I am arguing that everyone has a *prima facie* reason to trust all others, a majority of whom believe in God, and that gives us a *prima facie* reason to believe in God. That is a reason that can be defeated by the discovery of the lack of conscientiousness among believers, and it can be strengthened by the discovery of the conscientiousness of believers. An objector might think that when she believes conscientiously, she can identify a property of the believer that makes a belief formed out of that property untrustworthy, and that many theists in history have that property. If so, she must think either that this property prevents the believer from being conscientious, or she trusts the truth-conduciveness of that property more than that of conscientiousness. There are many other ways in which aspects of the self that one trusts can defeat one's reason for having a certain belief, but my purpose is not to investigate the particular defeaters one could have, but to propose a structure that a reasonable person should use based on self-trust.

The idea of God common among all peoples is exceedingly vague. Common consent clearly cannot support specific theological claims about God, not even the unicity of God, although that attribute has wider acceptance than such traditional attributes as personhood, omnipotence, and perfect goodness. Aristotle observed that there is greater satisfaction in a lesser grasp of "celestial things" than a complete grasp of mundane matters, just as a half glimpse of someone we love is more important than a full view of other things (*Parts of Animals* 644b32–24). I think that what we get from widespread agreement is closer to the "half glimpse" mentioned by Aristotle than to a clear view of the object. The peoples of the world give different descriptions of the object glimpsed, but they agree that there is a glimpse of something important. Perhaps the vagueness of the idea of God makes the *consensus gentium* argument uninteresting to some people, but I agree with Aristotle that even a veiled glance at something tremendous is more valuable than a complete grasp of ordinary objects.

This brings me to my final point. Given that self-trust commits us to trust those who have the qualities we trust in ourselves, disagreement with those we trust is a problem. The popular problem of reasonable disagreement is usually posed in terms of what a reasonable person should do when she is aware of other persons who have a belief that conflicts with her own when those other persons seem to her to be as reasonable as she is herself. The argument I have given here suggests that this problem in its most critical form arises from self-trust. When I am believing conscientiously, I come to believe that there are many others who are as conscientious as I am and who therefore deserve the same level of trust I have in myself when I am as conscientious as I can be. In fact, it is not even necessary to accept my argument that the feature of myself in virtue of which I trust myself the most epistemically is epistemic conscientiousness. For any quality I have in virtue of which I trust myself epistemically, whether it is particular intellectual virtues, the best exercise of my reason, or some other epistemically trustworthy property, when I believe in a way that arises from that quality, I will invariably come to believe that there are many other people who have the same trustworthy quality, and who have beliefs that arise from that quality that conflict with some of my own beliefs. I owe them trust because of consistent trust in myself.

I believe that the only way to resolve this problem is to become as self-conscious as we can about the things we trust. Trusting what I trust upon reflection when I am being conscientious is all I can do. Doing so seems to me to be very close to what Kant meant by an autonomous agent. But autonomy of intellect, like autonomy of will, should not be confused with self-reliance. Human intellects have been searching for truth for thousands of years. We are all different selves, so it is inevitable that we will not all have the same beliefs, but it is important that we are all part of a communal project to get closer and closer to a grasp of the world. What millions of people believe cannot be reasonably dismissed without dismissing our trust in ourselves.

Notes

1. Alston says, that he will pursue the discussion in terms of the "more dramatically attractive" skeptical challenge. His response to epistemic circularity two pages later is therefore framed as a reply to the Pyrrhonian skeptic.
2. In Zagzebski (2012), chapter 2, I argue that trust has a third component, a component of feeling trusting.
3. Note that as I define conscientiousness, it has no relation to duty.
4. Hume does this in his essay, "On Miracles." After giving an argument against the reasonableness of belief on testimony that a miracle occurred, he gives an example of something that it would be reasonable to believe which has some of the features of a miracle. He postulates that many people testified that darkness fell over the earth for a period of eight days long before the birth of the person making the judgment. There are several features of the situation that Hume thinks increase the reasonableness of believing their testimony. One of the most important is widespread agreement in the testimony.
5. See, for instance, Richard Dawkins (2008), 128.

VIII
GOD, TRINITY, AND THE METAPHYSICS OF MODALITY

17
What if the Impossible Had Been Actual? (1990)

17.1. Counterpossibles: The standard view

What would have happened if 2 + 2 had equaled 5? What if I were to go backwards in time and change my lecture last week? What if it had both rained and not rained here at this moment? I assume that each of these states of affairs is impossible, and impossible in as strong a sense as you like. None of them could have obtained, no matter what. Likewise, each of the following propositions is necessarily false:

1. 2 + 2 = 5.
2. I go backwards in time and change my lecture last week.
3. It is both raining and not raining here at this moment.

But even if it is assumed that some state of affairs could never have obtained, can anything interesting be said about what would have been the case if it had? That is the question I wish to investigate in this paper.

According to the standard semantics of counterfactual conditionals, one of the peculiar features of a necessarily false proposition is that it counterfactually implies every proposition whatever. For example, since proposition (3) is necessarily false, Lewis and Stalnaker hold that the following propositions are both true:

4. If it were both raining and not raining here at this moment, then I would be the Pope.
5. If it were both raining and not raining here at this moment, then I would not be the Pope.

Since a necessarily false proposition is one whose truth is impossible, I shall call such propositions "impossible propositions." So, according to the standard view, for any such impossible proposition, pi: $pi > q$ and $pi > \neg q$ are both true for any q.[1] Let us call a "would" counterfactual with an impossible antecedent a "counterpossible."

My reaction to the standard view applied to (4) and (5) is not very strong. If every counterfactual conditional with an explicitly contradictory antecedent turns out to be true, I might find that acceptable. Much more worrisome, though, is the status of counterpossibles with antecedents that are more interesting because they are not explicitly contradictory. Consider (2) for a moment. If it is necessarily false, then on the standard view, both of the following are true:

6. If I were to go backwards in time and change my lecture last week, then I would reach the same moment of time twice.
7. If I were to go backwards in time and change my lecture last week, then I would not reach the same moment of time twice.

I am inclined to think that (6) is true, and true in a non-trivial way, and that (7) is false.

Those philosophers interested in the nature of God often maintain that God exists necessarily and is essentially good. If so, the propositions

8. God does not exist

and

9. God is not good

are necessarily false. But again, on the standard view this means that all the following four propositions are true:

10. If God did not exist, matter would not exist.
11. If God did not exist, matter would exist anyway.
12. If God were not good, there would be more evil in the world than there is.
13. If God were not good, there would be less evil in the world than there is.

I am strongly inclined to say that (10) and (12) are true and (11) and (13) are false. If so, there ought to be a way of showing this in the logic of counterfactual conditionals.

There have, of course, been attempts to justify the standard view that every counterpossible is true. The strongest justification I know of is by way of the following inference:

i. Every impossible proposition p_i entails any proposition q.
ii. If a proposition p entails some proposition q, then $p > q$.

So,

> iii. Every impossible proposition *pi* is such that *pi* > *q*.

Proposition (i) is obviously true if entailment is understood as strict implication, in which case it is one of the so-called Paradoxes of Strict Implication hotly debated during the 1950s.[2] In the standard modal systems, to say *p* strictly implies *q* is to say that it is impossible for *p* to be true and *q* false. But of course, if it is impossible for *p* to be true, it is impossible for *p* to be true and *q* false, no matter what *q* is.

But even if entailment is understood more narrowly than strict implication, there is still reason for thinking (i) is true. On any account, we shall regard *q* as entailed by *p* if it can be derived from *p* by impeccable principles of deductive inference. But the following principles seem intuitively unassailable:

(A) A conjunction entails each of its conjuncts.
(B) Any proposition *p* entails *p* v *q*, no matter what *q* is.
(C) The propositions *p* v *q* and ¬ *p* entail *q*.
(D) If *p* entails *q* and *q* entails *r*, then *p* entails *r*.

Lewis, Langford, and Lamprecht (1959) and, much earlier, the author of *Quaestriones Exactissimae in Universam Aristotelis Logicam*, formerly attributed to Duns Scotus, showed that using just these four principles, any proposition is formally deducible from a contradiction by a derivation that has become familiar:[3]

1. *p* & ¬ *p*   Assumption
2. *p*   1, principle A
3. *p* v *q*   2, principle B
4. ¬ *p*   1, principle A
5. *q*   4 principle C

So, by principle D:

> iv. A contradiction *p* & ¬ *p* entails any proposition *q*.

If it is assumed that

> v. Every impossible proposition *pi* entails an explicit contradiction, *p* & ¬ *p*,

it follows from principle D that

> vi. Every impossible proposition *pi* entails any proposition *q*.

There are those who deny the validity of the preceding deduction and are willing to pay the price of a radical departure from ordinary logic.[4] My aim, though, is to see if reasonable truth conditions for counterpossibles can be provided in a way that is less drastic.

So (i) is true as long as either entailment is understood as strict implication, or if every necessarily false proposition is self-contradictory and principles A to D are valid principles of deductive inference. This means, of course, that the truth of such a proposition $pi \rightarrow q$ is trivial.

Let us turn now to (ii), a principle proposed by David Lewis and treated by John Pollock as an axiom of the logic of counterfactuals.[5] On this principle, any counterfactual in which the antecedent logically implies the consequent is true. Pollock says the principle is "clear" and, to my knowledge, does not defend it. Lewis does not defend it either, but says instead: "Further, it seems that a counterfactual in which the antecedent logically implies the consequent ought always to be true; and *one sort of impossible antecedent*, a self-contradictory one, logically implies any consequent" (emphasis mine) (1973, 24). Here he merely asserts (ii) and uses it to support (iii). But it is interesting that the support for (iii) just quoted would not apply to those cases, if any, in which the antecedent is impossible but not self-contradictory. Lewis himself thinks there are necessarily false propositions from which we cannot derive a contradiction. For example, he suggests that it is a necessary truth known *a priori* that there are talking donkeys in some possible world, but to deny that there are talking donkeys in some possible world is not self-contradictory (1986, 112). We will return to these cases presently.

I know of no extended discussion of (ii), although it has been mentioned by other philosophers in connection with (iii).[6] If entailment is understood as strict implication, then I believe the examples I gave at the beginning of this paper show it to be false. In a much more restricted sense of entailment, it is probably true, but in that sense I would no doubt deny (i). However, rather than go through the different notions of entailment that might be relevant here, I prefer to simply point out that the argument of (i)–(iii) is inconclusive, and will turn to a different approach in the next two sections.

Aside from that argument, what other justification is there for the standard view (iii)? Lewis gives two other reasons. One is motivated by the desire to preserve the *reductio ad absurdum*, a common and valuable form of argument. If we want to show that a certain supposition is absurd, we sometimes argue that if it were true, then something ridiculous would follow. If p were true, q would be true; q is impossible; hence, p is impossible as well. This form of reasoning requires the truth of counterpossibles.

But the reductio procedure does not require that for every q, if p is impossible, $p > (q \,\&\, \neg q)$. It is enough that there be some impossibility that would be true if p were true. It is not necessary that *every* contradiction of the form $q \,\&\, \neg q$

be such that it would be true if some impossible proposition *pi* were true. So, the need to preserve the reductio form of argument does not require that every counterpossible be true.

Finally Lewis justifies (iii) as follows: "There is at least some intuitive justification for the decision to make a 'would' counterfactual with an impossible antecedent come out vacuously true. Confronted by an antecedent that is not really an entertainable supposition, one may react by saying, with a shrug: If that were so, anything you like would be true!" (1973, 24).

I agree that we often say something like this, but the justification for it is not perfectly plain. Perhaps our reasoning is as follows: The supposition that this impossible proposition is true is so absurd, that any other proposition might just as well be supposed true. In other words, the supposition that any arbitrary proposition q is true is no worse than the supposition that *pi* is true.

On the other hand, we can just as well find intuitive support for the contrary position. If some state of affairs Φ could not have obtained no matter what, we might say there is literally nothing that would have been the case if Φ had obtained. There simply is no "what if" in such a case. But this suggests that no counterfactual conditional with an impossible antecedent would be true. By the Law of Excluded Middle, they would all be false.

Lewis considers just this option to his view (iii). He considers as an alternative that a counterfactual conditional is true only if there is at least one possible world in which the antecedent is true (1973, 25). This means that all counterpossibles would end up false. But he rejects this possibility because of the desirability of defining "might" counterfactuals in terms of "would" counterfactuals.

"q might be true if p were true," symbolized as "q M p" (Pollock's notation) is defined as follows:

$$q \, M \, p =_{df} \neg \, (p > \neg \, q)^7$$

which reads in English: "it is false that if p were true, q would not be true."

That means that since all "would"' counterpossibles are trivially true on Lewis's view, all "might" counterpossibles are trivially false. That is, since $pi > \neg \, q$ is true for every *pi* and q, $\neg \, (pi > \neg \, q)$ is false. By the preceding definition, "q might be true if *pi* were true" is false for every q and *pi*. But on the alternative account of "would" counterpossibles in which they are all trivially false, the "might" counterpossibles all come out trivially true by the same reasoning.

But the interdefinability of "would" and "might" counterfactuals leads to even stranger results than the ones we considered at the beginning of this paper. Although it is true, on Lewis's view, that

(4) If it were both raining and not raining here at this moment, then I would be the Pope,

it is nonetheless false that:

(14) If it were both raining and not raining here at this moment, then I might be the Pope.

And although it is true that:

(5) If it were both raining and not raining here at this moment, then I would not be the Pope,

it is false that:

(15) If it were both raining and not raining here at this moment, then I might not be the Pope.

The pair of true (4) and false (14) and the pair of true (5) and false (15) seem to me to be very strange.

But just what does the interdefinability of "would" and "might" counterfactuals have to do with Lewis's defense of (iii)? He has given us two pairs of counterpossibles to consider. On his position, the "would" counterpossibles are all true and the "might"' counterpossibles are all false. On the alternative view, the "would" counterpossibles are all false and the "might" counterpossibles all true. Lewis says simply that the pair he prefers is "somewhat better intuitively" than the alternative pair. And, he says, the simple interdefinability of "would"' and "might" seems plausible enough to destroy the appeal of a mixed pair of the Lewis "would" and the alternative "might." Lewis continues: "There seems not to be much more to be said; perhaps ordinary usage is insufficiently fixed to force either choice, and technical convenience may favor one or the other pair depending on how we choose to formulate our truth conditions" (1973, 25–26).

However, it seems to me that there is more to be said. If the examples I have given are convincing, Lewis's alternative pair is no better than the one he prefers, and neither is a mix of the two. If it is a bad idea to have "would" or "might" counterpossibles all come out trivially true, it is also a bad idea to have them all come out trivially false. Some counterpossibles seem to be non-trivially true, and others non-trivially false. And for similar reasons, some "might" counterpossibles seem to be non-trivially true and others non-trivially false. Ideally, we should have truth conditions that reflect these intuitions. Furthermore, even though I am not committed to the interdefinability of "would" and "might" counterfactuals, it seems to me that if we can preserve it in the truth conditions, so much the better.

So far, then, the defense of the general thesis (iii) is less than persuasive. Furthermore, neither Lewis nor Stalnaker gains anything technically by (iii). It is not something they are forced into by their respective accounts of counterfactuals, and it makes their formulation of the truth conditions for counterfactuals rather inelegant. Counterpossibles are treated somewhat arbitrarily.[8] This in itself would not be so bad if we did not need to use these propositions in metaphysical arguments. In section 17.4, however, I will argue that their treatment can make a great deal of difference to metaphysics and, no doubt, to other areas of philosophy as well.

17.2. Interesting impossible propositions

The standard semantics of modal and counterfactual logic allows no logically relevant distinctions among necessary falsehoods or among necessary truths. They have exactly the same logical entailments and counterfactual implications. On some views, such as those of John Pollock and David Lewis, they are even the same proposition. And the same can be said about necessary states of affairs. John Pollock (1984), for example, says that logically equivalent states of affairs are the same state of affairs. He says:

> Counterfactual conditionals tell us what would have been the case if something else had been the case. They are about "counterfactual situations" or states of affairs in a sense that requires that logically equivalent propositions describe the same situation. (1984, 141)

This means, of course, that if propositions (1) to (3) are necessary falsehoods, they are logically equivalent, and on Pollock's account, they describe the same situation. For the same reason, the negations of (1) to (3) all describe the same situation. This strikes me as extremely implausible.

I am suggesting that it is not correct to say that if the impossible had been the case, then anything goes. We *can* say coherently and truly that certain things would have been the case had some impossible state of affairs obtained and that certain other things would not have been the case. The reason, I think, is connected with the fact that it is a mistake to think of one necessary state of affairs as the same as any other, and for the same reason, it is a mistake to think of one impossible situation as the same as any other. In particular, it is reasonable to think that some necessary states of affairs can enter into relations, including causal relations, with other states of affairs. Christians, in fact, are probably committed to this view. The necessary state of affairs of God's being good is no doubt causally related to the existence of a physical universe (although it is probably not causally sufficient). But it is surely not the case that the necessary state of affairs of its being the case that 2 + 2 = 4 is causally related to the existence of a physical universe in that way. Furthermore, some philosophers, such as Thomas V. Morris (1987a), have suggested that God's existence is a necessary state of affairs that is causally related to other necessary states of affairs, such as the existence of numbers. And even if it is thought that the claims made in these two examples are false, surely it is not because necessary states of affairs all have the same relations to other states of affairs. This leads me to think that there are connections between impossible propositions that are independent of their status as logical impossibilities. Even if propositions have certain relations simply because one of them is a logical falsehood, there are still other connections between propositions that are independent of logical falsehood.

To see why it is natural to expect this to be the case, try the following thought experiment. Imagine for a moment that a large set of false propositions is numbered in lists as follows:

1.0	2.0	3.0	4.0
1.1	2.1	3.1	4.1
1.2	2.2	3.2	4.2
1.3 ...	2.3 ...	3.3 ...	4.3 ...

Suppose further that if proposition 1.1 had been true, proposition 1.2 might have been true, proposition 1.3 would have been true, but all the propositions numbered 2 would have remained false. Suppose also that if 1.1 had been true, since 2.0 and 3.0 would still be false, 3.1 would have been false. This seems to me to be a perfectly coherent set of relations among some imagined set of false propositions.

But suppose further that the propositions in lists 1 and 2 are all necessary falsehoods, while those in list 3 are all contingent falsehoods. Would this in any way destroy the coherence of the relations among this set of propositions as just described? It seems to me that it would not. If it would not, then it is not impossible that there are counterfactual implications between propositions that are independent of their individual necessity, contingency, or impossibility. In addition to the first three lists, there might be a fourth list of propositions, each of which entails a contradiction. It might then be the case that if any of these propositions were true, every proposition would be true. If so, this would be a limiting case.

Of course, it might simply be denied that there are any propositions in lists 1 or 2. It might be held that all necessary falsehoods are in list 4 since all entail contradictions. But what reason do we have to think so?

I would like to propose an *a priori* argument that it is possible that there is some proposition that is impossible, but not self-contradictory. I will assume that to say a proposition is not self-contradictory is to say that no proposition of the form "*p* & not *p*" can be derived only from it and truths of logic in some adequate formal system. I shall call such a proposition an Interesting Impossible Proposition (IIP).

(1) Assume that it is not possible that there is an IIP.
(2) Then there are no IIPs.
(3) So, every impossible proposition is self-contradictory.
(4) The proposition *There is a proposition that is false in all possible worlds but does not entail a contradiction* is not self-contradictory.
(5) Thus, the proposition *There is an IIP* is not self-contradictory.
(6) So, *There is an IIP* is not impossible (3, 5).
(7) Therefore, it is possible that there is an IIP.
(8) It is possible that there is an IIP and it is not possible that there is an IIP (1, 7).
(9) Therefore, it is possible that there is an IIP (RAA).

The conclusion of this argument is curious because it means that if there are no IIPs, it is merely a matter of contingent fact. But we can go farther. If it is possible that there is an IIP, that is to say that there is an IIP relative to some world possible relative to the actual world. But in a modal system at least as strong as S4, the accessibility relation is transitive. So if there is an IIP relative to any world possible relative to the actual world, there is an IIP relative to the actual world, which is to say, if it is possible that there is an IIP, there is one. It is possible by the preceding argument; hence, there is one.

17.3. What to do?

I have given an *a priori* argument that it is at least possible that there are impossible propositions from which no contradiction can be derived in an adequate formal system, and if the correct modal system is at least as strong as S4, there are in fact such propositions. I have also argued by examples that counterfactual conditionals with such interesting impossible propositions as antecedents are sometimes non-trivially true and sometimes non-trivially false. That is to say, there is some interesting impossible proposition pi and some proposition q for which $pi > q$ is true and $pi > \neg q$ is false. I have also offered the conjecture that some counterfactual implications between propositions hold independently of their modal status. Whatever the correct truth conditions for counterfactual conditionals may be, they should not be tied to the contingency or impossibility of the antecedent. How can this be expressed in the semantics of counterfactuals? In what follows I will give two suggestions, one adapted from Stalnaker and the other adapted from Lewis.

The basic idea behind Stalnaker's semantics is fairly simple. We say $A > B$ is true just in case if we add A to the stock of true propositions and modify them so as to make them consistent with A, but make the modifications as small as possible, the resulting set of propositions includes B.

We can retain this idea for counterfactual conditionals with IIPs as antecedents. Suppose we take the list of all true propositions, propositions true in the actual world, and add A. There are many things we can do with the resulting set of propositions. We can alter the truth value of individual propositions in the set in any number of ways, some of which constitute more serious changes in the set than others. One alternative is not to change anything. We can simply retain *not A* in the set along with A. This ought to count as a major mutilation in the set. Or we could eliminate *not A*, which in some cases means denying a necessary truth. But even then, this should not be considered as great a mutilation as retaining *not A*. The intuition I am relying on here is that it is a more serious change in the set of true propositions to alter them in a way that formally entails a contradiction than in a way that does not, even if the alternative also involves the denial of a necessary truth. Other adjustments in the truth value of propositions in the set would have to be made, and again, some alterations ought to be considered more serious than others. We ought to consider a change in the truth value of a necessary proposition, one true in all possible worlds, a greater change than any number of changes in contingent propositions. The relative degree of change for other changes could be handled as it is in standard counterfactual logic. Though each alternative set of propositions is maximal, in the case in which A is an impossible proposition, we need not think of them as descriptions of possible worlds.

We then say that if it takes a smaller change in the set of propositions true in the actual world to make B true than to make B false, then $A > B$ is true. If it takes a smaller change in the set to make B false than to make B true, then $A > \neg B$ is true. On this approach, it would never turn out that both $A > B$ and $A > \neg B$ are true. If we do not assume that there is a unique case of minimal change, it may turn out that the changes required to make B true are equal to those needed to make B false. If so, then neither $A > B$ nor $A > \neg B$ is true. If we retain the definition of "might" counterfactuals given earlier, this procedure will also yield the truth value of such conditionals. It will never turn out that "If A were the case, B would be the case" is true, while "If A were the case, B might be the case" is false, a problem I mentioned in the Lewis semantics.

The procedure just outlined is very close to the standard approach. Intuitively we think that degree of closeness to the actual world is measured by the degree of change from the actual world, although some degrees of change produce a description that, while intuitively consistent, do not describe possible worlds. As long as any maximal set of descriptions containing an impossible proposition represents a greater degree of change from the actual world than any maximal set of descriptions that does not contain an impossible proposition, the results of the procedure I have suggested for counterfactuals with possible antecedents ought to be exactly the same as those we get from the Lewis/Stalnaker approach.[9]

Suppose by way of illustration of the procedure I have outlined, we consider propositions (10) and (11). If we took a complete description of the actual world, substituted the proposition expressed by "God does not exist" for "God exists," and made minimal changes in the truth value of other propositions, what would be the result? If one of the necessary truths in the actual world is something like:

(16) Any contingent object in the world exists only because it was created by God,

since a change in the truth value of a necessary truth constitutes a greater change than the change in the truth value of any contingent truths, it follows that it is less drastic to change "Matter exists" to "Matter does not exist" than to deny (16). Therefore, (10) is true and (11) is false, as we would expect.

Similarly, if we substitute "God is not good" for "God is good," and if there is a necessary truth to the effect that a good being is motivated to produce good, and non-good beings are not, this would have the consequence that the least drastic change in the resulting set of propositions would result in truths that entail that the world has a degree of good that is less than what it in fact has. And so (12) is true and (13) is false.

It seems to me that Lewis's formal model of counterfactuals can also be extended in a natural way to include counterpossibles. Lewis assigns to each world i a set $\$i$ of sets of possible worlds, called a *system of spheres* around i. For each such world i, i is centered, nested, closed under unions, and closed under nonempty intersections. Any particular sphere around i is to contain just those worlds that resemble i to at least a certain degree. This degree is different for different spheres around i. The smaller a sphere, the more similar to i is a world that falls within it. On Lewis's model, each world in the system of spheres $\$i$ is accessible from i, which is to say, it is possible relative to i. Once he sets up his Ptolemaic astronomic system, he is able to give truth conditions for $A > B$ as follows:

$A > B$ is true at i if and only if either there are no A-worlds in any sphere in the system of spheres $\$i$, or there is a sphere in the system of spheres i in which there are A-worlds and in which every A-world is a B-world.

We can modify the model by specifying that the set of worlds accessible from i is a sphere that is a subset of the system of spheres $\$i$ around i, so every accessible world is closer to i than is any inaccessible world. On the modified model we think of the "worlds" in which some IIP is true as farther removed from the actual world than any possible world. A "world" in which a contradiction is true would be farther away still.

We may retain the Lewis assignment of truth conditions for the modal operators and $\Diamond$. p is true at a world i if and only if p is true in every world accessible from i. $\Diamond p$ is true if and if p is true in some world accessible from i. When i is the actual world, we say that "worlds" in which an IIP is true are not possible relative to the actual world.

Since for any A, there will always be some world in the modified $\$i$ in which A is true, we can eliminate the first disjunct of Lewis's truth conditions for preceding counterfactuals. The second disjunct alone is therefore sufficient to give the truth conditions for counterfactuals in this model, including counterpossibles.

As far as I can tell, this procedure also gives us the desired results for "might" counterfactuals in the typical cases. It does not, however, say anything about the proper treatment of counterfactuals with antecedents that are self-contradictory. For example, I do not know how to resolve the difficulty of a true (4) and a false (14), noted earlier.

17.4. What difference does it make?

Since counterpossibles have generally been considered uninteresting, it might be thought that even if the Lewis/Stalnaker treatment of them is a trifle eccentric, what harm can it do? In this section I would like to give some reason to think that it could do quite a lot of harm. I will briefly give examples of cases in which the truth value of a counterpossible affects the outcome of a metaphysical argument or position. I believe there are many such examples, and there is nothing special about these few in particular.

The first example, from Aquinas (*De Veritate*, q. 1, art. 2), is mentioned by Alfred J. Freddoso (1986). Thomas argues that truth consists in a certain relation between world and intellect, so that if, *per impossibile*, there were no intellects but there were other things, there would be no truths. Aquinas is surely thinking of the truth of such a counterpossible as non-trivial, both because he would most assuredly deny the same counterpossible with consequent negated, and because his claim rests on there being a special relationship between the existence of truths and the existence of God, a relationship that does not obtain between the existence of truths and 2 + 2 = 4. So, Aquinas's conceptual account of the nature of truth depends upon the fact that this counterpossible is true, and true in a non-trivial way.

Another example can be found in van Frassen's (1970) discussion of Kant's First Analogy. The First Analogy says that all change consists in alteration in the determinations of an enduring substance. Commenting on Kant's discussion, van Frassen says:

> Suppose, however, that all substances cease to be and other substances whose states are not simultaneous with any states of the former come into being. The way in which we have phrased this supposition suggests that the other substances exist after the former. But close scrutiny will show that this is not entailed: there is no ground for asserting any temporal relation between the states of the former and those of the latter, except nonsimultaneity. So there would be no way of ordering them all together into a single world history. Since we suppose that such an ordering is always possible, this supposition is absurd. (1970, 48)

A crucial step in this argument is the assertion of the counterpossible: *If all substances ceased to be and other substances came into being, there would be no way to order them all into a single world history.* Unlike the Aquinas example, this counterpossible is asserted without the assumption that the antecedent is impossible. Nonetheless, the counterpossible is neither denied nor reinterpreted in a trivial sense once it is concluded that the antecedent is impossible, and its non-trivial truth is necessary to get the desired conclusion.

A third example is theological. Thomas V. Morris (1987b) argues that although it is true that God could not have done evil since it is incompatible with his nature to want to, it is false that God could not have done evil even if he wanted to. This may be important if it is thought that perfect power requires that a being who has it not only can do anything he wants, but he *could* do anything he *wanted*. As Morris sees it, this point is important since it calls attention to the fact that the lack of the possibility of God's doing evil resides in his firmness of will, not in any lack of power. Without the non-trivial truth of the counterpossible, "If God had wanted to do evil, he would have been able to," there does not seem to be any way to capture the difference between impossibility due to lack of power and impossibility due to lack of willing.

Another example arises in the account of God's omniscience. It seems to me that it is true that

(17) If God were not omniscient, he might not have believed that p (where p is some true contingent proposition)

and false that

(18) If God were not omniscient, he would still have believed p,

and it is important for one of my proposed solutions to the dilemma of divine foreknowledge and human free will that this be the case (1991, chapter 6). I am not alone in requiring that (17) is true and (18) false. But that cannot be the case on the standard semantics of counterfactuals.

17.5. Conclusion

The impossible is sometimes said to be the same as the unthinkable. David Lewis even suggests that the possibility operator ◊ be read as: "It is entertainable that..." This is to suggest that we cannot even entertain the impossible, so maybe the less said about it, the better. Of course, it is generally admitted that there are propositions expressing impossible states of affairs, although Lewis admits only one such, and so something has to be said about *them*. But whether they are thought to be one or many, it is usually agreed that they are indistinguishable from each other in their logical relations.

I have argued in this paper that the category of the impossible is much more interesting than this and that we have good reason to think that impossible propositions do not all have the same relationships to other propositions. In particular, I have argued that there are impossible propositions that are not self-contradictory. It seems to me that these propositions are not only entertainable, but that we can say some interesting things about what would have been the case had certain ones obtained. I have suggested a way to extend the standard analysis of counterfactuals to take into account that some counterpossibles are non-trivially true and some are non-trivially false. Finally, I have claimed by way of examples that the treatment of the truth conditions of these propositions can make a difference to metaphysical arguments.

My remarks in this paper have covered only a small part of the territory of the impossible. I suggest that the impossible is an ontological category of great interest, and may turn out to be important to an understanding of many metaphysical problems.[10]

Notes

1. I will follow John Pollock in using the symbol > for "would" counterfactual implication. $A > B$ is to be read as: If it were the case that A, then it would be the case that B. I will discuss "might" counterfactuals presently.
2. For a discussion of this issue, see J. F. Bennett (1954); Peter Geach (in Lewy et al. 1958); C. Lewy (1950); John Pollock (1966); T. J. Smiley (1958); P. F. Strawson (1948); and G. H. von Wright (1957).

3. For discussion, see Kneale (1956), 239.
4. Nicholas Rescher and Robert Brandom (1980) deny the validity of the preceding deduction. They claim that it fails at step 4 and that we can allow the truth of a single contradiction without committing ourselves to logical anarchy. If so, of course, there is no reason to think that a contradiction counterfactually implies every proposition either. Anderson and Belnap (1962) deny (i) on the grounds that the relationship of entailment between p and q requires a condition of relevance in the content of p and q.
5. Pollock (1984), 128; also in Pollock (1975), 55.
6. Igal Kvart (1986) agrees with Lewis's principle (ii), but he rejects the idea that this is a good reason to take counterpossibles as true. Instead, he denies (i). On the other hand, Alfred Freddoso (1986, 44) says that he is inclined to the position that although a necessarily false proposition strictly implies every proposition, it does not counterfactually imply every proposition. He therefore accepts (i) on the broad interpretation of entailment, but rejects (ii). Neither Kvart nor Freddoso gives a justification for his rejection of (i) or (ii) apart from counterexamples to (iii) and the need to reject one or the other.
7. Stalnaker (1980) dissents from this definition.
8. Stalnaker (1968, 103) invents a possible world that he calls "the absurd world" in which all propositions are true in order to get (iii) to come out true.
9. Lewis and Stalnaker differ slightly from each other. Stalnaker thinks that there will always be a world that is closer than any others, and hence, for any A and B, either $A >$ B or $A > \neg B$ is true. Lewis does not make the uniqueness assumption and so does not accept the Law of Conditional Excluded Middle.
10. This paper was written during the fall of 1987 while I was a senior fellow at the Center for Philosophy of Religion at the University of Notre Dame. I am grateful to the Center for its support and to the Notre Dame Philosophy Department for inviting me to present the paper at a philosophy colloquium. I am indebted to several people for help in its preparation: Aron Edidin, Howard Wettstein, Philip Quinn, Robert Audi, and especially Michael Kremer.

18
Christian Monotheism (1989)

18.1. A principle of identity and four kinds of properties

Christians believe that there is but one God, and there are both philosophical and religious defenses of this doctrine. On the philosophical side there are arguments such as those of Aquinas that certain attributes constitutive of the concept of God could only apply to one being. These include self-existence, pure actuality, perfection, omnipotence, and simplicity. Each of these attributes can be used to generate an argument to the effect that it is not possible for more than one being to have such an attribute. William Wainwright (1986) has given very cogent and, in some cases, original arguments that monotheism is a necessary consequence of some of these attributes. The defense of monotheism from the requirements of religion is also persuasive. Only one being could be the object of total devotion and worship. Even if God turns out not to be "the God of the philosophers" and lacks some of the traditional attributes, there is still good reason to think God wouldn't be God if he were not unique.

Christian monotheism, unlike the Islamic and Judaic varieties which have used similar arguments for the numerical oneness of God, includes another doctrine which constrains the way Christians can argue for monotheism. That is the doctrine of the Trinity. According to this doctrine, there is numerically one God, yet there are three Persons who are correctly called "God." This doctrine does not seem to sit well with some of the traditional monotheistic arguments, such as the ones from aseity, from omnipotence, and from simplicity. That is because these arguments are most naturally interpreted as showing not merely that at most one *being* can have an attribute such as simplicity, omnipotence, or aseity, but also that at most one *person* can have such an attribute. So, for example, the argument from omnipotence usually includes a premise to the effect that if two beings are numerically distinct and have the capacity to will, then it is logically possible that there be a conflict in their wills. But presumably whatever reasons one has for such a principle would also be reasons for asserting the same principle with "persons" substituted for "beings." In fact, Wainwright explicitly uses the term "persons" in his argument from omnipotence (1986, 302). I am not denying that simplicity, omnipotence, and aseity are attributes—in fact, essential attributes—of the divine nature, nor am I denying that there may be sound unicity arguments that begin with one or another of these attributes. My

God, Knowledge, and the Good. Linda Trinkaus Zagzebski, Oxford University Press. © Oxford University Press 2022.
DOI: 10.1093/oso/9780197612385.003.0019

concern is not to refute any of these arguments, but to call attention to a methodological point for a Christian philosopher. If the Trinity is a much more important belief religiously than the premises of the unicity arguments mentioned earlier, then it is not a good idea to begin with such premises and worry later about accommodating the Trinity to their conclusions. Instead, it should be the other way around.

Some would say that it is no wonder that the doctrine of the Trinity is not harmonious with the divine attributes since it is not harmonious with anything, and that is why it is a mystery. But this seems to be too pessimistic. The Trinity is not flatly self-contradictory and there is no reason to shun the attempt to give an interpretive theory of it. In fact, it may even be important to do so. Therefore, I propose to give an argument for monotheism that makes as few assumptions as possible about the attributes included in Divinity, that allows for an interpretation of the Trinity that is logically prior to the arguments for particular attributes, and which consequently better reflects the relative importance of these beliefs in Christian theology.

The argument for one God that I will give makes no particular assumptions about the attributes included in Divinity. The argument in sections 18.2.1 and 18.2.2 is general enough to apply to any natural kind of thing, not only Divinity. The argument in section 18.2.3 makes an assumption about the semantic function of "Divinity," but no particular attribute is assumed to be included in Divinity. The explanation of the Trinity in section 18.3 requires only the assumption that Divinity includes absolute independence. My strategy will be to argue from the Identity of Indiscernibles and a Principle of Plenitude that two Gods could not be distinguished by their properties. Arguments of this type are rejected by Wainwright in part II of Wainwright (1986).

In every possible world let Φ be a variable ranging over complete sets H of the properties of an object in that world. For any property P, H contains either P or $\overline{P}$ (the complement of P). Assume the minimum restrictions on the properties in H to prevent triviality.[1] We can then formulate the principle of the identity of indiscernibles as follows:

(1) **Principle of the Identity of Indiscernibles**
$(x)(\Phi)[\Diamond \Phi x \rightarrow \sim \Diamond (\exists y)(\Phi y \,\&\, y \neq x)]$

This principle says that necessarily, if any object x has a certain complete set of properties in one world, there is no distinct object in any world with just that set of properties. Not only does no other actual object have exactly the same set of properties as this object, it is not even possible that some other object have this same set of properties. Any object in any world that has these properties is this object. The properties uniquely identify the object.

This principle is, of course, not uncontroversial. However, it seems to me to be true and less problematic than premises that assert that God has one or another of the "philosophers' attributes." That God has some of these other attributes may be derivable from the argument I will give, but that is the topic of another paper.

Before beginning the argument, I wish to distinguish four categories of properties:

> *Contingent property* = a property that is not necessarily instantiated, although it is instantiated in at least one world.
> *Necessary property* = a property that is instantiated in all possible worlds.
> *Essential property of S* = a property that an individual S has in all possible worlds in which S exists.
> *Accidental property of S* = a property that is not essential to some individual S, but that S has in some possible world.

We can also define the categories of essential and accidental properties *simpliciter*:

> An *essential property* = a property which is such that necessarily it is possessed essentially by any possible object that possesses it at all.
> An *accidental property* = a property which is such that it is possessed accidentally by any possible object that possesses it at all.[2]

Contingent properties may or may not be accidental to whatever beings possess them. The property of being human, for example, is contingent but not accidental. The property of being a philosopher is both contingent and accidental to all the beings who are philosophers. If a necessary being has a contingent property, it is accidental to it. That is because in some world a contingent property is not instantiated. But since a necessary being exists in all worlds, there must be some world in which such a being exists but does not have the property in question. If a necessary being has an accidental property, we would probably expect it to be contingent, but it may not be if there is some other being who possesses it. In fact, that other being would not even have to have it essentially so long as in every possible world *some* being has it (e.g., being the most powerful). So it is not clear whether there are necessary properties that are accidental to God. Later I will discuss this set of properties. Wainwright maintains without argument that all God's accidental properties must be contingent (1986, 293, n.8).

So there are four categories of properties for each S: necessary and essential to S, necessary and accidental to S, contingent and essential to S, and contingent and accidental to S. Since a necessary being can have no contingent essential property, there are at most three categories of properties as applied to a necessary being.

18.2. Why there can be only one God

In this paper I will use "God" not as a proper name, but as a descriptive designator applying to whatever being or beings are divine. The question, then, is whether two beings can be divine. I will argue that the answer is no, although a qualification about the status of internal essential relations leaves room for an interpretation of the doctrine of the Trinity.

18.2.1. Why two Gods could not differ only in a contingent property

Any contingent property of a God would also have to be accidental to it since there are no contingent properties essential to a necessary being and I am assuming that any God is a necessary being. Wainwright says that he can see no reason to think two necessary beings could not be distinguished on the basis of a difference in contingent accidental properties (1986, 293). However, I think there is an argument which does provide such a reason. Before presenting the argument, the logical connections between an object and its accidental properties should be made clear. I am assuming that what we mean by an accidental property entails the following principle:

(2) **First Principle of Plenitude (PP1)**
 If some property Pl is compatible with the set of essential properties E of an object O, and if O has P1 in some world w, there is another world w' in which O has Pl and is as similar to w as is compatible with O's having Pl in w'.

The intuition behind PP1 is that every property that is compatible with the essence of an object is something it is possible for it to have. Furthermore, given some possible world in which it lacks that property, it is possible for it to possess it even though everything else remains as much the same as is logically possible. So the essence of an object alone sets the limits of the possible properties of that object. It is assumed, though, that the essential properties of an object include the necessary truths. So, for example, each object is essentially such that 2 + 2 = 4, the Identity of Indiscernibles holds, etc.

The same intuition allows us to form a parallel principle for pairs of objects as follows:

(3) **Second Principle of Plenitude (PP2)**
 If properties Pl and P2 are respectively compatible with the set of essential properties E1 and E2 of objects O1 and O2, respectively, and if in some possible

world w O1 has P1 and O2 has P2, and O1's having P1 is compossible with O2's having P2, then there is another possible world w' in which O1 has P1 and O2 has P2, and which is as similar to w as is compatible with O1's having P1 and O2's having P2.

From principles (1), (3), and the hypothesis that two divine beings can differ only in a contingent accidental property and what is entailed by that difference, we can derive a contradiction as follows:

1. Assume the principles of the Identity of Indiscernibles (1) and the Second Principle of Plenitude (PP2).
2. Suppose that there is a world $w1$ in which God 1 and God 2 have all necessary properties in common. They therefore have the same set of essential properties, and also the same set of necessary accidental properties, if there are any of this kind. They differ only in contingent property Cl. God 1 has Cl; God 2 has $\overline{Cl}$.
3. Since God 1 and God 2 have the same essence E, there is nothing in E that precludes God 2 from having Cl and there is nothing in E that precludes God 1 from having $\overline{Cl}$.
4. By PP2 there is another world $w2$ where God 2 has Cl and God 1 has $\overline{Cl}$ and $w2$ is as much like $w1$ as is compatible with God 2's having Cl and God 1's having $\overline{Cl}$.
5. This contradicts the Identity of Indiscernibles (1) twice over. The complete set of properties H1 that God 1 has in $w1$ is possessed by God 2 in $w2$, and the complete set of properties H2 that God 2 has in $w1$ is possessed by God 1 in $w2$. There is nothing that makes God 1 God 1 and God 2 God 2 if what is unique about each is something the other one could have had instead.
6. The hypothesis that two divine beings can differ only in a contingent property and what is entailed by it is therefore false.

By the same reasoning it can be shown that two Gods cannot differ only in some set of contingent accidental properties. The reason is just that if any member of a set of properties is contingent, so is the set. The argument is parallel to the preceding one except that Cl and $\overline{Cl}$ stand for sets of contingent properties.

18.2.2. Why two Gods cannot differ only in a necessary accidental property

It is not clear that it is possible for a property to be necessary but accidental to God. The only candidates that come to mind are comparative properties such as being such that no other being is more powerful. If there is power in some world, there ought to be the greatest degree of it, although, of course it is an open question whether more than one being instantiates the greatest degree, and the same goes for benevolence, mercy, and any other property that admits of degree. So, there are candidates for properties that are instantiated in every possible world but in different beings in different worlds. But why should every world have a most powerful being? It would have such a being only if power is necessarily instantiated. One reason power might be necessarily instantiated is that it could be included or entailed by the essential properties of some necessary being. Then the putative property must be essential to at least one being. If it is essential to anyone, we would expect it to be essential to God, although this is probably not obvious. There is, however, at least some reasonable doubt that there is any property that is necessary but accidental to God. And if there is no such property, then, of course, there can be no question of two Gods differing in the possession of such a property. However, assuming that there is a property of this kind, we can still construct an argument parallel to the one in the previous section for the conclusion that two Gods could not differ only in such a property and what is entailed by that difference:

1. Assume 1 (the Identity of Indiscernibles) and PP2.
2. Suppose that in world $w1$ God 1 and God 2 have all essential properties in common and all contingent accidental properties in common. They differ only in necessary accidental property N1. God I has N1; God 2 has $\overline{N1}$.
3. Since God 1 and God 2 have the same essence, God 1 is not precluded by his essence from having $\overline{N1}$, nor is God 2 precluded by his essence from having N1.
4. By PP2 there is another possible world $w2$ in which God 1 has $\overline{N1}$ and God 2 has N1, and which is as much like $w1$ as is compatible with God 1's having N1 and God 2's having N1.
   But this contradicts II twice over. The complete set of properties H1 that God 1 has in $w1$ is possessed by God 2 in $w2$, and the complete set of properties H2 that God 2 has in $w1$ is possessed by God 1 in $w2$.
5. Therefore, two divine beings cannot differ only in a necessary accidental property and what is entailed by that difference.

By the same reasoning, two Gods cannot differ in some set of necessary accidental properties. The argument is exactly parallel to the preceding one except that N1 and $\overline{N1}$ stand for sets of necessary accidental properties.

Therefore, although it is not clear that there are any necessary accidental properties, if there are, God 1 and God 2 cannot differ in those properties alone since the supposition that they do violates the two principles I have proposed: a principle of identity and a principle of plenitude.

A parallel argument can also be used to show that two Gods cannot differ in any combination of contingent and necessary accidental properties. Any difference of accidental properties would lead to the consequence that there exists a world in which God 1 has exactly the same set of properties as those possessed by God 2 in some other world. But by the foregoing argument, this is impossible. Therefore, since God 1 and God 2 cannot differ in any set of contingent or necessary accidental properties, they cannot differ merely in accidental properties at all.

If the argument in this and the previous sections are right, they show not only that two Gods cannot differ only in accidental properties, but that no two beings of any sort can differ only in accidental properties. No two individual objects can share exactly the same set of essential properties. There are, therefore, individual essences. The implications of this consequence for metaphysics are interesting and I have examined them elsewhere (Zagzebski 1988), but for the purposes of this paper I wish to concentrate only on its application to a divine being.

If there are two Gods, they must differ in some essential property. Since by hypothesis both Gods are divine, if there are two Gods, one has an essential property that is not part of the divine essence and which the other one lacks. The next section will propose an argument that this is not possible.

18.2.3. Why two Gods cannot differ in an essential property

Wainwright says, "It is not clear why two necessary beings could not be distinguished by a difference in their essential properties, that is, it is not clear why two necessary beings must have the *same* essential properties. Indeed, if the doctrine of the Trinity is coherent, the thesis is false" (1986, 292). In this section I will try to show why two divine necessary beings cannot be distinguished by their essential properties, but in section 18.3 an exception will be made for essential internal relations, the properties that distinguish the members of the Trinity from each other. I will then give an interpretation of the relation between objects and their properties that does not preclude the persons of the Trinity from being numerically one being.

My argument that two Gods could not differ in an essential property rests on a particular view of the function of the concept of Divinity. It seems clear that we have a variety of ways of referring to a God, either directly or by description. When we use the name "God" we may mean to refer directly to the being worshipped by those in our religious community, or we may mean to refer indirectly to whatever being or beings have some attribute or attributes we are considering, such as omnipotence, omniscience, or perfection. The concept of Divinity, however, is used when we wish to refer to the *nature* of such a being or beings, and when it is asked whether there can be two Gods or two divine beings, what is meant is whether two beings can share such a nature. Divinity, then, can refer to either the nature of the being those in our religious community worship, picked out by a direct reference, or alternatively, it can refer indirectly to the nature of whatever being or beings have some particular attributes.

I will argue that "Divinity" refers to the *complete* nature of such a being. Divinity includes the complete set of properties essential to any divine being, so even though we may sometimes fix the reference of "God" by such descriptions as "the being we worship" or "the absolutely perfect creator of the universe," we use "Divinity" to refer to the whole nature of such a being. I have two arguments for this claim. One appeals to the way the term is actually used, while the other is purely theoretical.

Consider first some features of the ways "Divinity" and "God" are actually used. Sometimes "God" refers directly to a particular individual whom we come to know by revelation or the religious experience of our faith community. Call such an individual "Yahweh." Suppose we come to believe that Yahweh is essentially good. If it were possible for Yahweh to have essential properties that are not included in Divinity, then we would expect there to be a theological debate over the question of whether goodness is included in the properties that constitute Divinity, or whether instead it is essential only to Yahweh. But we do not have such a debate. In practice, if some property P is taken to be essential to Yahweh, that is *ipso facto* assumed to be sufficient to show it is essential to (any) God.

The same observation holds for those uses of "God" in which "God" is taken to refer indirectly to whatever being or beings have some specific attribute, such as absolute perfection, omnipotence, or independence. If it is discovered through some argument that such a being must have some other essential attribute—say omniscience—this attribute also is taken to be constitutive of Divinity. In fact, it seems to me that this procedure and the one mentioned in the previous paragraph are two important ways we *find out* what properties are contained in Divinity. It seems, then, that our usage of "God" and "Divinity" supports my position. Although there have been discussions in which it was taken to be an open question whether Yahweh's possession of some essential property P is necessary for P's being a divine attribute, it is almost always taken to be sufficient. Divinity, then, includes all the essential properties of a particular divine being. If follows that no two divine beings can differ in an essential property.

The second argument for this position is theoretical. It seems plausible that the existence of individual essential differences among members of a natural kind indicate that such individuals fall short of the perfection of the kind. Suppose, for example, that humanity is a proper subset of the essential properties of individual humans; that is, humans possess individual essences. This suggests that no individual human possesses the whole of humanity. Contained in the identity of each is a way of being human that is not possessed by any other. If a being were essentially everything a human could be, there would only be one human. The same point can be made even if the idea of individual essences is unacceptable. All we need do is switch the discussion to higher-order natural kinds such as the kind rational creature. It is reasonable to think of rational creature as a higher-level kind under which the kinds Angel and Human fall. But given that there are properties constitutive of being human and therefore essential to individual humans that are distinct from some of the properties essential to Angels, neither the kind Human nor the kind Angel exhausts the kind rational creature. Only one set of essential properties could exhaust the kind rational creature; so if more than one perfectly rational creature existed, they would have the same set of essential properties.

If Divinity can be considered a natural kind by analogy with the kind rational creature, and if it is assumed that any divine being contains the whole of Divinity, or is perfectly divine, it follows that two divine beings could not differ in an essential property. Since it was shown in the previous section that two divine beings could not differ in an accidental property, it follows that two divine beings could not differ at all. Therefore, by the Identity of Indiscernibles, there is only one God.

18.3. The Trinity

The proper use of reason in placing the doctrine of the Trinity within a general metaphysical interpretation of such concepts as essence, attribute, person, and numerical identity is a difficult and sensitive issue. It seems to me that Aquinas was right in saying that what we can expect from reason in a discussion and defense of the Trinity is quite different from what we can expect from reason in an argument for the unicity of God. To put it briefly, for the latter we can expect fairly cogent direct arguments, whereas for the former we can hope only for a coherent explanation.[3] In this section I will need to assume that the attribute of absolute independence is included in Divinity.

In attempting an explanation of the Trinity, I will present a theory on the relationship between individuals and their properties. I will use this theory to suggest a criterion for distinctness between individual beings that allows for a unique case in which numerically identical beings differ in some essential internal relations.

18.3.1. The distinction between an attribute, expressed by a simple, one place predicate, and the general category of properties

What I call a simple one-place predicate stands for a property that is non-relational in two senses. First, it does not purport to relate the object to another object, and second, it does not purport to relate the object to a moment or moments of time. I call the first sense in which a predicate can be relational object-relational (rel_0), and the second sense time-relational (rel_t).

Let us define the notions of non-rel_0 and non-rel_t as follows:

> To say that a predicate Φ is non-rel_0 is to say that for any x, the result of predicating Φ of x does not entail the existence of any object that is not entailed by saying of x that it exists.
>
> To say that a predicate Φ is non-rel_t is to say that necessarily for any x, if the result of predicating Φ of x is true at one moment of time, it is true at every moment of time at which x exists.

When I say that R entails S, I mean that it is impossible in the broadly logical or metaphysical sense for R to be true and S to be false. If R entails S, then the truth of R depends upon the truth of S.

We can define the notion of a simple one-place predicate as follows:

> A predicate Φ is a simple one-place predicate $\leftrightarrow$ Φ is non-rel_0, is non-rel_t, and is simple in structure.

Let us call the property expressed by a simple one-place predicate an *attribute*.

To have a simple structure would ordinarily mean that it is a single word. Such a predicate cannot have a complex structure, nor can it be an abbreviation of an expression with a complex structure. Predicates that are non-rel_0 and non-rel_t would include "human," "water," "daffodil," "is either awake or asleep," and "is such that if it does not exist, then it exists." With the criterion of simplicity added, the last two examples would be excluded. The criterion of simplicity is intended to remove contrived properties, Boolean combinations of other properties that intuitively are not what was intended by the classical notion of a property (e.g., being either a fish or a worm).

Examples of predicates that are non-rel_0 but rel_t are "blue," "asleep," "tadpole," and "is either angry or frightened." Examples of predicates that are rel_0 but non-rel_t are "carnivorous" and "was born after Christ." Predicates that are both rel_0 and rel_t include "philosopher," "squash player" and "is decorated with flowers." "Mother" is rel_0 and has two senses, one rel_t, one not. The first is the sense in which we say that a woman becomes a mother only when her child is born. The second is the sense in which we call a woman the mother of someone timelessly.

It is my position that the category of predicates I have just defined pick out what we intuitively consider to be natural kind terms, although it is not important for the purposes of this paper to insist on this point. The paradigm cases of natural kind terms fit this category. Some questionable ones such as artifact terms may also fit it, although I do not believe any clearly non-natural kind terms are simple one-place predicates in my sense. In the case of a contingent temporal object, we usually think that either it falls under a unique natural kind, or that if it falls under more than one, they are related as species and genus. On my view it is possible for an object to fall under more than one natural kind when the definition of the kind includes a set of distinct properties. Each of those properties is an attribute and would in turn define a natural kind. So, each of us primarily falls under the natural kind Human Being, but if such a kind includes both rationality and temporality as defining characteristics, we would also fall under the natural kind Rational Being, as well as the kind Temporal Being. So, when an object falls under more than one natural kind, they are connected by relations of entailment from one primary kind. To be human entails that one is an animal, and it entails that one is a rational being.

Contingent objects will include in the class of their attributes those which relate the object to other objects without which the object cannot exist. This is because no contingent object is purely independent. Consider some particular daffodil. For this daffodil to exist, certain other things must exist as a matter of physical necessity—earth, air, water, light, and so on. Perhaps this particular earth, air, water, and sunlight is not necessary, but certainly something is that provides for the plant what these things provide. What this plant needs as a matter of logical necessity is much more difficult to answer. It seems that we could imagine a possible world in which daffodils grow without water, light, and air, but perhaps it would be incorrect to call them daffodils, but only something "like" daffodils. A stronger case could be made for the claim that a given daffodil could not exist, i.e., it is logically impossible that it exist, unless matter of a certain kind existed. Many philosophers would even say that the particular matter of which this daffodil is composed is logically necessary to it. It could not exist without it. So, a given daffodil cannot exist unless other things of certain kinds exist, and its existence may even be dependent upon the existence of other particulars such as other daffodils, this matter, etc. In each case predicating the natural kind term "daffodil" of a daffodil entails the existence of other objects. But it does not entail the existence of any object not entailed by the *de re* predication of existence to the daffodil. "Daffodil," therefore, is non-rel$_0$.

I assume that each contingent object, including, of course, each of us, cannot exist without God. This means that to say of me that I exist entails the existence of that being without whom I could not exist. So, all contingent objects have relationality built into them. Their one-place predicates express this. On my view, essential relations, i.e., relations that an object has in every world in which it exists, such as "is created by God," express properties that are non-rel$_0$.

God also has attributes in the technical sense I have defined. Many of the traditional attributes would probably qualify as attributes in my sense as well, although some of them might not. If objects of knowledge exist apart from God, and if omniscience entails the existence of such objects, then God's omniscience is not an attribute in my sense, although God could still be omniscient. Being the creator would not be an attribute, although omnipotence, goodness, simplicity, freedom, immutability, and timelessness would all be candidates. (Some are probably actually second-order attributes, or attributes of attributes.)

Unlike the attributes of all other beings, the predication of an attribute of God does not entail the existence of any distinct object at all. It does not entail the existence of any contingent object. Furthermore, it does not entail the existence of a distinct necessary object. God's non-relational properties cannot entail the existence of any distinct being because that would mean that it is impossible for God to exist without that other being and that would make God dependent, contrary to the assumption of this section. It follows that none of God's attributes entails the existence of anything but God. Since the predication of attributes to God entails the existence of necessary objects such as numbers, it follows that such necessary objects are not distinct from God.

God is therefore unique among all other beings, including all other necessary beings. The predication of attributes to any being other than God entails the existence of something distinct from that being, and in every case, it entails the existence of God. God is, of course, more than a number, so to say that the existence of numbers entails the existence of God is to say that the existence of numbers entails the existence of something distinct from, or more precisely, something over and above, themselves. But to say that the existence of God entails the existence of numbers is not to say that the existence of God entails the existence of anything distinct from or over and above himself. I am not proposing any specific theory on the nature of necessary objects other than God and the way in which they depend upon God's nature. It is natural to think of them as objects in his mind or something of the sort, but I am suggesting only that they are not independent beings; they are not distinct from God himself.

18.3.2. Relational properties in the Divinity

Relational properties can be either internal or external. Call the set of attributes of some object A Φ. Let us define an internal relation of A as a relation that does not entail the existence of anything other than an object that possesses Φ. Relations to other beings in the same natural kind are internal relations in my sense. An external relation of A is a relation that entails the existence of an object that possesses some properties not contained in Φ. I argued in section 18.2.3 that two Gods could not differ in their essential properties and that would include any essential relations. But the distinction just drawn between internal and external essential relations has an interesting consequence when applied to God.

Let us review some of the important differences between the way God is related to his properties and we are related to ours. First of all, none of God's attributes entails the existence of any distinct being, whereas our attributes, and the attributes of all contingent beings, do. That follows immediately from the notion that Divinity entails complete independence and created or contingent beings entail dependence. This feature of the relation between God and his attributes distinguishes him not only from beings that are contingent in the sense of existing in only some possible worlds, but it also distinguishes him from other necessary beings. Beings like numbers are necessary in the sense that they exist in all possible worlds, but they are nevertheless dependent beings that owe their existence to God and are not distinct from God.

Another difference in the relation between God and his attributes and the relation between us and our attributes is that two contingent objects A and B can share one-place properties, but the existence of A entails the existence of different objects than are entailed by the existence of B. These differences in entailment generate criteria of distinctness between the different members of the kind. Each daffodil entails the existence of different particulars, although the relation between each daffodil and the particulars its existence entails is formally the same since they are in the same natural kind. In the case of God, however, no other particular is entailed by God's existence. Therefore, there can be no distinction between one God and another on the basis of different entailments. Different members of an ordinary natural kind will be alike in their attributes, but each attribute when applied to a particular member of the kind will entail the existence of different particulars. This leads to the conclusion that different members of the same natural kind have different essential external relations (relations to things outside the kind). In God, however, there are no essential external relations.

In the case of ordinary natural kinds, the members of the kind differ in their internal relations as well—their relations to other members of the kind. But it can never happen that two contingent objects that are members of the same natural kind and hence have the same attributes differ only in their essential internal relations. They will always differ as well in their essential external relations. For this reason, the criterion of distinctness for individual beings that belong to the same natural kind, and hence have the same attributes, is difference of essential external relations. We can use this to formulate a criterion of distinctness for individual objects:

Criterion of Object Distinctness
If object a and object b belong to the same natural kind, then if a is distinct from b, there exists some relation R and object x outside the natural kind to which a and b belong, such that aRx and $-bRx$.

On this criterion for distinctness between individuals with the same attributes, there can be only one God and the different members of the Trinity are numerically one individual being. On the other hand, the fact that they differ in internal essential relations means that there is *some* important difference of individual being. The tradition, of course, calls it a difference of person since the only differences between the members of the Trinity are person-like characteristics.[4]

Could there be other internal essential relations between the members of the Trinity in which they differ other than the ones that are traditionally used to distinguish Father, Son, and Holy Spirit? I cannot think of any reason of logic that would prevent such a possibility, although perhaps the lack of such a distinction might be argued from the Principle of Sufficient Reason. In any case, I think it reasonable to say that we get our concept of identity for individuals from contingent objects or other dependent beings, and on this concept, differences in internal essential relations do not by themselves give a difference of object identity, although they give a difference of identity in some other sense. I propose that this other sense is what is intended by the distinction within the Trinity.

Even though the persons of the Trinity do not differ in essential external relations, they will differ in accidental external relations. For example, the accidental property of being prayed to by Anselm may be a property of the Father, not the Son. That would be the case if Anselm prays to the Father *qua* Father, i.e., his intentional state is essentially connected to his perception of God as having that property that distinguishes him from the Son. If the Father, Son, and Holy Spirit differ in some essential relational properties, then they will also differ in some accidental relational properties. This is not a problem, however, since accidental relational properties do not figure in the identity of a being. The only problematic ones are the essential relational properties, and I have argued that these are important enough to give a difference of person, but not of numerical being.

I concluded from the discussion in sections 18.2.1 and 18.2.2 that two Gods cannot differ in an accidental property, whether contingent or necessary. In section 18.2.3, I argued that two Gods could not differ in an essential property. Hence, by the principle of the Identity of Indiscernibles, there can be only one God. In section 18.3, I presented a theory of things and kinds which, when combined with the assumption that God is absolutely independent of all other beings, allows us to conclude that in the single case of Divinity, being A can have exactly the same essential external relations as being B, and hence, be numerically identical with B, but A and B differ in essential internal relations. The identity of A and B, therefore, differs in some sense of identity. It is plausible to call this a difference of persons. I conclude that although in a plausible sense of being there is at most one divine being, the Trinity is not contrary to reason.[5]

Notes

1. This excludes any property of being identical with one of the individuals in the domain of the individual variables picked out by a *de re* reference, such as being-identical-with-Socrates. It also excludes any world-indexed property uniquely satisfied by an individual, such as being-the-first-president-of-the-U.S.-in-world $w1$.
2. There may be properties that are essential to possible object S yet accidental to possible object R. If so, there are properties that are neither essential properties simpliciter nor accidental properties simpliciter.
3. Aquinas writes:

    Reason may be employed in two ways to establish a point: firstly, for the purpose of furnishing sufficient proof of some principle, as in natural science, where sufficient proof can be brought to show that the movement of the heavens is always of uniform velocity. Reason is employed in another way, not as furnishing a sufficient proof of a principle, but as confirming an already established principle, by showing the congruity of its results, as in astrology the theory of eccentrics and epicycles is considered as established, because thereby the sensible appearances of the heavenly movements can be explained; not, however, as if this proof were sufficient, forasmuch as some other theory might explain them. In the first way we can prove that God is one, and the like. In the second way, reasons avail to prove the Trinity; as when assumed to be true, such reasons confirm it. We must not, however, think that the Trinity of persons is adequately proved by such reasons. (ST I q 32, a.1, reply obj. 2).

4. As Aquinas expresses it:

    Therefore person in any nature signifies what is distinct in that nature; thus in human nature it signifies this flesh, these bones, and this soul, which are the individuating principles of a man, and which, though not belonging to person in general, nevertheless do belong to the meaning of a particular human person.

    Now distinction in God is only by relation of origin, as stated above [q 28, a 2, 3] while relation in God is not as an accident in a subject, but is the divine essence itself; and so is subsistent, for the divine essence subsists. (ST I q 29, a 4, corpus).

    Now as there is no quantity of God, for He is great without quantity, as Augustine says (De Trin. i 1), it follows that a real relation in God can be based only on action. Such relations are not based on the actions of God according to any extrinsic procession, forasmuch as the relations of God to creatures are not real in Him [q. 13 a.7]. Hence, it follows that real relations in God can be understood only in regard to those actions according to which there are internal, and not external, processions in God. These processions are two only, as above explained, one derived from the action of the intellect, the procession of the Word; and the other from the action of the will, the procession of love. (ST I q. 28, a. 4, corpus).

5. I am grateful to a number of people for their generous and helpful comments on an earlier version of this paper, including Alvin Plantinga, Philip Quinn, Richard Swinburne, Robert Adams, Norman Kretzmann, William Wainwright, James Hanink, Peter van Inwagen, Stephen Davis, and Charles Taliaferro.

Bibliography

Adams, M. M. (1986). "Redemptive Suffering: A Christian Solution to the Problem of Evil," in R. Audi and W. J. Wainwright (eds.), *Rationality, Religious Belief, and Moral Commitment*. Ithaca, NY: Cornell University Press, 248–267.

Adams, M. M. (1988). "Problems of Evil: More Advice to Christian Philosophers." *Faith and Philosophy*, 5, 121–143.

Adams, M. M. (1999). *What Sort of Human Nature? Medieval Philosophy and the Systematics of Christology*. Aquinas Lecture. Milwaukee: Marquette University Press.

Adams, M. M. (2006). *Christ and Horrors: The Coherence of Christology*. Cambridge, UK: Cambridge University Press.

Adams, R. M. (1976). "Motive Utilitarianism." *The Journal of Philosophy*, 73(14), 467.

Adams, R. M. (1977). "Middle Knowledge and the Problem of Evil." *American Philosophical Quarterly*, 14(2), 109–117.

Adams, R. M. (1979). "Divine Command Metaethics Modified Again." *The Journal of Religious Ethics*, 7, 66–79.

Adams, R. M. (1984). "Saints." *Journal of Philosophy*, 81, 392–401.

Alston, W. P. (1986). "Epistemic Circularity." *Philosophy and Phenomenological Research* 47, 1–30; repinted in *Beyond Justification: Dimensions of Epistemic Evaluation*. Ithaca, NY: Cornell University Press, 2005.

Alston, W. P. (2005). *Beyond "Justification": Dimensions of Epistemic Evaluation*. Ithaca, NY: Cornell University Press.

Anderson, A. R., and Belnap, N. D., Jr. (1962). "The Pure Calculus of Entailment." *Journal of Symbolic Logic* 27:1 (March), 19–52.

Annas, J. (1993). *The Morality of Happiness*. New York: Oxford University Press.

St. Thomas Aquinas. (1974). *Summa Theologica*, translated by the Dominican Fathers of the English Province. Allen, TX: Christian Classics.

St. Augustine. (1948). *The City of God*. Trans. J. J. Smith. In *Basic Writings of St Augustine, II*. New York, Modern Library.

St. Augustine. (1953). *On the Free Choice of the Will*. Trans. J. H. Burleigh. In *The Library of Christian Classics, VI: Augustine: Earlier Writings*. Louisville, KY: Westminster John Knox Press.

Bandura, A. (1971). *Social Learning Theory*. Morristown, NJ: General Learning Press.

Bandura, A. (1986). *Social Foundations of Thought and Action*. Englewood Cliffs, NJ: Prentice-Hall.

Bennett, J. F. (1954). "Meaning and Implication." *Mind*, 63(252), 451–463.

Blum, L. (1980). *Friendship, Altruism, and Morality*. London: Routledge and Kegan Paul.

Boethius, A. M. S. (2009). *The Consolation of Philosophy*. Cambridge, MA: Harvard University Press.

Bonhoeffer, D. (1995). *Ethics*. New York: Simon & Schuster.

Brody, B. (1974). *Readings in the Philosophy of Religion: An Analytic Approach*. Englewood Cliffs, NJ: Prentice-Hall.

Browne, B. (1992) "A Solution to the Problem of Moral Luck." *Philosophical Quarterly*, 42, 345–356.
Catholic Church. (1995). *Catechism of the Catholic Church*. 2nd edition. Vatican City: Libreria Editrice Vaticana.
Cicero, M. T. (1942). *On the Orator, Bk 3, On Fate, Stoic Paradoxes*. Trans. H. Rackham. (Loeb Classic Library #349). Cambridge, MA: Harvard University Press.
Cicero. (1998). *On the Nature of the Gods*. Trans. P. G. Walsh. New York: Oxford University Press.
Clarke, S. G., and Simpson, E. (eds.). (1989). *Anti-Theory in Ethics and Moral Conservatism*. Albany: State University of New York Press.
Dostoevsky, F. (1992). *The Brothers Karamazov*. Trans. R. Pevear and L. Volokhonsky. New York: Alfred A. Knopf.
Dalai Lama. (1999). *Ethics for the New Millennium*. New York: Penguin (Riverhead Books).
Davis, S. T. (1983). *Logic and the Nature of God*. Grand Rapids, MI: Eerdmans.
Dawkins, R. (2008). *The God Delusion*. New York: Houghton Mifflin.
Dummett, M. (2003) *Truth and the Past*. New York: Columbia University Press.
Edwards, J. (1974). "Freedom of the Will," in B. Brody (ed.), *Readings in the Philosophy of Religion*. Englewood Cliffs, NJ: Prentice-Hall.
Ehring, D. (1982). "Causal Asymmetry." *Journal of Philosophy*, LXXIX(12), 761–774.
Engstrom, S., and Whiting, J. (1996). *Aristotle, Kant, and the Stoics*. Cambridge: Cambridge University Press.
Feinberg, J. (1970). "Problematic Responsibility in Law and Morals," in J. Feinberg, *Doing and Deserving*. Princeton, NJ: Princeton University Press, 25–37.
Finch, A., and Warfield, T. (1999). "The Mind Argument against Libertarianism." *Mind*, 107, 515–528.
Fischer, J. M. (1983). "Freedom and Foreknowledge." *Philosophical Review*, 92(1) (January), 67–89.
Fischer, J. M., and P. Todd (eds.). (2015). *Freedom, Fatalism, and Foreknowledge*. New York: Oxford University Press.
Flint, T. (2006). *Divine Providence: The Molinist Account*. Ithaca, NY: Cornell University Press.
Foley, R. (2001). *Intellectual Trust in Oneself and Others*. Cambridge: Cambridge University Press.
Frankfurt, H. (1969). "Moral Responsibility and the Principle of Alternative Possibilities." *Journal of Philosophy*, 66, 828–839.
Freddoso, A. J. (1983). "Accidental Necessity and Logical Determinism." *Journal of Philosophy*, LXXX(5), 257–278.
Freddoso, A. J. (1986). "Human Nature, Potency and the Incarnation." *Faith and Philosophy*, 3(1), 27–53.
Frege, G. (1956). "The Thought: A Logical Inquiry." *Mind*, 65(259), 289–311.
Fricker, E. (2006). "Testimony and Epistemic Autonomy," in Jennifer Lackey and Ernest Sosa (eds.), *The Epistemology of Testimony*. New York: Oxford University Press, 225–250.
Geach, P. (1977). *Providence and Evil*. Cambridge: Cambridge University Press.
Grim, P. (1979). "Against Omniscience: The Case from Essential Indexicals." *Nous*, 19, 151–180.

Gunderson, K. (ed.). (1975). *Language, Mind, and Knowledge*. Minneapolis: University of Minnesota Press.
Hare, J. (1996). *The Moral Gap*. Oxford: Clarendon Press.
Harper, W., et al. (eds.). (1980). *Ifs*. Dordrecht: Reidel.
Hartshorne, C. (1982). *The Divine Relativity: A Social Conception of God*. New Haven, CT: Yale University Press.
Hasker, W. (1989). *God, Time, and Knowledge*. Ithaca, NY: Cornell University Press.
Hasker, W. (1983). "Concerning the Intelligibility of 'God Is Timeless.'" *The New Scholasticism*, LVII(2), 170–195.
Hewitt, H., Jr. (ed.). (1991). *Problems in the Philosophy of Religion: Critical Studies of the Work of John Hick*. New York: St. Martin's Press.
Hick, J. (1966). *Evil and the God of Love*. New York: Harper and Row.
Hick, J. (1978). *Evil and the God of Love*. 2nd edition. London: Macmillan; New York: Harper and Row.
Hick, J. (1983). *Philosophy of Religion*. 3rd edition. Englewood Cliffs, NJ: Prentice-Hall.
Hick, J. (2000). "Religious Pluralism and Salvation," in P. L. Quinn and K. Meeker (eds.), *The Philosophical Challenge of Religious Diversity*. New York: Oxford University Press.
Hick, J. (2004). *An Interpretation of Religion: Human Responses to the Transcendent*. New Haven, CT: Yale University Press.
Howard-Snyder, D. (1999). "God, Evil, and Suffering," in M. J. Murray (ed.), *Reason for the Hope Within*. Grand Rapids, MI: Eerdmans, 217–237.
Hume, D. (1990). *Dialogues Concerning Natural Religion*. London: Penguin Books.
Hume, D. (2000). *An Inquiry Concerning Human Understanding*. Ed. Thomas L. Beauchamp. Oxford: Oxford University Press.
Hunt, D. (1998). "What *Is* the Problem of Theological Fatalism?" *International Philosophical Quarterly*, XXXVIII(1), 17–30.
Hunt, D. (1999). "On Augustine's Way Out." *Faith and Philosophy*, 16(1) (January), 3–26.
Hunt, D. (2000). "Moral Responsibility and Unavoidable Action." *Philosophical Studies*, 97(2), 195–227.
Hurley, P. (2008). *A Concise Introduction to Logic*. Belmont, CA: Wadsworth.
Jackson, F. (1986). "What Mary Didn't Know." *Journal of Philosophy*, LXXXIII(5), 291–295.
Jackson, F. (2003). "Mind and Illusion," in Anthony O'Hear (ed.), *Minds and Persons*. Cambridge: Cambridge University Press, 251–271.
Kellner, M. (1991). "Jewish Ethics," in Peter Singer (ed.), *A Companion to Ethics*. Blackwell, 82–90.
Kelly, T. (2016). "Evidence," in Edward N. Zalta (ed.), *The Stanford Encyclopedia of Philosophy* (Winter 2016 Edition), https://plato.stanford.edu/archives/win2016/entries/evidence/.
Kenny, A. (1974). "Divine Foreknowledge and Human Free Will," in Baruch Brody (ed.), *Readings in the Philosophy of Religion*. Englewood Cliffs, NJ: Prentice-Hall, 403–413.
Kenny, A. (1979). *The God of the Philosophers*. Oxford: Clarendon Press.
Kneale, W., and Kneale, M. (1962). *The Development of Logic*. Oxford: Clarendon Press.
Kretzmann, N. (1997). *The Metaphysics of Theism: Aquinas's Natural Theology in Summa contra gentiles I*. Oxford: Clarendon Press.
Kripke, S. (1980). *Naming and Necessity*. Oxford: Blackwell.
Kvart, I. (1986). *A Theory of Counterfactuals*. Indianapolis: Hackett.

Kneale, W. C. (2003). "The Province of Logic," in H. D. Lewis (ed.), *Contemporary British Philosophy*. London: Routledge.
Leftow, B. (1991). *Time and Eternity*. Ithaca, NY: Cornell University Press.
Lewis, C. I., C. H. Langford, and P. Lamprecht. (1959). *Symbolic logic*. New York: Dover Publications.
Lewis, C. S. (1996). *The Problem of Pain*. New York: Touchstone.
Lewis, D. (1973). *Counterfactuals*. Oxford: Blackwell.
Lewis, D. (1986). *On the Plurality of Worlds*. Oxford: Blackwell.
Lewy, C. (1950). "Entailment end Necessary Propositions," in Max Black (ed.), *Philosophical Analysis*. Ithaca, NY: Cornell University Press, 195–210.
Lewy, C., J. Watling, and P. T. Geach. (1958). "Symposium: Entailment." *Proceedings of the Aristotelian Society*, Supplementary Volume 32, 123–172.
Locke, J. (1996). *An Essay Concerning Human Understanding*. Indiana: Hackett.
Locke. J. (2000). "A Discourse of Miracles," in *John Locke: Writings on Religion*. Oxford: Clarendon Press, 114–120.
Locke, J. (2009). *A Letter Concerning Toleration*. New York: Classic Book America.
Hurley, P. (2008). *A Concise Introduction to Logic*. Belmont, CA: Wadsworth.
Mackie, J. L. (1955). "Evil and Omnipotence." *Mind*, LXIV(254), 200–212.
Mackie, J. L. (1966). "The Direction of Causation." *Philosophical Review*, 75(4), 441–466.
Mavrodes, G. (1984). "Is the Past Unpreventable?" *Faith and Philosophy*, I(2), 131–146.
Mavrodes, G. (2000). "Polytheism," in P. L. Quinn and K. Meeker (eds.), *The Philosophical Challenge of Religious Diversity*. New York: Oxford University Press.
McMyler, B. (2011). *Testimony, Trust, and Authority*. New York: Oxford University Press.
Mill, J. S. (2002). *Utilitarianism*. Indianapolis: Hackett.
Molina, L. (1988). *On Divine Foreknowledge: Part IV of the Concordia*. Trans. Alfred J. Freddoso. Ithaca, NY: Cornell University Press.
Moran, R. (2001). *Authority and Estrangement: An Essay on Self-Knowledge*. Princeton, NJ: Princeton University Press.
Moran, R. (2006). "Getting Told and Being Believed," in Jennifer Lackey and Ernest Sosa (eds.), *The Epistemology of Testimony*. New York: Oxford University Press, 272–306.
Morris, T. V. (1986). *The Logic of God Incarnate*. Ithaca, NY: Cornell University Press.
Morris, T. V. (1987a). "Absolute Creation," in *Anselmian Explorations*. Notre Dame, IN: University of Notre Dame Press, 161–178.
Morris, T. V. (1987b). "Perfection and Power," in *Anselmian Explorations*. Notre Dame, IN: University of Notre Dame Press, 70–75.
Murdoch, I. (1970). "The Sovereignty of Good," in *The Sovereignty of Good and Other Essays*. London: Routledge & Kegan Paul.
Nagel, T. (1974). "What Is It like to Be a Bat?" *Philosophical Review*, 83, 435–450.
Nagel, T. (1978). *The Possibility of Altruism*. Princeton, NJ: Princeton University Press.
Nagel, T. (1979). *Mortal Questions*. Cambridge: Cambridge University Press.
Nagel, T. (1986). *The View from Nowhere*. New York: Oxford University Press.
Nock, A. D. (1998). *Conversion*. Baltimore, MD: Johns Hopkins University Press.
Ockham, W. (1983). *Predestination, God's Foreknowledge, and Future Contingents*. 2nd edition, translated, introduction, and notes by M. M. Adams and N. Kretzmann. Indianapolis: Hackett.
O'Connor, T. (1993). "On the Transfer of Necessity." *Noûs*, 27(2) (June), 204–218.
O'Connor, T. (2002). *Persons and Causes: The Metaphysics of Free Will*. New York: Oxford University Press.

Parfit, D. (1984). *Reasons and Persons.* Oxford: Oxford University Press.
Parfit, D. (2003). "Why Our Identity Is Not What Matters," in R. Martin and J. Barresi (eds.), *Personal Identity.* Oxford: Blackwell, 115–143.
Perry, J. (1978). *A Dialogue on Personal Identity and Immortality.* Indianapolis: Hackett.
Perry, J. (1979). "The Problem of the Essential Indexical." *Nous*, 13(1), 3–21.
Pike, N. (1965). "Divine Omniscience and Voluntary Action." *The Philosophical Review*, 74(January), 27–46.
Pike, N. (1970). *God and Timelessness.* London: Routledge and Kegan Paul.
Pike, N. (1977). "Divine Foreknowledge, Human Freedom, and Possible Worlds." *Philosophical Review*, 86(April), 209–216.
Pinnock, C., et al (1994). *The Openness of God: A Biblical Challenge to the Traditional Understanding of God.* Downers Grove, IL: InterVarsity Press.
Plantinga, A. (1974a). *God, Freedom, and Evil.* New York: Harper and Row.
Plantinga, A. (1974b). *The Nature of Necessity.* New York: Oxford University Press.
Plantinga, A. (1980). *Does God Have a Nature?* Aquinas Lecture. Milwaukee: Marquette University Press.
Plantinga, A. (1986). "On Ockham's Way Out." *Faith and Philosophy*, 3(3), 235–269.
Plantinga, A. (1993a). *Warrant: The Current Debate.* New York: Oxford University Press.
Plantinga, A. (1993b). *Warrant and Proper Function.* New York: Oxford University Press.
Plantinga, A. (2000a). "Pluralism: A Defense of Religious Exclusivism," in P. L. Quinn and K. Meeker (eds.), *The Philosophical Challenge of Religious Diversity.* New York: Oxford University Press.
Plantinga, A. (2000b). *Warranted Christian Belief.* New York: Oxford University Press.
Pollock, J. L. (1966). "The Paradoxes of Strict Implication." *Logique et analyse*, 9(34), 180–196.
Pollock, J. L. (1975). "Four Kinds of Conditionals." *American Philosophical Quarterly*, 12(1), 51–59.
Pollock, J. L. (1984). *The Foundations of Philosophical Semantics.* Princeton, NJ: Princeton University Press.
Purtill, R. (1974). "Foreknowledge and Fatalism." *Religious Studies*, 10(September), 319–324.
Putnam, H. (1975). "The Meaning of 'Meaning,'" in *Mind, Language, and Reality (Philosophical Papers), vol. 2* Cambridge: Cambridge University Press.
Putnam, H. (2004). *The Collapse of the Fact/Value Dichotomy.* Cambridge, MA: Harvard University Press.
Quine, W. V. O. (1970). *Philosophy of Logic.* Englewood Cliffs, NJ: Prentice-Hall.
Quinn, P. L. (1989). "Tragic Dilemmas, Suffering Love, and the Christian Life." *Journal of Religious Ethics*, 17(1), 151–183.
Rawls, J. (1974–1975). "The Independence of Moral Theory." *Proceedings of the American Philosophical Association*, 48, 5–22.
Raz, J. (1986). *The Morality of Freedom.* Oxford: Clarendon Press.
Rescher, N., and R. Brandom (1980). *The Logic of Inconsistency* Oxford: Basil Blackwell.
Rice, H. (2005). "Zagzebski on the Arrow of Time." *Faith and Philosophy*, 22(3), 363–369.
Ridge, M. (2017). "Reasons for Action: Agent-Neutral vs. Agent-Relative," in Edward N. Zalta (ed.), *The Stanford Encyclopedia of Philosophy (Fall 2017 Edition)*, <https://plato.stanford.edu/archives/fall2017/entries/reasons-agent/>.
Roberts, R. C. (1988). "What an Emotion Is: A Sketch." *The Philosophical Review*, 97(2), 183–209.

Roberts, R. C. (1997). "Narrative Ethics," in P. L. Quinn and C. Taliaferro (eds.), *Companion to Philosophy of Religion*. Wiley-Blackwell, 473–480.
Rouner, L. S. (ed.). (1997). *Is There a Human Nature?* Notre Dame, IN: University of Notre Dame Press.
Rowe, W. L. (1979). "The Problem of Evil and Some Varieties of Atheism." *American Philosophical Quarterly*, 16, 335–341.
Rowe, W. (1990). "The Problem of Evil and Some Varieties of Atheism," in M. M. Adams and R. M. Adams (eds.), *The Problem of Evil*. Oxford: Oxford University Press.
Runzo, J. (1981). "Omniscience and Freedom for Evil." *International Journal for the Philosophy of Religion*, 12, 131–147.
Schlesinger, G. (1988). *New Perspectives on Old-Time Religion*. Oxford: Clarendon Press.
Schoeck, H. (1966). *Envy*. New York: Harcourt Brace, 237–238.
Slote, M. (1995). "Agent-Based Virtue Ethics." *Midwest Studies in Philosophy*, 20, 83–101.
Smart, J. J. C., and B. Williams. (1973). *Utilitarianism: For and Against*. Cambridge: Cambridge University Press.
Smiley, T. J. (1958). "Entailment and Deducibility." *Proceedings of the Aristotelian Society*, 59, 233–254.
Stalnaker, R. C. (1968). "A Theory of Counterfactuals." In Nicholas Rescher (ed.), *Studies in Logical Theory*. Oxford: Basil Blackwell, 98–112.
Stalnaker, R. C. (1980). "A Defense of Conditional Excluded Middle," in William L. Harper et al. (eds.), *Ifs: Belief, Decision, Chance, and Time*. Dordrecht: Springer, 87–104.
Stocker, M. (1976). "The Schizophrenia of Modern Ethical Theories." *Journal of Philosophy*, 73(14), 453–466.
Strawson, P. F. (1948). "Necessary Propositions and Entailment-Statements." *Mind*, 57(226), 184–200.
Stump, E. (1986). "Dante's Hell, Aquinas' Moral Theory, and the Love of God." *Canadian Journal of Philosophy*, 16(2), 181–198.
Stump, E. (1990). "Intellect, Will, and the Principle of Alternate Possibilities," in M. Beaty (ed.), *Christian Theism and Problems of Philosophy*. Notre Dame, IN: University of Notre Dame Press, 254–285.
Stump, E. (2003). *Aquinas*. New York: Routledge.
Stump, E. (2010). *Wandering in Darkness: Narrative and the Problem of Suffering*. New York: Oxford University Press.
Stump, E., and N. Kretzmann. (1981). "Eternity." *The Journal of Philosophy*, 78(8), 429–458.
Stump, E., and N. Kretzmann. (1985). "Absolute Simplicity." *Faith and Philosophy*, 2, 353–382.
Stump, E., and N. Kretzmann. (1988). "Being and Goodness," in Thomas V. Morris (ed.), *Divine and Human Action*. Ithaca, NY: Cornell University Press, 281–312.
Swartz, N., & Bradley, R. (1979). *Possible Worlds: An Introduction to Logic and Its Philosophy*. Hackett Publishing.
Swinburne, R. (1977). *The Coherence of Theism*. Oxford: Clarendon Press.
Swinburne, R. (1983). "A Theodicy of Heaven and Hell," in Alfred J. Freddoso (ed.), *The Existence of God*. Notre Dame, IN: University of Notre Dame Press, 37–54.
Swinburne, R. (1986). *The Evolution of the Soul*. Oxford: Oxford University Press.
Swinburne, R. (1994). *The Christian God*. Oxford: Oxford University Press.
Talbott, T. (1990). "The Doctrine of Everlasting Punishment." *Faith and Philosophy*, 7(1), 19–42.

Thomson, J. J. (1989). "Morality and Bad Luck." *Meta-philosophy*, 20(3–4), 203–221.
Tooley, M. (2013). "The Problem of Evil," in Edward N. Zalta (ed.), *The Stanford Encyclopedia of Philosophy* (Summer 2013 Edition), <http://plato.stanford.edu/archives/sum2013/entries/evil/>.
Vacek, E. (1994). *Love, Human and Divine: The Heart of Christian Ethics*. Washington, DC: Georgetown University Press.
van Frassen, B. C. (1970). *An Introduction to the Philosophy of Time and Space*. New York: Random House.
van Inwagen, P. (1983). *An Essay on Free Will*. New York: Oxford University Press.
van Inwagen, P. (1992). "The Possibility of Resurrection," in Paul Edwards (ed.), *Immortality*. New York: Macmillan, 242–246.
van Inwagen, P. (2008). "What Does an Omniscient Being Know About the Future?," in Jonathan Kvanvig (ed.), *Oxford Studies in Philosophy of Religion* 1. New York: Oxford University Press, 216–230.
von Balthasar, H. U. (ed.). (1990). *The Scandal of the Incarnation*. Trans. John Saward. San Francisco: Ignatius Press.
von Hildebrand, D. (1953). *Christian Ethics*. Philadelphia: David McKay.
von Wright, G. H. (1957). "The Concept of Entailment," in *Logical Studies*. London: Routledge & Kegan Paul, 165–191.
von Wright, G. H. (1971). *Explanation and Understanding*. Ithaca, NY: Cornell University Press.
Wainwright, W. (1986). "Monotheism," in Robert Audi and William J. Wainwright (eds.), *Rationality, Religious Belief, and Moral Commitment*. Ithaca, NY: Cornell University Press, 289–314.
Watson, G. (1990). "On the Primacy of Character," in O. Flanagan and A. O. Rorty (eds.), *Identity, Character, and Morality*. Cambridge, MA: MIT Press, 449–483.
Weithman, P. (ed.). (2008). *Liberal Faith: Essays in Honor of Philip Quinn*. Notre Dame, IN: University of Notre Dame Press.
Williams, B., & Nagel, T. (1976). "Moral Luck." *Proceedings of the Aristotelian Society, Supplementary Volumes*, 50, 115–151.
Williams, B. (1981a). "Moral Luck," in *Moral Luck and Other Essays*. Cambridge: Cambridge University Press, 20–39.
Williams, B. (1981b). "Persons, Character, and Morality," in *Moral Luck and Other Essays*. Cambridge: Cambridge University Press, 1–19.
Williams, B. (1985). *Ethics and the Limits of Philosophy*. Cambridge, MA: Harvard University Press.
Wittgenstein, L. (1998). *Culture and Value: A Selection from the Posthumous Remains*. Trans. P. Winch, ed. G. H. von Wright. Oxford: Blackwell.
Wolf, S. (1982). "Moral Saints." *Journal of Philosophy*, 7, 419–439.
Wolff, R. P. (1998). *In Defense of Anarchism*. Berkeley: University of California Press.
Wolterstorff, N. (1982). "God Everlasting," in Steven M. Cahn and David Shatz (eds.), *Contemporary Philosophy of Religion*. Oxford University Press, 181–203.
Zagzebski, L. T. (1985). "Divine Foreknowledge and Human Free Will." *Religious Studies*, 21 (Fall), 279–298.
Zagzebski, L. T. (1988). "Individual Essence and the Creation," in T. V. Morris (ed.), *Divine and Human Action*. Ithaca, NY: Cornell University Press, 119–144.
Zagzebski, L. T. (1989). "Christian Monotheism." *Faith and Philosophy*, 6(1), 3–18.

Zagzebski, L. T. (1990). "What if the Impossible Had Been Actual?," in M. Beaty (ed.), *Christian Theism and the Problems of Philosophy*. Notre Dame, IN: University of Notre Dame Press, 165–183.

Zagzebski, L. T. (1991). *The Dilemma of Freedom and Foreknowledge*. New York: Oxford University Press.

Zagzebski, L. T. (1994). "Religious Luck." *Faith and Philosophy*, 11(3), 397–413.

Zagzebski, L. T. (1996a). *Virtues of the Mind: An Inquiry into the Nature of Virtue and the Ethical Foundations of Knowledge*. Cambridge: Cambridge University Press.

Zagzebski, L. T. (1996b). "An Agent-Based Approach to the Problem of Evil." *International Journal for the Philosophy of Religion*, 39, 127–139.

Zagzebski, L. T. (1997). "Perfect Goodness and Divine Motivation Theory." *Midwest Studies in Philosophy*, 21, 296–309.

Zagzebski, L. T. (1998). "The Virtues of God and the Foundations of Ethics." *Faith and Philosophy*, 15(4), 538–552 (Special issue on "Virtues and Virtue Theories from a Christian Perspective").

Zagzebski, L. T. (2000). "Does Libertarian Freedom Require Alternate Possibilities?" *Noûs: Philosophical Perspectives*, 14, 231–248.

Zagzebski, L. T. (2001). "Religious Diversity and Social Responsibility." *Logos: A Journal of Catholic Thought and Culture*, 4(1), 135–155.

Zagzebski, L. T. (2002a). "Omniscience and the Arrow of Time." *Faith and Philosophy*, 19(4), 503–519.

Zagzebski, L. T. (2002b). "The Incarnation and Virtue Ethics," in S. T. Davis, D. J. Kendall, SJ, and G. O'Collins, SJ (eds.), *The Incarnation*. New York: Oxford University Press, 313–331.

Zagzebski, L. T. (2003). "Emotion and Moral Judgment." *Philosophy and Phenomenological Research*, 66(1), 104–124.

Zagzebski, L. T. (2004a). *Divine Motivation Theory*. Cambridge: Cambridge University Press.

Zagzebski, L. T. (2004b). "The Epistemology of Religion: The Need for Engagement," in W. Loffler and P. Weingartner (eds.), *Proceedings of the Twenty-Sixth Annual Wittgenstein Symposium: Knowledge and Belief*. Vienna: Holder-Pichler-Tempsky, 386–398.

Zagzebski, L. T. (2005). "Sleeping Beauty and the Afterlife," in A. Chignell and A. Dole (eds.), *God and the Ethics of Belief: New Essays in the Philosophy of Religion*. Cambridge: Cambridge University Press, 59–76.

Zagzebski, L. T. (2006). "Self-Trust and the Diversity of Religions." *Philosophic Exchange*, 36(1), 62–76.

Zagzebski, L. T., and J. Seachris. (2007). "Weighing Evils: The C. S. Lewis Approach." *International Journal for Philosophy of Religion*, 62(2), 81–88.

Zagzebski, L. T. (2008). "Omnisubjectivity," in J. L. Kvanvig (ed.), *Oxford Studies in Philosophy of Religion 1*. New York: Oxford University Press, 231–247.

Zagzebski, L. T. (2011a). "Eternity and Fatalism," in C. Tapp and E. Runggaldier (eds.), *God, Eternity, and Time*. Farnham, UK and Burlington, VT: Ashgate, 65–80.

Zagzebski, L. T. (2011b). "First Person and Third Person Reasons and Religious Epistemology." *European Journal for Philosophy of Religion*, 80(Fall), 285–304.

Zagzebski, L. T. (2011c). "Epistemic Self-Trust and the *Consensus Gentium* Argument," in K. Clark and R. van Aragon (eds.), *Evidence and Religious Belief*. Oxford: Clarendon Press: 22–36.

Zagzebski, L. T. (2012). *Epistemic Authority: A Theory of Trust, Authority, and Autonomy in Belief.* New York: Oxford University Press.
Zagzebski, L. T. (2013). *Omnisubjectivity: A Defense of a Divine Attribute.* Aquinas Lecture. Milwaukee: Marquette University Press.
Zagzebski, L. T. (2014a). "Divine Foreknowledge and the Metaphysics of Time," in A. Ramelow (ed.), *God: Reason, and Reality. Philosophia series: Basic Philosophical Concepts.* Munich: Philosophia Verlag, 275–302.
Zagzebski, L. T. (2014b). "Trust, Anti-Trust, and Reasons for Religious Belief," in L. F. Callahan and T. O'Connor (eds.), *Religious Faith and Intellectual Virtue.* New York: Oxford University Press, 231–245.
Zagzebski, L. T. (2014c). "First Person and Third Person Reasons and the Regress Problem," in J. Turri and P. Klein (eds.), *Ad Infinitum: New Essays on Epistemological Infinitism.* Oxford: Oxford University Press, 243–255.
Zagzebski, L. T. (2015). *Epistemic Authority: A theory of Trust, Authority, and Autonomy in Belief.* New York: Oxford University Press.
Zagzebski, L. T. (2016a). "Divine Motivation Theory and Exemplarism." *European Journal for Philosophy of Religion,* 8(3), 109–121.
Zagzebski, L. T. (2016b). "Omnisubjectivity: Why It is a Divine Attribute." *Nova et vetera,* 14(2), 435–450.
Zagzebski, L. T. (2016c). "A Modern Defense of Religious Authority." *Logos: A Journal of Catholic Thought and Culture,* 19(3), 15–28.
Zagzebski, L. T. (2016d). "Divine Motivation theory and Exemplarism." *European Journal of Philosophy of Religion,* 8(3), 109–121.
Zagzebski, L. T. (2017a). "Good Persons, Good Aims, and the Problem of Evil," in J. Sterba (ed.), *Ethics and the Problem of Evil.* Bloomington, IN: Indiana University Press, 43–56.
Zagzebski, L. T. (2017b). *Exemplarist Moral Theory.* New York: Oxford University Press.
Zagzebski, L. T. (2017c). "Foreknowledge and Free Will," in Edward N. Zalta (ed.), *The Stanford Encyclopedia of Philosophy* (Spring 2021 Edition), <https://plato.stanford.edu/archives/spr2021/entries/free-will-foreknowledge/>.
Zagzebski, L. T. (2020). *Epistemic Values: Collected Papers in Epistemology.* New York: Oxford University Press.
Zagzebski, L. T. (2021). *The Two Greatest Ideas: How Our Grasp of the Universe and Our Minds Changed Everything.* Princeton, NJ: Princeton University Press.
Zimmerman, D. (1999). "The Compatibility of Materialism and Survival: The 'Falling Elevator' Model." *Faith and Philosophy,* 16(2), 194–212.

Sources

I. Foreknowledge and Fatalism

1. "Divine Foreknowledge and Human Free will," in *Religious Studies*, 21(Fall 1985), 279–298.
2. "Eternity and Fatalism," in *God, Eternity, and Time*, edited by Christian Tapp and Edmund Runggaldier, Ashgate, 2011, 65–80. Reprinted with permission.
3. "Divine Foreknowledge and the Metaphysics of Time," in *God: Reason, and Reality*, edited by Anselm Ramelow, in the *Philosophia* series: Basic Philosophical Concepts, Philosophia Verlag, Munich, 2014, 275–302. Reprinted with permission.

II. The Problem of Evil

4. "An Agent-Based Approach to the Problem of Evil," in *International Journal for the Philosophy of Religion* 39(June 1996), 127–139. Reprinted with permission.
5. "Good Persons, Good Aims, and the Problem of Evil," in *Ethics and the Problem of Evil*, edited by James Sterba, Indiana University Press, 2017, 43–56. Reprinted with permission.
6. "Weighing Evils: The C. S. Lewis Approach," coauthor Joshua Seachris, in *International Journal for Philosophy of Religion* 62(2) (October 2007), 81–88. Reprinted with permission.

III. Death, Hell, and Resurrection

7. "Sleeping Beauty and the Afterlife," in *God and the Ethics of Belief: New Essays in the Philosophy of Religion*, edited by Andrew Chignell and Andrew Dole, Cambridge University Press, 2005, 59–76.
8. "Religious Luck" in *Faith and Philosophy*, 11(3) (July 1994), 397–413.

IV. God and Morality

9. "The Virtues of God and the Foundations of Ethics," in *Faith and Philosophy* 15(4) (October 1998), 538–552. (Special issue on "Virtues and Virtue Theories from a Christian Perspective").
10. "The Incarnation and Virtue Ethics," in *The Incarnation*, edited by Stephen T. Davis, Daniel J. Kendall, SJ, and Gerald O'Collins, SJ, Oxford University Press, 2002, 313–331. Reprinted with permission.

V. Omnisubjectivity

11. "The Attribute of Omnisubjectivity," expanded version of *Omnisubjectivity: A Defense of a Divine Attribute* (Aquinas Lecture 2013), Milwaukee: Marquette University Press, 2013. Reprinted with permission. Sec. 9 taken from "Omnisubjectivity: Why It Is a Divine Attribute," in *Nova et vetera*, 14(2), (2016), 435–450.

VI. The Rationality of Religious Belief

12. "The Epistemology of Religion: The Need for Engagement," in *Proceedings of the Twenty-Sixth Annual Wittgenstein Symposium: Knowledge and Belief*, edited by Winfried Loffler and Paul Weingartner, Holder-Pichler-Tempsky, 2004, 386–398.
13. "First-Person and Third-Person Reasons and Religious Epistemology," in *European Journal for Philosophy of Religion* (Fall 2011), 285–304. Reprinted with permission.
14. "Religious Diversity and Social Responsibility," in *Logos: A Journal of Catholic Thought and Culture*, 4(1) (2001), 136–156. Reprinted with permission.

VII. Rational Religious Belief, Self-Trust, and Authority

15. "A Modern Defense of Religious Authority, in *Logos: A Journal of Catholic Thought and Culture*, 19(3) (2016), 15–28. Reprinted with permission.
16. "Epistemic Self-Trust and the *Consensus Gentium* Argument," in *Evidence and Religious Belief*, edited by Kelly Clark and Raymond van Aragon, Oxford: Clarendon Press, 2011, 22–36. Reprinted with permission.

VIII. God, Trinity, and the Metaphysics of Modality

17. "What if the Impossible Had Been Actual?", in *Christian Theism and the Problems of Philosophy*, edited by Michael D. Beaty, Notre Dame, IN: University of Notre Dame Press, 1990, 165–183. Reprinted with permission.
18. "Christian Monotheism," in *Faith and Philosophy*, 6(1) (January 1989), 3–18.

Index

accidental necessity, 20, 34n8, 55–56, 60–61, 64–65
acts, moral status of, 77–78, 81, 89–90, 93–96, 155, 176, 180
actual world, properties/features of, 198–200
Adams, Marilyn, 98
Adams, Robert, 29, 164
admiration, as epistemic reason, 232
agency. *See* free will; motives/motivations
agent-based virtue ethics
    advantages of, 78–79
    Christian theology in relation to, 79–80
    concept of, 86n4
    overview of, 77–80
    and problem of evil, 80–86
    virtue–good relationship in, 77–78
    virtue–rightness relationship in, 77
agent-relative reasons, 235–36
Alston, William, 1, 275–76
American Philosophical Association, 8
anarchism, 264–66
Anderson, A. R., 305n4
Anderson, Paul Thomas, *There Will Be Blood*, 204
Anglo-American philosophy, 214
Annas, Julia, 166n2
Anselm, Saint, 34n11, 170, 190, 319
Apollo, 226
a posteriori truths, 173–75
Aquinas, Thomas
    and counterpossibles, 302
    on divine foreknowledge and human free will, 17–19, 23–24
    on God's knowledge, 59, 189
    on God's nature, 159, 162, 165, 306
    on God's omnipresence, 190–91, 196
    on God's relation to time, 39
    on grace and moral luck, 137
    on the Incarnation, 170
    and monotheism, 306, 314
    and morality, 151, 157, 165
    on reason, 314, 320n3
    on the resurrection, 125, 129
    on substance and form, 117, 130n3
    in thought experiment about resurrection, 115
    and the Trinity, 314, 320n3, 320n4

Aquinas/Calvin model (A/C model), 215, 219, 226
Aristotle
    on character traits, 135
    on ethics, 153
    and exemplarism, 172, 174
    on form, 116–17
    on hierarchy of objects of inquiry, 287
    and *phronesis*, 85, 174, 182n12, 224
    on truth of future-tensed propositions, 19
    virtue ethics and, 77, 85, 151, 177
arrow of time, 3, 55, 64–66
atheism, 213, 227n1, 251–52, 285, 286
Atomists, 63
Audi, Robert, 1
Augustine, Saint, 16, 52n2, 137
Austen, Jane, 91
authority
    autonomy in relation to, 10, 264–68, 272
    dilemmas involving, 267–68
    epistemic, 9–10, 226, 267–68
    modern rejection of, 10, 242, 263–65
    moral, 268–70
    political, 10, 263, 265–68, 271
    preemption thesis, 266–68
    reasons for rejection of, 263–65
    religious, 10, 241–42, 270–72
    theoretical vs. deliberative reasons and, 241–42
autonomy
    authority in relation to, 10, 264–68, 270, 272
    conceptions related to, 264
    intellectual, 279–80, 288
    personal, 81, 85

backwards causation, 26–28, 44–45, 65–66, 120, 125–28
Bathsheba, 255
belief. *See* Christian beliefs; religious beliefs
Belnap, N. D., Jr., 305n4
bifurcation, and identity, 123, 129
body, thought experiment about resurrection of, 5, 115–30
Boethius, 39, 44, 48
Bonaventure, Saint, 170
Bonhoeffer, Dietrich, 171, 180

Brandom, Robert, 305n4
Browne, Brynmor, 141

Cassandra, 226–27
Catholicism, 139, 191, 265, 269–70
causal closure, 67–68
causal contingency
  backwards, 26–28
  concept of, 20–21
  defined, 25
  divine foreknowledge and, 21–22, 24–28
causality
  asymmetry of, 31–33, 66
  backwards, 26–28, 44–45, 65–66, 120, 125–28
  and fatalism, 37–38
  and the past, 3, 55–56, 66–70
  time in relation to, 27
  See also arrow of time
causal necessity, 55–56
certainty, 20
character traits
  God's traits as model for, 157
  and intellectual virtues, 224–25
  as moral foundation, 77–78, 83, 153, 176–77
  moral luck and, 133, 135–37, 139, 145
  motives associated with, 154–55
  virtue ethics and, 77–78, 83, 153
Chinese philosophy, 78
Christian beliefs
  authority as grounds for, 241–42
  external rationality of, 219–21
  Holy Spirit as agent/source of, 215, 219–20, 250
  internal rationality of, 216–18
  justification of, 216–18
  Plantinga on, 8, 215–22
  warrant of, 219–21
  See also religious beliefs
Christian ethics
  Christocentric nature of, 168, 169, 182n2
  and imitation of Christ, 162–63, 168, 171–72, 180
  importance of theory for, 168–69
  Incarnation and, 168
  luck in relation to, 5, 132, 136–47
  types of moral theory in relation to, 152
Christian theology
  agent-based theories in relation to, 79–80
  metaphysics in relation to, 71
  and moral luck, 5, 132–33, 138–47
  timelessness of God's knowledge as principle of, 18
Christology, 6, 98, 166

Cicero, 52n2, 284, 286
circularity of arguments
  Aristotle and *phronesis*, 174
  epistemic, 10, 231, 240, 274–80
  in moral theory, 175
Clifford, W. K., 245–46
Confucius, 78
conscience, 269
consciousness
  counterfactual, 197–200
  emotions as states of, 159
  and identity, 124, 127
  knowing another's, 189
  pain experienced in, 105, 107
  prayer and, 192–93
  relationship of God's and humans', 192–93
  subjectivity as one's experience of, 187
consensus gentium argument for God's existence, 10, 273, 284–88
consequentialist theories, 79, 93, 97, 101. *See also* utilitarianism
contingency, 19–20, 22–24. *See also* causal contingency
contingent objects, 316–17
conversion, 242, 244n16
correspondence theory of truth, 19
counterfactual conditionals, 10–11, 291–92, 295, 297, 299–300. *See also* subjunctive counterfactual conditionals
counterfactuals, 134–35, 142, 294–97, 300–304. *See also* subjunctive counterfactual conditionals
counterfactual subjectivity, 197–200
counterpossibles, 10–11, 291–97, 301–2
creation, God's acts of, 80
credibility, 226
critical detachment/self-reflection, 251–59, 275. *See also* epistemic conscientiousness
culture
  and pluralism, 252–53
  and shared rationality, 245–46, 248–50, 256–57
  social responsibility to those of another, 9, 245–59
Culture-Sensitivity Principle, 9, 256

Dalai Lama, 248, 249, 258
David (Israelite king), 254–56
Davis, Stephen T., 148n7
Day-Lewis, Daniel, 204
deliberative (first-person) reasons
  and authority, 241–42
  concept of, 229–30
  and conversion, 242

and disagreement, 240–41
executive control over, 234
and experience, 230, 236–37
first- and second-order, 235
and intuition, 230–31
relationship of theoretical to, 233–34
and religious experience, 237
and self-trust, 231–32
and testimony, 237–39
theoretical reasons contrasted with, 233–36
trust or admiration as basis for, 231–32, 242
Dennett, Daniel, 227
deontological theories, 79, 165
Descartes, René, 20, 187
desires, natural, 273
determinism, 15, 17, 19. *See also* fatalism
Diodorus Cronus, 52n1
direct reference, theory of, 172–74
disagreement, 239–41, 246, 287
diversity. *See* religious diversity
Divine Command theory
  agent-based theories and, 79–80, 86n9
  and Christian ethics, 168
  DM theory compared to, 6, 77, 152, 163–66
  and problem of evil, 76–77
  in traditional Christian philosophy, 180
  will as foundation of, 76, 79, 163–65, 181
divine foreknowledge
  Aquinas's solution to reconciling free will with, 17–19
  causal contingency in relation to, 24–28
  compatibility of free will with, 2, 15–19, 30–34, 49–52
  counterfactuals and, 28–30
  logical contingency in relation to, 22–24
  metaphysics of time and, 54–71
  problem of reconciling free will with, 15, 21–22, 54–64
  pseudo-problems in relation to, 19–21
  theory of explanation compatible with, 30–34
  timelessness of, 2
  weak notions of, 17
  See also omniscience
divine justice, 143–45
Divine Motivation (DM) theory
  advantages of, 6, 164–66
  Divine Command theory compared to, 6, 77, 152, 163–66
  as exemplarist moral theory, 168, 177–78
  goodness of God as primary in, 4
  human moral theory grounded in, 161
  and the Incarnation, 6, 162, 179
  overview of, 3–6, 161–63, 178

and perfect goodness, 6
personal relationship of God with humans as component of, 4
structure of, 152
and Trinity concept, 162
divine revelation, 238–39
division of linguistic labor, 173, 174
DM theory. *See* Divine Motivation (DM) theory
Dostoevsky, Fyodor, 103, 110, 181
dualism, 129
duty, 155

Ehring, Douglas, 27
L'Elegant criminel (film), 145
emotions, 153–54, 157, 159–60, 167n8, 167n9, 203–4
empathy, 7, 193–97
  as acquisition of emotion like that of another, 193–94
  as expressive virtue, 155
  God and, 7, 193–97, 201–4, 207–8
  morality/immorality of, 203–4
  novels or movies as models of, 194, 201, 203–4, 209n10
  omnisubjectivity as, 195–96, 207–8
  total, 195
Endo, Shusaku, *Silence*, 147n3
Enlightenment, 213, 214, 217, 253–54
Epicurus, 19
epistemic agency
  and authoritativeness, 226
  community context for, 222–26
  and credibility, 226
  duty and responsibility in, 217–18, 221
  emulation as means of improving, 215, 224
  features of, 222
  importance of, 215
  and intellectual virtues, 224–25
  and trustworthiness, 225–26, 231, 234
epistemic authority, 9–10, 226, 267–68
epistemic conscientiousness, 278–82, 286–88
epistemic reasons
  agent-relative and agent-neutral, 235–36, 243n8, 244n9
  and authority, 241–42
  and conversion, 242
  and disagreement, 239–41
  first-order, 232, 235
  first-person (deliberative) vs. third-person (theoretical), 8–9, 229–36, 242–43
  and religious experience, 237
  second-order, 231, 235
  and testimony, 237–39

epistemic trustworthiness
  conscientiousness as component of, 278
  of one's faculties, 231, 274, 276–79
  of others, 225–26, 234, 241, 280–84
epistemic universalism, 282
epistemology. *See* knowledge; rationality; religious epistemology; *entries beginning with* epistemic
essences, 11
eudaimonia (human flourishing), 151, 177
Euthyphro problem, 6
evidence
  for beliefs, 245
  defined, 229
  and disagreement, 239–41
  experiences or intuitions treated as, 231
  and testimony, 237–38
  trust in relation to, 234, 278–79
evidentialism, 245
evil. *See* problem of evil
excluded middle, law of, 17, 19
exclusivism
  about rationality, 248–50, 257
  about salvation, 247–48
  about truth, 247–51, 257
  pluralism compared to, 253
exemplarism and exemplarist moral theory, 6
  Aristotelian ethics compared to, 177
  Christian ethics as, 168
  definition and, 172–74
  DM theory as, 168, 177–78
  grounding of, 175
  imitation of Christ as instance of, 177–80
  narrative as feature of, 175–76
  in non-Christian religions, 179
  personhood as vehicle of, 175, 176–77
existence of God
  consensus gentium argument for, 10, 273, 284–88
  problem of evil and, 4, 75–76, 81, 82, 103–7, 110
  traditional arguments for, 160
experience, 230–31, 236. *See also* religious experience
explanation
  classical account of, 32–33
  and divine foreknowledge, 30–34
Eyre, Ronald, 250

fatalism
  arguments of, 36–38
  causal, 37–38
  infallibility and, 60–61

  knowledge in relation to, 35n12
  logical, 36–40, 42–43, 48–49, 51–52
  and mind–world relation, 58–59
  theological, 37–44, 47–52, 55, 58–59, 67, 69
  time in relation to, 2, 3, 34n4, 36, 38–52, 59
  See also determinism
Feinberg, Joel, 5, 132, 134–37, 140, 142–43, 145–46
first-person epistemic reasons, 8–9
Fischer, John Martin, 24, 63
Fixed Past Constraint (FPC), 24–26
Foley, Richard, 274–76
foreknowledge. *See* divine foreknowledge
form, 116–30
foundationalism, 274–75, 277
FPC. *See* Fixed Past Constraint
Frankfurt, Harry, 72n9
Freddoso, Alfred J., 302, 305n6
freedom
  as essential to personhood, 82
  God's, 6
  personal relationships based on, 4
  See also free will
free will
  Aquinas's solution to reconciling divine foreknowledge with, 17–19
  Augustine on, 16
  causal contingency in relation to, 24–26
  compatibility of determinism with, 15, 17
  compatibility of divine foreknowledge with, 2, 15–19, 30–34, 49–52
  compatibility of infallible (not necessarily divine) foreknowledge with, 58–60
  counterfactuals and, 28–30
  defined, 15–16
  God's motivation for personal relationship with humans as basis of, 4
  incompatibilist, 15, 21, 50, 139
  logical contingency in relation to, 22–24
  metaphysics of time and, 54–71
  and moral luck, 139
  and problem of evil, 82
  problem of reconciling divine foreknowledge with, 15, 21–22, 54–64
  pseudo-problems in relation to, 19–21
  weak notions of, 16–17
Frege, Gottlob, 208n8
Fricker, Elizabeth, 280
future contingent propositions, 17, 19, 27, 58

Geach, Peter, 139
God
  attributes of, 287, 317

creation by, 80
emotions of, 157, 159–60
and empathy, 7, 193–97
freedom of, 6
and free will, 4
goodness of, 4, 6, 79–80, 92, 99–101
imitation of, 162, 170
life of, 97–98
love shown by, 82, 158, 164, 165, 207
monotheistic conception of, 11, 306–20
motives of, 79–80, 152, 158
not a deceiver, 42
and possible worlds, 30
relational properties in, 317–18
relationship of, with humans, 4, 97–98, 106
usage of the term, 312–13
virtues of, 157–62
See also existence of God; *entries beginning with* divine; *entries beginning with* omni
God's-eye view, 7
Golden Rule, 163
goodness
of aims/motives, 3–4, 75–77, 81–86, 88–96, 156–57
of God, 4, 6, 79–80, 92, 99–101
God's freedom in relation to, 6
motivations for, 3–4, 5–6, 75–77
omnipotence in relation to, 6
perfect, 6, 76, 79, 82, 207, 287
of persons, 4, 91–100
of states of affairs, 3–4, 90–96, 156
virtue in relation to, 77–78
Gospels, 168, 169, 179
grace, and moral luck, 5, 132, 137–39, 145
Grosseteste, Robert, 170
Gustafson, James, 182n2

habitus (state of having), 160
Hare, John, 182n3
Hartshorne, Charles, 193, 209n9
Hasker, William, 34n3, 50
heaven and hell
God's attributes in relation to notions of, 139, 146
and moral luck, 5, 132, 137–38, 139, 141, 145–46
hedonic calculus, 104
hell. *See* heaven and hell
Hempel, C. G., 32–33
Hick, John, 81, 139, 252–53
Holy Spirit, 215, 217, 219–20, 250
Howard-Snyder, Daniel, 103, 110, 110n1
human nature, 151, 161, 177, 249, 320n4

Hume, David, 103, 110, 253, 286, 288n4
Hunt, David, 61
Hurley, Patrick, 263

identity, of objects/individuals, 116–30, 314, 319
Identity of Indiscernibles, 11, 307–11, 314, 319
immutability, 200–201
impassibility, 202
impossible propositions, 291–304
inalterability, 20–21
Incarnation
as atonement for sin, 168, 169–70, 172
and Christian ethics, 168
and Christ's knowledge, 43, 52
DM theory and, 6, 162, 179
and imitation of Christ, 6, 162, 168
as manifestation of divine goodness, wisdom, and power, 170
moral purpose of, 168, 169, 171–72, 178, 180
incompatibilist free will, 15, 21, 50, 139
infallibility
and fatalism, 60–61
and free will, 58–60
and time, 61–63
Institute in Philosophy of Religion, 1
integrity, 97–98, 101
intentions. *See* motives/motivations
intersubjectivity
omnisubjectivity as perfection of, 7, 206–7
and second-person rationality, 9
as solution to subjective and objective perspectives, 7, 254
and the Trinity, 205–7
intuition, 230–31
Irenaeus, 170–71

Jackson, Frank, 188, 208n2
Jesus Christ
ethics centered on life of, 168, 169
imitation of, 6, 157, 162–63, 168, 170–72, 177–80
knowledge of, 2, 43, 52
as moral exemplar, 178, 180
and motives, 162–63
and problem of evil, 98
John Paul II, Pope, 269
justice. *See* divine justice
justification, 216–18, 225
Justification of Epistemic Authority thesis, 268, 269

Kant, Immanuel, and Kantian ethics
and autonomy, 264, 288
Categorical Imperative in, 87n11, 153

Kant, Immanuel, and Kantian ethics (*cont.*)
   and Christ as moral exemplar, 181
   and Christian ethics, 137
   and counterpossibles, 303
   and moral luck, 135, 182n3
   noumenal/phenomenal distinction of, 252–53
   respect as key concept in, 85
   will as key concept in, 133
Kenny, Anthony, 16–17, 18, 20, 29
knowledge
   fatalism in relation to, 35n12
   timeless, 2, 18, 49–52
   See also divine foreknowledge; religious epistemology; truth; *entries beginning with* epistemic
Kretzmann, Norman, 159, 160, 165, 209n12
Kripke, Saul, 172–73
Kvart, Igel, 305n6

Lamprecht, P., 293
Langford, C. H., 293
Leftow, Brian, 209n12
Leibniz, Gottfried Wilhelm, 63
Lewis, C. I., 293
Lewis, C. S., 4, 104–7, 109–10
Lewis, David, 11, 291, 294–97, 300–302, 304, 305n9
Locke, John, 238, 263–64
logic
   counterfactual, 297
   facts/logic dichotomy, 214
   impossibility and, 291–304
   modal, 37, 56, 61, 297
   properties of systems of, 17, 19
logical contingency, 22–24
The Long Search (video series), 250
love
   as basis of motivation, 81–85, 162–63, 165
   empathy and, 207–8
   expressed in the Trinity, 207
   God's, 82, 158, 164, 207–8
   imitative nature of, 170
   Jesus's teaching of, 162–63, 180
   omnisubjectivity and, 207–8
   parental, 81, 83
   respect compared to, 84–85
   in the Trinity, 207
   understanding as prerequisite for, 207
luck. *See* moral luck
Lukasiewicz, J., 19

Mackie, J. L., 88–89, 91
Martineau, James, 78
Mavrodes, George, 253
McMyler, Benjamin, 244n10
Mencius, 78
metaphysics
   academic treatment of, 214
   of actual and possible worlds, 199–200
   and counterpossibles, 302–4
   divine foreknowledge and, 32–33, 54–71
   epistemic value of, 169
   of good and evil, 77, 79, 92–99
   infallibility and problems of, 58–60, 62–63, 71
   of noumenal/phenomenal distinction, 252–53
   religious, 214
   of theism, 11
   of time, 3, 54–71
   and the Trinity, 314
   of value, 152, 157, 164, 179
Middle Knowledge, 29, 57, 71n4, 142–43
Mill, John Stuart, 86n6, 153
Molina, Luis de, 29–30
Molinism, 57
monotheism, 11, 306–20
   attributes of God and, 306–7
   and contingent properties, 309–10
   and essential properties, 312–14
   Identity of Indiscernibles principle and, 307–8
   and necessary accidental properties, 310–12
   Principle of Plenitude and, 309–10
   the Trinity and, 306–7, 314, 319–20
moral authority, 268–70
moral luck, 132–47
   attitudes toward, 132, 135, 142, 169
   Christian ethics and, 136–47
   Christian theology and, 5, 132–33, 138–47
   in circumstances, 133–44
   in consequences, 133, 136, 142, 147n2
   in constitution (character traits), 133, 135–37, 139, 145
   controversy over, 132
   and divine justice, 143–45
   grace and, 5, 132, 137–39, 145
   and heaven/hell, 5, 132, 137–38, 139, 141, 145–46
   inequality as issue in, 132, 138, 140–42
   Middle Knowledge and, 142–43
   personal control as factor in, 143
   philosophical case for, 133–36
   problems in, 139–42
   religious forms of, 137–47
   secular morality incapable of accounting for, 132–33
   universal salvation and, 145–46
moral particularism, 169

moral theory, importance of, 151–52, 168–69, 174–75. *See also* Christian ethics; consequentialist theories; deontological theories; utilitarianism; virtue ethics
Moran, Richard, 244n12
More, Thomas, 179
Morris, Thomas V., 53n8, 298, 303
motives/motivations
  character traits associated with, 154–55
  defined, 5, 152, 154
  emotions in relation to, 154
  expressive, 80–81, 95, 155
  as foundation of moral theory, 5–6, 80, 152–57, 177–78
  God's, 79–80, 152, 158
  of a good being, 3–4, 75–77, 81–86, 88–96
  goodness of, 156–57
  Jesus and, 162–63
  love as basis of, 81–85
  moral theories' treatments of, 78–80
  of parents, 81–84
  productive, 155
  respect as basis of, 84–85
  will contrasted with, 80, 165
  See also Divine Motivation theory
movies, as model of empathy, 209n10
multi-valued logics, 17, 19
Murdoch, Iris, 181

Nagel, Thomas, 5, 132–41, 143, 145–46, 169, 188, 243n8, 244n9, 254
narrative ethics, 6, 163, 168, 175–76
Nathan (prophet), 255
National Endowment for the Humanities (NEH), 1
natural kinds, 158, 160, 174, 175, 177, 179, 307, 313–14, 318
natural kind terms, 172–73, 182n10, 316
Natural Law theory, 168, 180
necessity
  accidental, 20, 34n8, 55–56, 60–61, 64–65
  causal, 55–56
  of the past, 3, 46, 48–49, 55–56, 59–60, 64–66, 70
  truth not equivalent to, 20
Necessity of Eternity, 2, 46, 48–49, 52
negative theology, 253
Nock, A. D., 244n16
Normal Justification thesis, 10, 266–68
novels, as model of empathy, 194, 201, 203–4, 209n10

objective perspective, 254
Ockham, William of, 20–21, 34n8, 55–56, 59–62, 64

Old Testament, Divine Command theory/ethic of law associated with, 166, 180
omnipotence, 6, 76, 80, 190, 207, 287, 306, 312, 313, 317
omnipresence, 7, 187, 190–91, 196–97, 200, 207, 208n6
omniscience
  as attribute of God, 59, 80, 187, 207
  and counterfactuals, 28–30
  and counterfactual subjectivity, 197–200
  and counterpossibles, 10–11, 303–4
  defined, 15
  moral luck in relation to, 140–41
  omnisubjectivity and, 7, 188–90, 196
  qualifications of, 17, 50, 52
  and subjectivity, 188–90
  See also divine foreknowledge
omnisubjectivity, 187–208
  advantages of concept of, 207
  and counterfactual conscious states, 197–200
  defined, 7, 187
  and doctrine of the Trinity, 7
  and empathy, 193–97
  immutability and, 200–201
  and impassibility, 202
  and love, 207–8
  moral objection to, 203–5
  omnipresence and, 7, 190–91, 196–97, 207
  omniscience and, 7, 188–90, 196, 207
  as perfection of intersubjectivity, 7, 206–7
  and prayer, 7, 191–93, 197
  timelessness and, 200–202
  and the Trinity, 205–7
Open theism, 50

pain
  additive approach (AA) to quantifying, 4, 104–7, 109
  gratuitous, 104, 107–10
PAP. *See* Principle of Alternate Possibilities
Paradoxes of Strict Implication, 293
Parfit, Derek, 131n10, 243n8, 244n9
Parmenides, 45
passions, 154, 159, 202
the past
  causality and, 3, 55–56, 66–70
  fatalism dependent on inability to control, 36–38, 44–45
  necessity of, 3, 46, 48–49, 55–56, 59–60, 64–66, 70
  timeless realm compared to, 45–48
  unpreventability of, 68–69
Paul, Saint, 163, 170

Pauline principle, 93–96, 98, 101
Pelagian heresy, 139
Perry, John, 208n5
personhood
　autonomous, 10, 81, 85, 264–68, 272
　conceptions of, 5, 129–30
　evil permitted for sake of, 81
　exemplarism and, 175, 176–77
　freedom as essential to, 82
　of God, 97–98
　goodness and, 4, 91–100
　imitation as issue for, 180–81
　integrity of, 97–98, 101
　as locus of moral theory, 153
　resurrection and, 5, 129–30
　and Trinity concept, 205–6, 306, 319
　uniqueness of, 205–6
　See also subjective perspective; subjectivity
philosophy
　academic, 213
　as community of inquirers, 213, 220–21, 224
　discovery of subjectivity in, 187
　religious epistemology's lack of engagement with, 213–14, 218, 220–21, 223–24, 227
　status of religion in, 213–14
　value of, 221
phronesis (practical wisdom), 85, 174, 182n12, 224, 257
Pike, Nelson, 2, 18, 21
Plantinga, Alvin, 1
　on contingency, 35n15
　and divine foreknowledge–free will problem, 17, 21, 24, 26, 29–30, 34n4, 53n7
　and exclusivism, 247, 251, 254
　on rationality of Christian beliefs, 213–27, 227n2
　and religious differences, 247, 250–51
　Warranted Christian Belief, 8, 213–27
Plato, 45
　Euthyphro, 164
pluralism, 252–53
political authority, 10, 263, 265–68, 271
Pollock, John, 294, 297
polytheism, 253
possible worlds
　actual vs., 198–200
　counterfactuals and, 300–302
　essences in, 11
　God's creation and, 30
　God's omniscience and, 15, 19–33, 198–200
　properties in, 307–11, 316
practical wisdom. *See phronesis*
prayer, 7, 191–93, 197

predestination, 138–39
presentism, 53n9
Principle of Alternate Possibilities (PAP), 56–58, 61, 64, 69, 72n9
Principle of Plenitude, 11, 309–11
Principle of Repeatable Reasons (PRR), 108–10
Principle of the Unpreventability of the Past, 68–69
Prior, A. N., 18, 20
problem of evil
　agent-based approach to, 80–86
　DM theory and, 6
　evil not permitted for the sake of some good, 80–81
　evil permitted for the sake of personhood, 81
　free will and, 82
　goodness of aims/motives as factor in, 3–4, 75–77, 81–86, 88–96
　logical dimension of, 75–77, 85
　meta ethical assumption concerning, 88–92
　Pauline principle and, 93–96, 98, 101
　problem of suffering compared to, 83–84, 88–89
　quantity of evil as factor in, 4, 88, 103–10
　and relationship of agency to state of affairs, 3–4, 90–96
problem of the gap (rationality–truth relationship), 249, 257–58
propositions
　future contingent, 17, 19
　God's knowledge and, 189
　temporal character of, 39, 48–49, 51
　theoretical vs. deliberative reasons for believing, 229–35
　timelessness of, 36–39, 51
Putnam, Hilary, 172–73, 214
Pyrrhonian skeptics, 273

Quaestriones Exactissimae in Universam Aristotelis Logicam, 293
Quine, W.V.O., 46
Quinn, Philip L., 147n3

Rahner, Karl, 248
rationality
　of Christian belief, 8
　and disagreement, 239–41, 246
　exclusivism about, 248–50, 257
　external, 8, 214, 219–22, 225
　internal, 8, 214, 216–18, 222–25
　Plantinga's treatment of, 214–27
　of religious beliefs, 258
　second-person, 9, 221, 254–59

shared among all humans, 245–46, 248–50, 256–57
social dimension of, 8, 9, 224–27
truth in relation to, 222–23, 248–49, 253, 257–58
See also epistemic agency; epistemic reasons
Rational-Recognition Principle, 9, 256–57
Rawls, John, 183n16
Raz, Joseph, 10, 241, 265–68, 271–72
The Morality of Freedom, 266
reductio ad absurdum, 294
Reformation, 15
Reid, Thomas, 238
relativism, 251–52
religious authority, 10, 241–42, 270–72
religious beliefs
critical reflection on, 251–59, 258
disagreement about, 246–48
and exclusivisms, 247–51
pluralism of, 252–53
rationality of, 258
relativism about, 251–52
second-person perspective and, 254–59
social responsibility concerning, 9, 245–59
See also Christian beliefs; religious epistemology
religious diversity, 9, 245–59
religious epistemology
authority in, 9–10
conceptual and linguistic issues in, 214
defensive character of, 213, 227
first-person and third-person reasons, 8–9
isolation as danger for, 8, 226–27
lack of engagement with wider epistemic community, 213–14, 218, 220–21, 223–24, 227
Plantinga on Christian belief, 215–22
problems in, 8–9
See also religious beliefs
religious experience, 236–37
religious luck
considerations for, 142–46
moral luck compared to, 138–42
replication, and identity, 122–23, 129
Rescher, Nicholas, 305n4
respect, as basis of motivation, 84–85
resurrection, thought experiment concerning, 5, 115–30
Rice, Hugh, 69, 72n11
Roberts, Robert C., 167n8
Rodrigues, Sebastian, 147n3
Ross, James, 87n10
Rowe, W. L., 88–89, 91, 103, 110, 111n2

Royce, Josiah, 78
Runzo, Joseph, 17, 21

saints, 179
salvation
religious authority and, 272
religious diversity and, 247–48, 252–53
universal, 145–46
Schindler, Oskar, 179
Schlesinger, George, 139, 143–45
Schoeck, Helmut, 140
scholasticism, 15
science, authority of, 263
Scotus, John Duns, 78, 153, 170, 293
Seachris, Joshua, 4
second-person rationality/reasons, 9, 221, 254–59
self-trust
belief in relation to, 10, 231
and *consensus gentium* argument, 285–87
and disagreement, 287–88
epistemic, 10, 231, 273–89
and evidence, 278–79
need for, 273–79
pre-reflective nature of, 275–76
and rational inquiry, 277–78
reasonableness of, 276–79
trust in others based on, 9, 10, 232, 280–82, 287–88
semantic shift, 46
Sidgwick, Henry, 153
sin, 137
Sinclair, Upton, *Oil*, 209n13
skepticism, 273, 274–76
Slote, Michael, 86n9
Smith, Wilfred Cantwell, 248
social responsibility, religious beliefs and, 9, 245–59
Society of Christian Philosophers, 1
Socrates, 269
Spinoza, Baruch, 63
Stalnaker, R. C., 291, 297, 300–301, 305n8, 305n9
states of affairs, moral status of, 3–4, 90–96, 156, 176
Stoics, 19, 264
Stump, Eleonore, 98, 139, 165, 209n12
Suarez, Francisco, 29
subjective perspective, 254
subjectivity
counterfactual, 197–200
defined, 187
features of, 187–88
knowledge of another's, 188–90

subjectivity (cont.)
   modern discovery of, 187
   omniscience and, 188–90
   and prayer, 191–93
   See also intersubjectivity; omnisubjectivity; personhood
subjunctive counterfactual conditionals, 28–30
substantial form, 5, 117, 120–27, 129–30, 130n3
suffering, 83–84, 88–89, 102n3
Swinburne, Richard, 17, 26–27, 53n8, 121, 139

Talbott, Thomas, 139
tense logics, 17
Teresa, Mother, 179
testimony, 237–39
theism
   consensus gentium argument for, 10
   and divine foreknowledge, 54, 58–60
   and metaphysics, 59, 71
   and problem of evil, 76, 82–85, 97, 103–4
   rationality of, 8
theodicies, 97–98, 101
theology. *See* Christian theology
theoretical (third-person) reasons
   and authority, 241–42
   concept of, 229
   deliberative reasons contrasted with, 233–36
   and disagreement, 239–40
   and experience, 230, 236–37
   first- and second-order, 235
   and intuition, 230–31
   relationship of deliberative to, 233–34
   and religious experience, 237
   and self-trust, 231
   and testimony, 237–39
theory. *See* moral theory
theory of direct reference, 172–74
third-person epistemic reasons, 8–9
Thomistic Ockhamism, 59
Thomson, Judith Jarvis, 147n2
time
   causality in relation to, 27
   fatalism in relation to, 2, 3, 36, 38–52
   infallibility and, 61–63
   knowledge in relation to, 2, 18
   metaphysics of, in relation to divine foreknowledge and free will, 54–71
   truth in relation to, 17–19
   See also future contingent propositions; the past; timelessness
timelessness
   Aquinas's arguments about God based on, 18–19, 39

   causation and, 44–46
   and divine foreknowledge–free will problem, 18–19, 38–52
   fatalist arguments under conditions of, 2, 38–52, 59
   omnisubjectivity and, 200–202
   the past compared to, 45–46
   reality of realm of, 45–46
TLC. *See* Transfer of Lack of Control
Tooley, M., 88–89, 91
traits. *See* character traits
Transfer of Accidental Necessity, 56–57, 61, 70, 71n2
Transfer of Lack of Control (TLC), 38–39, 44, 49
Transfer of Necessity, 37, 61–65
Transfer of Non-causability, 68, 70
Transfer of Unpreventability, 68–70, 72n11
Trinity
   DM theory and, 162
   and intersubjectivity, 205–7
   and monotheism, 306–7, 314, 319–20
   and omnisubjectivity, 7, 205–7
   and personhood, 205–6, 306, 319
   properties of, 320n4
   properties of members of, 11, 312, 319
   reasoning about, 314, 320n3
trust. *See* self-trust; trust in others, 242
trust in others, epistemic, 9, 10, 232, 237–39, 279–82, 287–88
trustworthiness. *See* epistemic trustworthiness
truth
   a posteriori, 173–75
   certainty not equivalent to, 20
   connection between inquiry/reasoning and, 277–78
   correspondence theory of, 19
   desire for, 273–77
   exclusivism about, 247–51, 257
   necessity not equivalent to, 20
   rationality in relation to, 222–23, 248–49, 253, 257–58
   time in relation to, 17–19
   timeless truth dilemma, 2, 48, 52
   See also knowledge

Uriah, 255
utilitarianism, 78–79, 86n6, 97–98, 104, 153. *See also* consequentialist theories

Vacek, Edward, 182n2
van Frassen, B. C., 303
van Inwagen, Peter, 40–43, 50, 52n2, 69, 72n12, 130n1

Vatican II, 245
virtue ethics
   anti-theory approach of, 151
   character traits (virtue) as fundamental concept in, 77–78, 83, 153, 176–77
   criticisms of, 151
   eudaimonia as fundamental moral concept in, 151
   examples of, 78
   features of, 153–57
   and moral luck, 136
   motivation-based, 152–57, 177–78
   practical wisdom as component of, 85
   and problem of evil, 77
   strong vs. weak forms of, 77, 152, 153
   theological foundation for, 152
   See also agent-based virtue ethics
virtues. *See* character traits; God: virtues of; motives/motivations
voodoo beliefs, 217–18, 222

Wainwright, William, 306, 307, 309, 312
warrant, 214, 219–21, 225
Watson, Gary, 183n16
will, moral theories based on, 80, 153, 163–66, 181
Williams, Bernard, 5, 81, 97–98, 101, 132–33, 143, 166n1, 167n8, 169
Wittgenstein, Ludwig, 105
Wolff, Robert Paul, 264–66